Came the Mirror & Other Tales

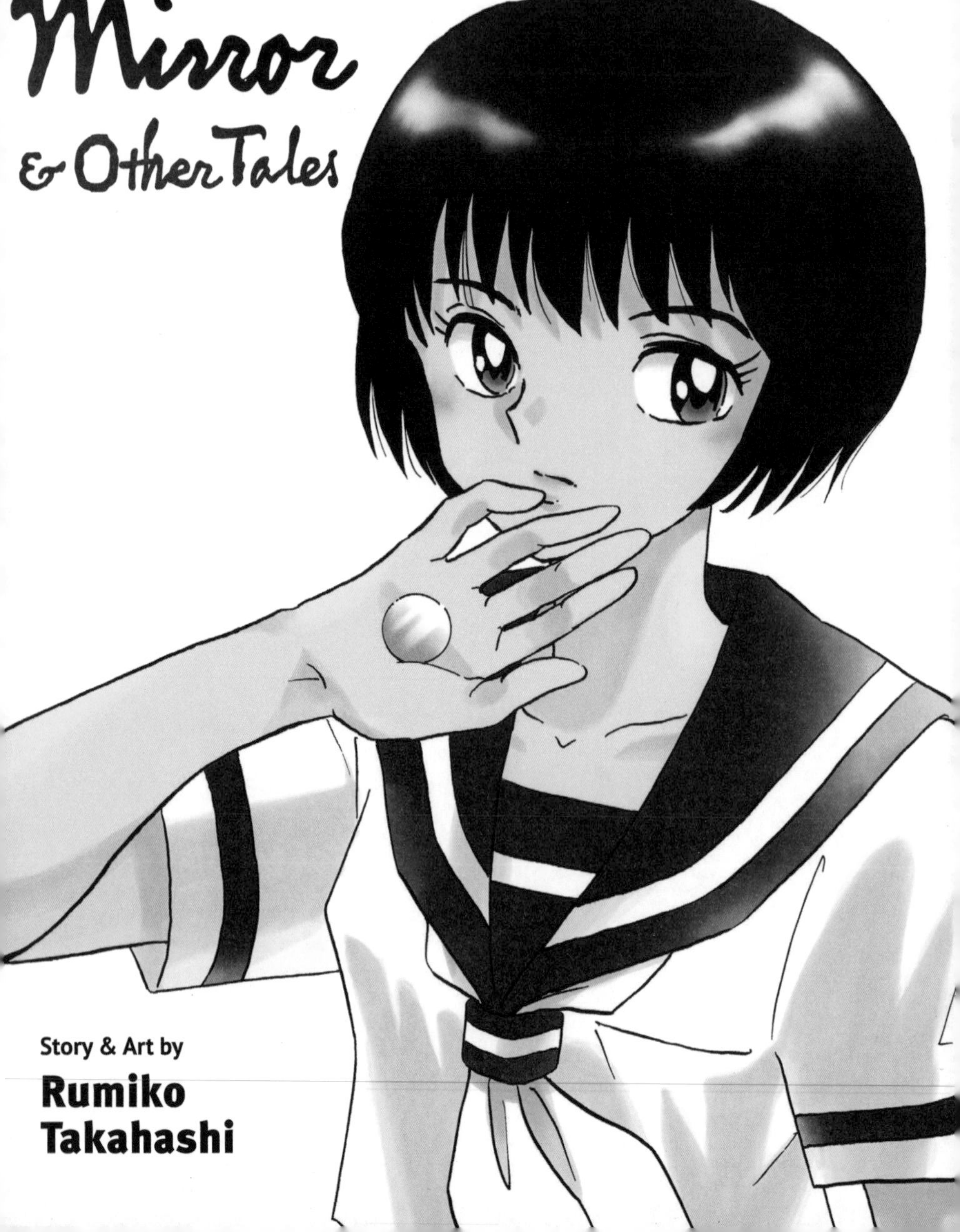

Story & Art by

Rumiko Takahashi

CONTENTS

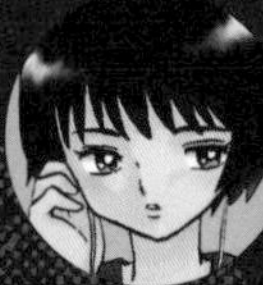

Came the Mirror

Big Comics Superior
July 25, 2014

3

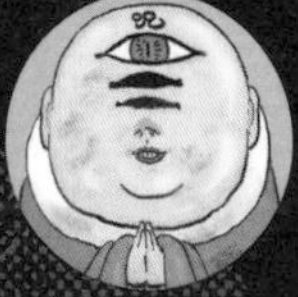

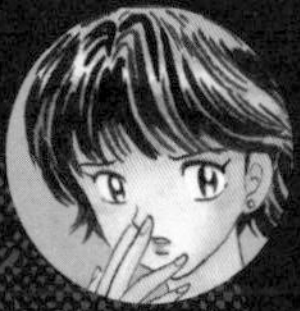

Lovely Flower

Big Comic
November 10, 2003

105

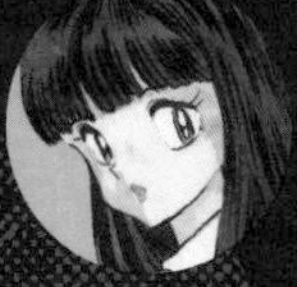

Revenge Doll

Big Comic
October 25, 2013

39

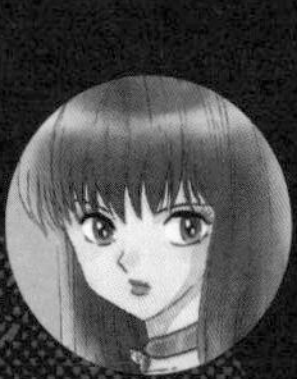

With Cat

Shonen Sunday
October 27, 1999

137

The Star Has a Thousand Faces

Big Comics Spirits
October 18, 2010

73

My Sweet Sunday

Mitsuru Adachi x Rumiko Takahashi

Shonen Sunday
April 1, 2009

171

Came the Mirror

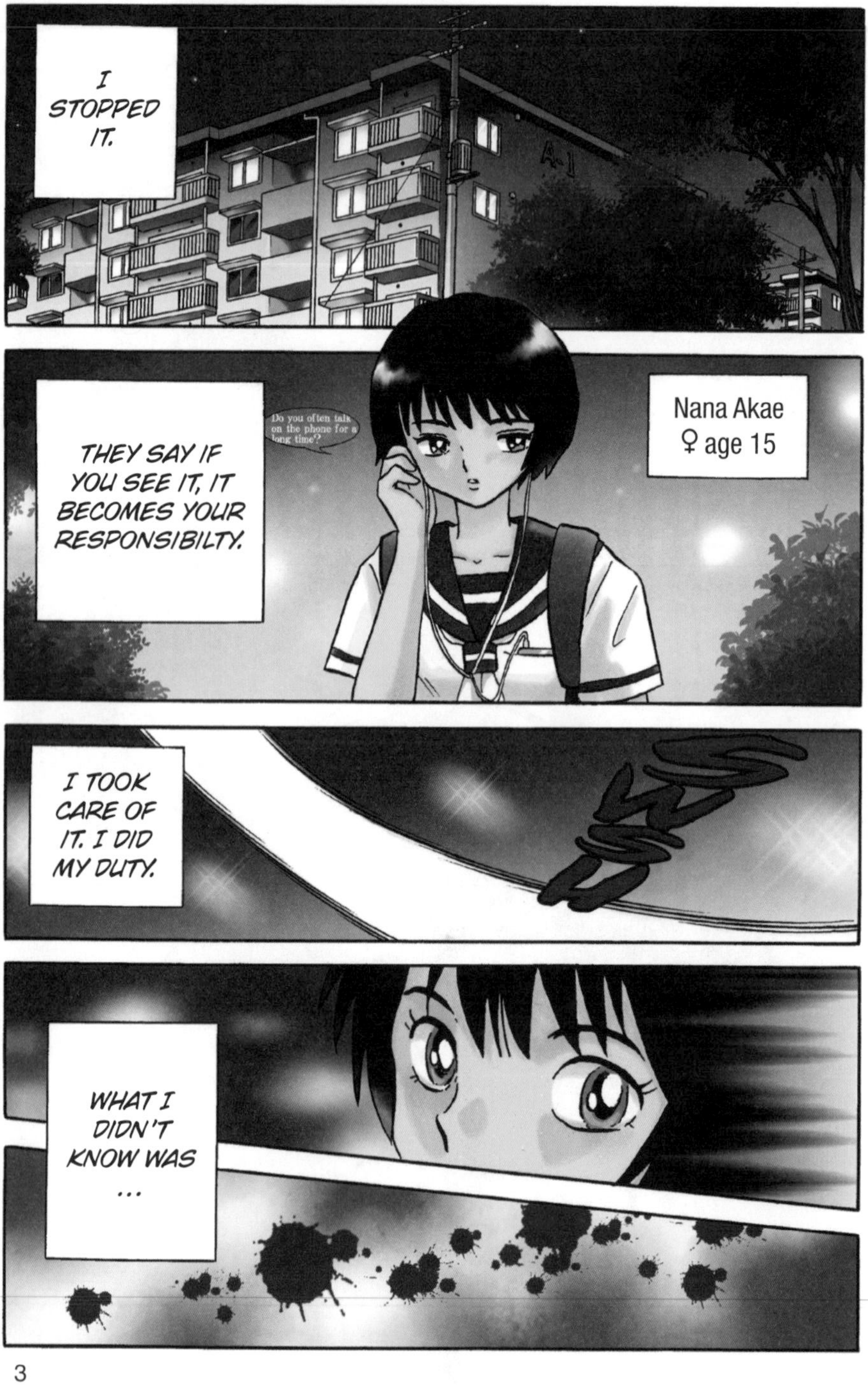
I STOPPED IT.
Nana Akae ♀ age 15
Do you often talk on the phone for a long time?
THEY SAY IF YOU SEE IT, IT BECOMES YOUR RESPONSIBILTY.
I TOOK CARE OF IT. I DID MY DUTY.
WHAT I DIDN'T KNOW WAS ...

Came the Mirror

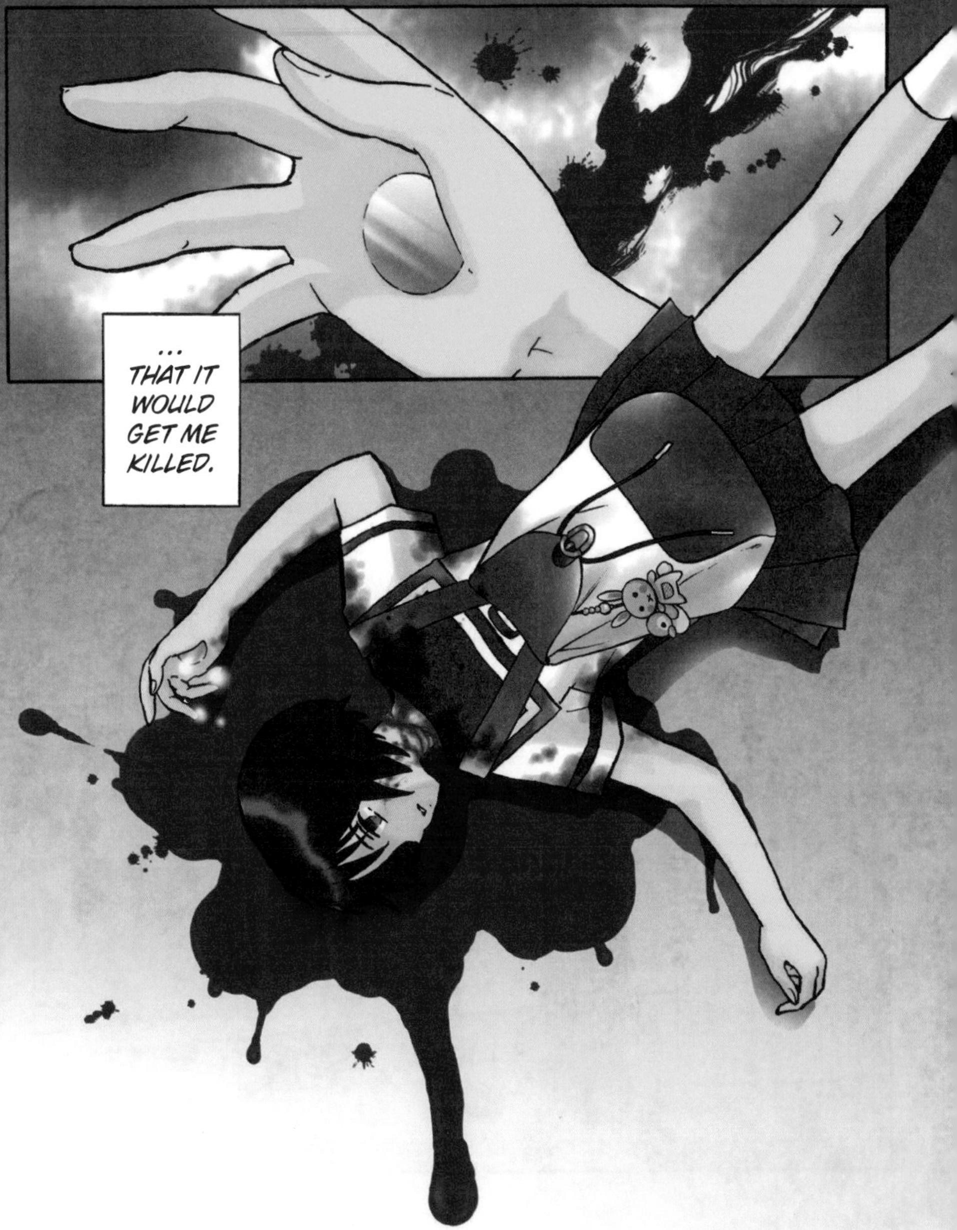
... THAT IT WOULD GET ME KILLED.

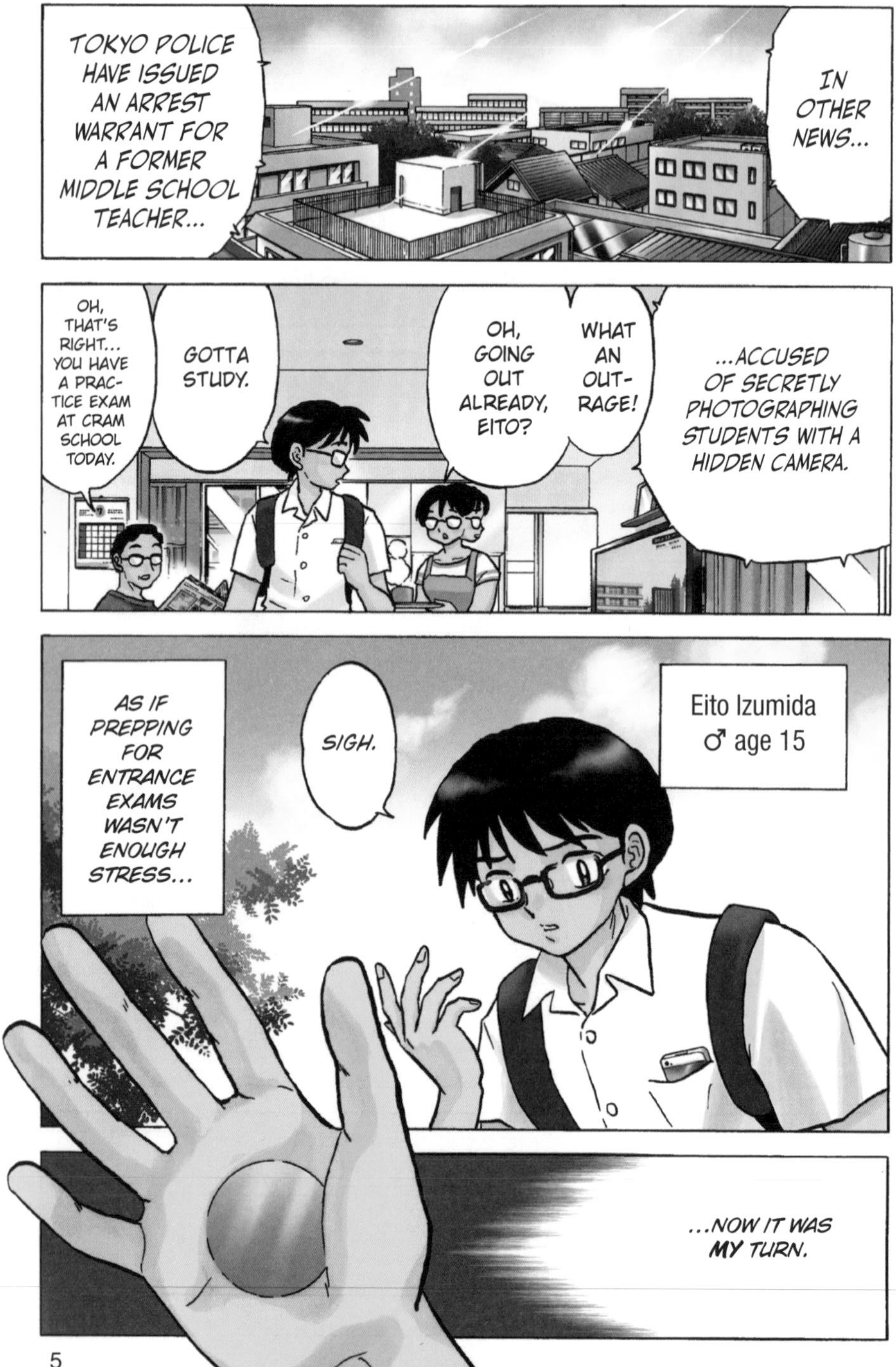
IN OTHER NEWS...
TOKYO POLICE HAVE ISSUED AN ARREST WARRANT FOR A FORMER MIDDLE SCHOOL TEACHER...
...ACCUSED OF SECRETLY PHOTOGRAPHING STUDENTS WITH A HIDDEN CAMERA.
WHAT AN OUT-RAGE!
OH, GOING OUT ALREADY, EITO?
GOTTA STUDY.
OH, THAT'S RIGHT... YOU HAVE A PRAC-TICE EXAM AT CRAM SCHOOL TODAY.
Eito Izumida ♂ age 15
SIGH.
AS IF PREPPING FOR ENTRANCE EXAMS WASN'T ENOUGH STRESS...
...NOW IT WAS MY TURN.

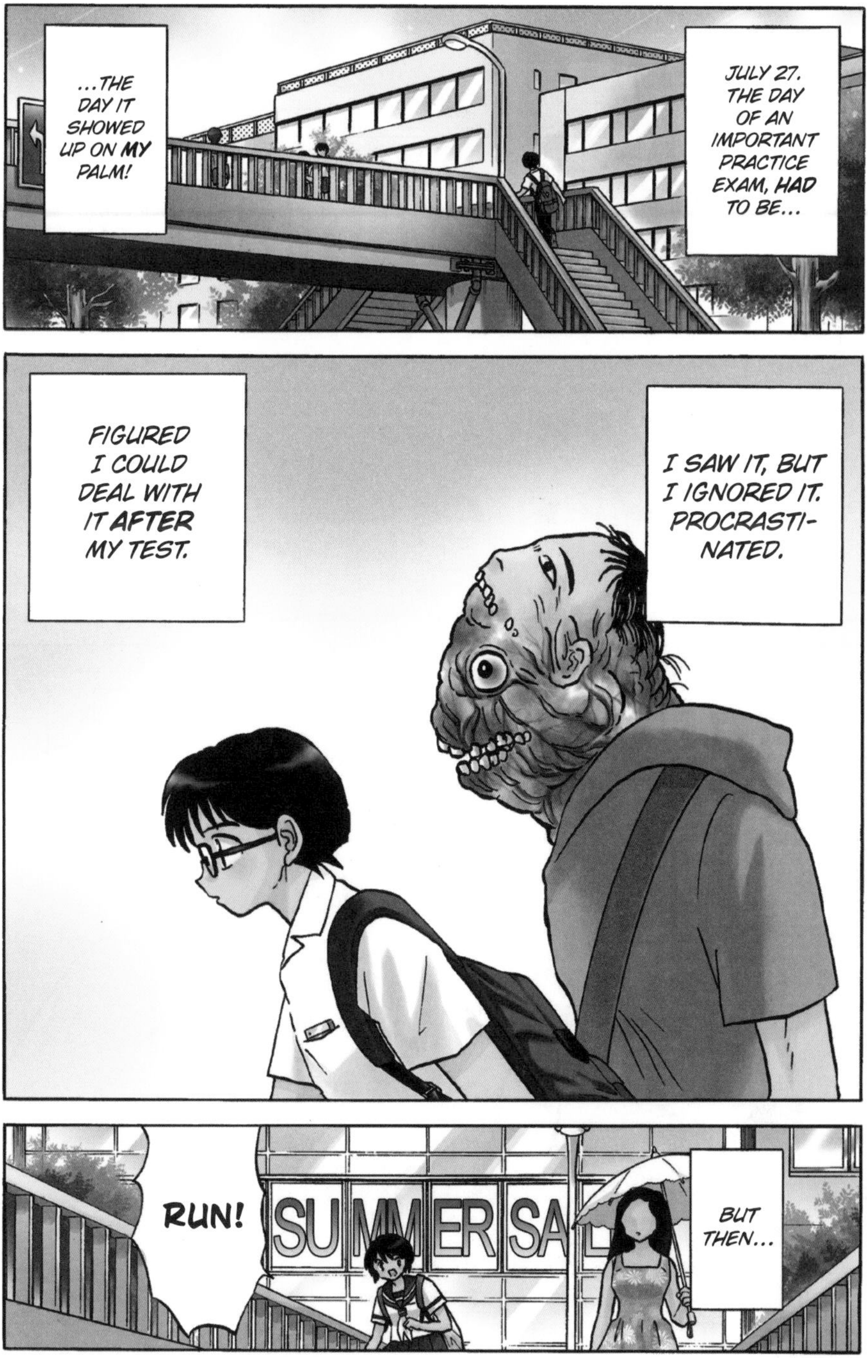
JULY 27. THE DAY OF AN IMPORTANT PRACTICE EXAM, HAD TO BE...
...THE DAY IT SHOWED UP ON MY PALM!
I SAW IT, BUT I IGNORED IT. PROCRASTINATED.
FIGURED I COULD DEAL WITH IT AFTER MY TEST.
BUT THEN...
RUN!

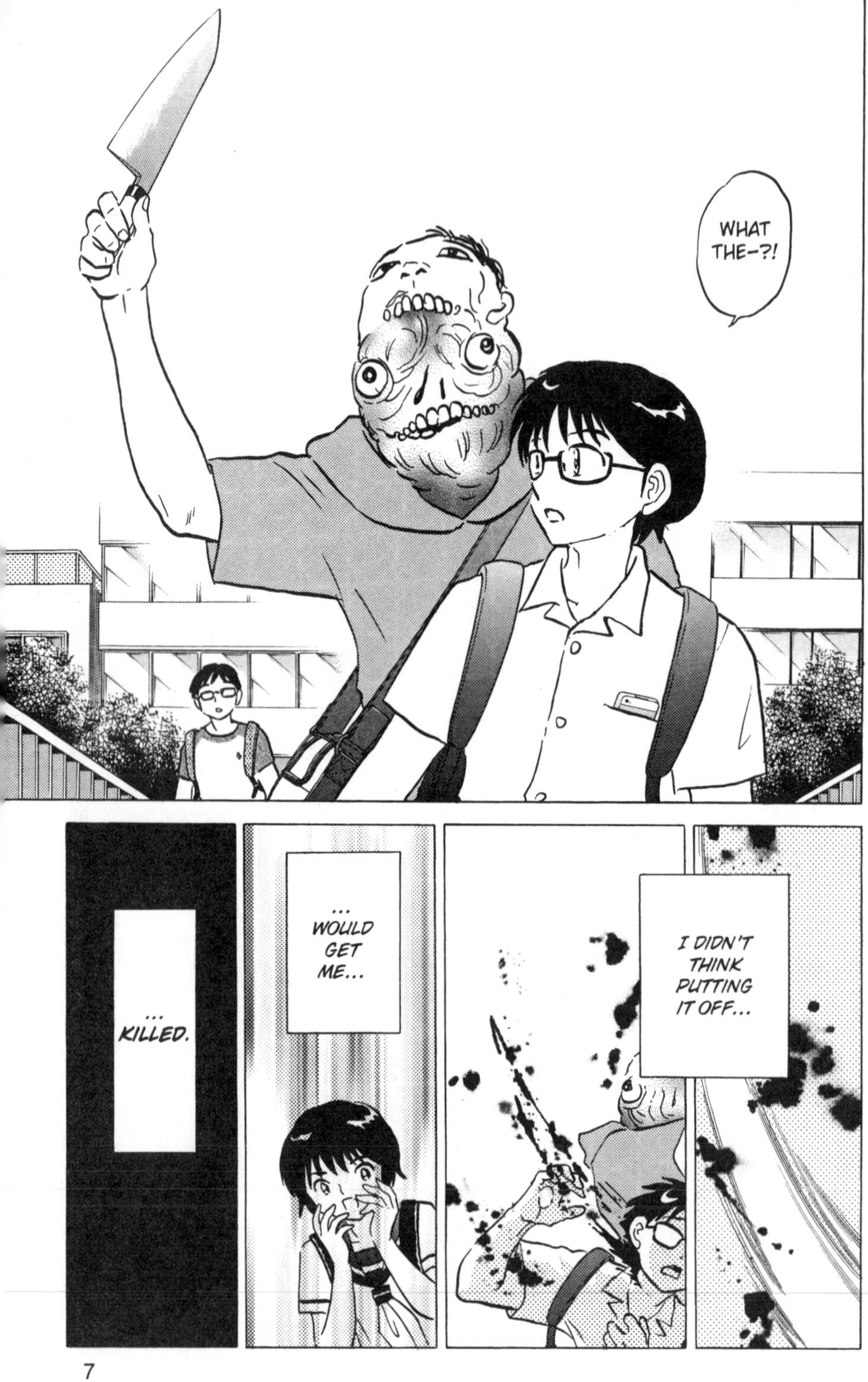
WHAT THE-?!
I DIDN'T THINK PUTTING IT OFF...
...WOULD GET ME...
...KILLED.

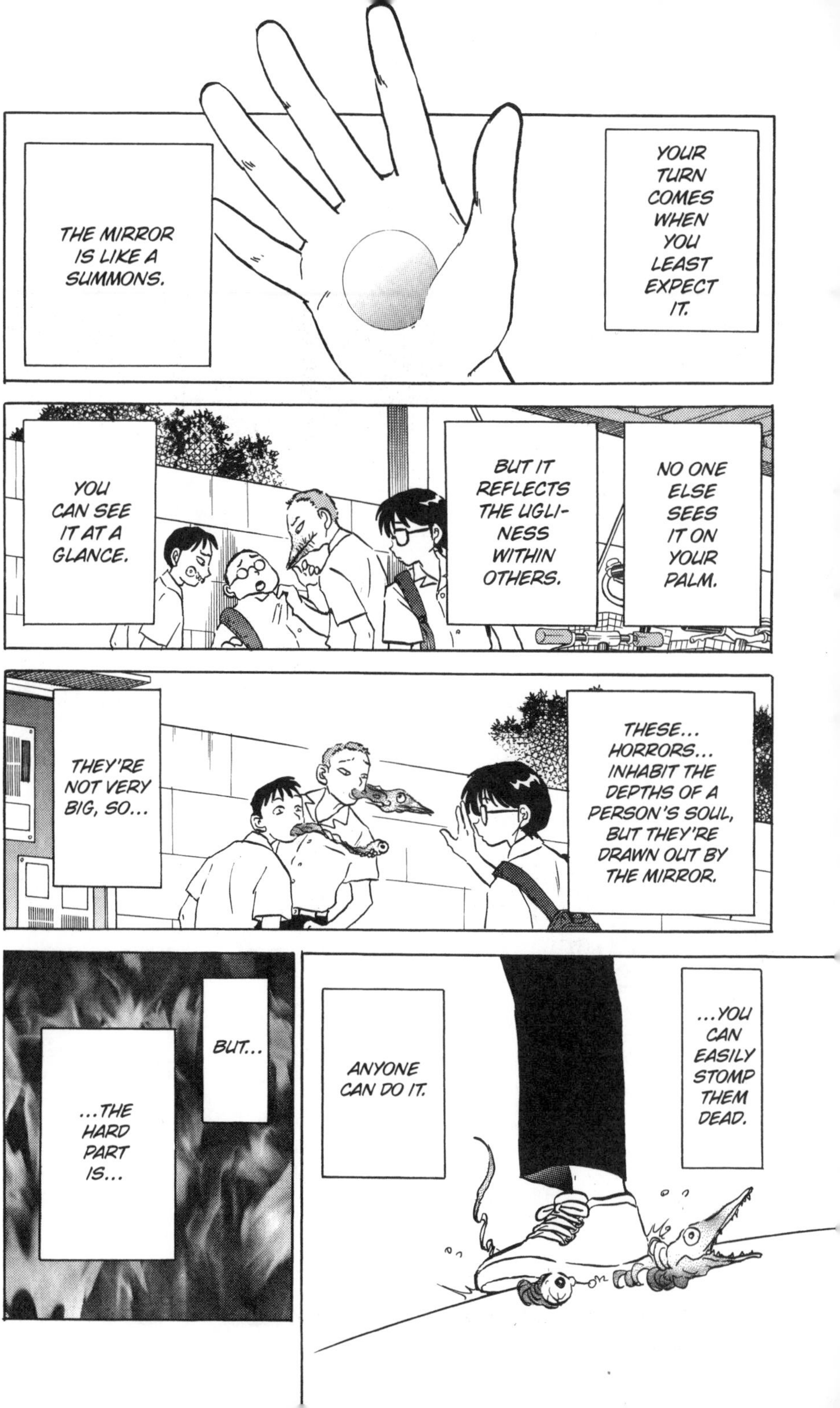
YOUR TURN COMES WHEN YOU LEAST EXPECT IT.
THE MIRROR IS LIKE A SUMMONS.
NO ONE ELSE SEES IT ON YOUR PALM.
BUT IT REFLECTS THE UGLI-NESS WITHIN OTHERS.
YOU CAN SEE IT AT A GLANCE.
THESE... HORRORS... INHABIT THE DEPTHS OF A PERSON'S SOUL, BUT THEY'RE DRAWN OUT BY THE MIRROR.
THEY'RE NOT VERY BIG, SO...
...YOU CAN EASILY STOMP THEM DEAD.
ANYONE CAN DO IT.
BUT...
...THE HARD PART IS...

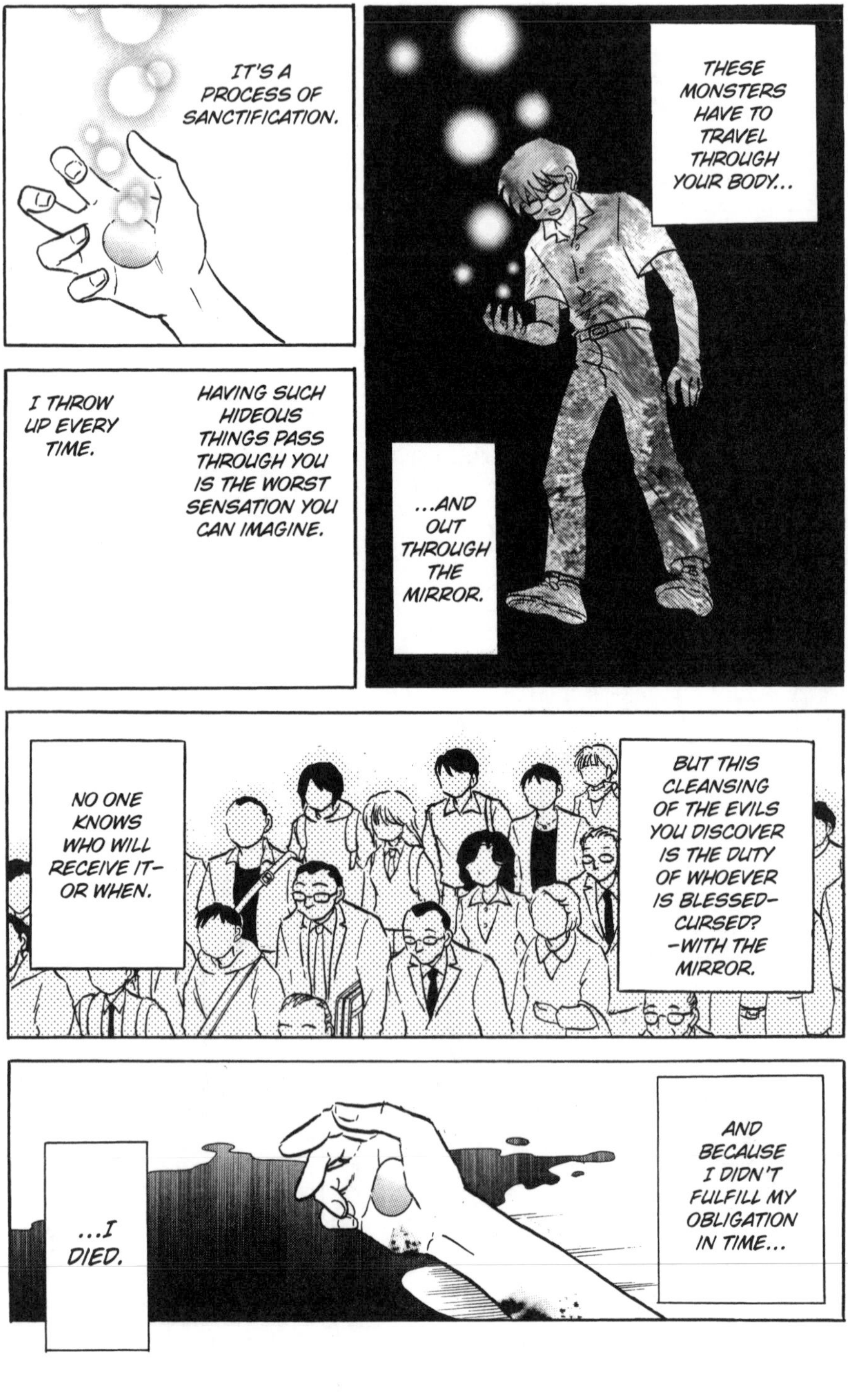
THESE MONSTERS HAVE TO TRAVEL THROUGH YOUR BODY...
...AND OUT THROUGH THE MIRROR.
IT'S A PROCESS OF SANCTIFICATION.
HAVING SUCH HIDEOUS THINGS PASS THROUGH YOU IS THE WORST SENSATION YOU CAN IMAGINE.
I THROW UP EVERY TIME.
BUT THIS CLEANSING OF THE EVILS YOU DISCOVER IS THE DUTY OF WHOEVER IS BLESSED-CURSED? -WITH THE MIRROR.
NO ONE KNOWS WHO WILL RECEIVE IT-OR WHEN.
AND BECAUSE I DIDN'T FULFILL MY OBLIGATION IN TIME...
...I DIED.

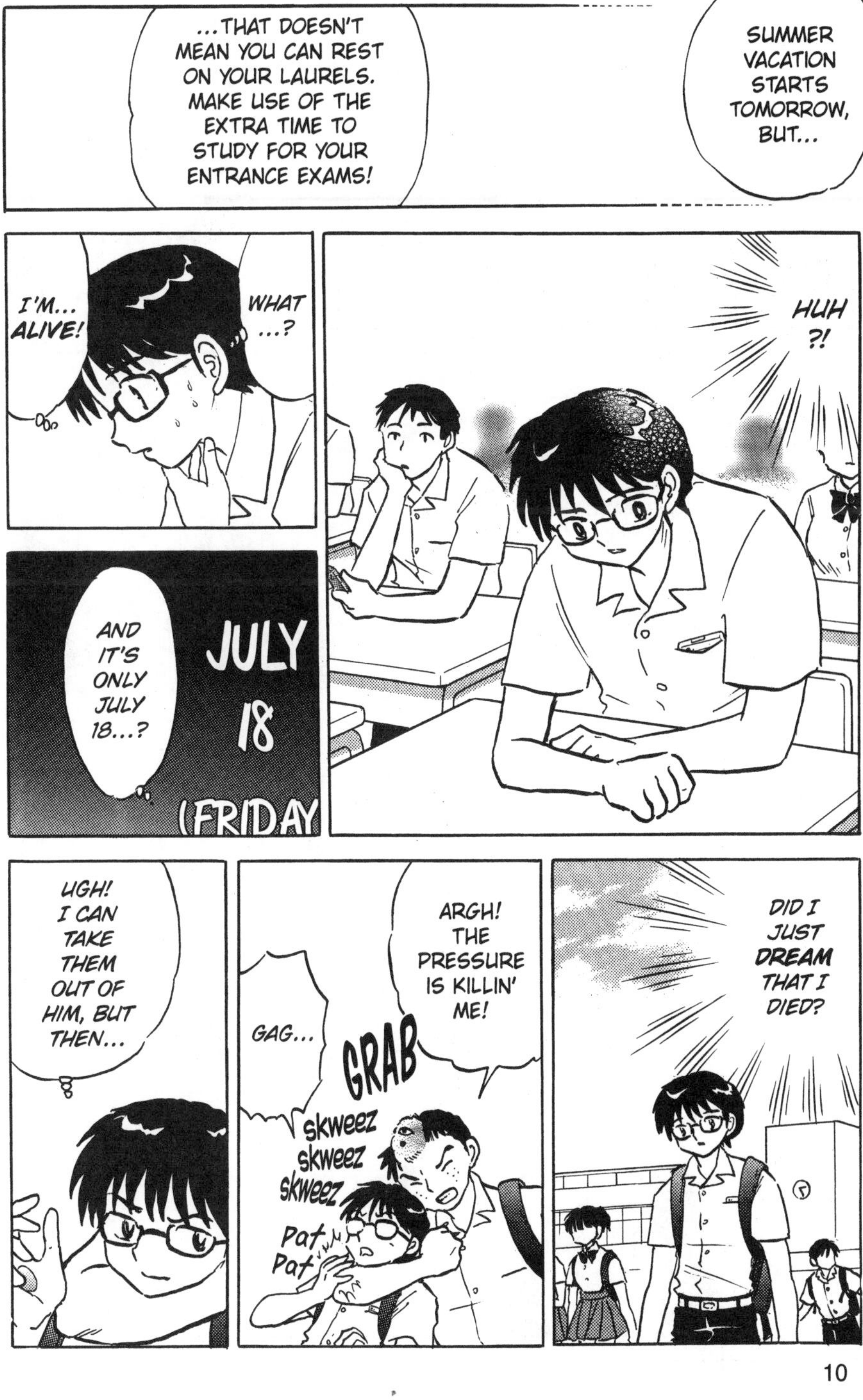
SUMMER VACATION STARTS TOMORROW, BUT...
...THAT DOESN'T MEAN YOU CAN REST ON YOUR LAURELS. MAKE USE OF THE EXTRA TIME TO STUDY FOR YOUR ENTRANCE EXAMS!
HUH ?!
WHAT ...?
I'M... ALIVE!
JULY 18 (FRIDAY
AND IT'S ONLY JULY 18...?
DID I JUST DREAM THAT I DIED?
ARGH! THE PRESSURE IS KILLIN' ME!
GRAB
GAG...
skweez skweez skweez
Pat Pat
UGH! I CAN TAKE THEM OUT OF HIM, BUT THEN...

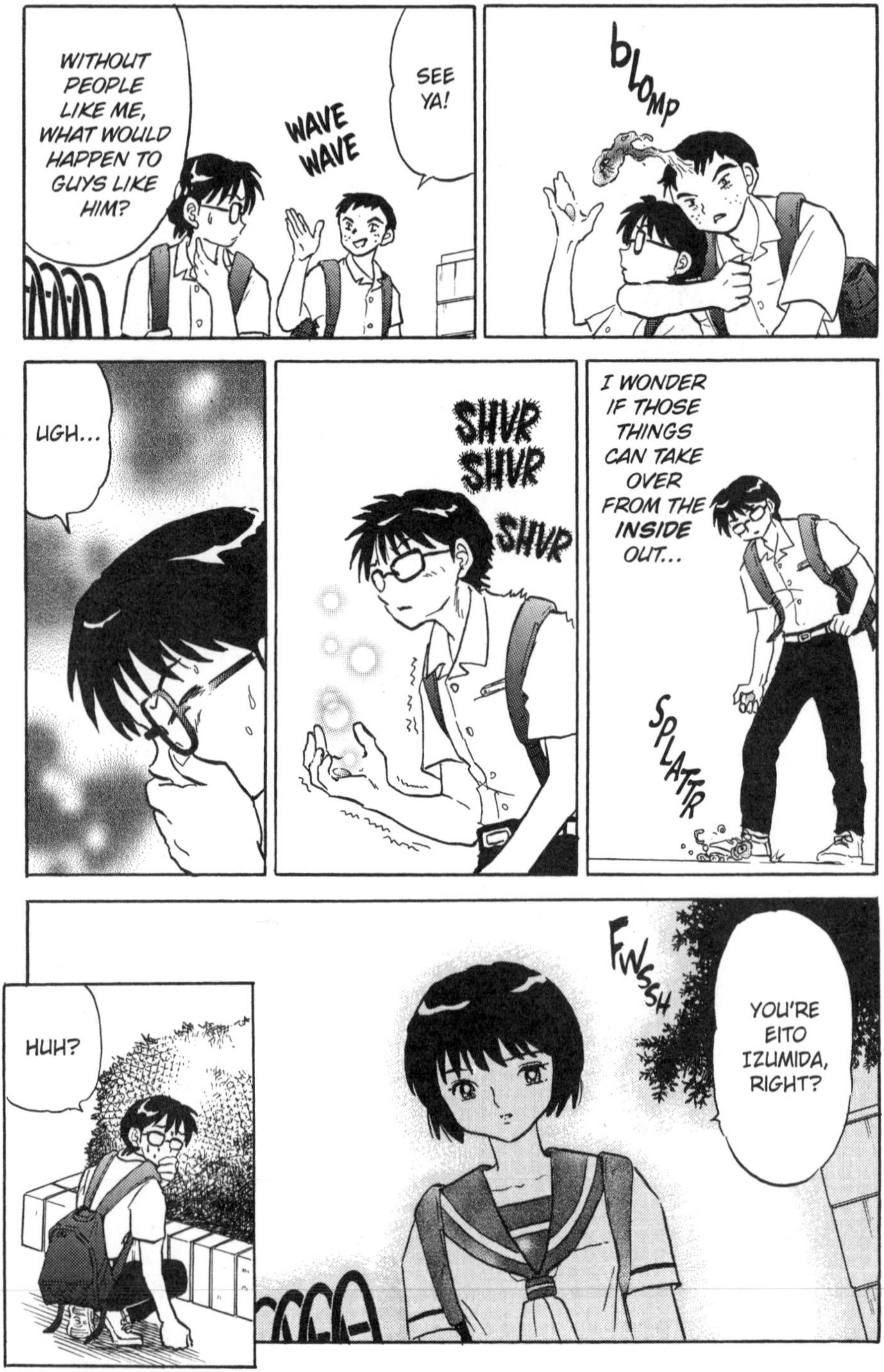
bLOMP
SEE YA!
WAVE WAVE
WITHOUT PEOPLE LIKE ME, WHAT WOULD HAPPEN TO GUYS LIKE HIM?
I WONDER IF THOSE THINGS CAN TAKE OVER FROM THE INSIDE OUT...
SPLATTR
SHVR SHVR
SHVR
UGH...
YOU'RE EITO IZUMIDA, RIGHT?
FWSSH
HUH?

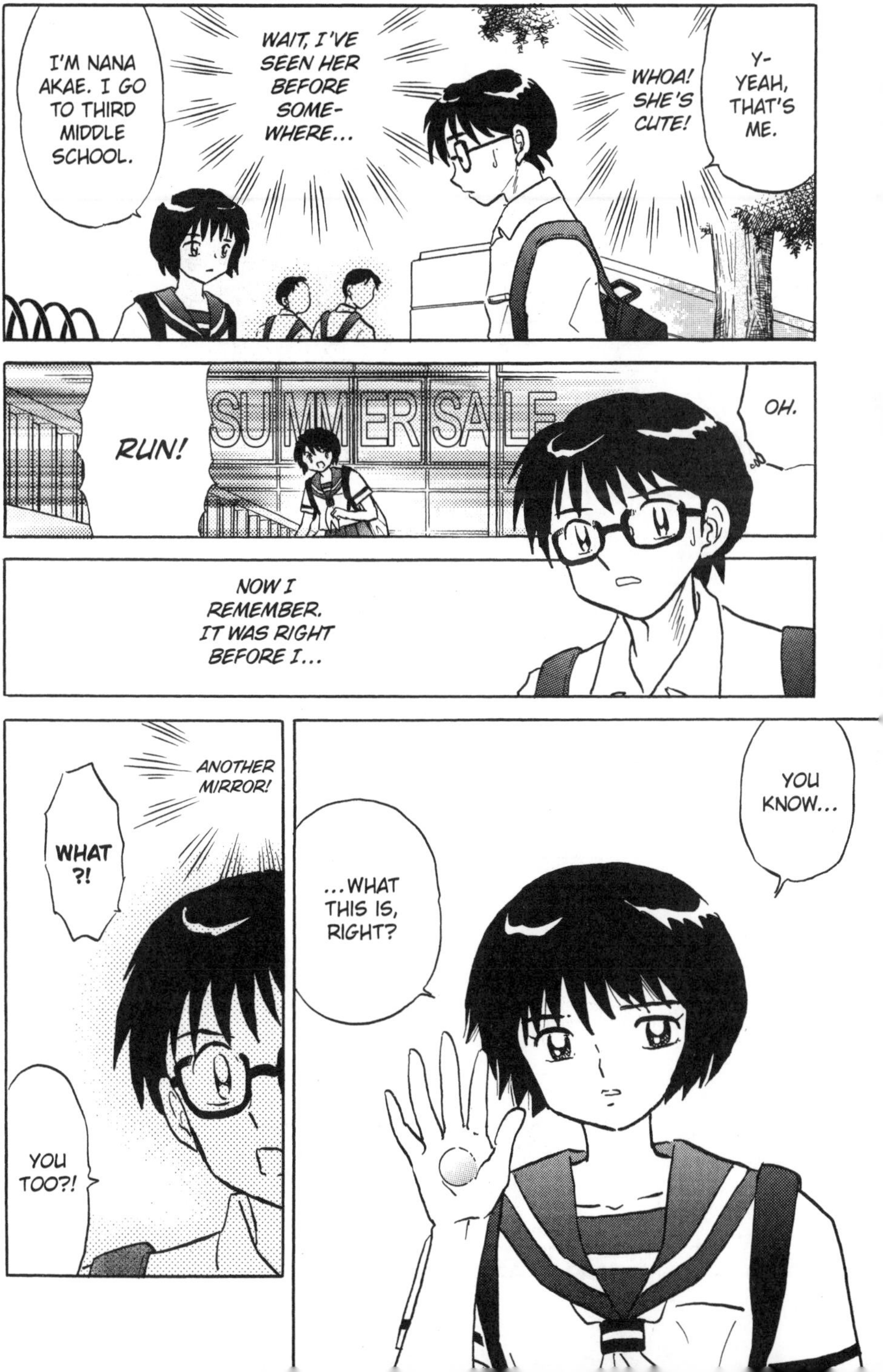
Y-YEAH, THAT'S ME.
WHOA! SHE'S CUTE!
WAIT, I'VE SEEN HER BEFORE SOME-WHERE...
I'M NANA AKAE. I GO TO THIRD MIDDLE SCHOOL.
OH.
SUMMER SALE
RUN!
NOW I REMEMBER. IT WAS RIGHT BEFORE I...
YOU KNOW...
...WHAT THIS IS, RIGHT?
ANOTHER MIRROR!
WHAT?!
YOU TOO?!

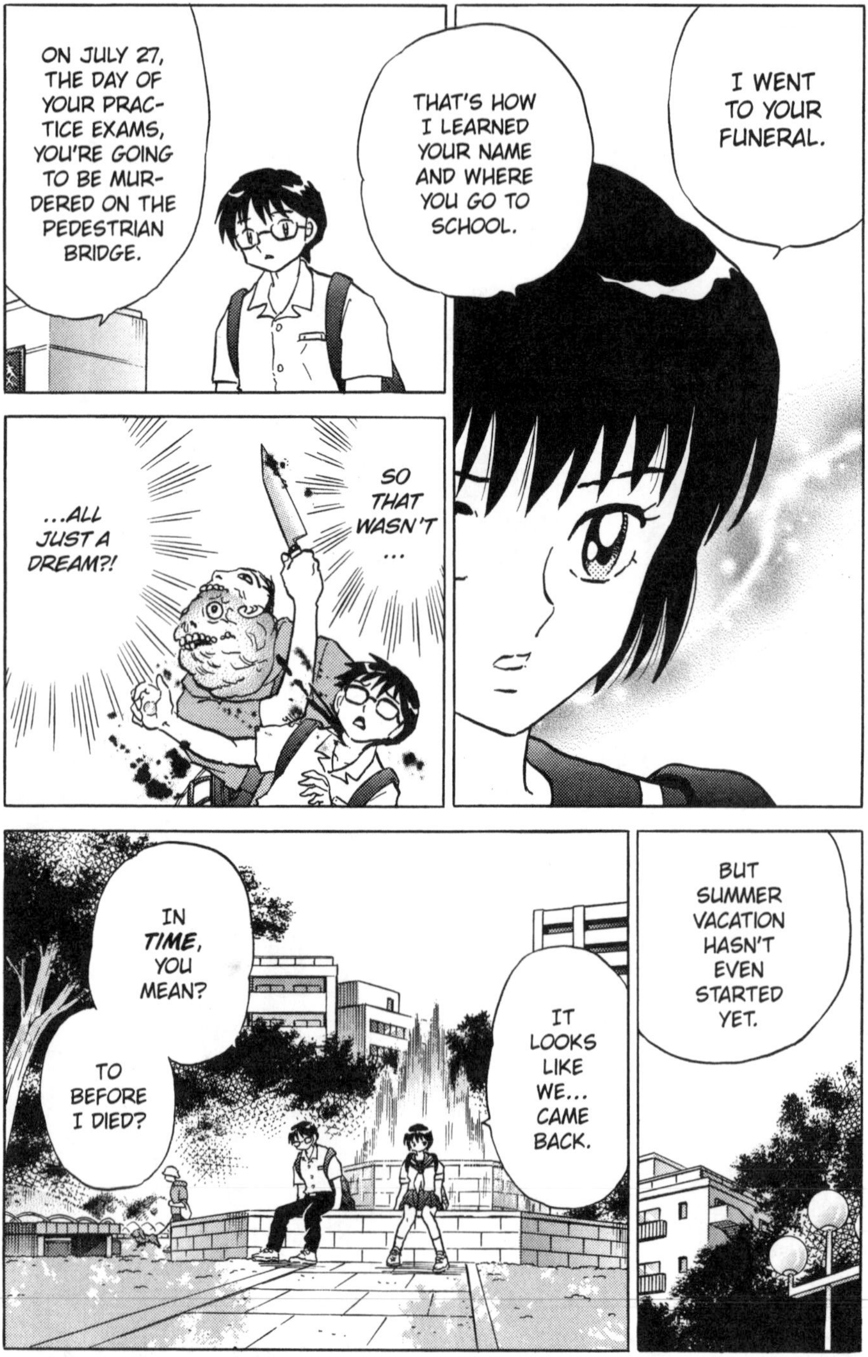
I WENT TO YOUR FUNERAL.
THAT'S HOW I LEARNED YOUR NAME AND WHERE YOU GO TO SCHOOL.
ON JULY 27, THE DAY OF YOUR PRAC-TICE EXAMS, YOU'RE GOING TO BE MUR-DERED ON THE PEDESTRIAN BRIDGE.
SO THAT WASN'T ...
...ALL JUST A DREAM?!
BUT SUMMER VACATION HASN'T EVEN STARTED YET.
IT LOOKS LIKE WE... CAME BACK.
IN *TIME*, YOU MEAN?
TO BEFORE I DIED?

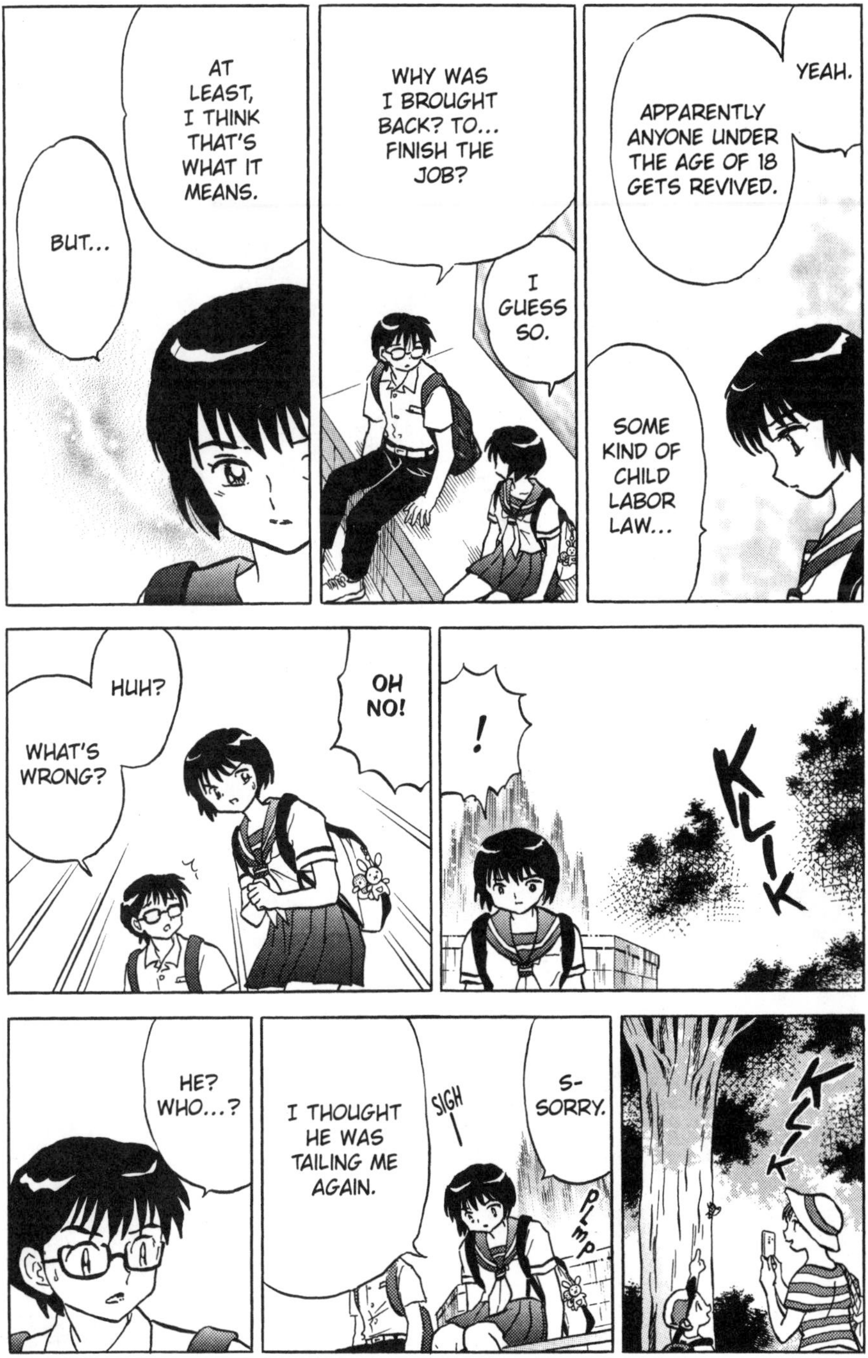
YEAH.
APPARENTLY ANYONE UNDER THE AGE OF 18 GETS REVIVED.
SOME KIND OF CHILD LABOR LAW...
WHY WAS I BROUGHT BACK? TO... FINISH THE JOB?
I GUESS SO.
AT LEAST, I THINK THAT'S WHAT IT MEANS.
BUT...
KLIK
!
OH NO!
HUH?
WHAT'S WRONG?
KLIK
PLMP
S-SORRY.
SIGH
I THOUGHT HE WAS TAILING ME AGAIN.
HE? WHO...?

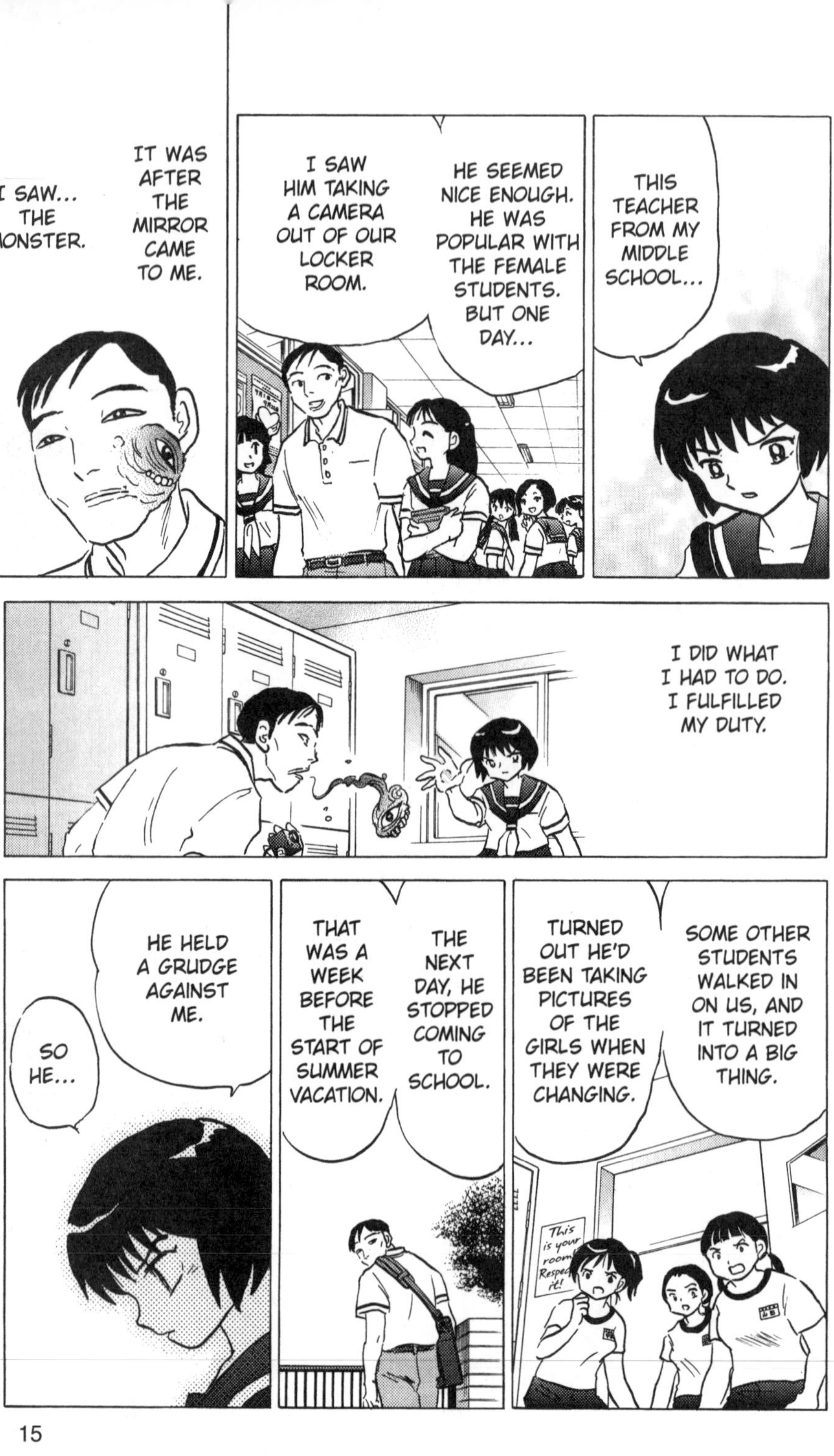
THIS TEACHER FROM MY MIDDLE SCHOOL...
HE SEEMED NICE ENOUGH. HE WAS POPULAR WITH THE FEMALE STUDENTS. BUT ONE DAY...
I SAW HIM TAKING A CAMERA OUT OF OUR LOCKER ROOM.
IT WAS AFTER THE MIRROR CAME TO ME.
I SAW... THE MONSTER.
I DID WHAT I HAD TO DO. I FULFILLED MY DUTY.
SOME OTHER STUDENTS WALKED IN ON US, AND IT TURNED INTO A BIG THING.
TURNED OUT HE'D BEEN TAKING PICTURES OF THE GIRLS WHEN THEY WERE CHANGING.
This is your
THE NEXT DAY, HE STOPPED COMING TO SCHOOL.
THAT WAS A WEEK BEFORE THE START OF SUMMER VACATION.
HE HELD A GRUDGE AGAINST ME.
SO HE...

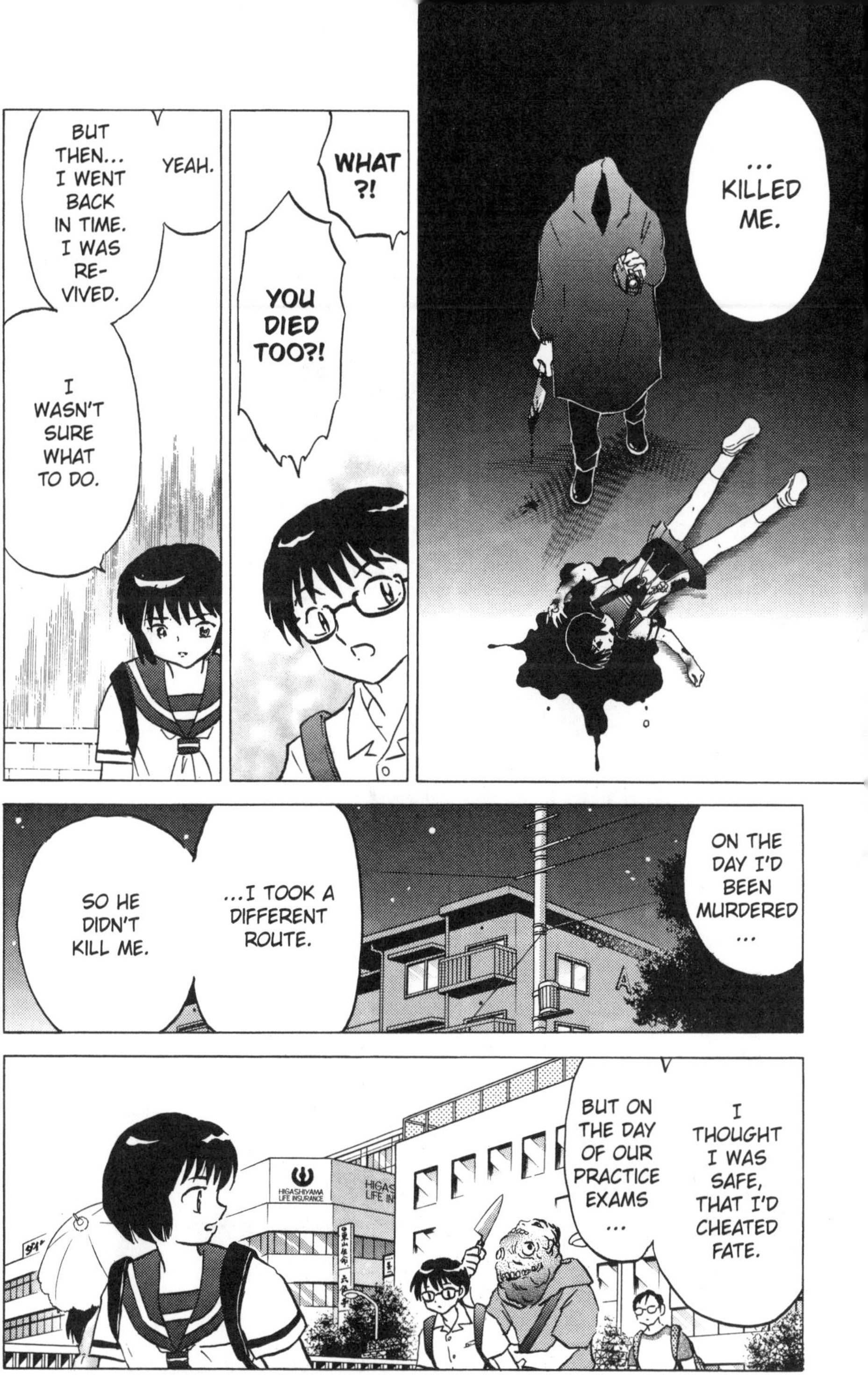
... KILLED ME.
WHAT ?!
YOU DIED TOO?!
YEAH.
BUT THEN... I WENT BACK IN TIME. I WAS RE-VIVED.
I WASN'T SURE WHAT TO DO.
ON THE DAY I'D BEEN MURDERED ...
...I TOOK A DIFFERENT ROUTE.
SO HE DIDN'T KILL ME.
I THOUGHT I WAS SAFE, THAT I'D CHEATED FATE.
BUT ON THE DAY OF OUR PRACTICE EXAMS ...
HIGASHIYAMA LIFE INSURANCE

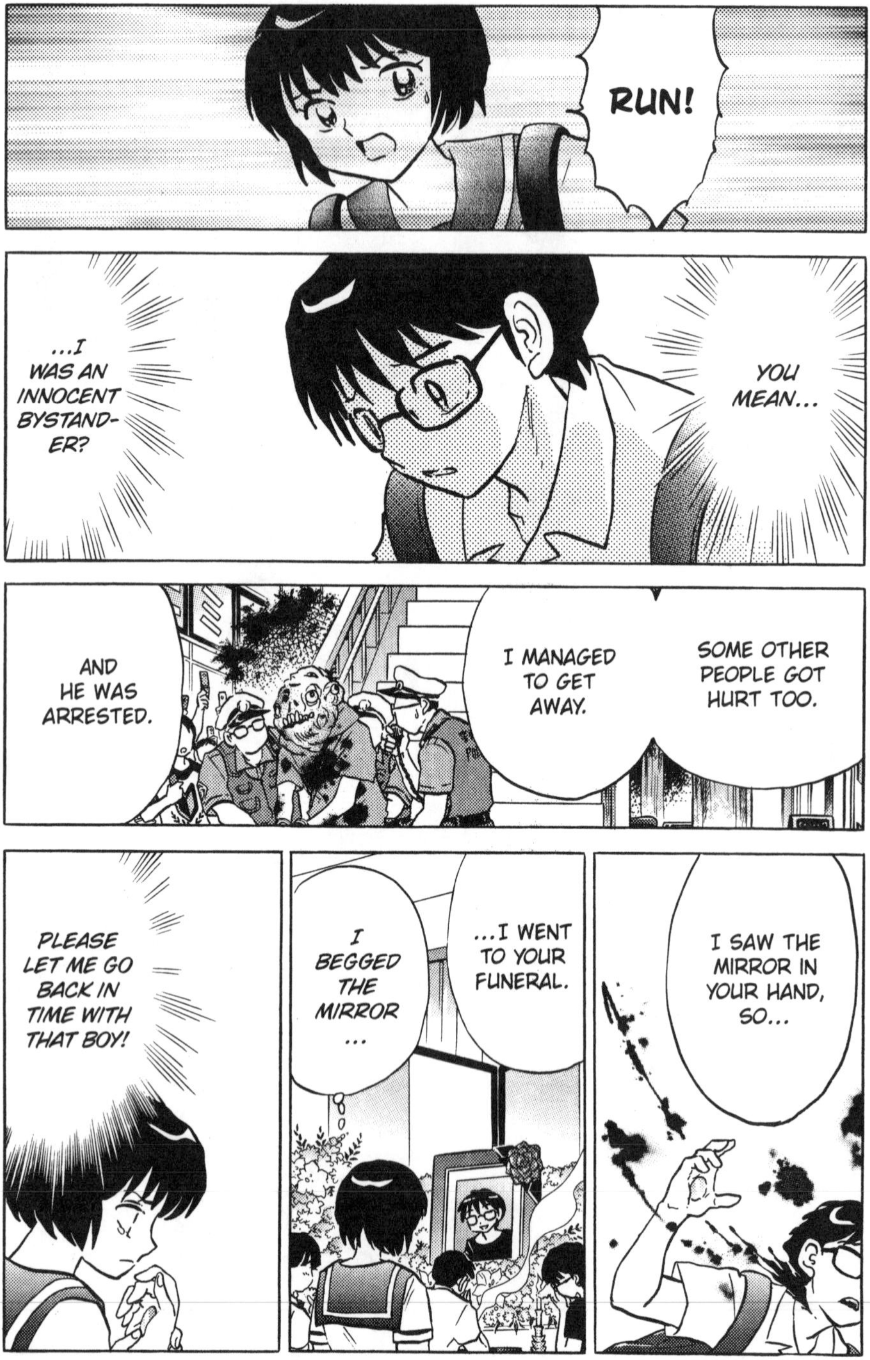
RUN!
YOU MEAN...
...I WAS AN INNOCENT BYSTANDER?
SOME OTHER PEOPLE GOT HURT TOO.
I MANAGED TO GET AWAY.
AND HE WAS ARRESTED.
I SAW THE MIRROR IN YOUR HAND, SO...
...I WENT TO YOUR FUNERAL.
I BEGGED THE MIRROR...
PLEASE LET ME GO BACK IN TIME WITH THAT BOY!

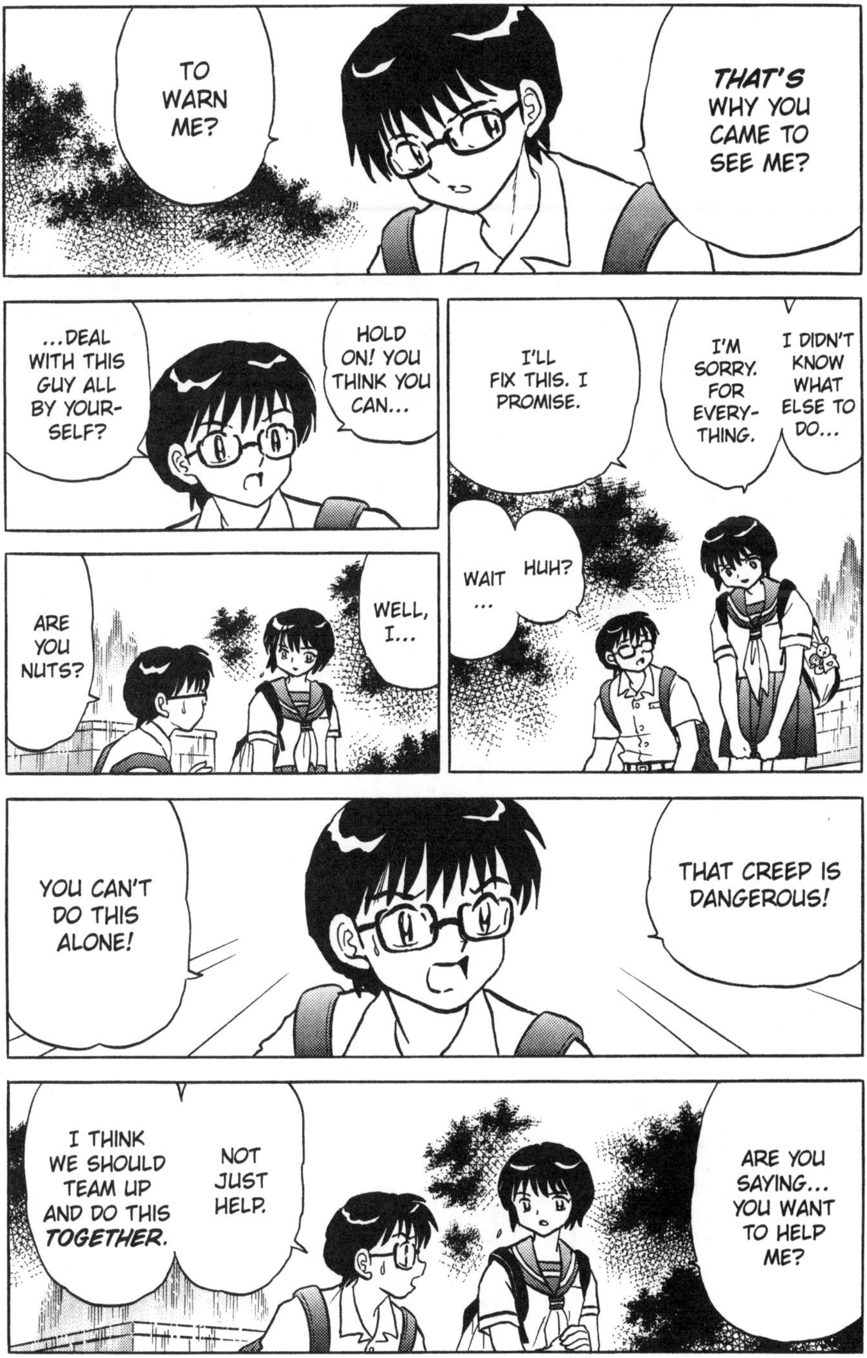
THAT'S WHY YOU CAME TO SEE ME?
TO WARN ME?
I DIDN'T KNOW WHAT ELSE TO DO...
I'M SORRY. FOR EVERY-THING.
I'LL FIX THIS. I PROMISE.
HUH?
WAIT ...
HOLD ON! YOU THINK YOU CAN...
...DEAL WITH THIS GUY ALL BY YOUR-SELF?
WELL, I...
ARE YOU NUTS?
THAT CREEP IS DANGEROUS!
YOU CAN'T DO THIS ALONE!
ARE YOU SAYING... YOU WANT TO HELP ME?
NOT JUST HELP.
I THINK WE SHOULD TEAM UP AND DO THIS TOGETHER.

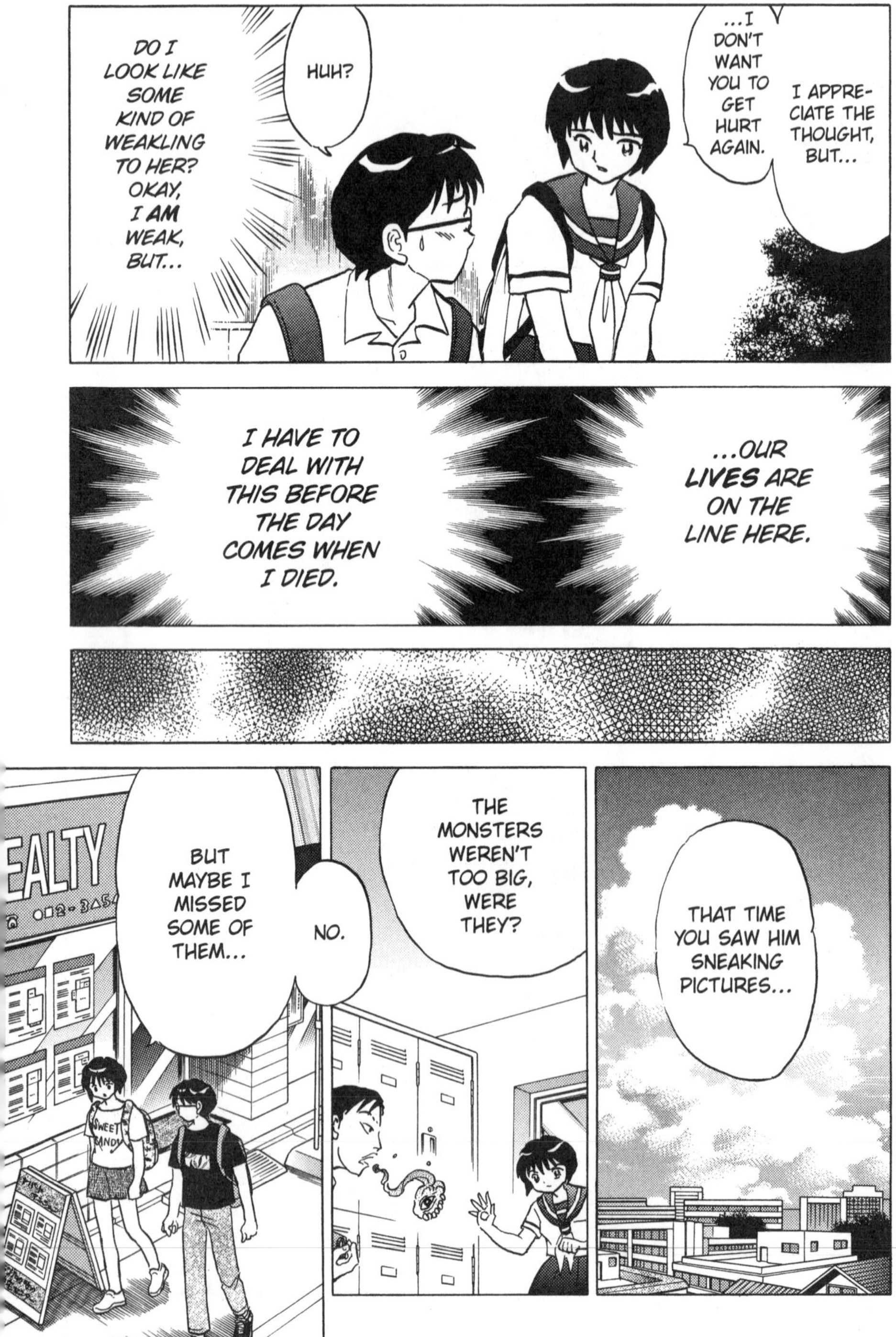
I APPRE-CIATE THE THOUGHT, BUT...
...I DON'T WANT YOU TO GET HURT AGAIN.
HUH?
DO I LOOK LIKE SOME KIND OF WEAKLING TO HER? OKAY, I AM WEAK, BUT...
...OUR LIVES ARE ON THE LINE HERE.
I HAVE TO DEAL WITH THIS BEFORE THE DAY COMES WHEN I DIED.
THAT TIME YOU SAW HIM SNEAKING PICTURES...
THE MONSTERS WEREN'T TOO BIG, WERE THEY?
NO.
BUT MAYBE I MISSED SOME OF THEM...

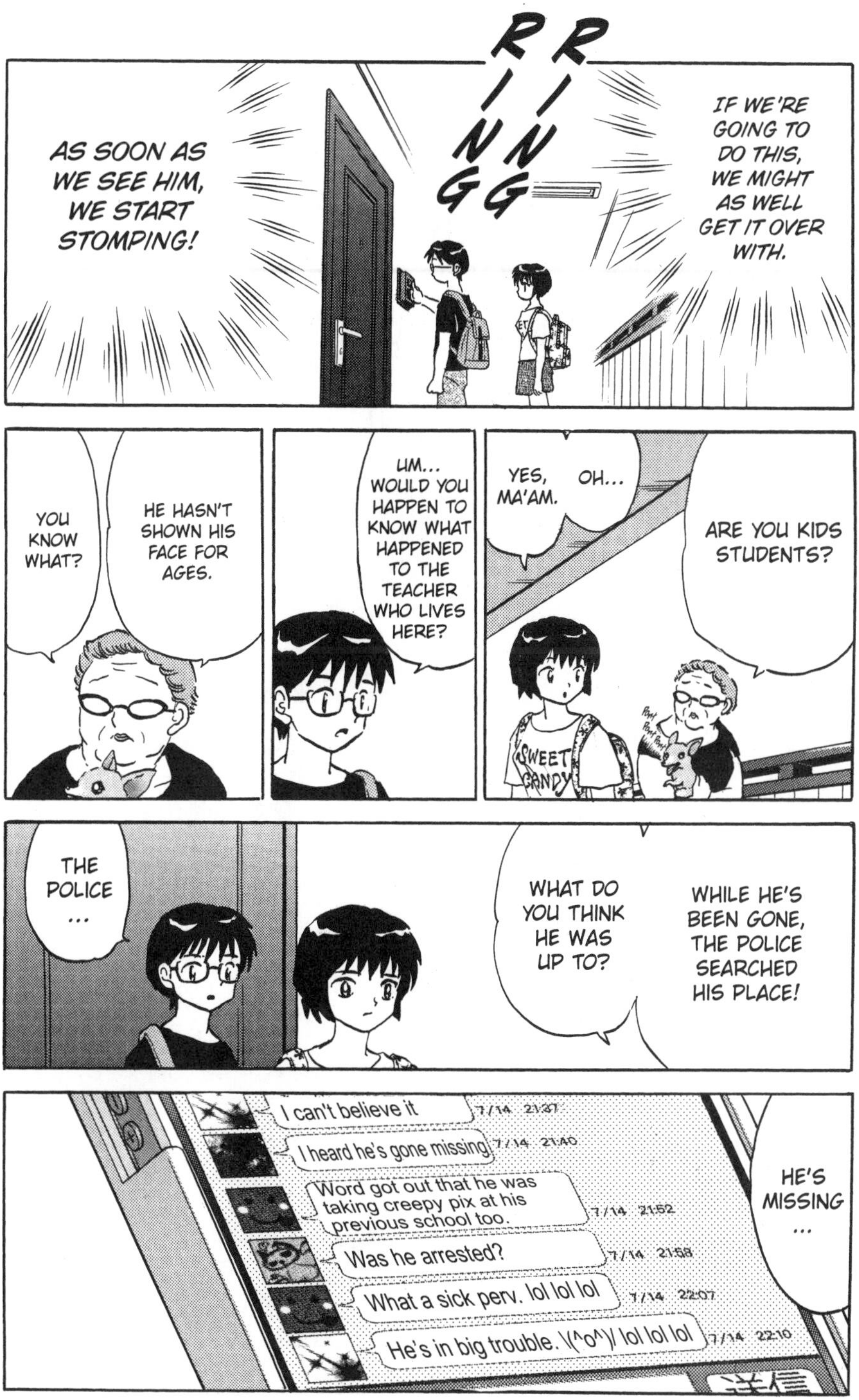
IF WE'RE GOING TO DO THIS, WE MIGHT AS WELL GET IT OVER WITH.
RRING RRING
AS SOON AS WE SEE HIM, WE START STOMPING!
OH...
ARE YOU KIDS STUDENTS?
YES, MA'AM.
UM... WOULD YOU HAPPEN TO KNOW WHAT HAPPENED TO THE TEACHER WHO LIVES HERE?
HE HASN'T SHOWN HIS FACE FOR AGES.
YOU KNOW WHAT?
WHILE HE'S BEEN GONE, THE POLICE SEARCHED HIS PLACE!
WHAT DO YOU THINK HE WAS UP TO?
THE POLICE...
HE'S MISSING...
I can't believe it 7/14 21:37
I heard he's gone missing 7/14 21:40
Word got out that he was taking creepy pix at his previous school too. 7/14 21:52
Was he arrested? 7/14 21:58
What a sick perv. lol lol lol 7/14 22:07
He's in big trouble. \(^o^)/ lol lol lol 7/14 22:10

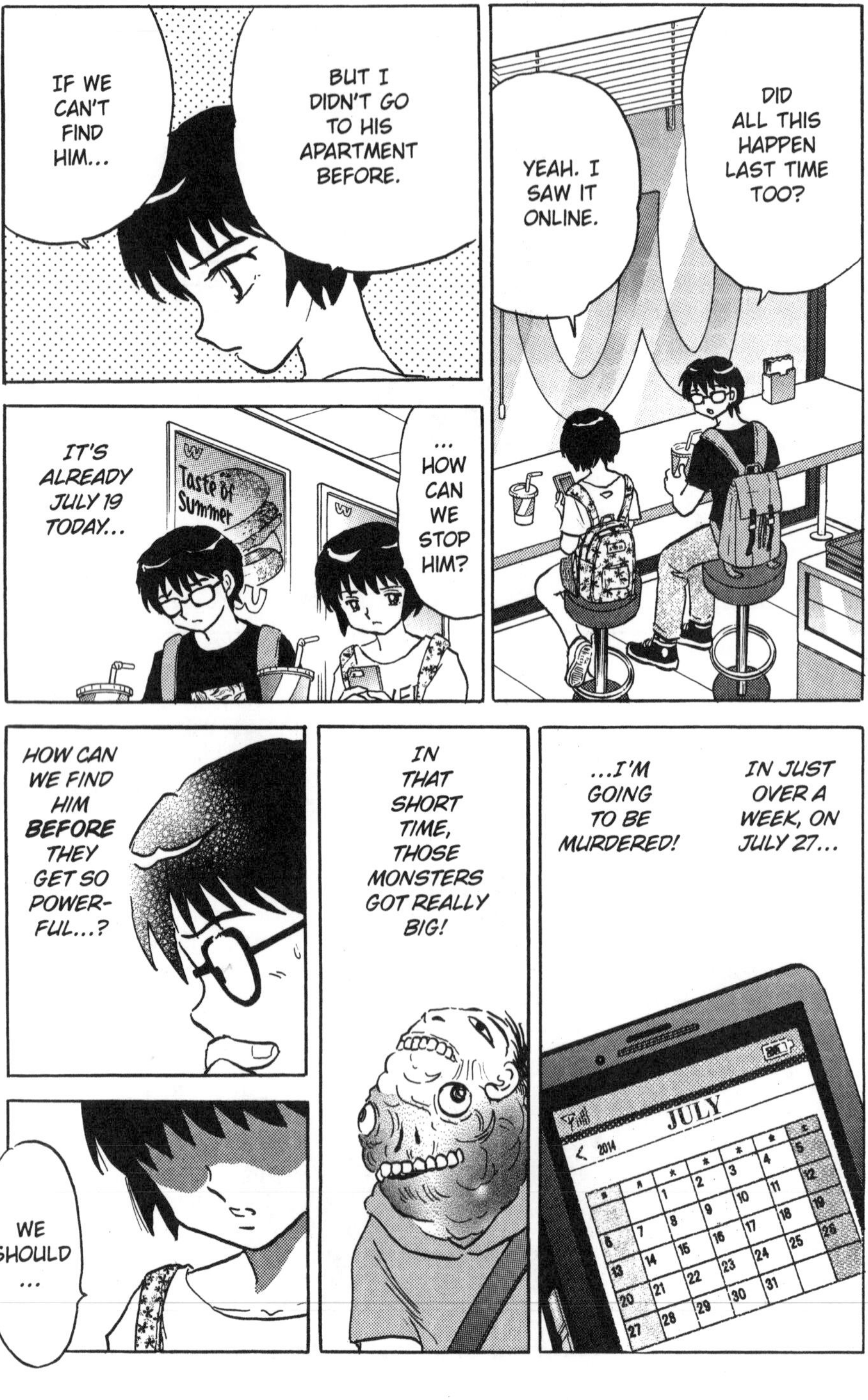
DID ALL THIS HAPPEN LAST TIME TOO?
YEAH. I SAW IT ONLINE.
BUT I DIDN'T GO TO HIS APARTMENT BEFORE.
IF WE CAN'T FIND HIM...
... HOW CAN WE STOP HIM?
Taste of Summer
IT'S ALREADY JULY 19 TODAY...
IN JUST OVER A WEEK, ON JULY 27...
...I'M GOING TO BE MURDERED!
JULY
2014
IN THAT SHORT TIME, THOSE MONSTERS GOT REALLY BIG!
HOW CAN WE FIND HIM **BEFORE** THEY GET SO POWER-FUL...?
WE SHOULD ...

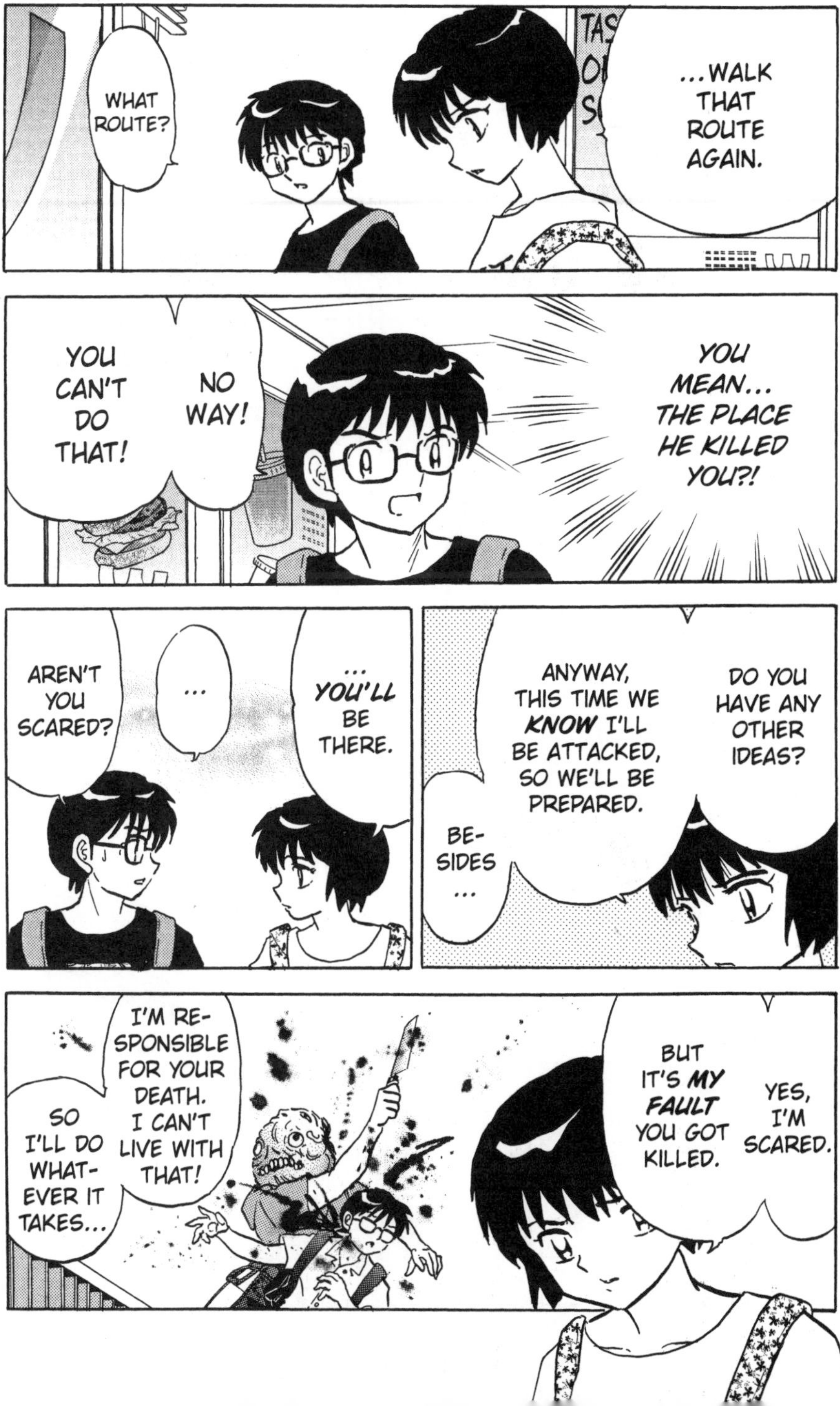
...WALK THAT ROUTE AGAIN.
WHAT ROUTE?
YOU MEAN... THE PLACE HE KILLED YOU?!
NO WAY!
YOU CAN'T DO THAT!
DO YOU HAVE ANY OTHER IDEAS?
ANYWAY, THIS TIME WE KNOW I'LL BE ATTACKED, SO WE'LL BE PREPARED.
BE-SIDES...
...YOU'LL BE THERE.
...
AREN'T YOU SCARED?
YES, I'M SCARED.
BUT IT'S MY FAULT YOU GOT KILLED.
I'M RE-SPONSIBLE FOR YOUR DEATH. I CAN'T LIVE WITH THAT!
SO I'LL DO WHAT-EVER IT TAKES...

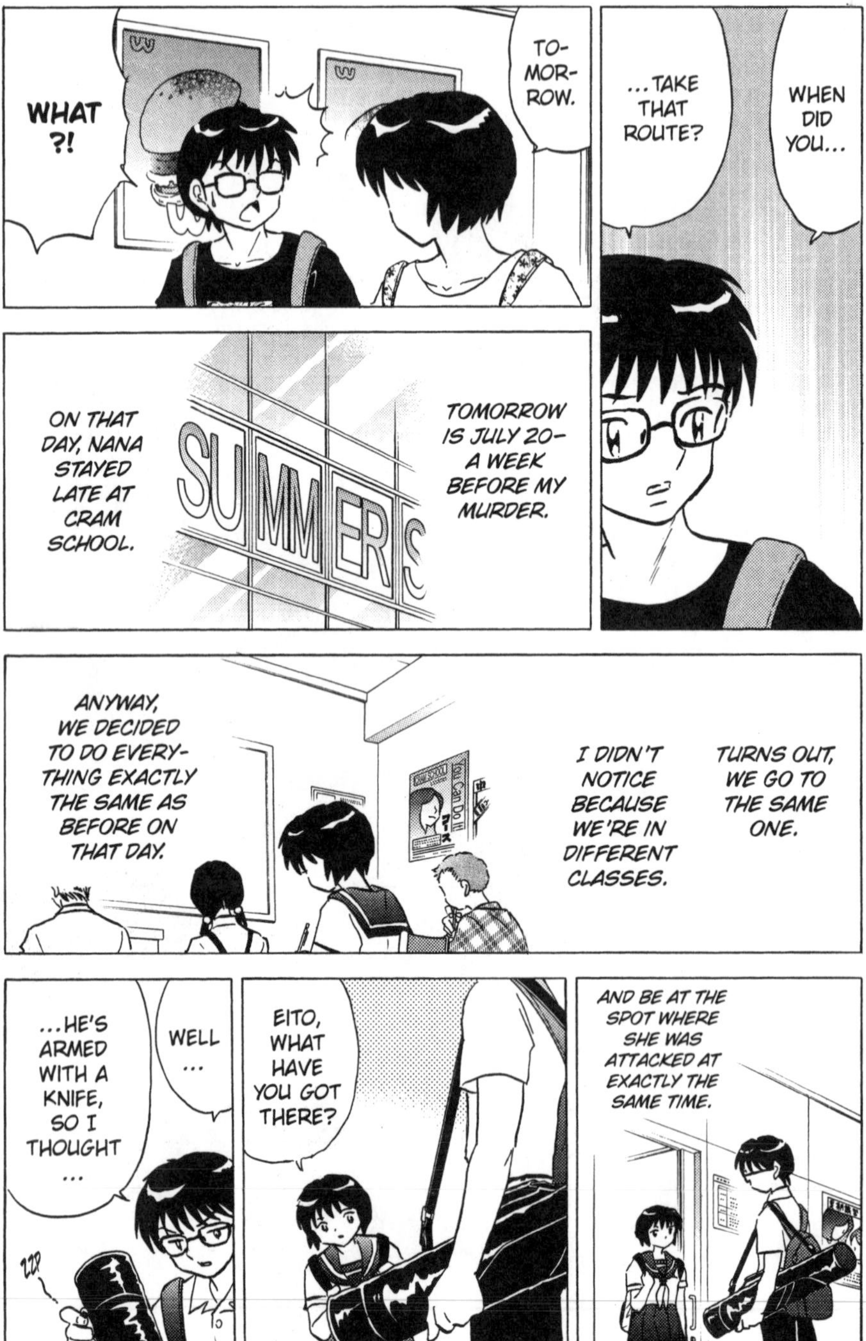
WHEN DID YOU…
…TAKE THAT ROUTE?
TO-MOR-ROW.
WHAT ?!
TOMORROW IS JULY 20— A WEEK BEFORE MY MURDER.
SUMMERS
ON THAT DAY, NANA STAYED LATE AT CRAM SCHOOL.
TURNS OUT, WE GO TO THE SAME ONE.
I DIDN'T NOTICE BECAUSE WE'RE IN DIFFERENT CLASSES.
CRAM SCHOOL
You Can Do It!
ANYWAY, WE DECIDED TO DO EVERYTHING EXACTLY THE SAME AS BEFORE ON THAT DAY.
AND BE AT THE SPOT WHERE SHE WAS ATTACKED AT EXACTLY THE SAME TIME.
EITO, WHAT HAVE YOU GOT THERE?
WELL …
…HE'S ARMED WITH A KNIFE, SO I THOUGHT …
ZZP

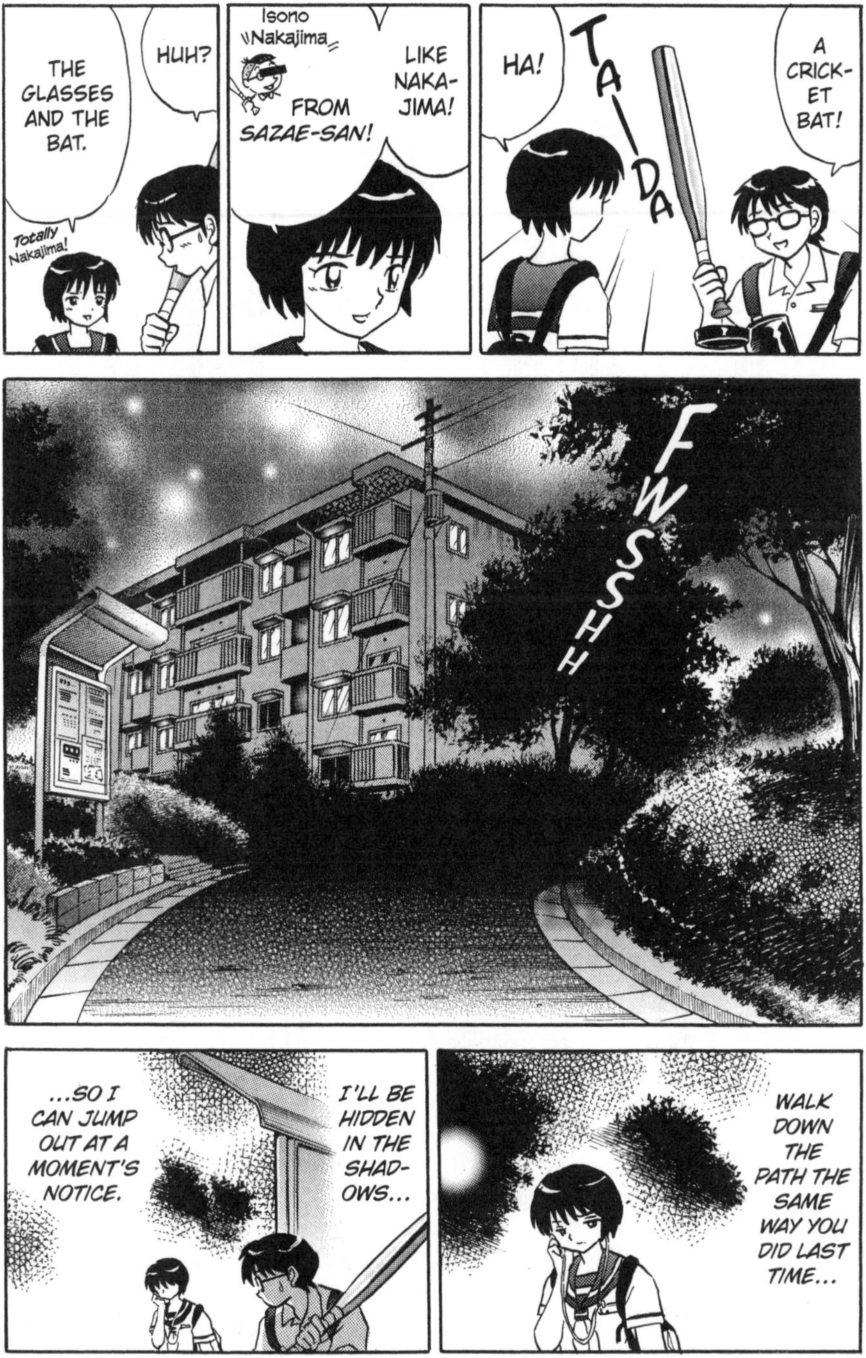
A CRICK-ET BAT!
TAIDA
HA!
LIKE NAKA-JIMA!
FROM SAZAE-SAN!
Isono Nakajima
HUH?
THE GLASSES AND THE BAT.
Totally Nakajima!
FWSSHH
WALK DOWN THE PATH THE SAME WAY YOU DID LAST TIME...
I'LL BE HIDDEN IN THE SHADOWS...
...SO I CAN JUMP OUT AT A MOMENT'S NOTICE.

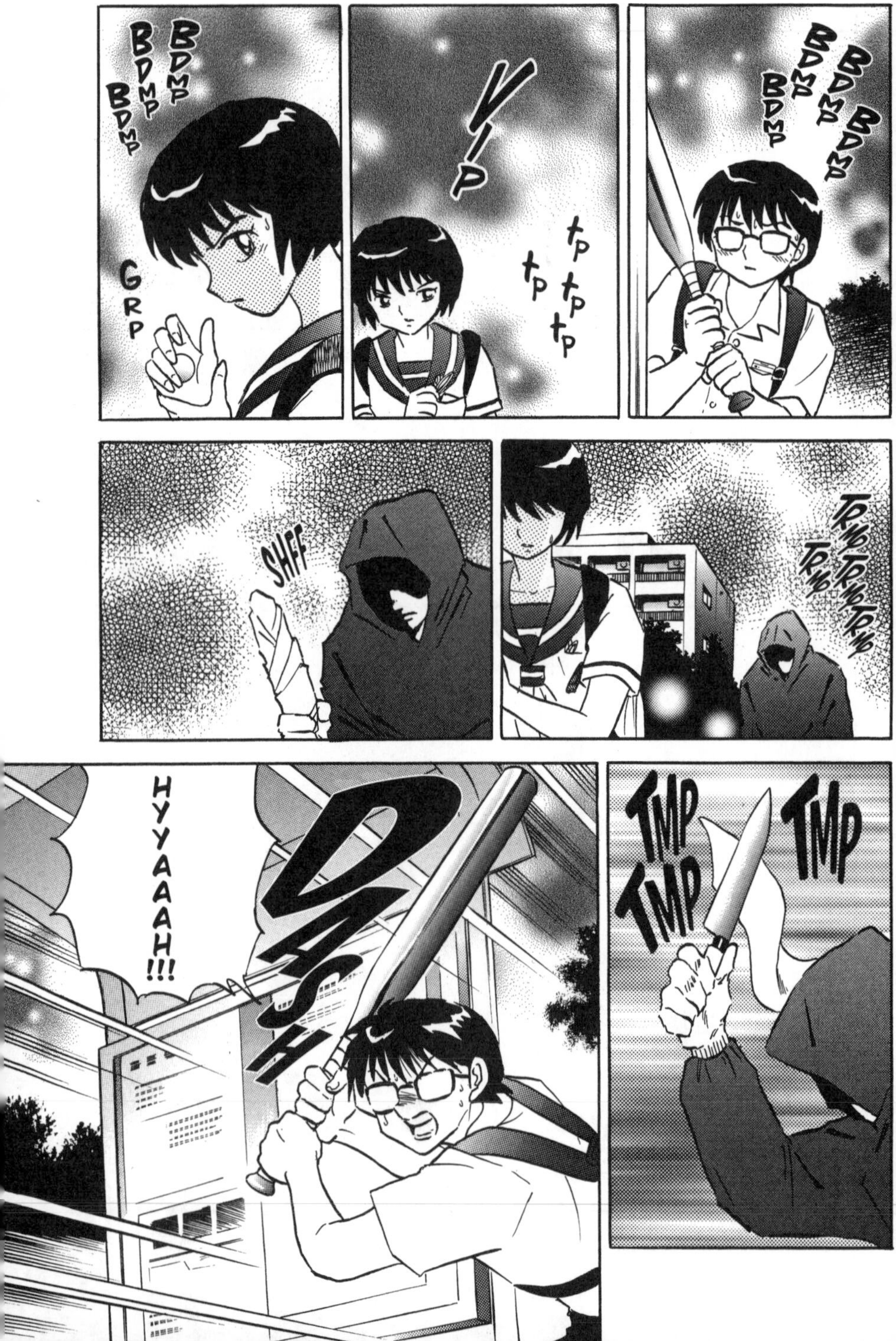

BDMP BDMP BDMP
VIP
tp tp tp tp tp
BDMP BDMP BDMP
GRP
TRMP TRMP TRMP TRMP
SHFF
TMP TMP TMP
HYYAAAAH!!!

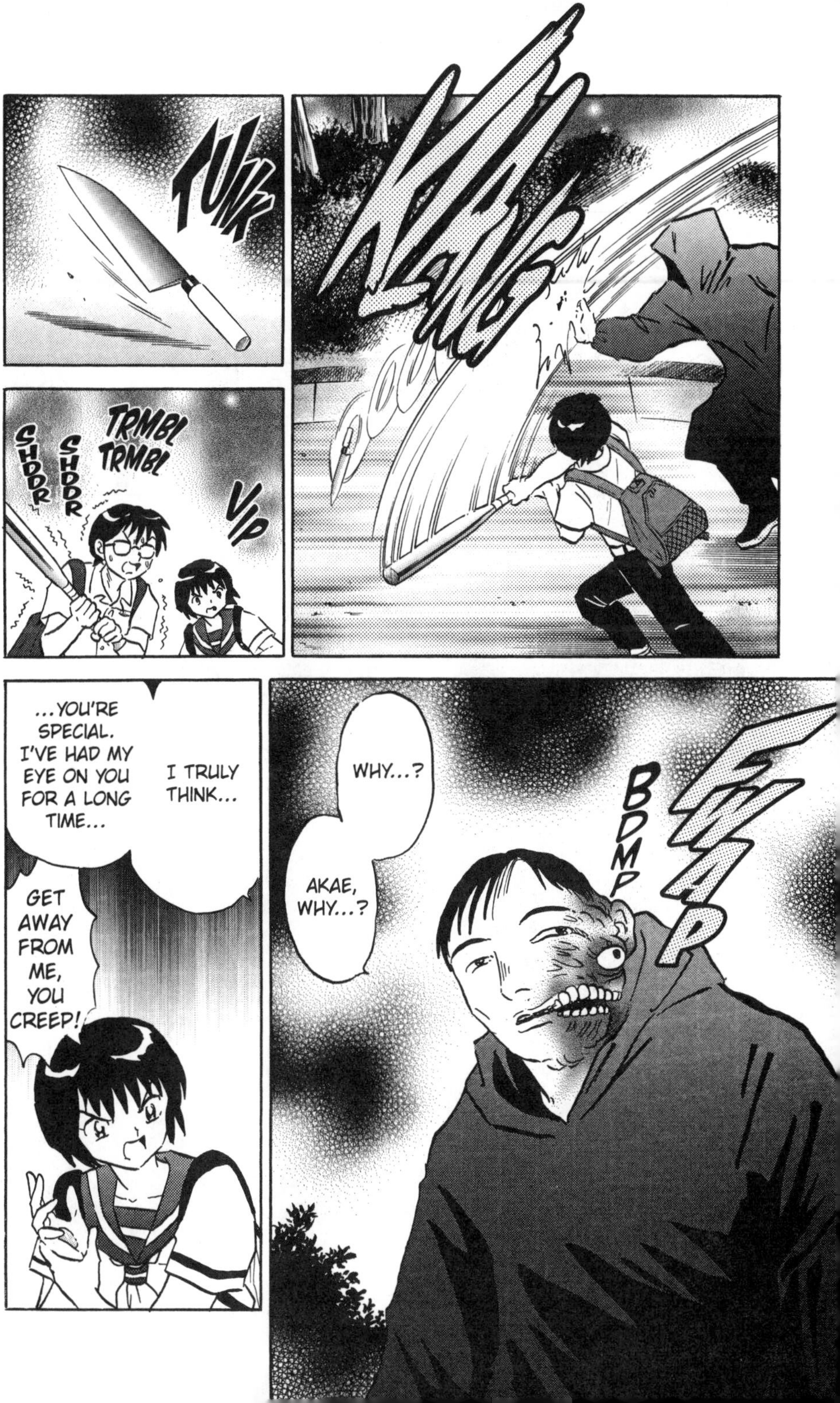
TUNK
SHDDR SHDDR
TRMBL TRMBL
VIP
BDMP
WHY...?
AKAE, WHY...?
I TRULY THINK...
...YOU'RE SPECIAL. I'VE HAD MY EYE ON YOU FOR A LONG TIME...
GET AWAY FROM ME, YOU CREEP!

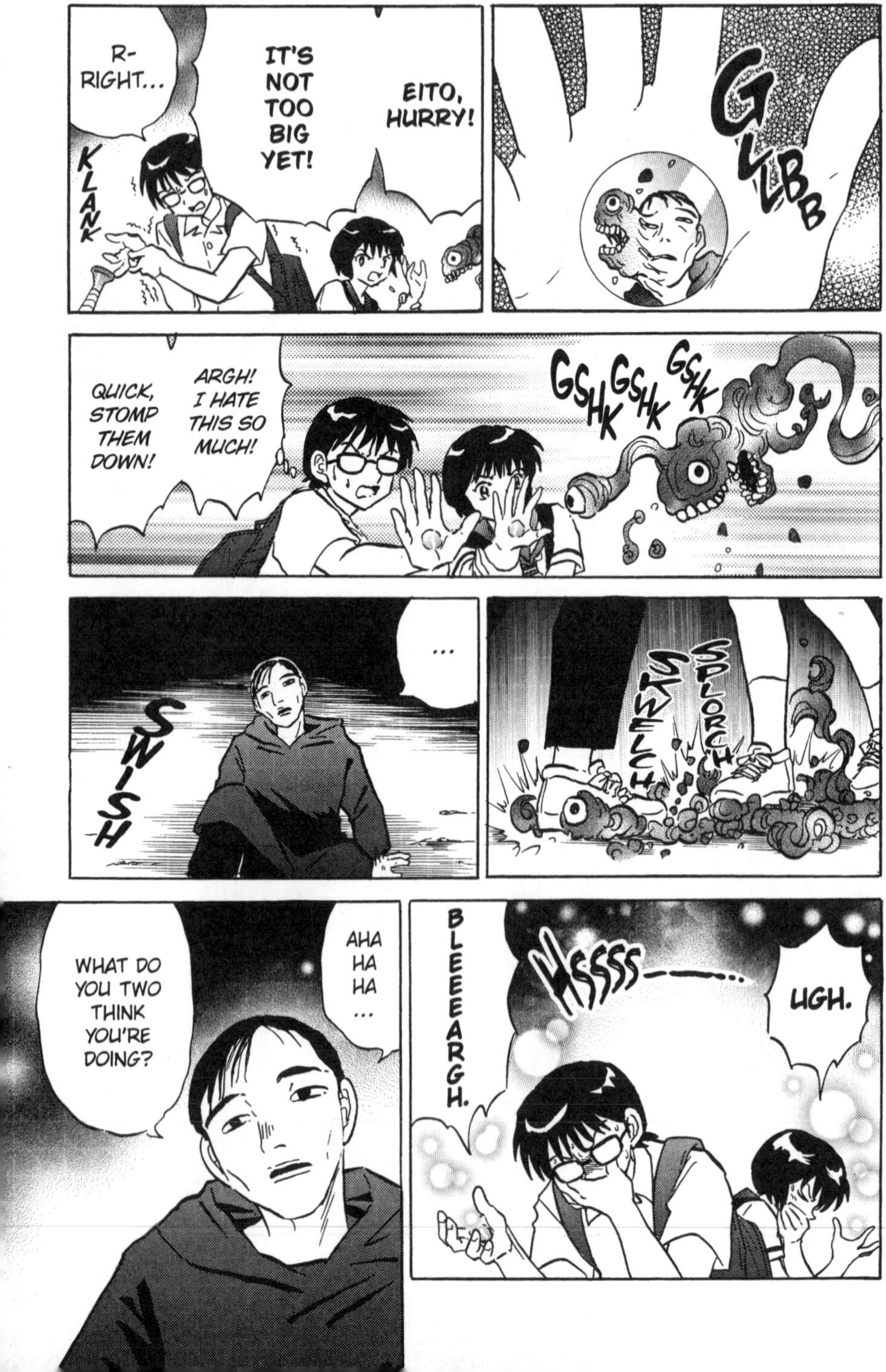
GLLBB
EITO, HURRY!
IT'S NOT TOO BIG YET!
R- RIGHT...
KLANK
GSHK GSHK GSHK
ARGH! I HATE THIS SO MUCH!
QUICK, STOMP THEM DOWN!
SPLORCH
SKWELCH
...
SWISH
UGH.
HSSSS—
BLEEEEARGH.
AHA HA HA...
WHAT DO YOU TWO THINK YOU'RE DOING?

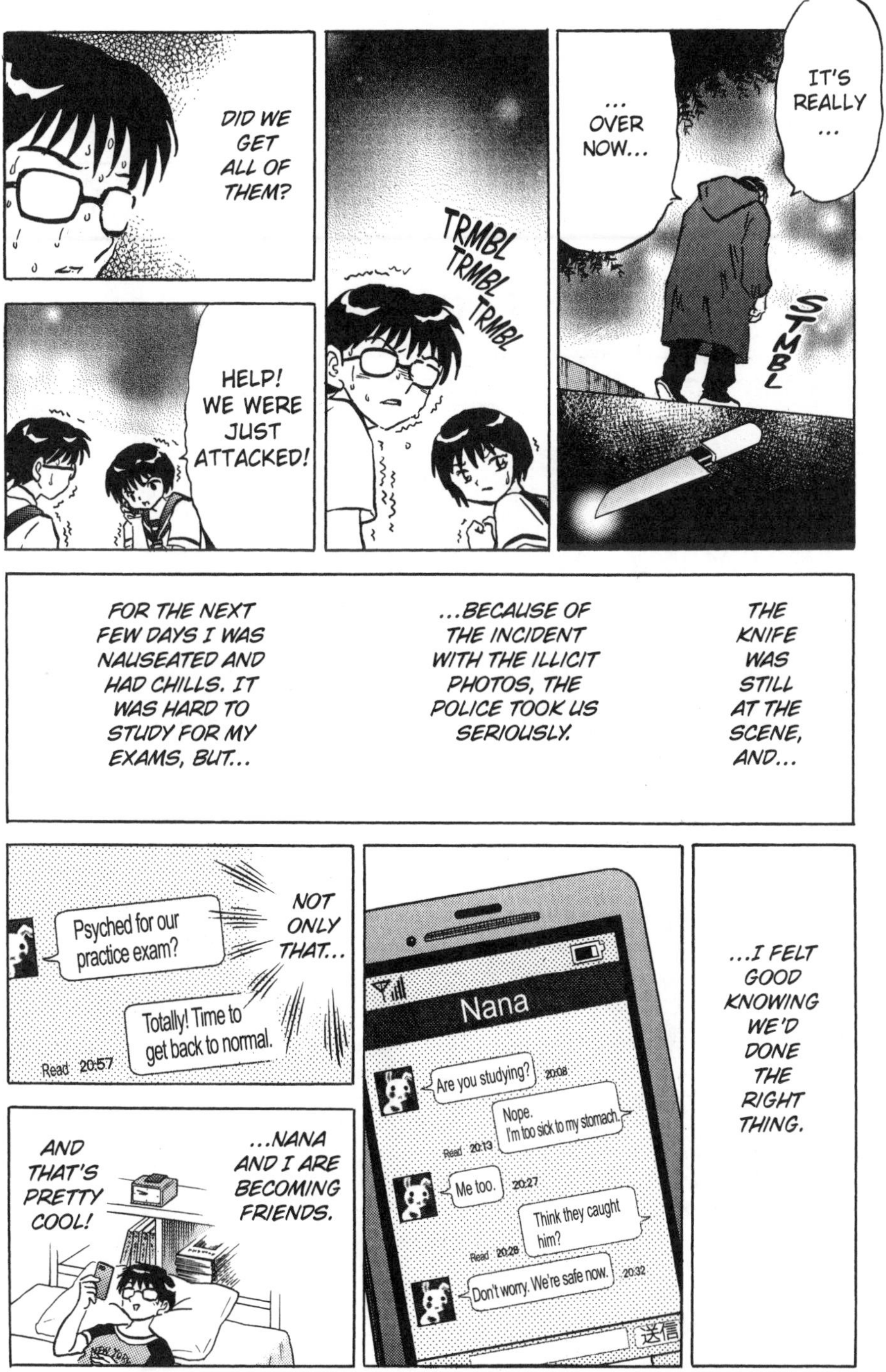
DID WE GET ALL OF THEM?
HELP! WE WERE JUST ATTACKED!
TRMBL TRMBL TRMBL
IT'S REALLY ...
... OVER NOW...
STMBL
FOR THE NEXT FEW DAYS I WAS NAUSEATED AND HAD CHILLS. IT WAS HARD TO STUDY FOR MY EXAMS, BUT...
...BECAUSE OF THE INCIDENT WITH THE ILLICIT PHOTOS, THE POLICE TOOK US SERIOUSLY.
THE KNIFE WAS STILL AT THE SCENE, AND...
Psyched for our practice exam?
Totally! Time to get back to normal.
Read 20:57
NOT ONLY THAT...
...NANA AND I ARE BECOMING FRIENDS.
AND THAT'S PRETTY COOL!
Nana
Are you studying? 20:08
Nope. I'm too sick to my stomach.
Read 20:13
Me too. 20:27
Think they caught him?
Read 20:28
Don't worry. We're safe now. 20:32
送信
...I FELT GOOD KNOWING WE'D DONE THE RIGHT THING.

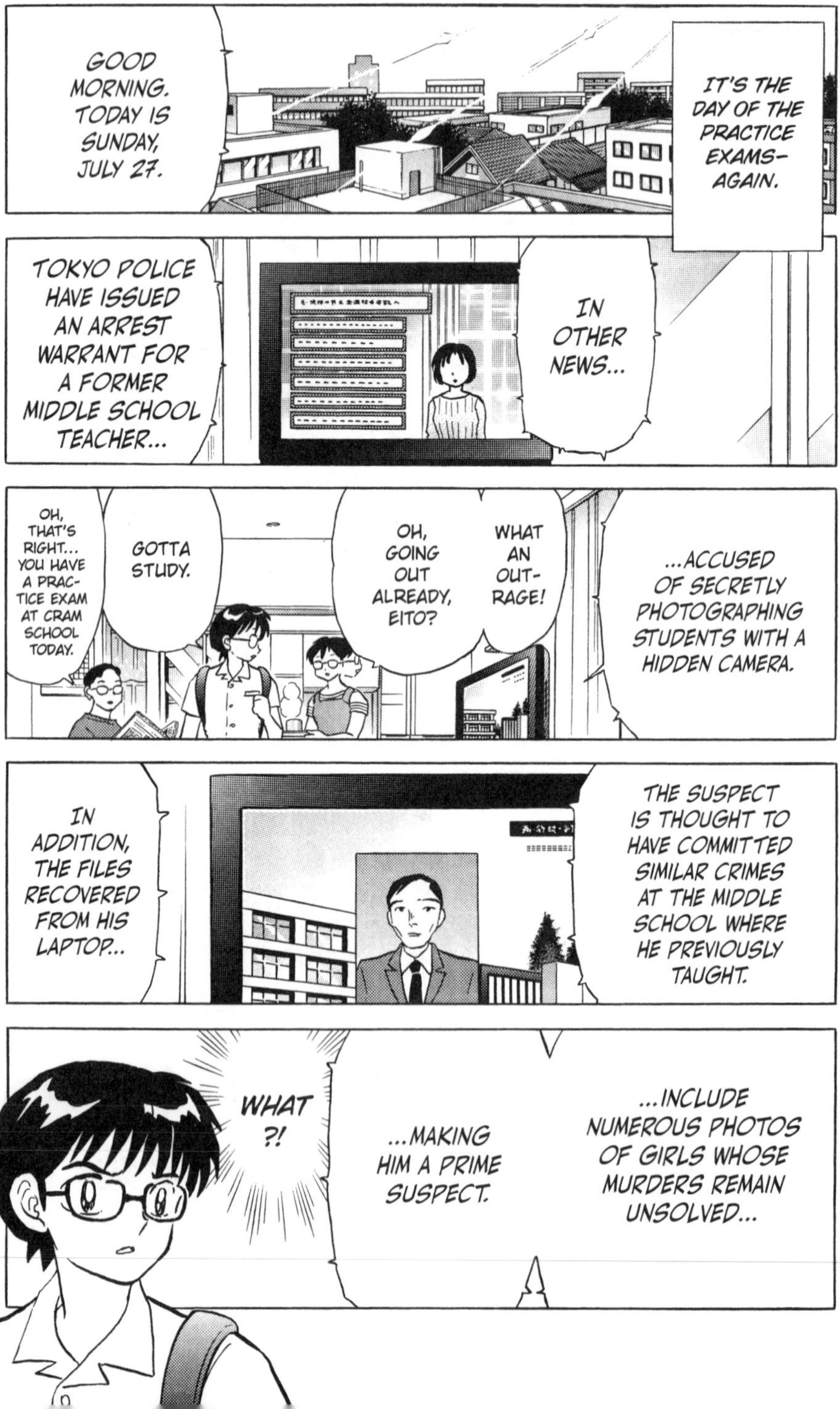
IT'S THE DAY OF THE PRACTICE EXAMS–AGAIN.
GOOD MORNING. TODAY IS SUNDAY, JULY 27.
IN OTHER NEWS...
TOKYO POLICE HAVE ISSUED AN ARREST WARRANT FOR A FORMER MIDDLE SCHOOL TEACHER...
...ACCUSED OF SECRETLY PHOTOGRAPHING STUDENTS WITH A HIDDEN CAMERA.
WHAT AN OUT-RAGE!
OH, GOING OUT ALREADY, EITO?
GOTTA STUDY.
OH, THAT'S RIGHT... YOU HAVE A PRAC-TICE EXAM AT CRAM SCHOOL TODAY.
THE SUSPECT IS THOUGHT TO HAVE COMMITTED SIMILAR CRIMES AT THE MIDDLE SCHOOL WHERE HE PREVIOUSLY TAUGHT.
IN ADDITION, THE FILES RECOVERED FROM HIS LAPTOP...
...INCLUDE NUMEROUS PHOTOS OF GIRLS WHOSE MURDERS REMAIN UNSOLVED...
...MAKING HIM A PRIME SUSPECT.
WHAT?!

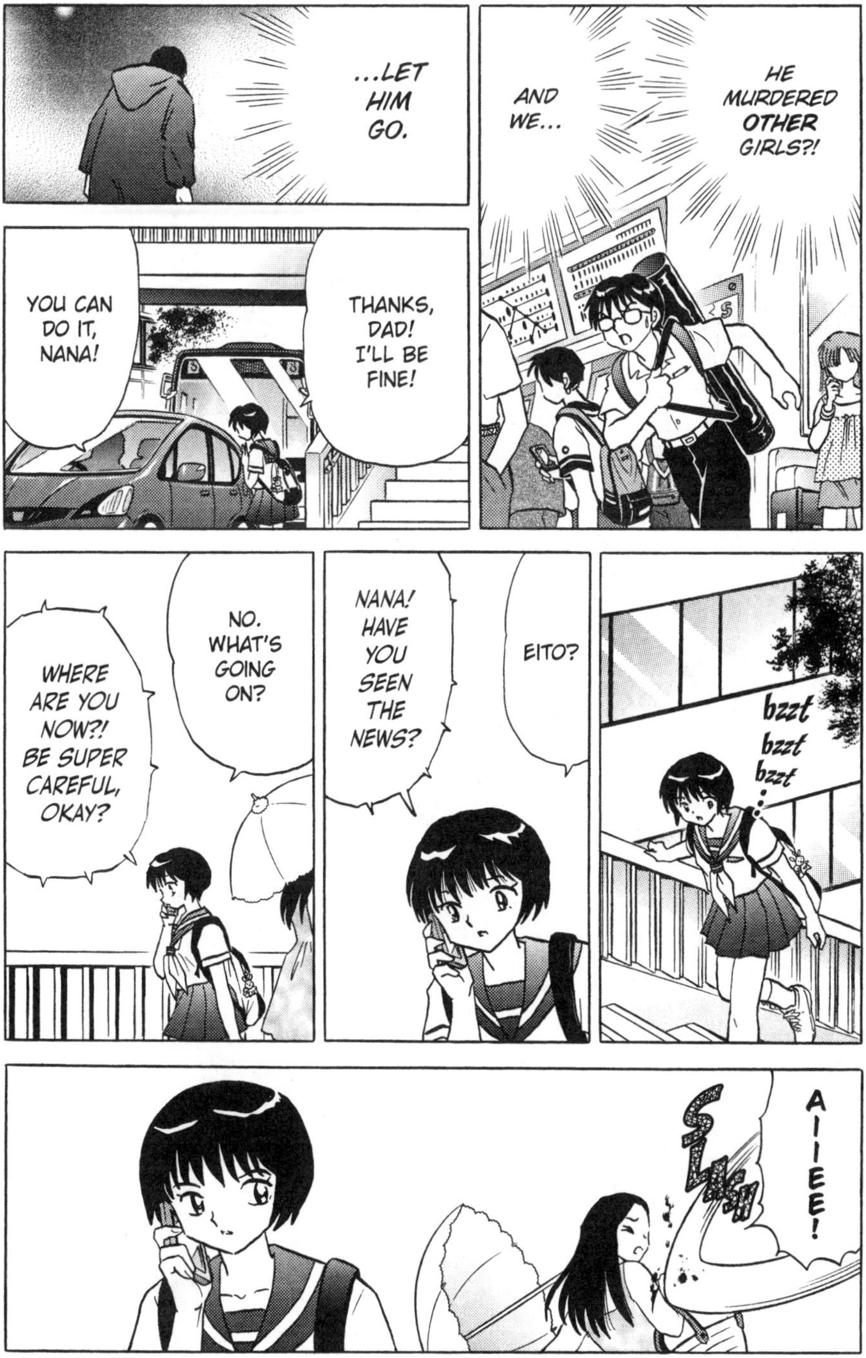
HE MURDERED OTHER GIRLS?!
AND WE...
...LET HIM GO.
YOU CAN DO IT, NANA!
THANKS, DAD! I'LL BE FINE!
bzzt
bzzt
bzzt
EITO?
NANA! HAVE YOU SEEN THE NEWS?
NO. WHAT'S GOING ON?
WHERE ARE YOU NOW?! BE SUPER CAREFUL, OKAY?
AIIEEE!
SLASH

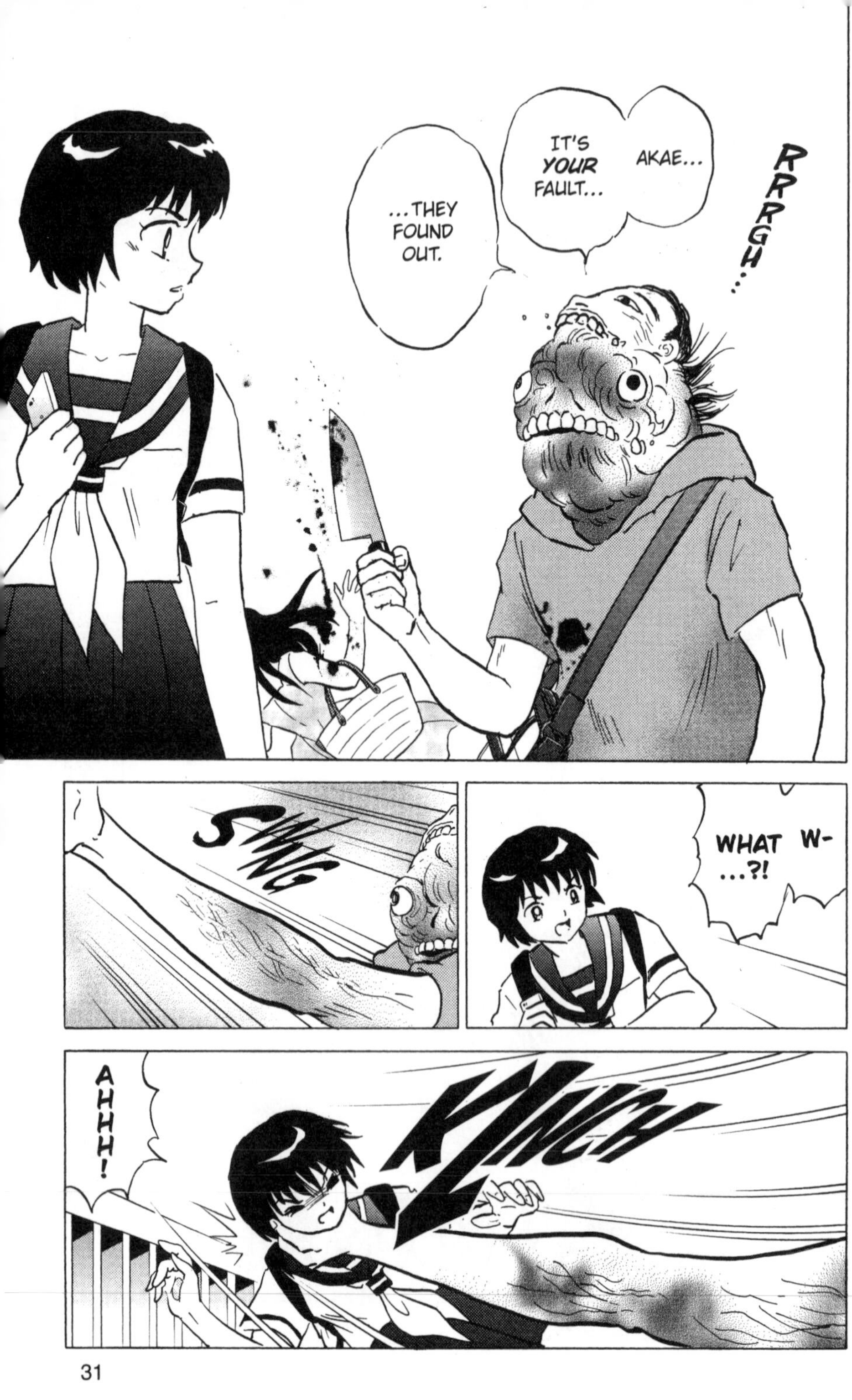
RRRGH...
AKAE...
IT'S YOUR FAULT...
...THEY FOUND OUT.
WHAT W- ...?!
SWING
AHHH!
KLINCH

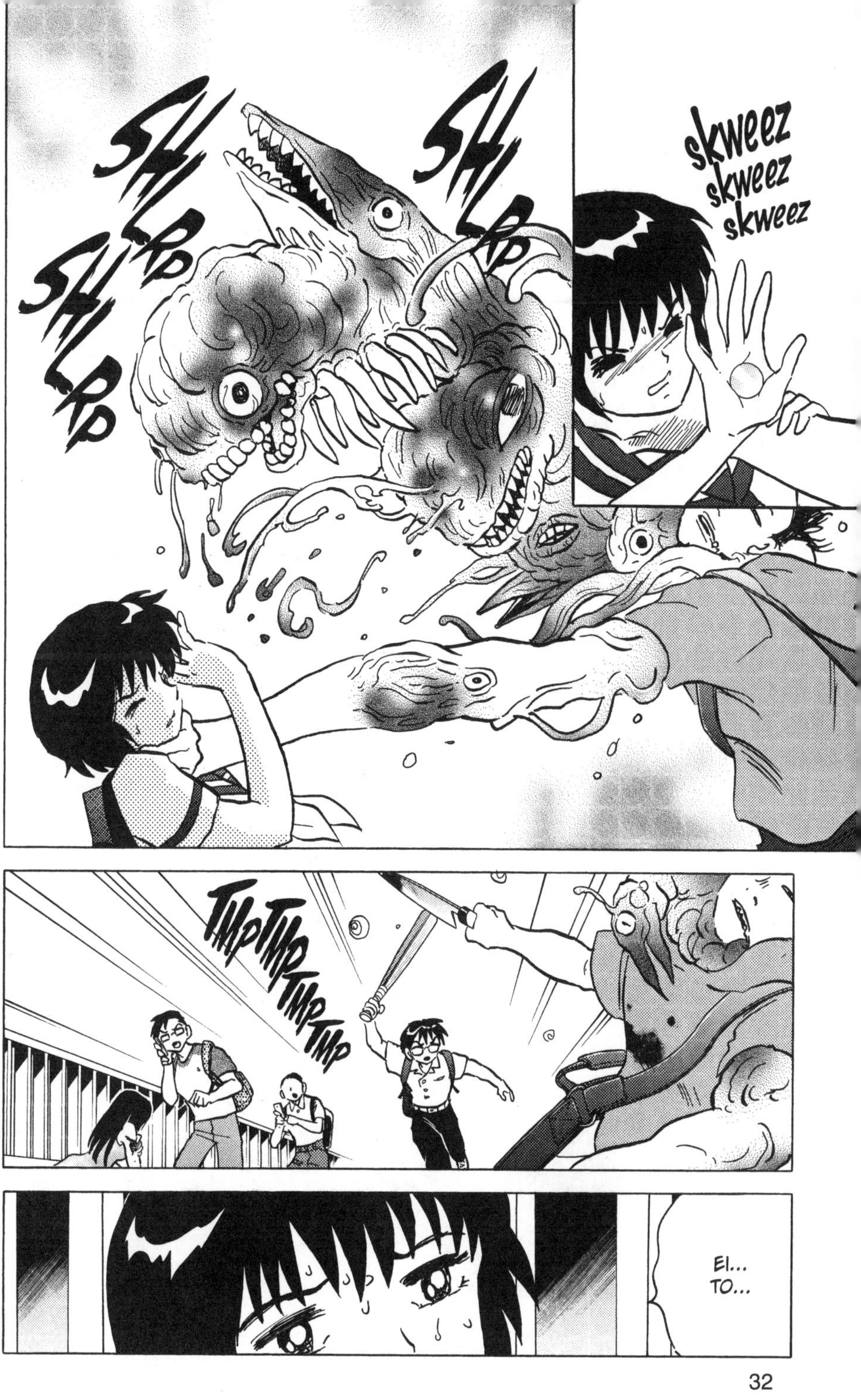
skweez
skweez
skweez
SHLRP
SHLRP
SHLRP
TMPTMPTMPTMP
EI... TO...

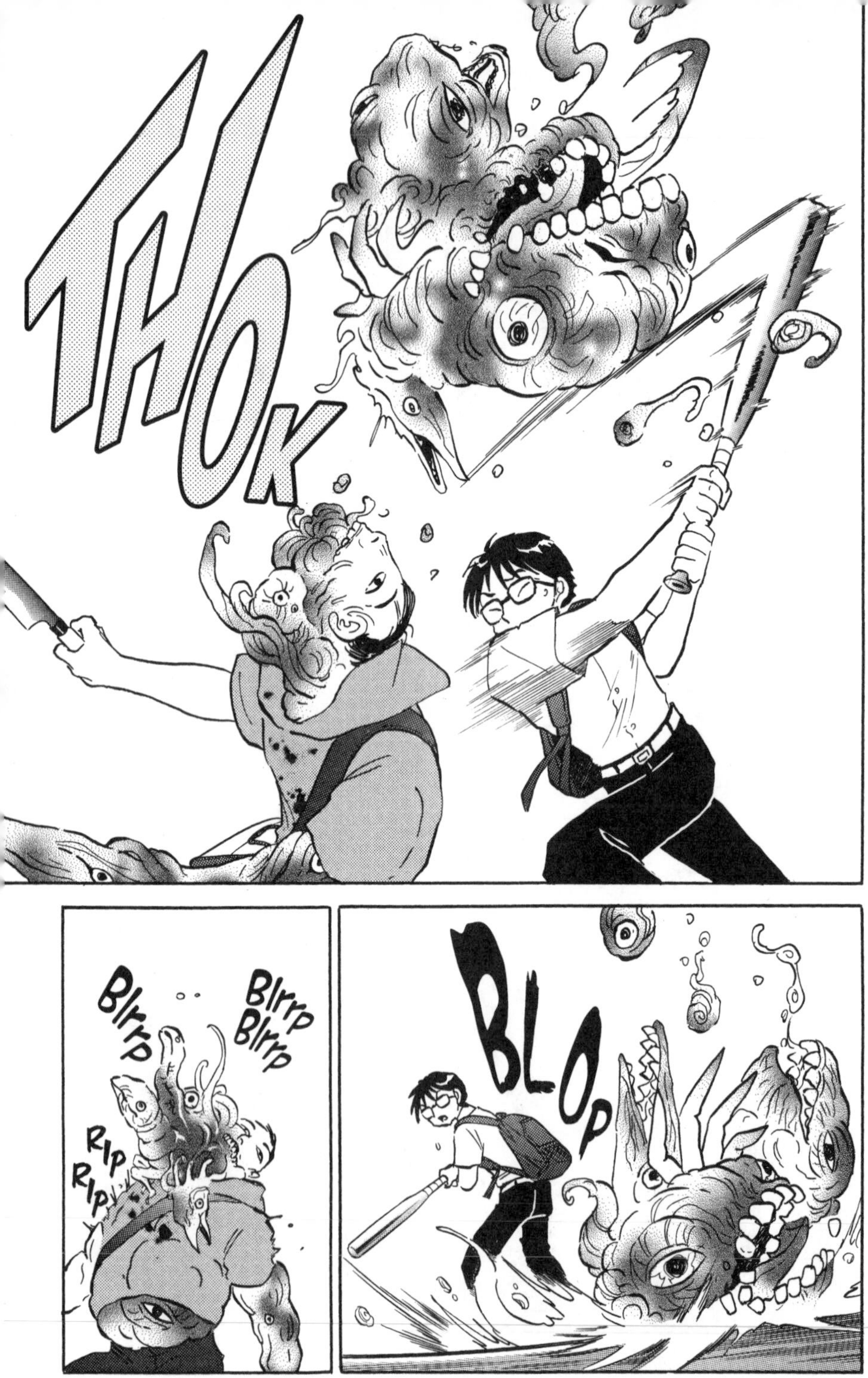
THOK
BLOP
Blrrp
Blrrp
Blrrp
RIP
RIP

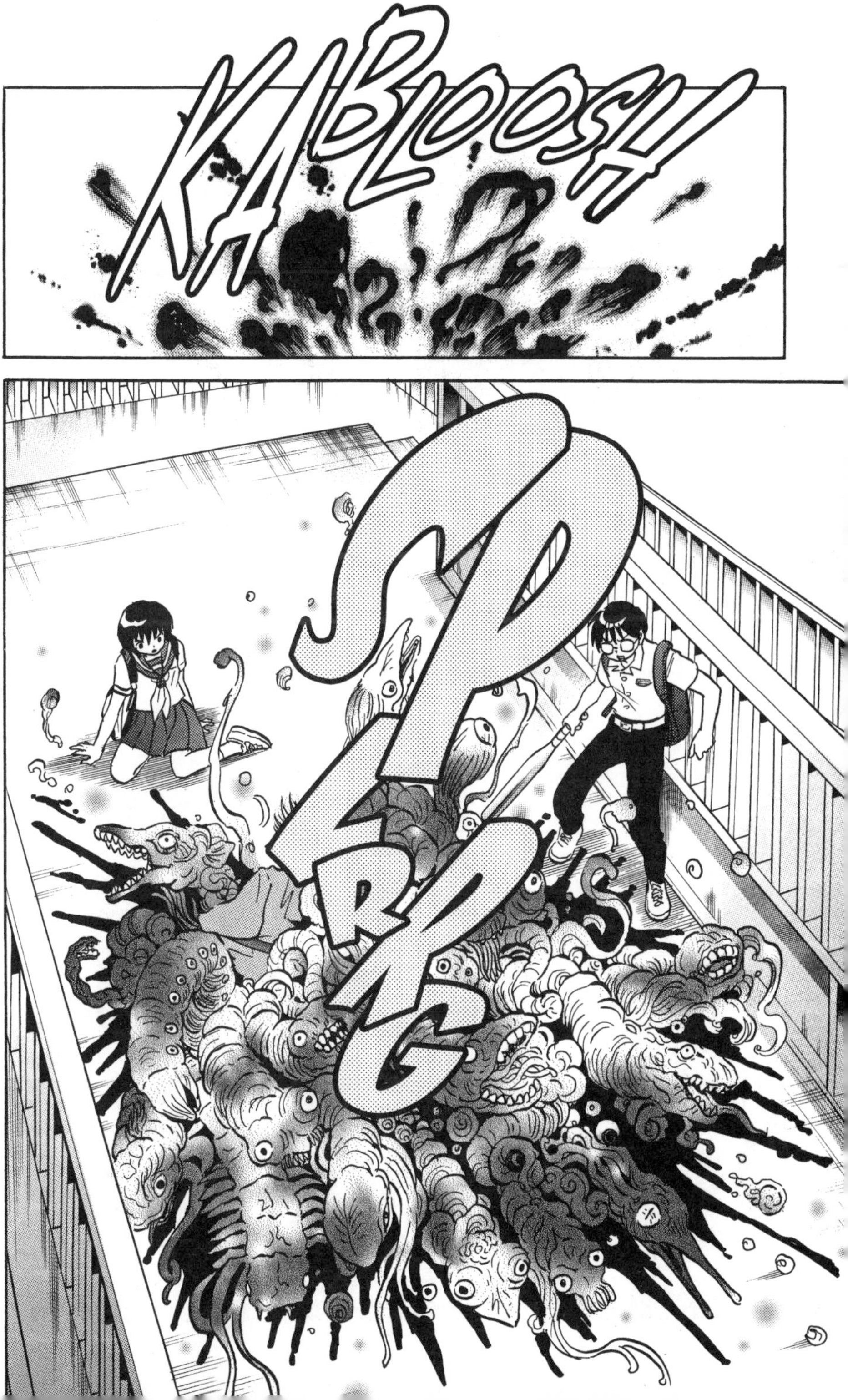
KABLOOSH

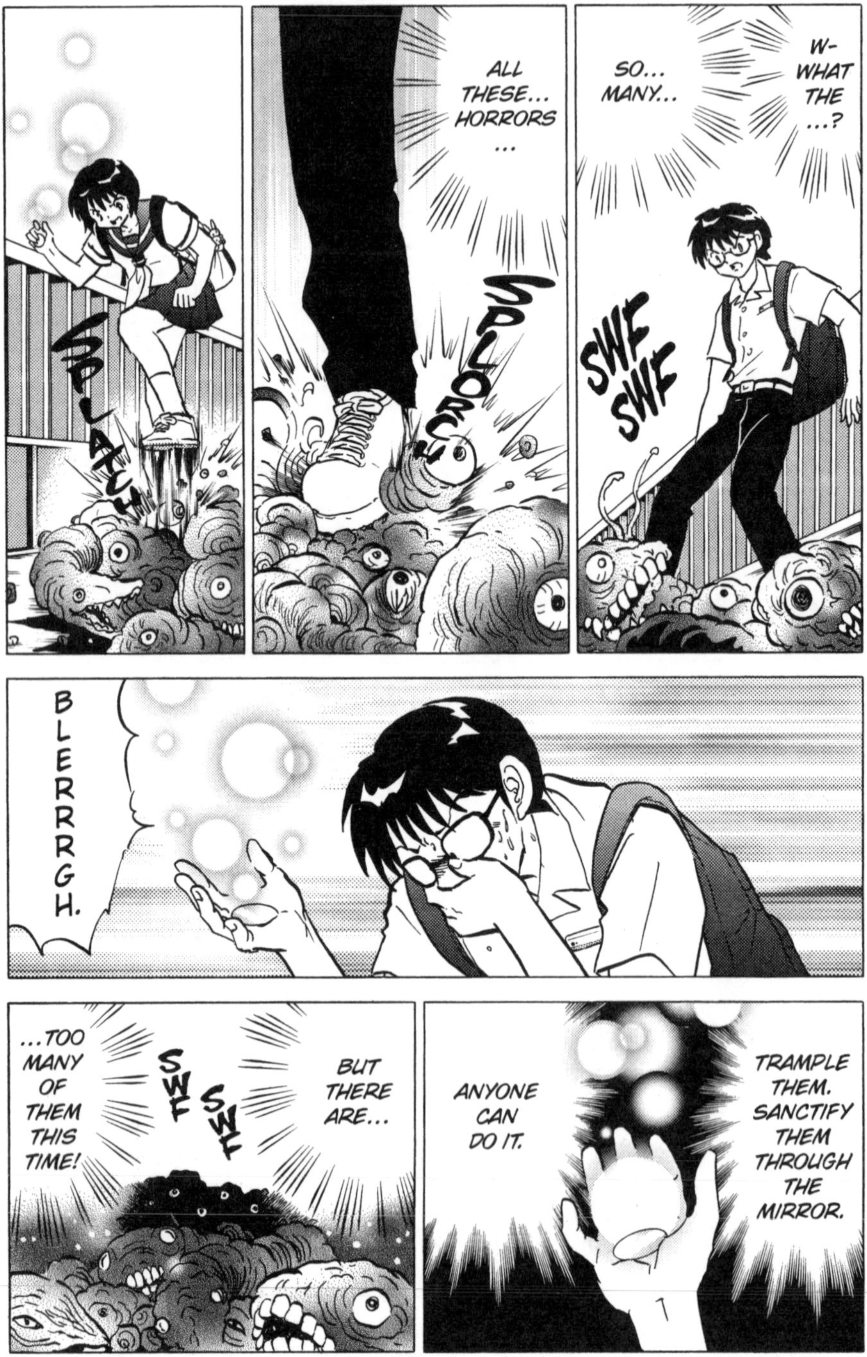
W-WHAT THE ...?
SO... MANY...
SWF SWF
ALL THESE... HORRORS ...
SPLORCH
SPLATCH
BLERRRGH.
TRAMPLE THEM. SANCTIFY THEM THROUGH THE MIRROR.
ANYONE CAN DO IT.
BUT THERE ARE...
SWF SWF
...TOO MANY OF THEM THIS TIME!

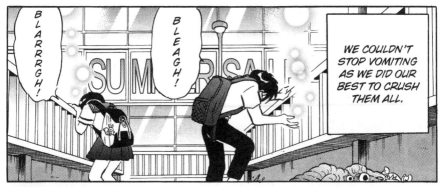

WE COULDN'T STOP VOMITING AS WE DID OUR BEST TO CRUSH THEM ALL.
BLEAGH!
BLARRRGH!
AND IN THE END...
KRIKKK
I CAN'T... ANYMORE...
I'M... DYING...
WEE-OO
WEE-OO
WEE-OO...
WHEN I CAME TO...
...I WAS IN NO CONDITION TO TAKE A PRACTICE EXAM.

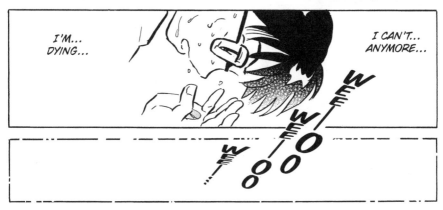

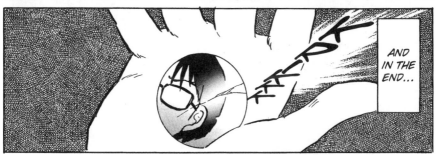

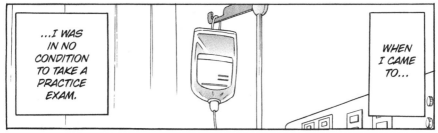

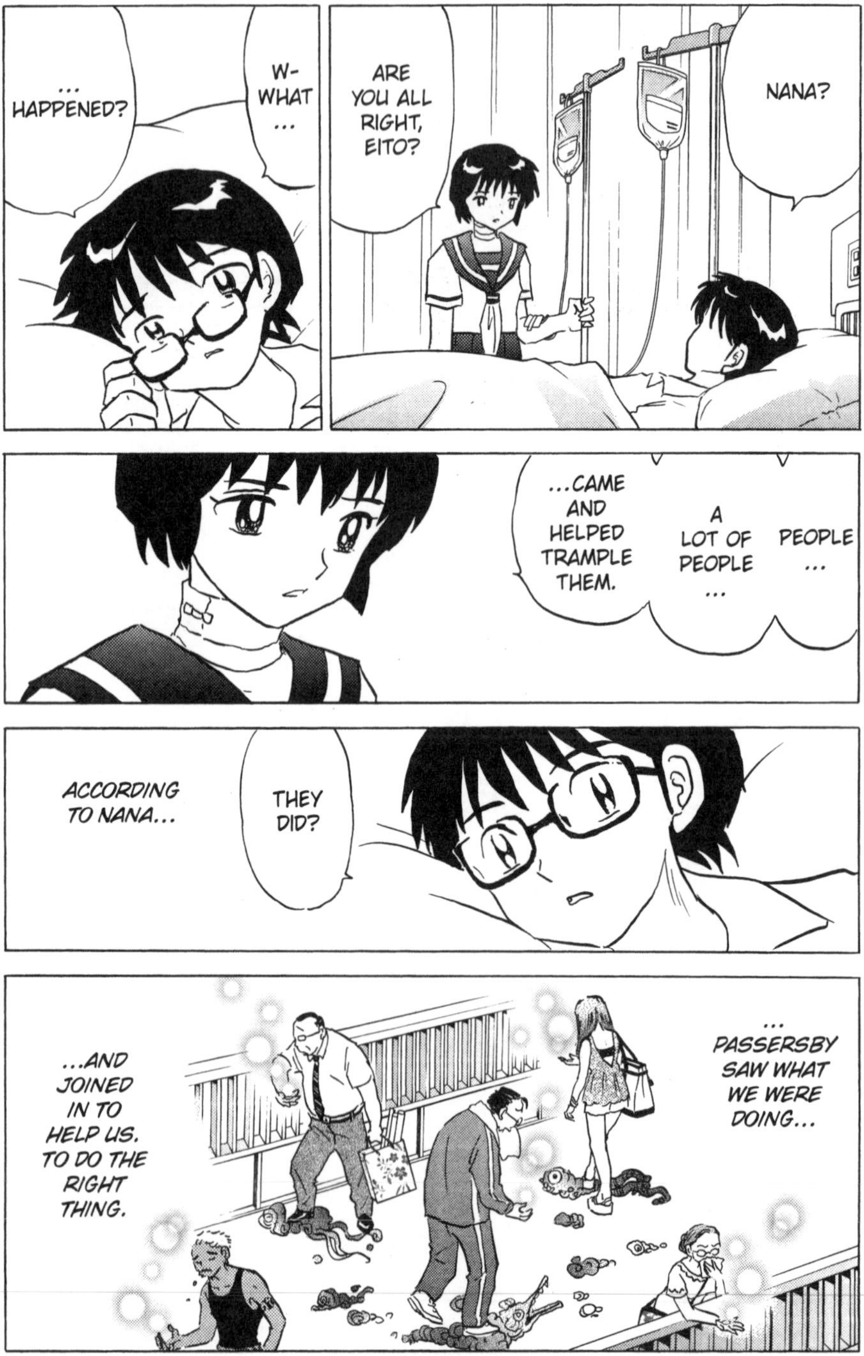
NANA?
ARE YOU ALL RIGHT, EITO?
W-WHAT ...
... HAPPENED?
PEOPLE ...
A LOT OF PEOPLE ...
...CAME AND HELPED TRAMPLE THEM.
THEY DID?
ACCORDING TO NANA...
... PASSERSBY SAW WHAT WE WERE DOING...
...AND JOINED IN TO HELP US. TO DO THE RIGHT THING.

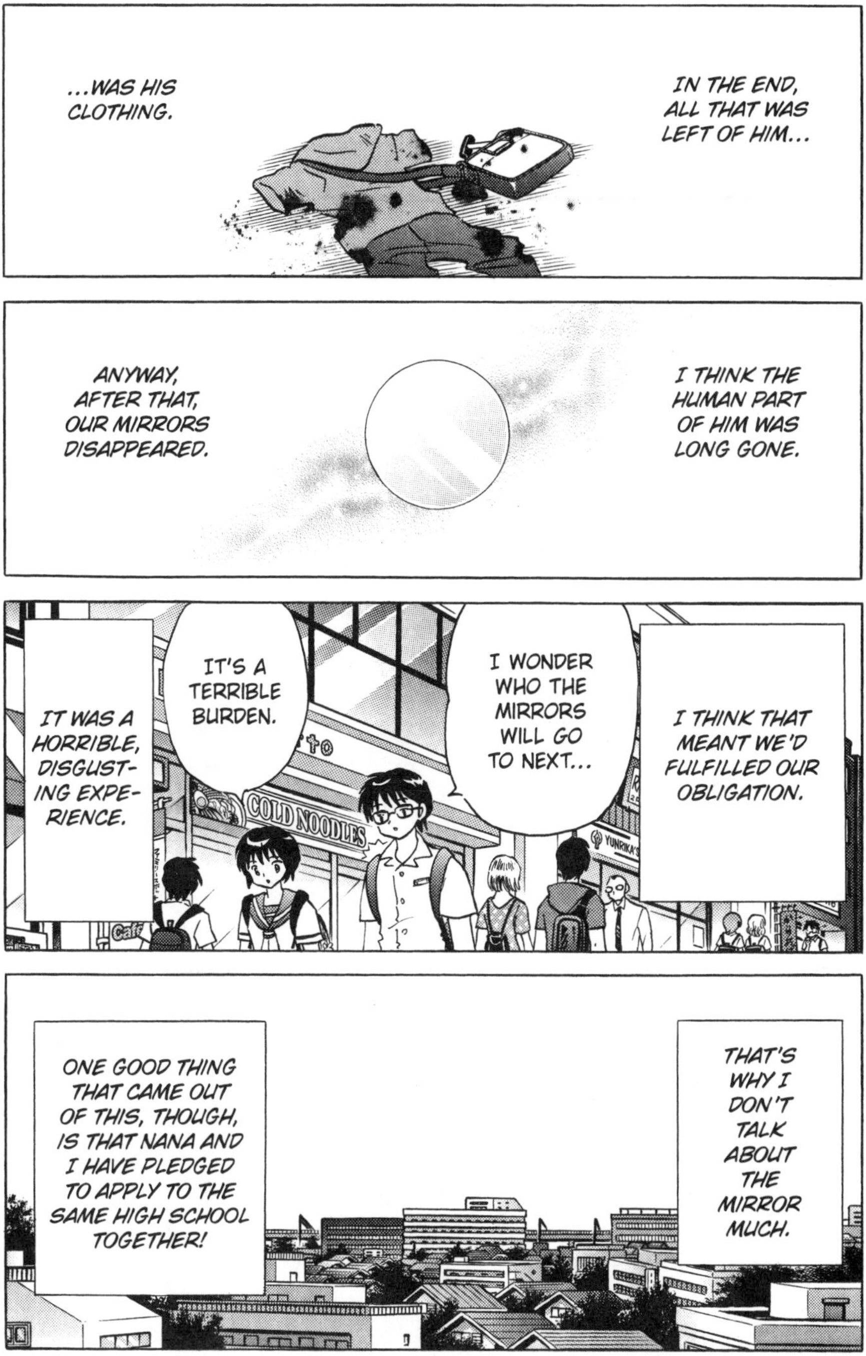
IN THE END, ALL THAT WAS LEFT OF HIM...
...WAS HIS CLOTHING.
I THINK THE HUMAN PART OF HIM WAS LONG GONE.
ANYWAY, AFTER THAT, OUR MIRRORS DISAPPEARED.
I THINK THAT MEANT WE'D FULFILLED OUR OBLIGATION.
YUNRIKA'S
I WONDER WHO THE MIRRORS WILL GO TO NEXT...
IT'S A TERRIBLE BURDEN.
COLD NOODLES
IT WAS A HORRIBLE, DISGUST-ING EXPE-RIENCE.
THAT'S WHY I DON'T TALK ABOUT THE MIRROR MUCH.
ONE GOOD THING THAT CAME OUT OF THIS, THOUGH, IS THAT NANA AND I HAVE PLEDGED TO APPLY TO THE SAME HIGH SCHOOL TOGETHER!

Revenge Doll

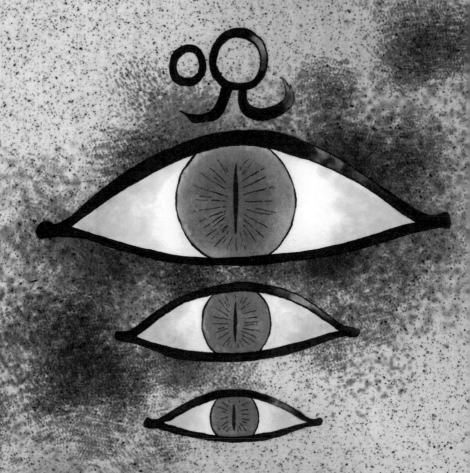

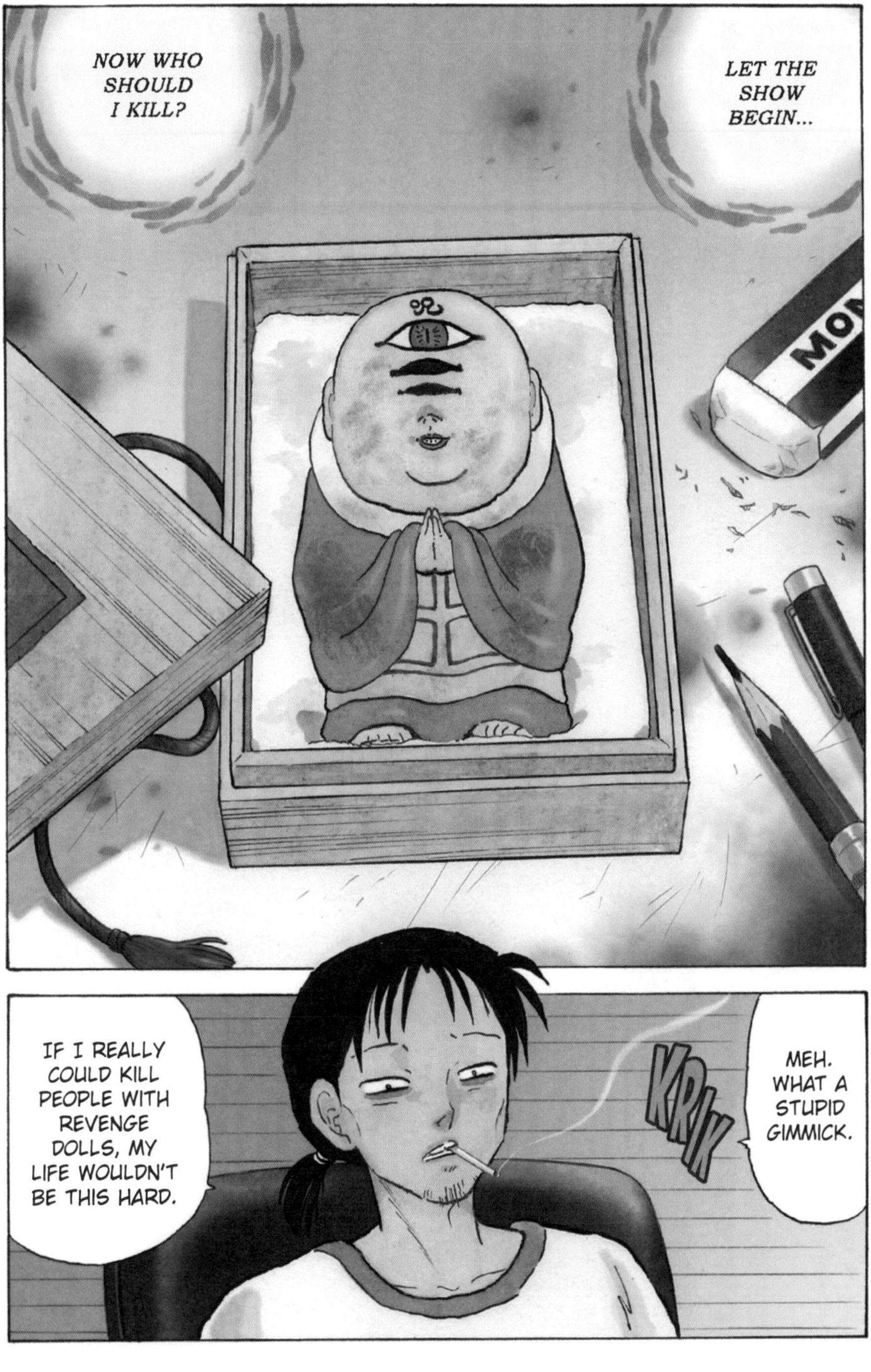
LET THE SHOW BEGIN...
NOW WHO SHOULD I KILL?
MEH. WHAT A STUPID GIMMICK.
KRIK
IF I REALLY COULD KILL PEOPLE WITH REVENGE DOLLS, MY LIFE WOULDN'T BE THIS HARD.

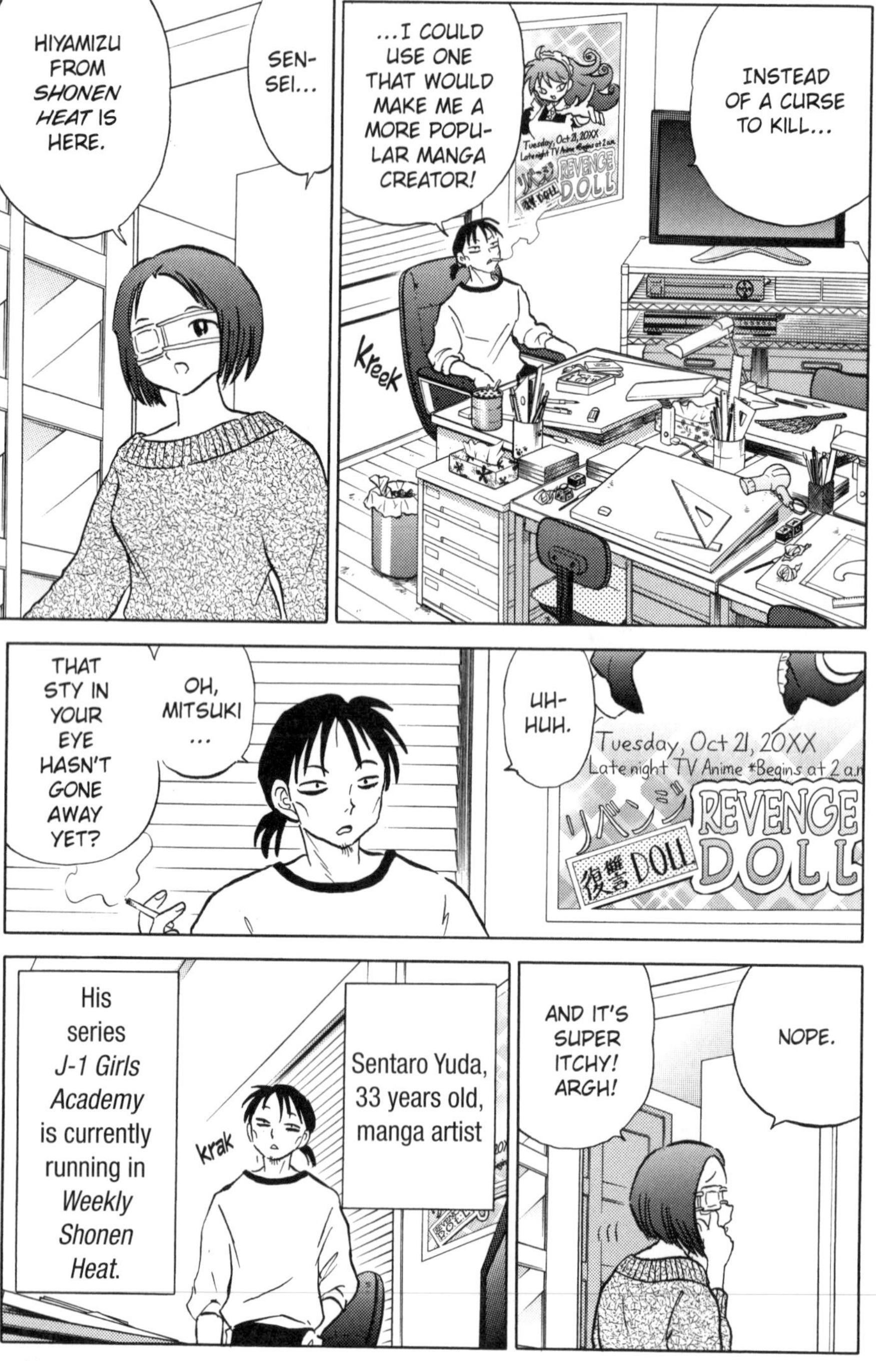
INSTEAD OF A CURSE TO KILL...
...I COULD USE ONE THAT WOULD MAKE ME A MORE POPULAR MANGA CREATOR!
Kreek
SEN-SEI...
HIYAMIZU FROM *SHONEN HEAT* IS HERE.
UH-HUH.
Tuesday, Oct 21, 20XX
Late night TV Anime *Begins at 2 a.m
リベンジ
REVENGE DOLL
復讐DOLL
OH, MITSUKI...
THAT STY IN YOUR EYE HASN'T GONE AWAY YET?
NOPE.
AND IT'S SUPER ITCHY! ARGH!
Sentaro Yuda, 33 years old, manga artist
krak
His series *J-1 Girls Academy* is currently running in *Weekly Shonen Heat*.

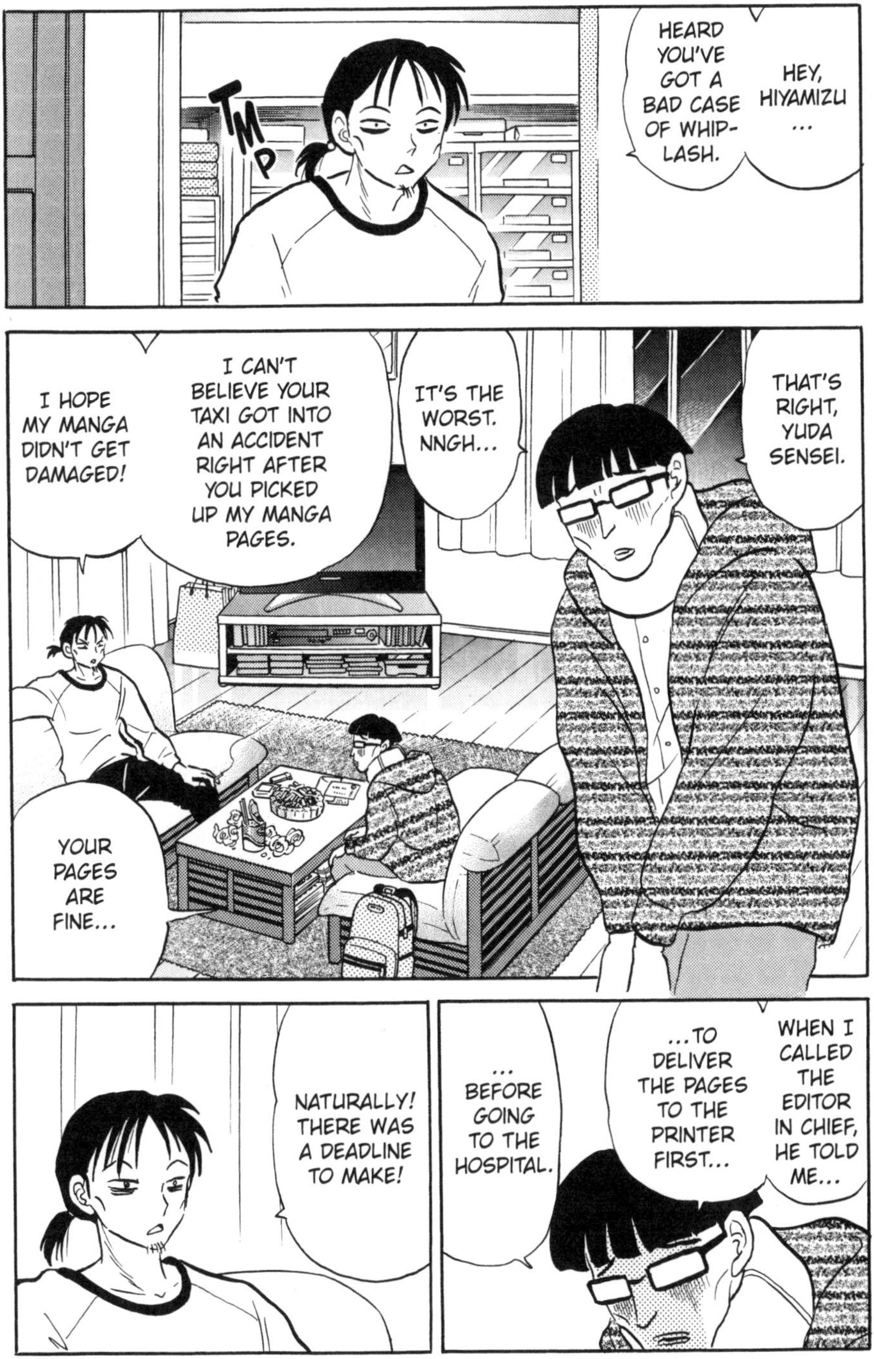
HEY, HIYAMIZU...
HEARD YOU'VE GOT A BAD CASE OF WHIP-LASH.
TMP
THAT'S RIGHT, YUDA SENSEI.
IT'S THE WORST. NNGH...
I CAN'T BELIEVE YOUR TAXI GOT INTO AN ACCIDENT RIGHT AFTER YOU PICKED UP MY MANGA PAGES.
I HOPE MY MANGA DIDN'T GET DAMAGED!
YOUR PAGES ARE FINE...
WHEN I CALLED THE EDITOR IN CHIEF, HE TOLD ME...
...TO DELIVER THE PAGES TO THE PRINTER FIRST...
... BEFORE GOING TO THE HOSPITAL.
NATURALLY! THERE WAS A DEADLINE TO MAKE!

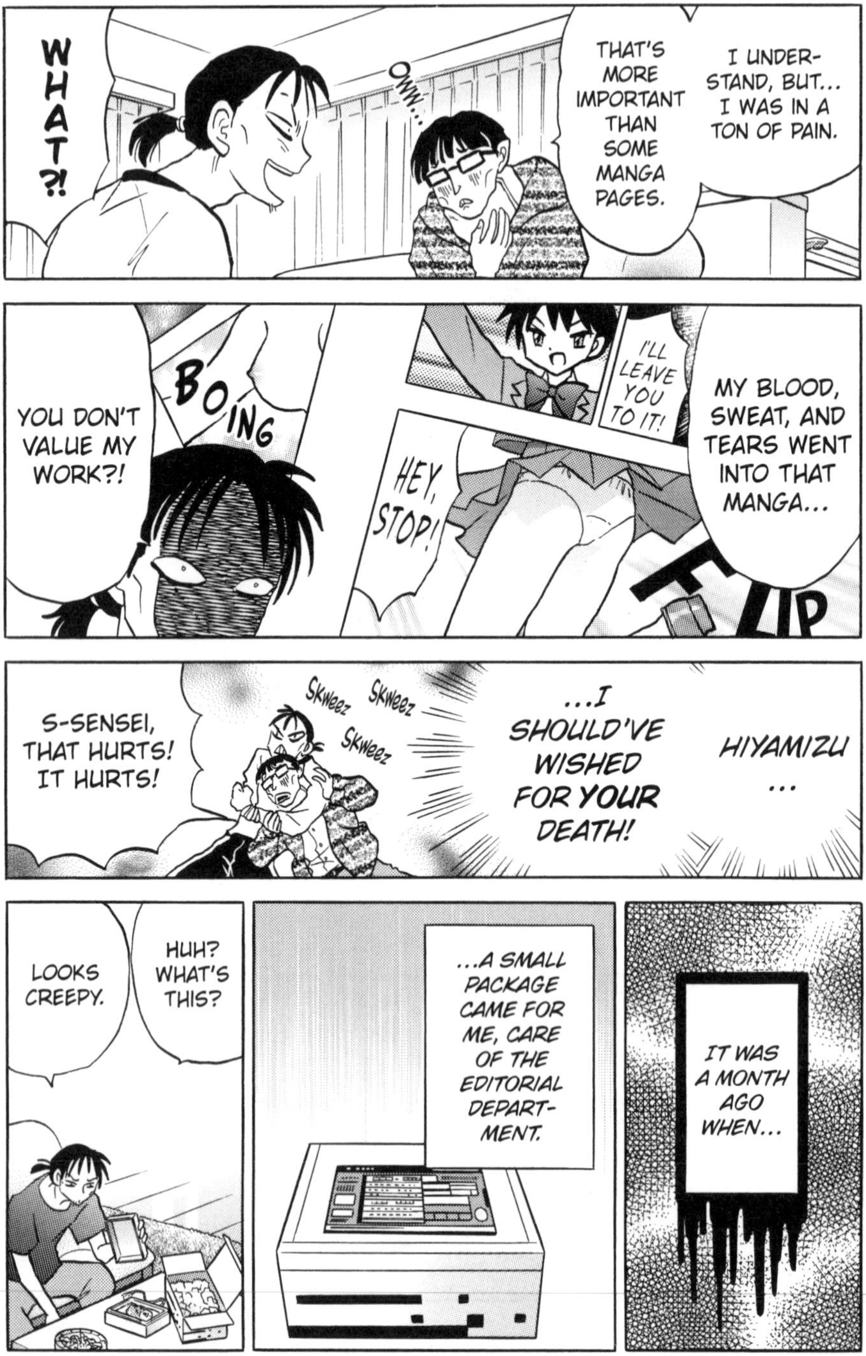
I UNDERSTAND, BUT... I WAS IN A TON OF PAIN.
THAT'S MORE IMPORTANT THAN SOME MANGA PAGES.
OWW...
WHAT?!
MY BLOOD, SWEAT, AND TEARS WENT INTO THAT MANGA...
I'LL LEAVE YOU TO IT!
HEY, STOP!
FLIP
BOING
YOU DON'T VALUE MY WORK?!
HIYAMIZU...
...I SHOULD'VE WISHED FOR YOUR DEATH!
Skweez
Skweez
Skweez
S-SENSEI, THAT HURTS! IT HURTS!
IT WAS A MONTH AGO WHEN...
...A SMALL PACKAGE CAME FOR ME, CARE OF THE EDITORIAL DEPARTMENT.
HUH? WHAT'S THIS?
LOOKS CREEPY.

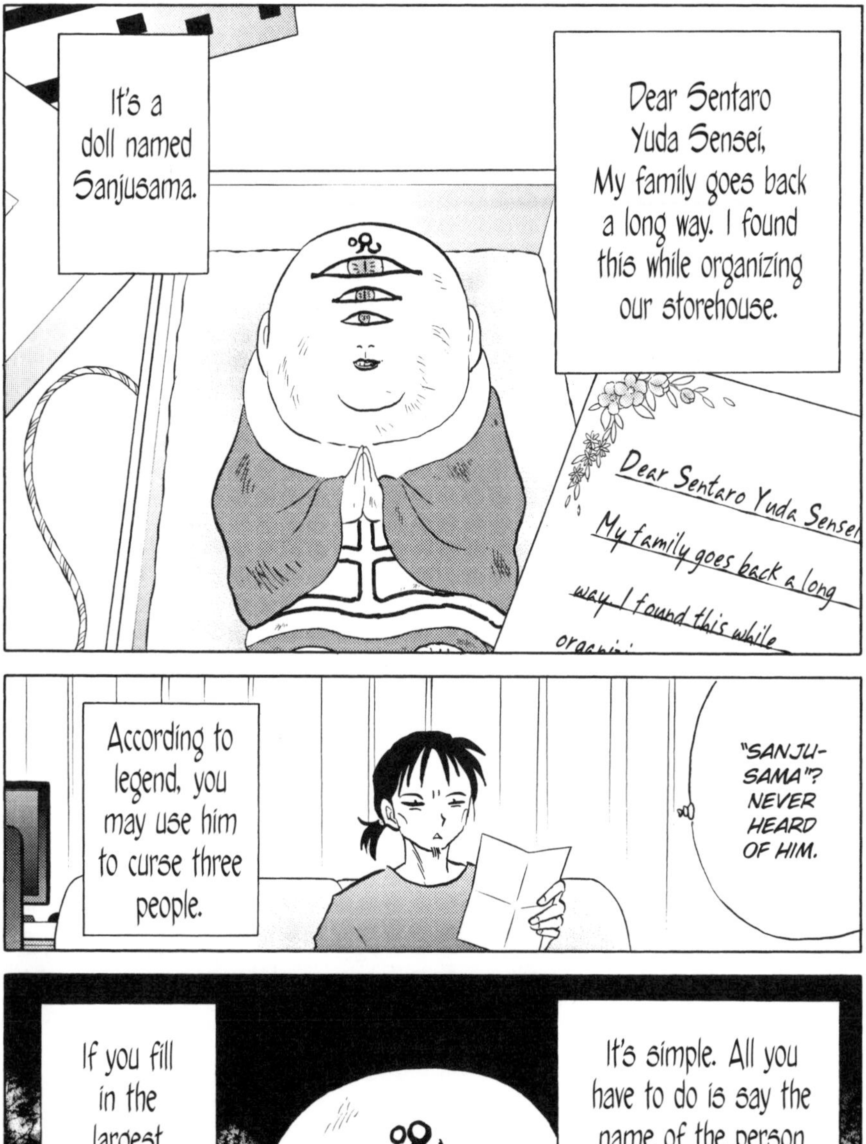
Dear Sentaro Yuda Sensei, My family goes back a long way. I found this while organizing our storehouse.
Dear Sentaro Yuda Sensei
My family goes back a long
way. I found this while
It's a doll named Sanjusama.
"SANJU-SAMA"? NEVER HEARD OF HIM.
According to legend, you may use him to curse three people.
It's simple. All you have to do is say the name of the person as you curse them while filling in one of the eyes with black ink.
If you fill in the largest eye, you can kill the person.

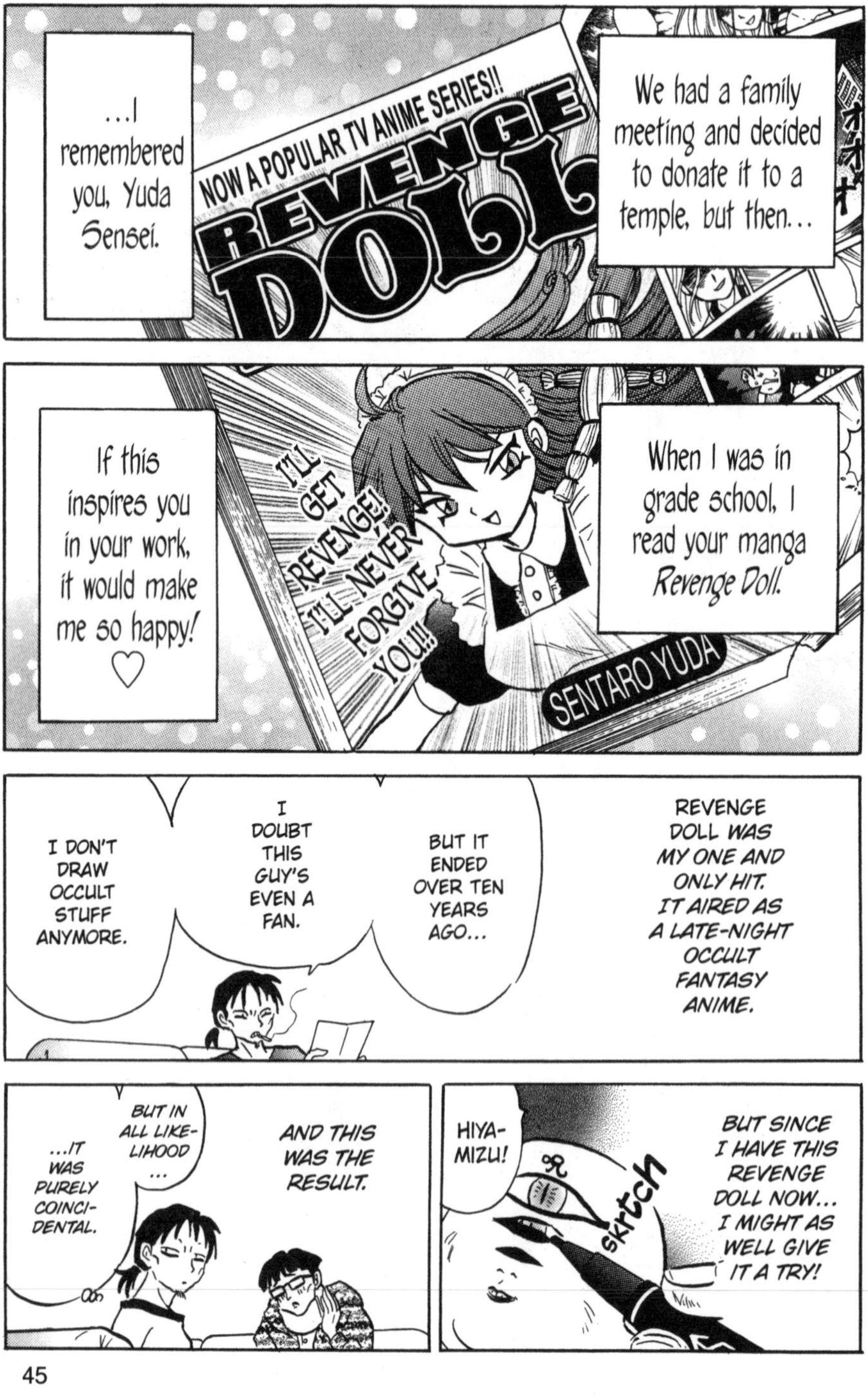
We had a family meeting and decided to donate it to a temple, but then...
NOW A POPULAR TV ANIME SERIES!!
REVENGE DOLL
...I remembered you, Yuda Sensei.
When I was in grade school, I read your manga *Revenge Doll.*
SENTARO YUDA
I'LL GET REVENGE! I'LL NEVER FORGIVE YOU!!
If this inspires you in your work, it would make me so happy! ♡
REVENGE DOLL WAS MY ONE AND ONLY HIT. IT AIRED AS A LATE-NIGHT OCCULT FANTASY ANIME.
BUT IT ENDED OVER TEN YEARS AGO...
I DOUBT THIS GUY'S EVEN A FAN.
I DON'T DRAW OCCULT STUFF ANYMORE.
BUT SINCE I HAVE THIS REVENGE DOLL NOW... I MIGHT AS WELL GIVE IT A TRY!
skrtch
HIYA-MIZU!
AND THIS WAS THE RESULT.
BUT IN ALL LIKE-LIHOOD ...
...IT WAS PURELY COINCI-DENTAL.

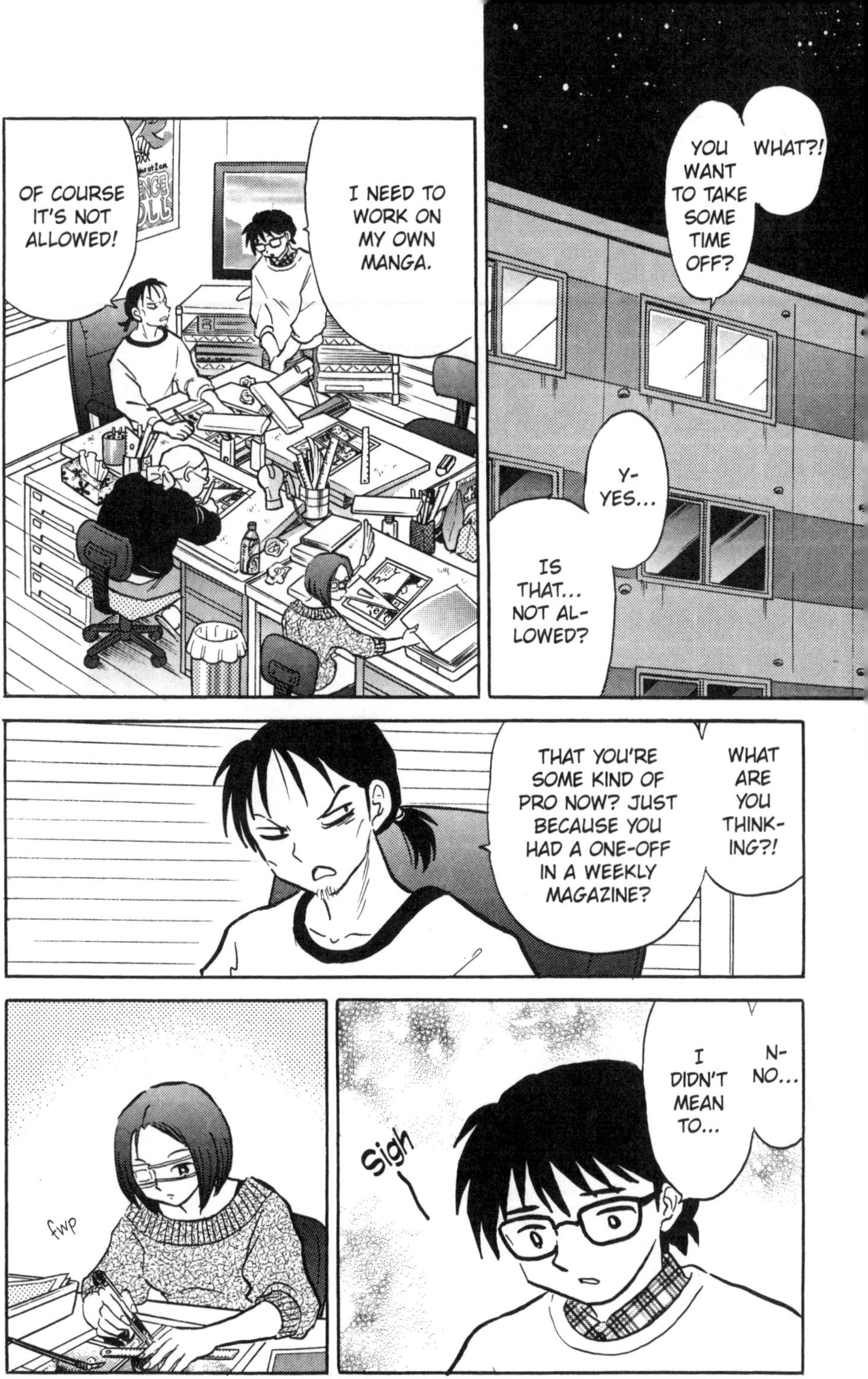
WHAT?!
YOU WANT TO TAKE SOME TIME OFF?
Y-YES...
IS THAT... NOT ALLOWED?
I NEED TO WORK ON MY OWN MANGA.
OF COURSE IT'S NOT ALLOWED!
WHAT ARE YOU THINKING?!
THAT YOU'RE SOME KIND OF PRO NOW? JUST BECAUSE YOU HAD A ONE-OFF IN A WEEKLY MAGAZINE?
N-NO...
I DIDN'T MEAN TO...
Sigh
fwp

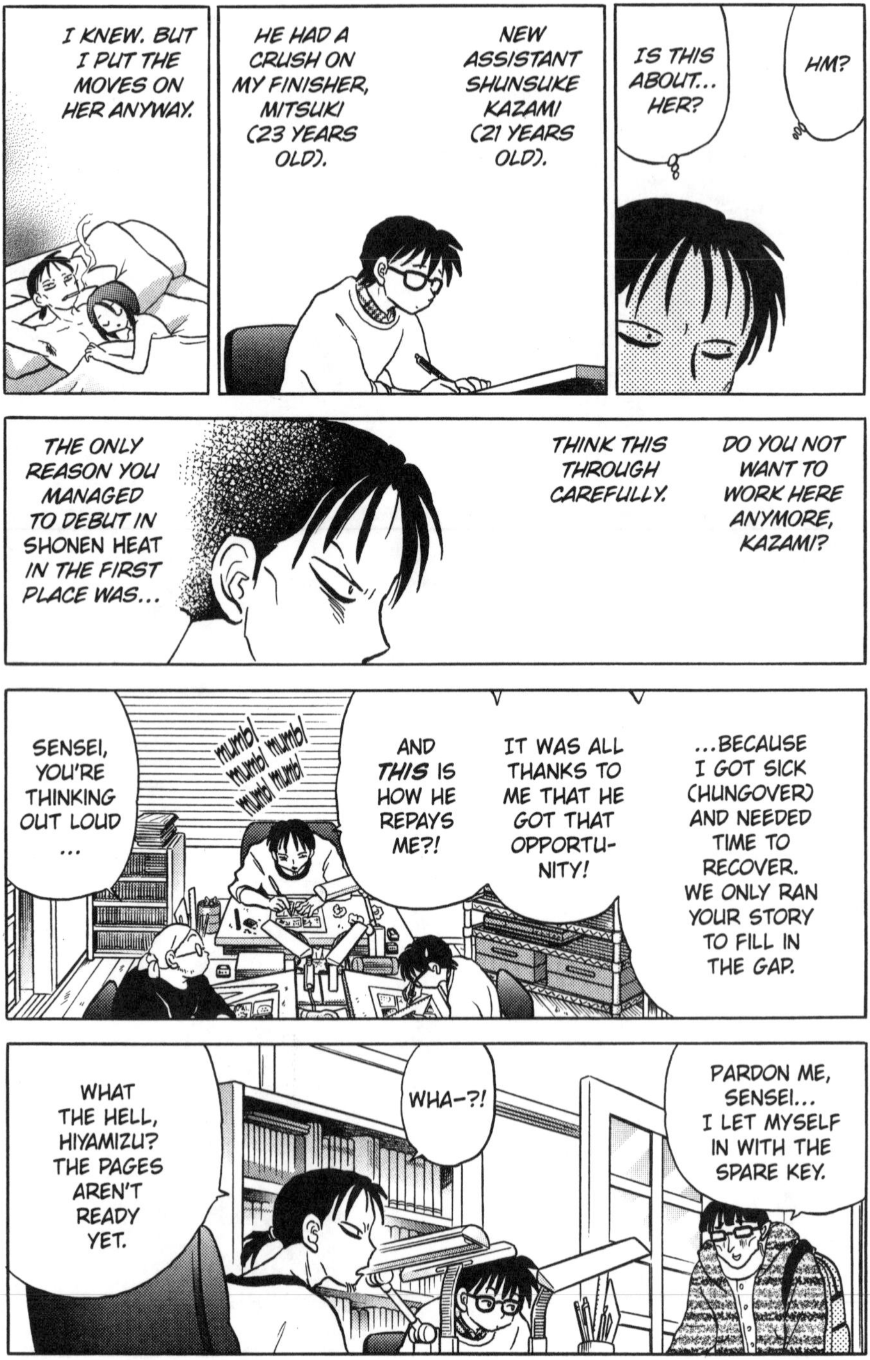
HM?
IS THIS ABOUT... HER?
NEW ASSISTANT SHUNSUKE KAZAMI (21 YEARS OLD).
HE HAD A CRUSH ON MY FINISHER, MITSUKI (23 YEARS OLD).
I KNEW. BUT I PUT THE MOVES ON HER ANYWAY.
DO YOU NOT WANT TO WORK HERE ANYMORE, KAZAMI?
THINK THIS THROUGH CAREFULLY.
THE ONLY REASON YOU MANAGED TO DEBUT IN SHONEN HEAT IN THE FIRST PLACE WAS...
...BECAUSE I GOT SICK (HUNGOVER) AND NEEDED TIME TO RECOVER. WE ONLY RAN YOUR STORY TO FILL IN THE GAP.
IT WAS ALL THANKS TO ME THAT HE GOT THAT OPPORTUNITY!
AND *THIS* IS HOW HE REPAYS ME?!
mumbl mumbl mumbl mumbl mumbl mumbl
SENSEI, YOU'RE THINKING OUT LOUD...
PARDON ME, SENSEI... I LET MYSELF IN WITH THE SPARE KEY.
WHA-?!
WHAT THE HELL, HIYAMIZU? THE PAGES AREN'T READY YET.

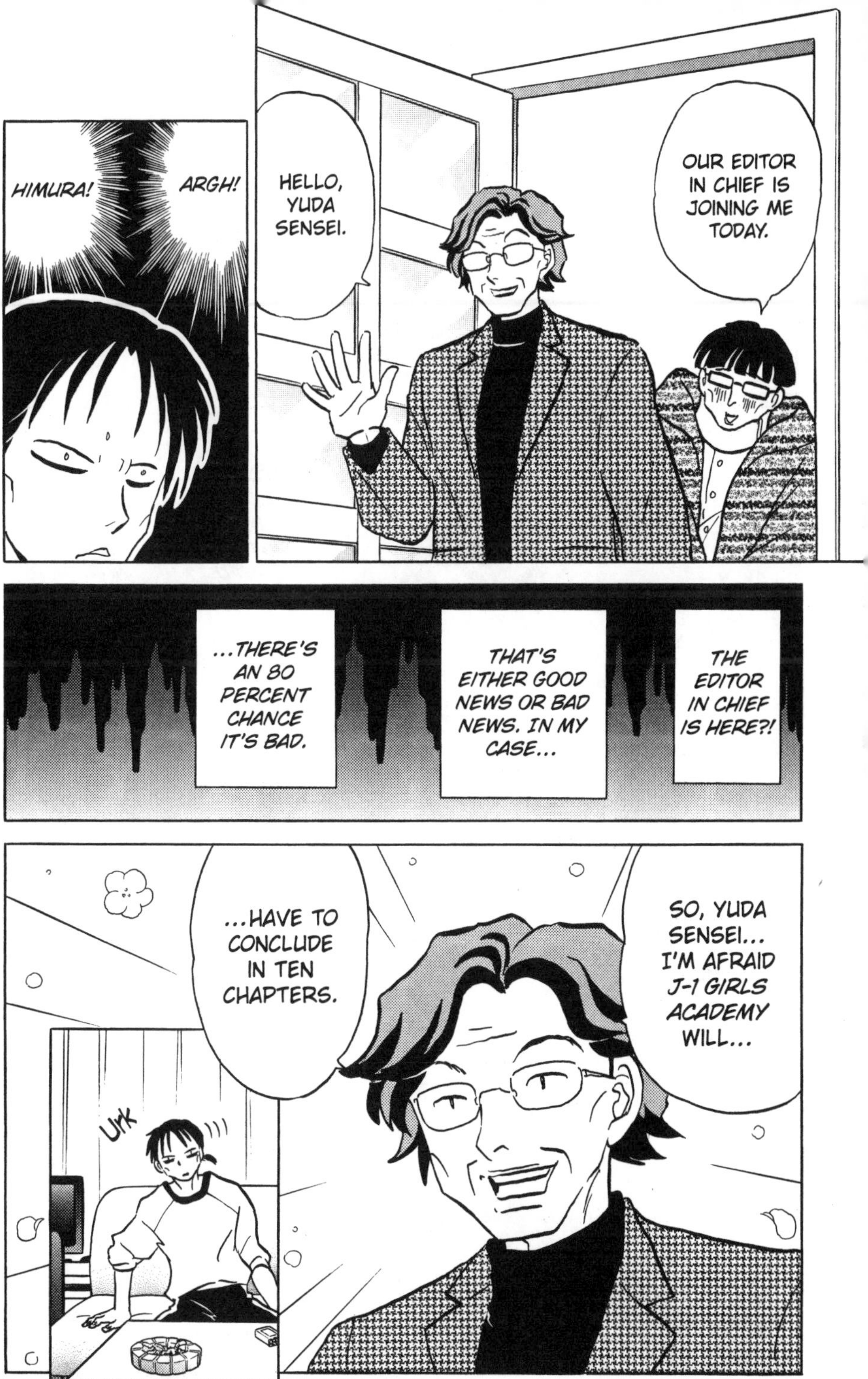
OUR EDITOR IN CHIEF IS JOINING ME TODAY.
HELLO, YUDA SENSEI.
ARGH!
HIMURA!
THE EDITOR IN CHIEF IS HERE?!
THAT'S EITHER GOOD NEWS OR BAD NEWS. IN MY CASE...
...THERE'S AN 80 PERCENT CHANCE IT'S BAD.
SO, YUDA SENSEI... I'M AFRAID J-1 GIRLS ACADEMY WILL...
...HAVE TO CONCLUDE IN TEN CHAPTERS.
Urk

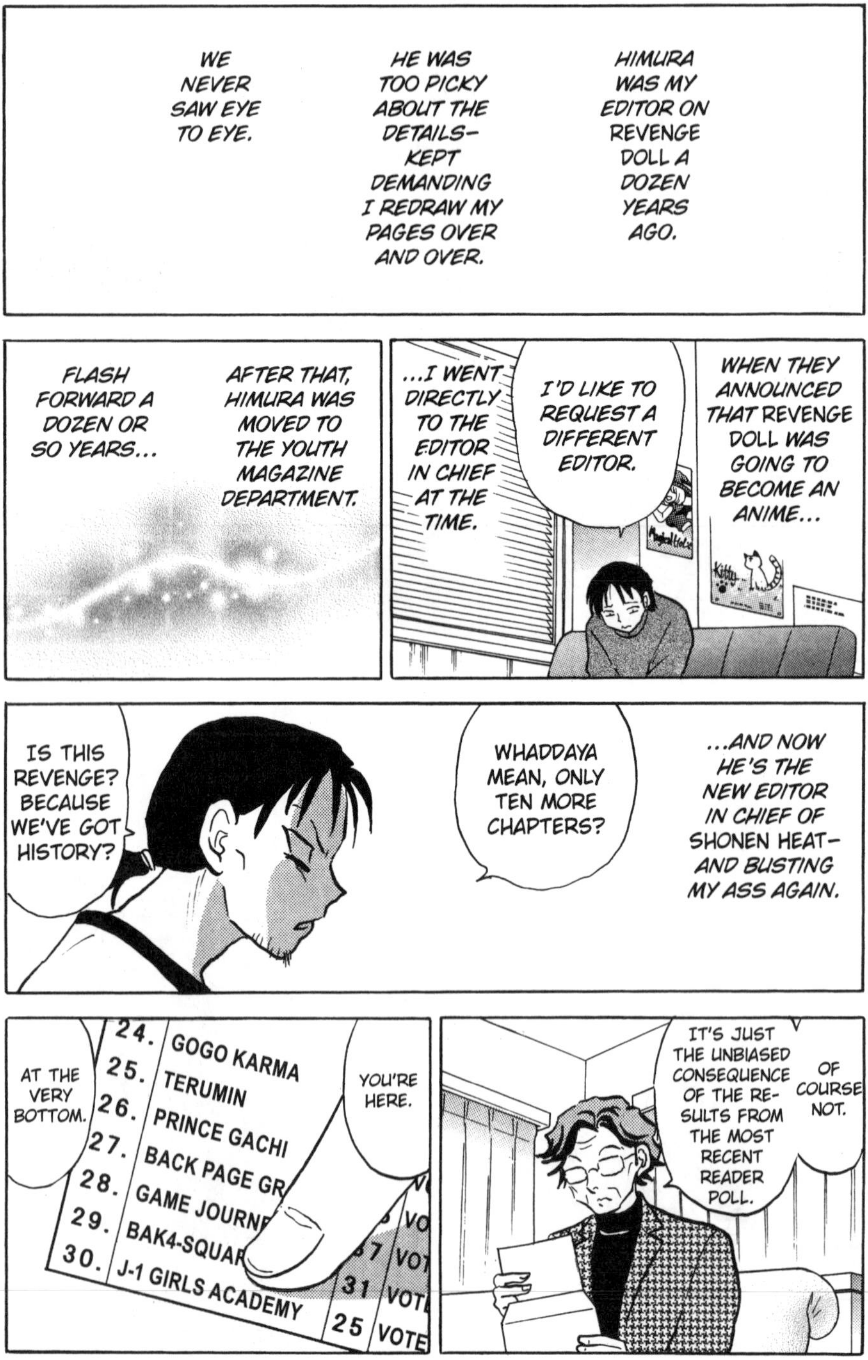
HIMURA WAS MY EDITOR ON REVENGE DOLL A DOZEN YEARS AGO.
HE WAS TOO PICKY ABOUT THE DETAILS—KEPT DEMANDING I REDRAW MY PAGES OVER AND OVER.
WE NEVER SAW EYE TO EYE.
WHEN THEY ANNOUNCED THAT REVENGE DOLL WAS GOING TO BECOME AN ANIME...
I'D LIKE TO REQUEST A DIFFERENT EDITOR.
...I WENT DIRECTLY TO THE EDITOR IN CHIEF AT THE TIME.
AFTER THAT, HIMURA WAS MOVED TO THE YOUTH MAGAZINE DEPARTMENT.
FLASH FORWARD A DOZEN OR SO YEARS...
...AND NOW HE'S THE NEW EDITOR IN CHIEF OF SHONEN HEAT—AND BUSTING MY ASS AGAIN.
WHADDAYA MEAN, ONLY TEN MORE CHAPTERS?
IS THIS REVENGE? BECAUSE WE'VE GOT HISTORY?
OF COURSE NOT.
IT'S JUST THE UNBIASED CONSEQUENCE OF THE RESULTS FROM THE MOST RECENT READER POLL.
YOU'RE HERE.
AT THE VERY BOTTOM.
24. GOGO KARMA
25. TERUMIN
26. PRINCE GACHI
27. BACK PAGE GR
28. GAME JOURN
29. BAK4-SQUA
30. J-1 GIRLS ACADEMY
31 VOTE
25 VOTE

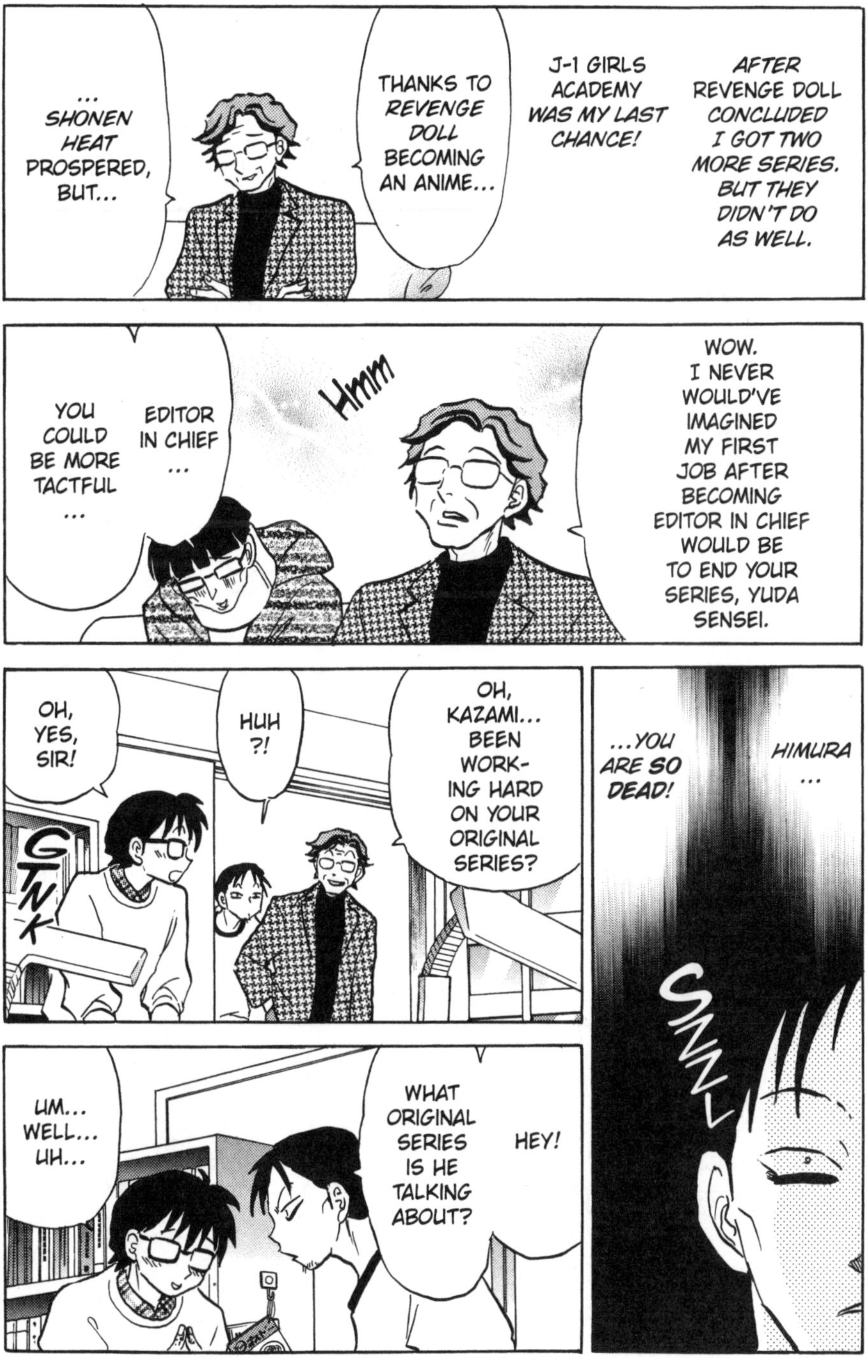
AFTER REVENGE DOLL CONCLUDED I GOT TWO MORE SERIES. BUT THEY DIDN'T DO AS WELL.
J-1 GIRLS ACADEMY WAS MY LAST CHANCE!
THANKS TO REVENGE DOLL BECOMING AN ANIME...
... SHONEN HEAT PROSPERED, BUT...
WOW. I NEVER WOULD'VE IMAGINED MY FIRST JOB AFTER BECOMING EDITOR IN CHIEF WOULD BE TO END YOUR SERIES, YUDA SENSEI.
Hmm
EDITOR IN CHIEF ...
YOU COULD BE MORE TACTFUL ...
HIMURA ...
...YOU ARE SO DEAD!
SZZZ
OH, KAZAMI... BEEN WORKING HARD ON YOUR ORIGINAL SERIES?
HUH ?!
OH, YES, SIR!
GTNK
HEY!
WHAT ORIGINAL SERIES IS HE TALKING ABOUT?
UM... WELL... UH...

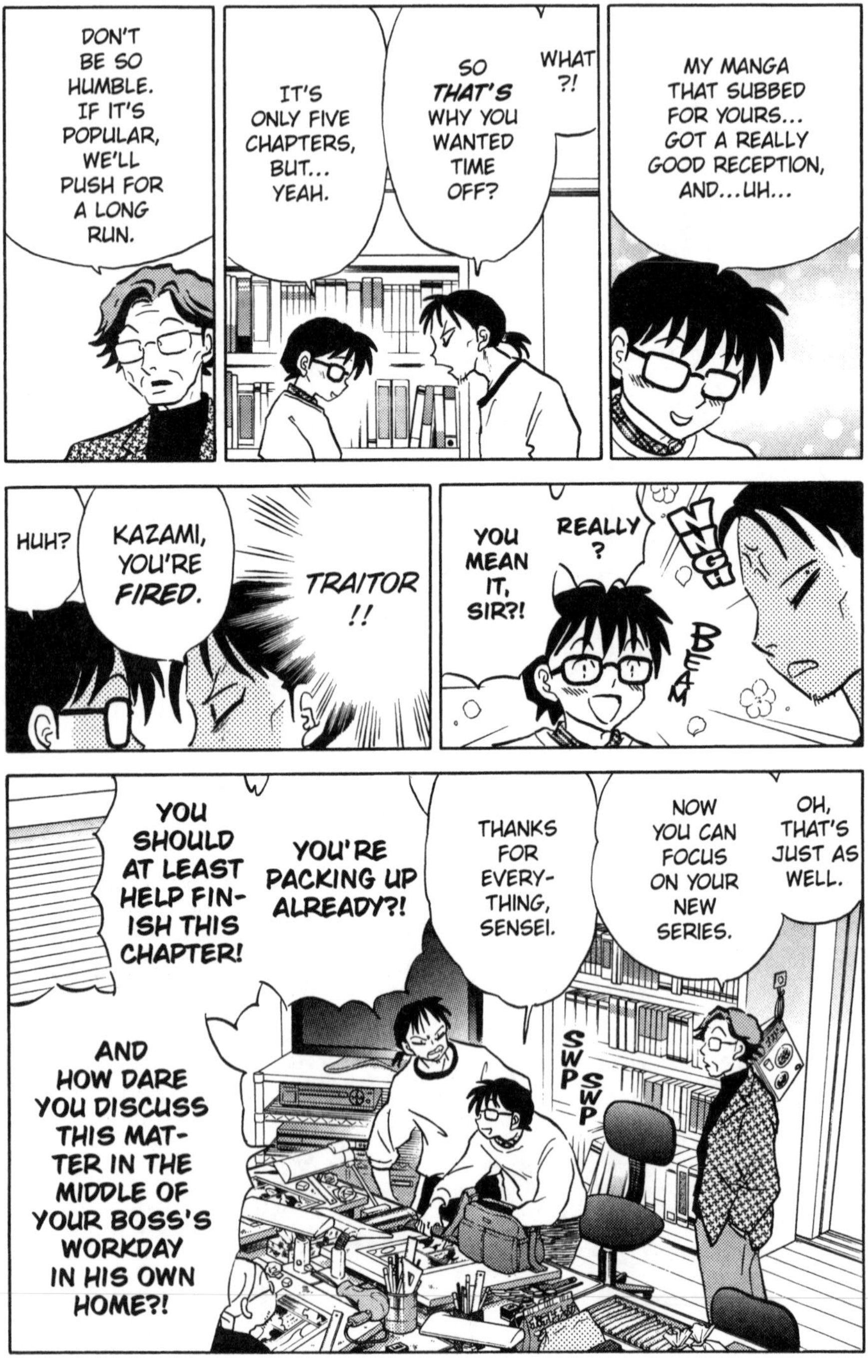
MY MANGA THAT SUBBED FOR YOURS... GOT A REALLY GOOD RECEPTION, AND...UH...
WHAT ?!
SO *THAT'S* WHY YOU WANTED TIME OFF?
IT'S ONLY FIVE CHAPTERS, BUT... YEAH.
DON'T BE SO HUMBLE. IF IT'S POPULAR, WE'LL PUSH FOR A LONG RUN.
NNGH
REALLY ?
YOU MEAN IT, SIR?!
BEAM
TRAITOR !!
KAZAMI, YOU'RE *FIRED*.
HUH?
OH, THAT'S JUST AS WELL.
NOW YOU CAN FOCUS ON YOUR NEW SERIES.
THANKS FOR EVERY-THING, SENSEI.
SWP SWP
YOU'RE PACKING UP ALREADY?!
YOU SHOULD AT LEAST HELP FIN-ISH THIS CHAPTER!
AND HOW DARE YOU DISCUSS THIS MAT-TER IN THE MIDDLE OF YOUR BOSS'S WORKDAY IN HIS OWN HOME?!

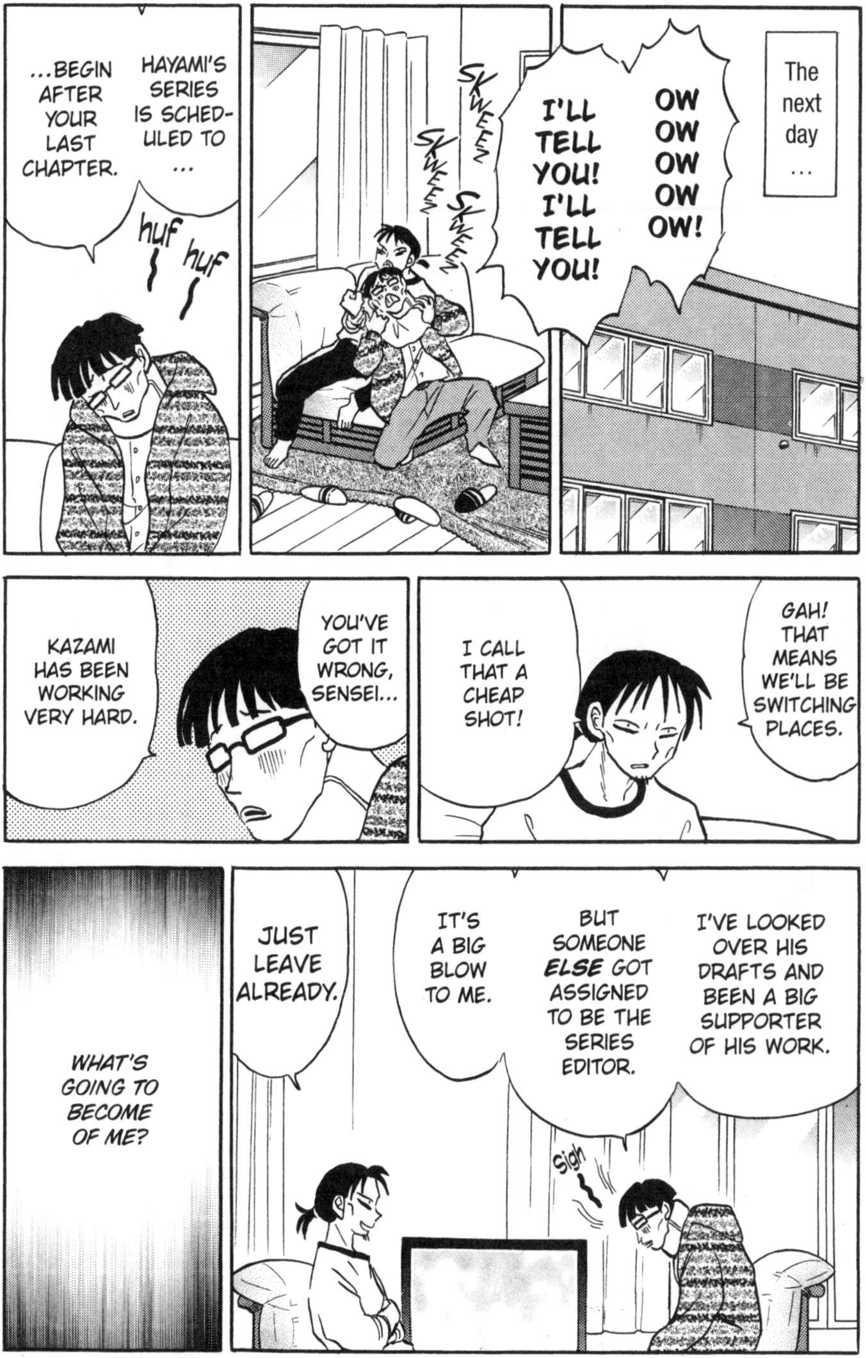
The next day …
OW OW OW OW OW!
I'LL TELL YOU! I'LL TELL YOU!
SKWEEN SKWEEN SKWEEN
HAYAMI'S SERIES IS SCHED-ULED TO …
…BEGIN AFTER YOUR LAST CHAPTER.
huf huf
GAH! THAT MEANS WE'LL BE SWITCHING PLACES.
I CALL THAT A CHEAP SHOT!
YOU'VE GOT IT WRONG, SENSEI…
KAZAMI HAS BEEN WORKING VERY HARD.
I'VE LOOKED OVER HIS DRAFTS AND BEEN A BIG SUPPORTER OF HIS WORK.
BUT SOMEONE ELSE GOT ASSIGNED TO BE THE SERIES EDITOR.
IT'S A BIG BLOW TO ME.
Sigh
JUST LEAVE ALREADY.
WHAT'S GOING TO BECOME OF ME?

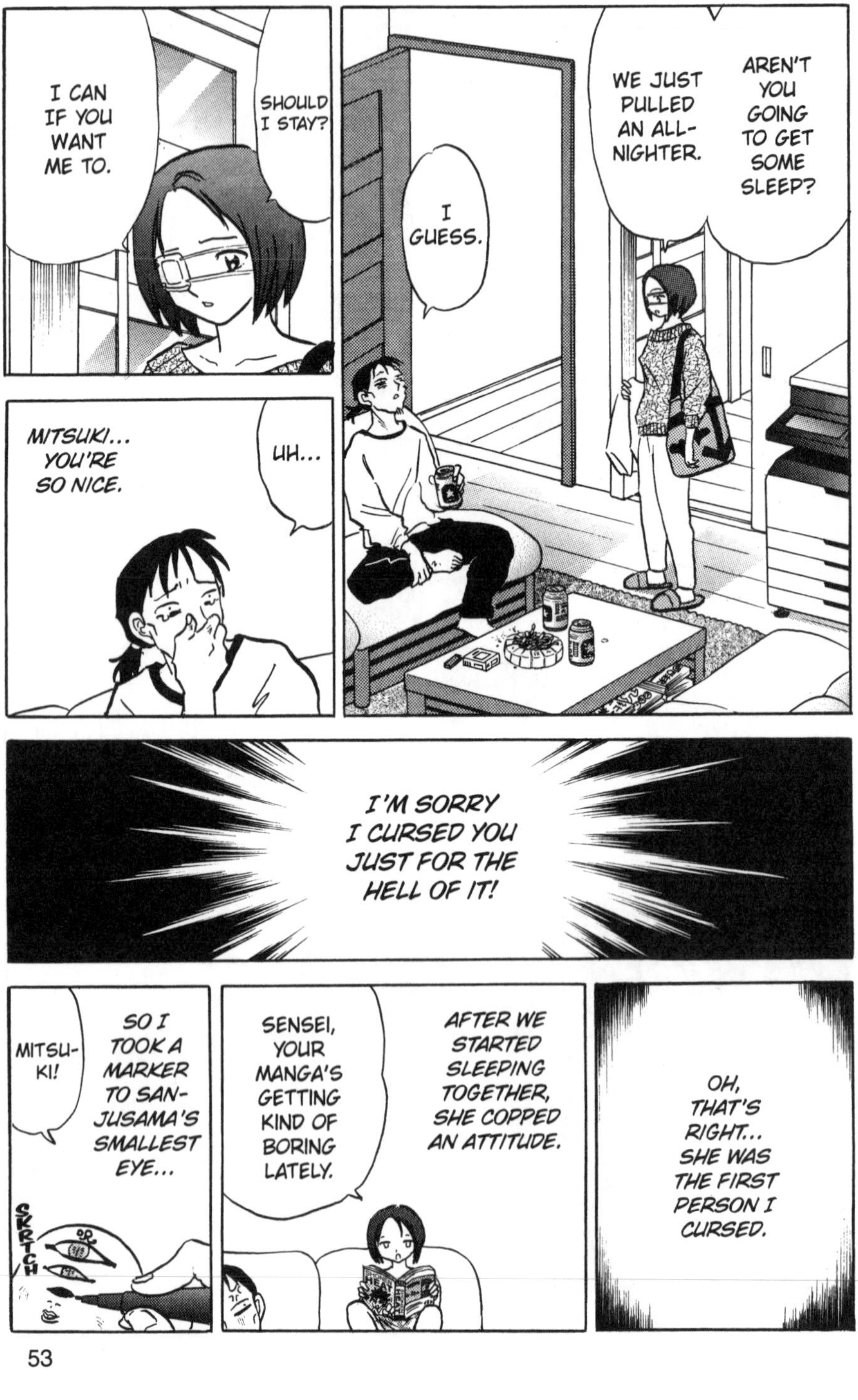
AREN'T YOU GOING TO GET SOME SLEEP?
WE JUST PULLED AN ALL-NIGHTER.
I GUESS.
SHOULD I STAY?
I CAN IF YOU WANT ME TO.
UH...
MITSUKI... YOU'RE SO NICE.
I'M SORRY I CURSED YOU JUST FOR THE HELL OF IT!
OH, THAT'S RIGHT... SHE WAS THE FIRST PERSON I CURSED.
AFTER WE STARTED SLEEPING TOGETHER, SHE COPPED AN ATTITUDE.
SENSEI, YOUR MANGA'S GETTING KIND OF BORING LATELY.
SO I TOOK A MARKER TO SAN-JUSAMA'S SMALLEST EYE...
MITSU-KI!
SKRTCH

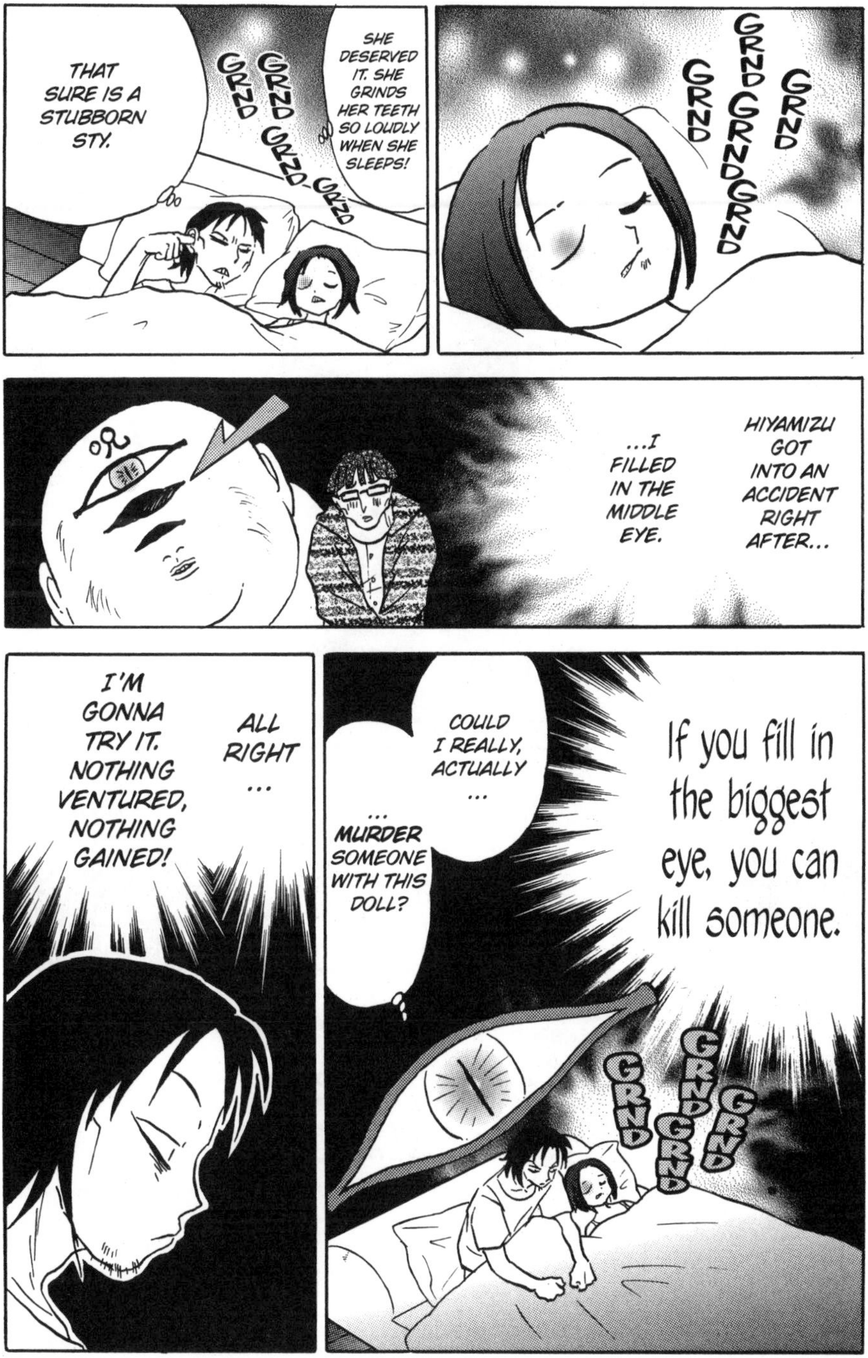
GRND GRND GRND GRND GRND GRND GRND
SHE DESERVED IT. SHE GRINDS HER TEETH SO LOUDLY WHEN SHE SLEEPS!
GRND GRND GRND GRND
THAT SURE IS A STUBBORN STY.
HIYAMIZU GOT INTO AN ACCIDENT RIGHT AFTER...
...I FILLED IN THE MIDDLE EYE.
If you fill in the biggest eye, you can kill someone.
COULD I REALLY, ACTUALLY ...
... MURDER SOMEONE WITH THIS DOLL?
GRND GRND GRND GRND GRND
ALL RIGHT ...
I'M GONNA TRY IT. NOTHING VENTURED, NOTHING GAINED!

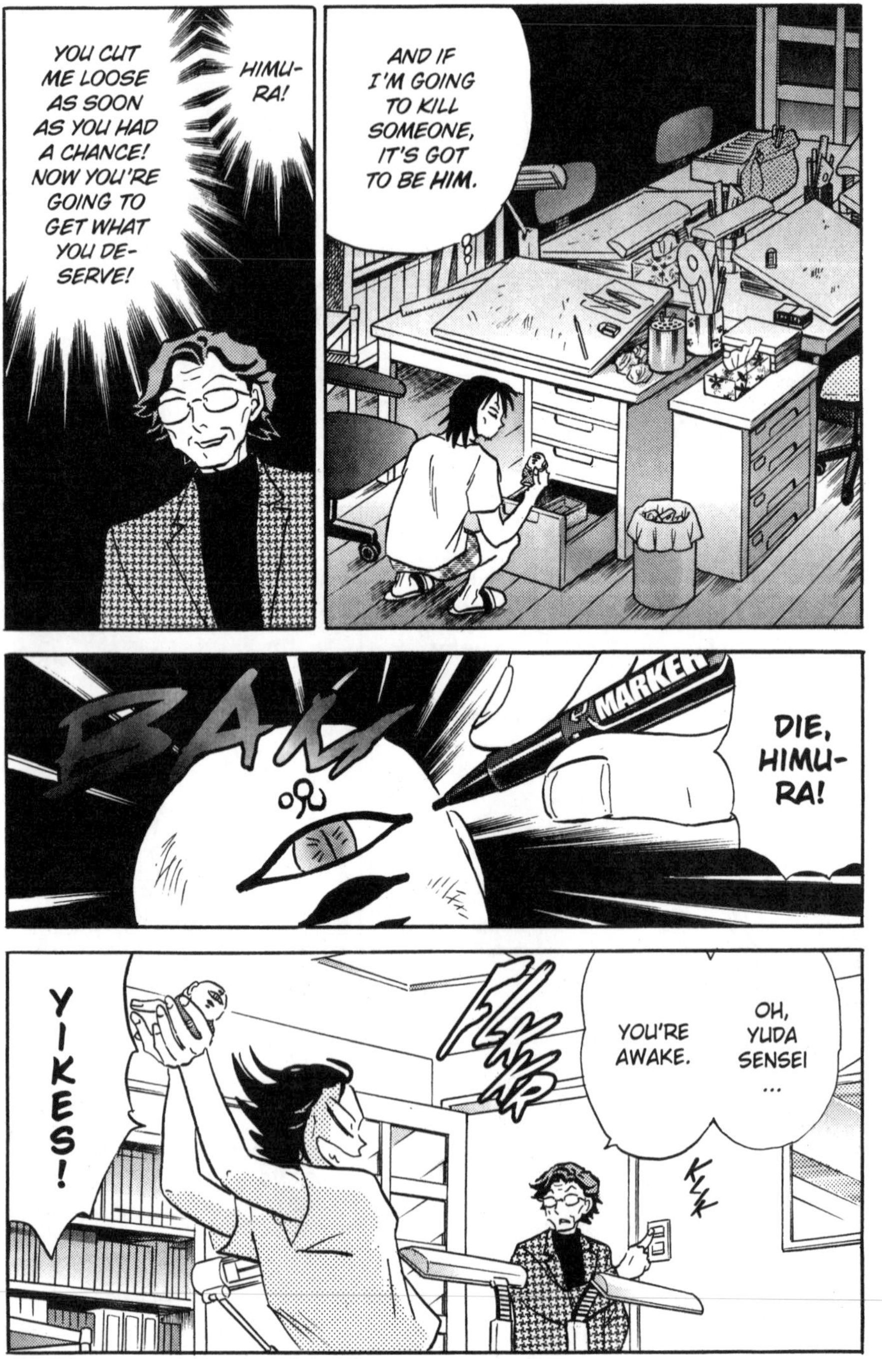
AND IF I'M GOING TO KILL SOMEONE, IT'S GOT TO BE HIM.
HIMU-RA!
YOU CUT ME LOOSE AS SOON AS YOU HAD A CHANCE! NOW YOU'RE GOING TO GET WHAT YOU DE-SERVE!
DIE, HIMU-RA!
MARKER
OH, YUDA SENSEI ...
YOU'RE AWAKE.
KLIK
YIKES!

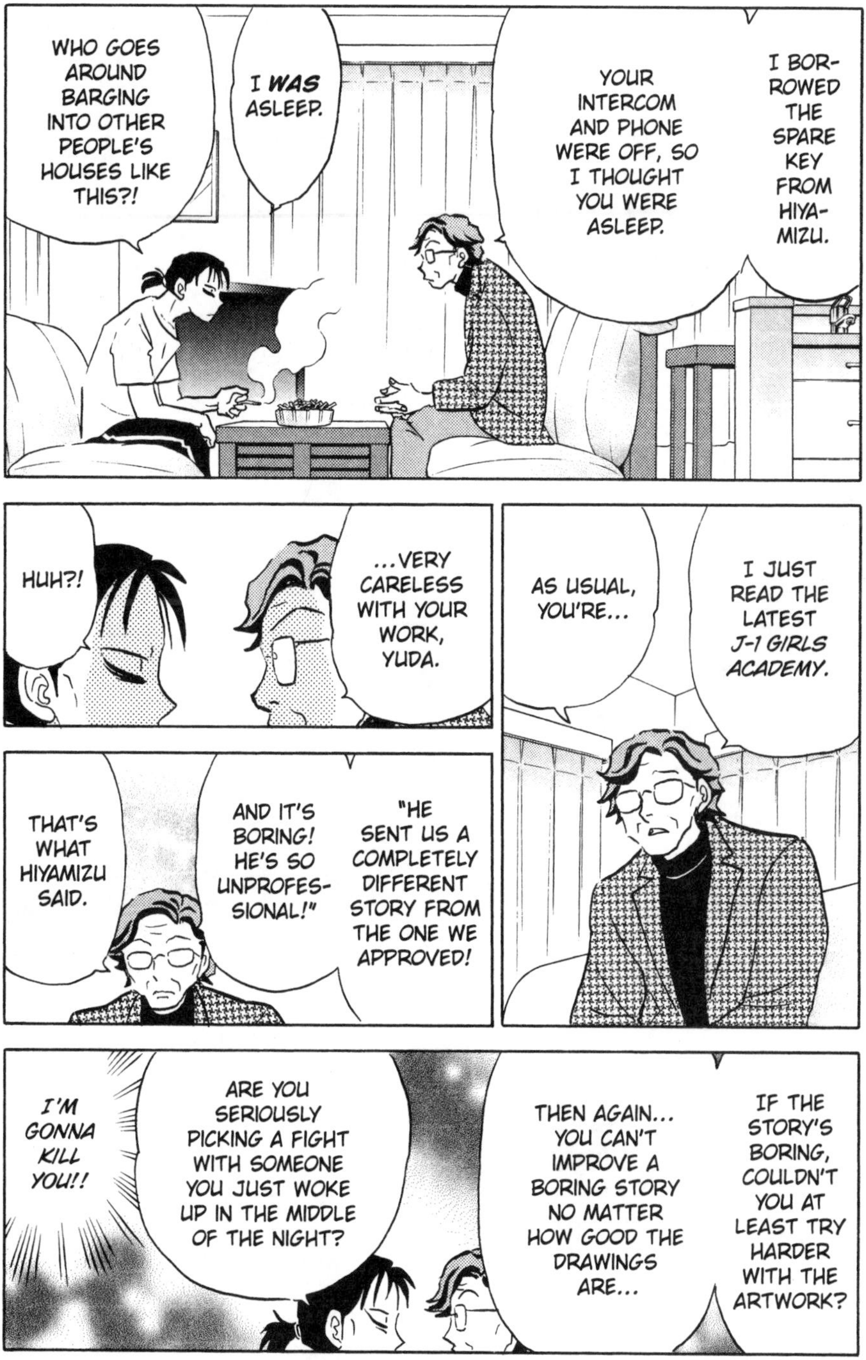
I BORROWED THE SPARE KEY FROM HIYAMIZU.
YOUR INTERCOM AND PHONE WERE OFF, SO I THOUGHT YOU WERE ASLEEP.
I *WAS* ASLEEP.
WHO GOES AROUND BARGING INTO OTHER PEOPLE'S HOUSES LIKE THIS?!
I JUST READ THE LATEST *J-1 GIRLS ACADEMY.*
AS USUAL, YOU'RE...
...VERY CARELESS WITH YOUR WORK, YUDA.
HUH?!
"HE SENT US A COMPLETELY DIFFERENT STORY FROM THE ONE WE APPROVED!
AND IT'S BORING! HE'S SO UNPROFESSIONAL!"
THAT'S WHAT HIYAMIZU SAID.
IF THE STORY'S BORING, COULDN'T YOU AT LEAST TRY HARDER WITH THE ARTWORK?
THEN AGAIN... YOU CAN'T IMPROVE A BORING STORY NO MATTER HOW GOOD THE DRAWINGS ARE...
ARE YOU SERIOUSLY PICKING A FIGHT WITH SOMEONE YOU JUST WOKE UP IN THE MIDDLE OF THE NIGHT?
I'M GONNA KILL YOU!!

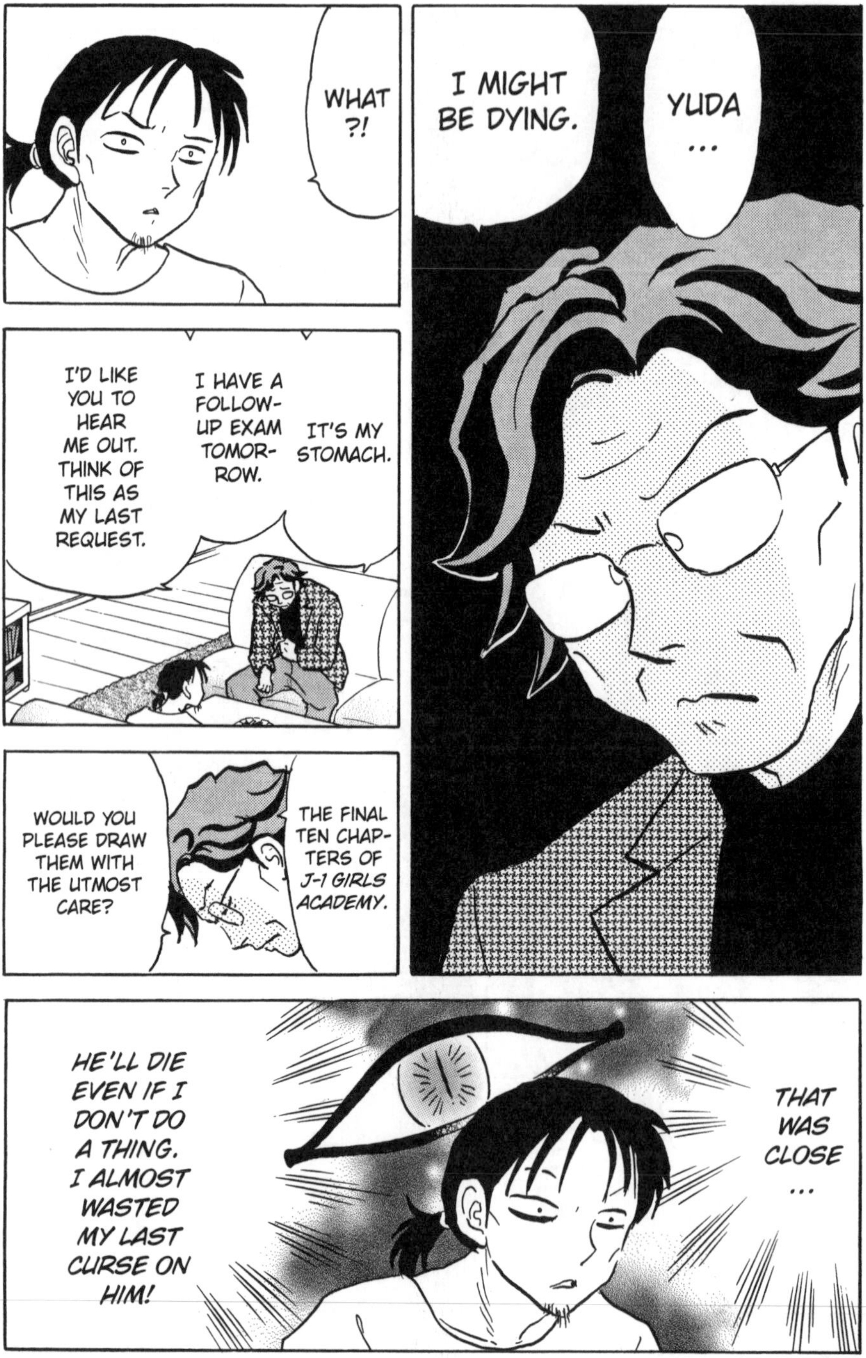
YUDA ...
I MIGHT BE DYING.
WHAT ?!
IT'S MY STOMACH.
I HAVE A FOLLOW-UP EXAM TOMORROW.
I'D LIKE YOU TO HEAR ME OUT. THINK OF THIS AS MY LAST REQUEST.
THE FINAL TEN CHAPTERS OF J-1 GIRLS ACADEMY.
WOULD YOU PLEASE DRAW THEM WITH THE UTMOST CARE?
THAT WAS CLOSE ...
HE'LL DIE EVEN IF I DON'T DO A THING. I ALMOST WASTED MY LAST CURSE ON HIM!

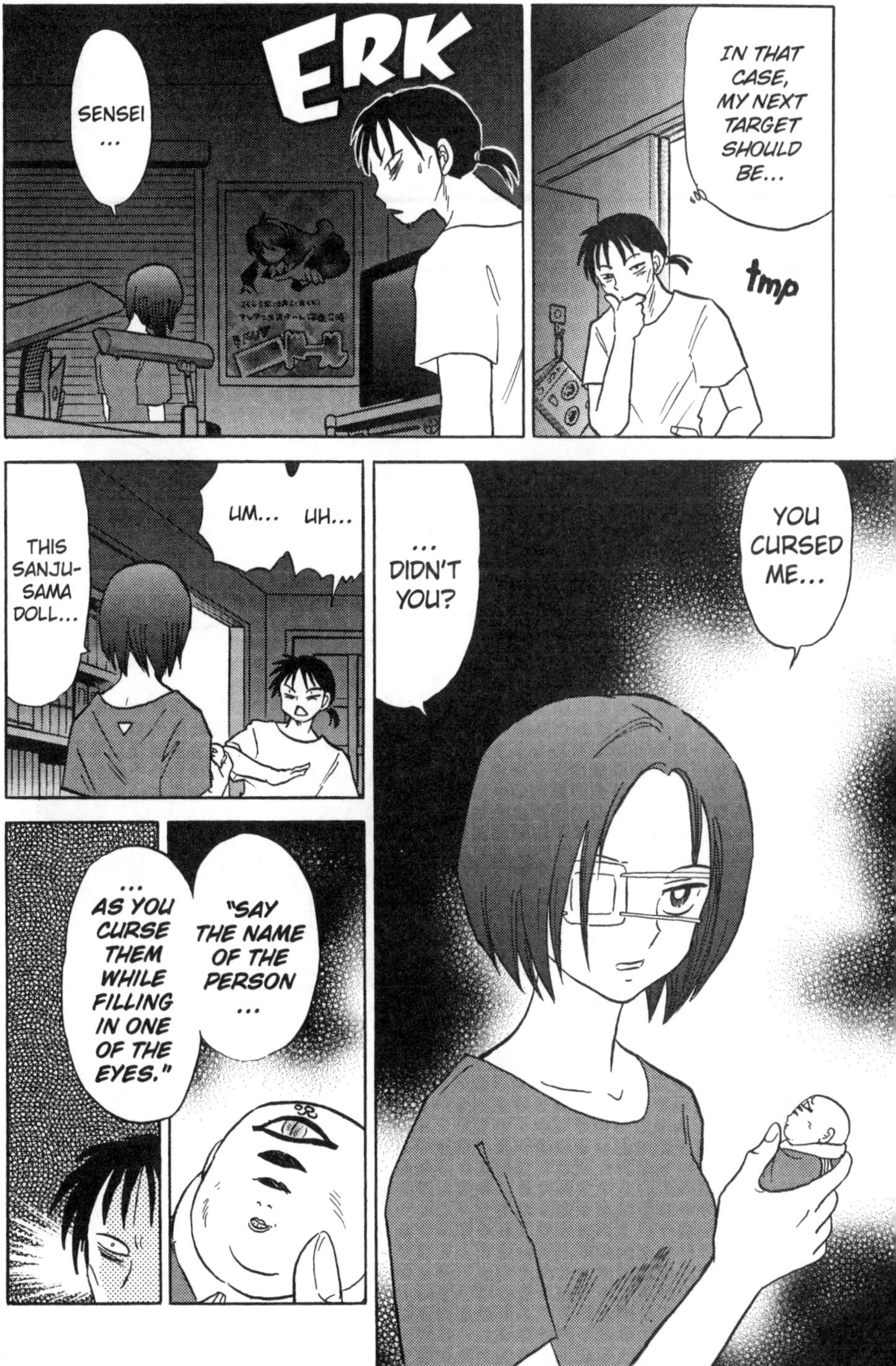
IN THAT CASE, MY NEXT TARGET SHOULD BE...
tmp
ERK
SENSEI...
YOU CURSED ME...
...DIDN'T YOU?
UM... UH...
THIS SANJU-SAMA DOLL...
"SAY THE NAME OF THE PERSON...
...AS YOU CURSE THEM WHILE FILLING IN ONE OF THE EYES."

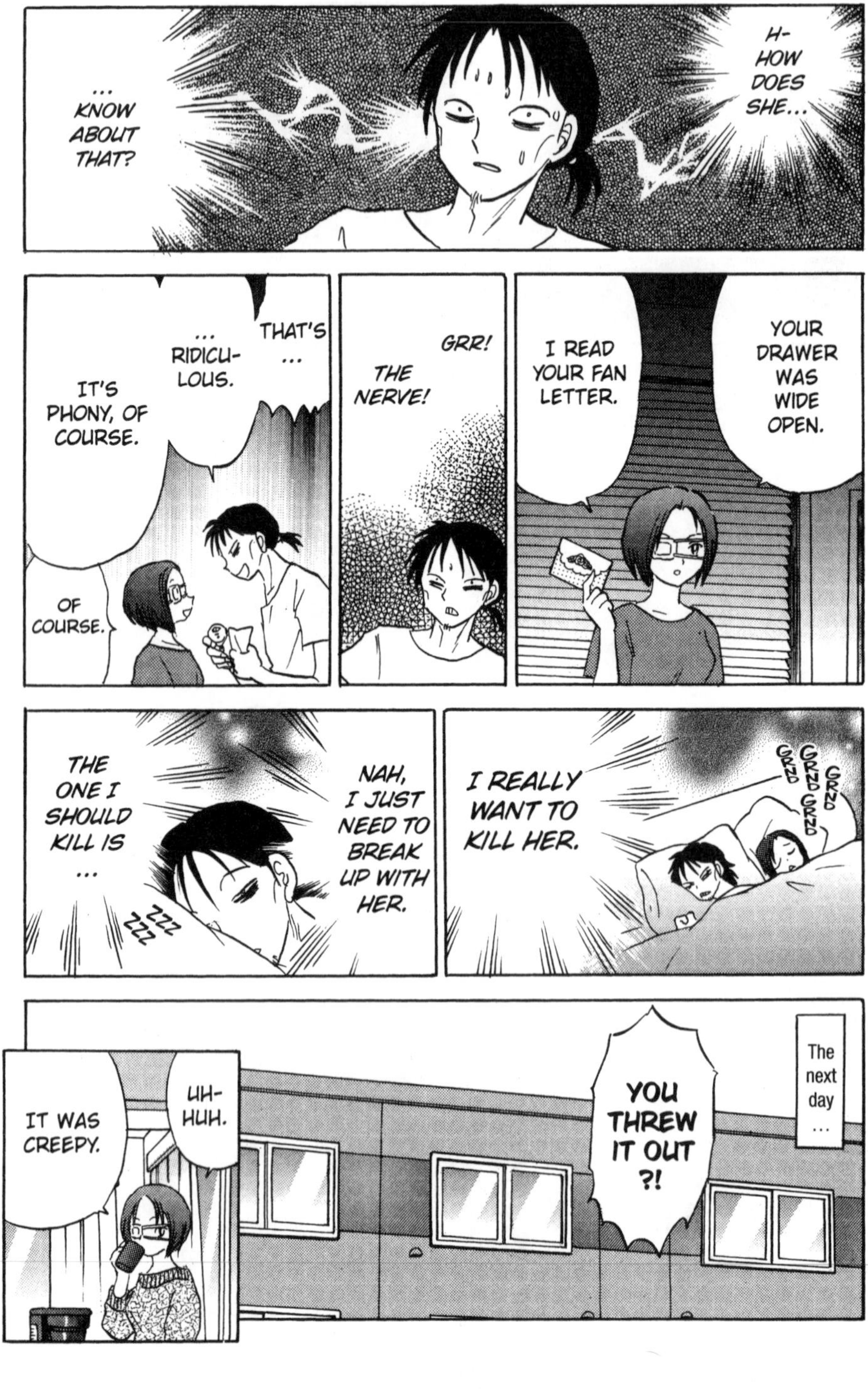

H- HOW DOES SHE…
… KNOW ABOUT THAT?
YOUR DRAWER WAS WIDE OPEN.
I READ YOUR FAN LETTER.
GRR!
THE NERVE!
THAT'S …
… RIDICU-LOUS.
IT'S PHONY, OF COURSE.
OF COURSE.
GRND GRND GRND GRND
I REALLY WANT TO KILL HER.
NAH, I JUST NEED TO BREAK UP WITH HER.
THE ONE I SHOULD KILL IS …
ZZZ ZZZ
The next day …
YOU THREW IT OUT ?!
UH-HUH.
IT WAS CREEPY.

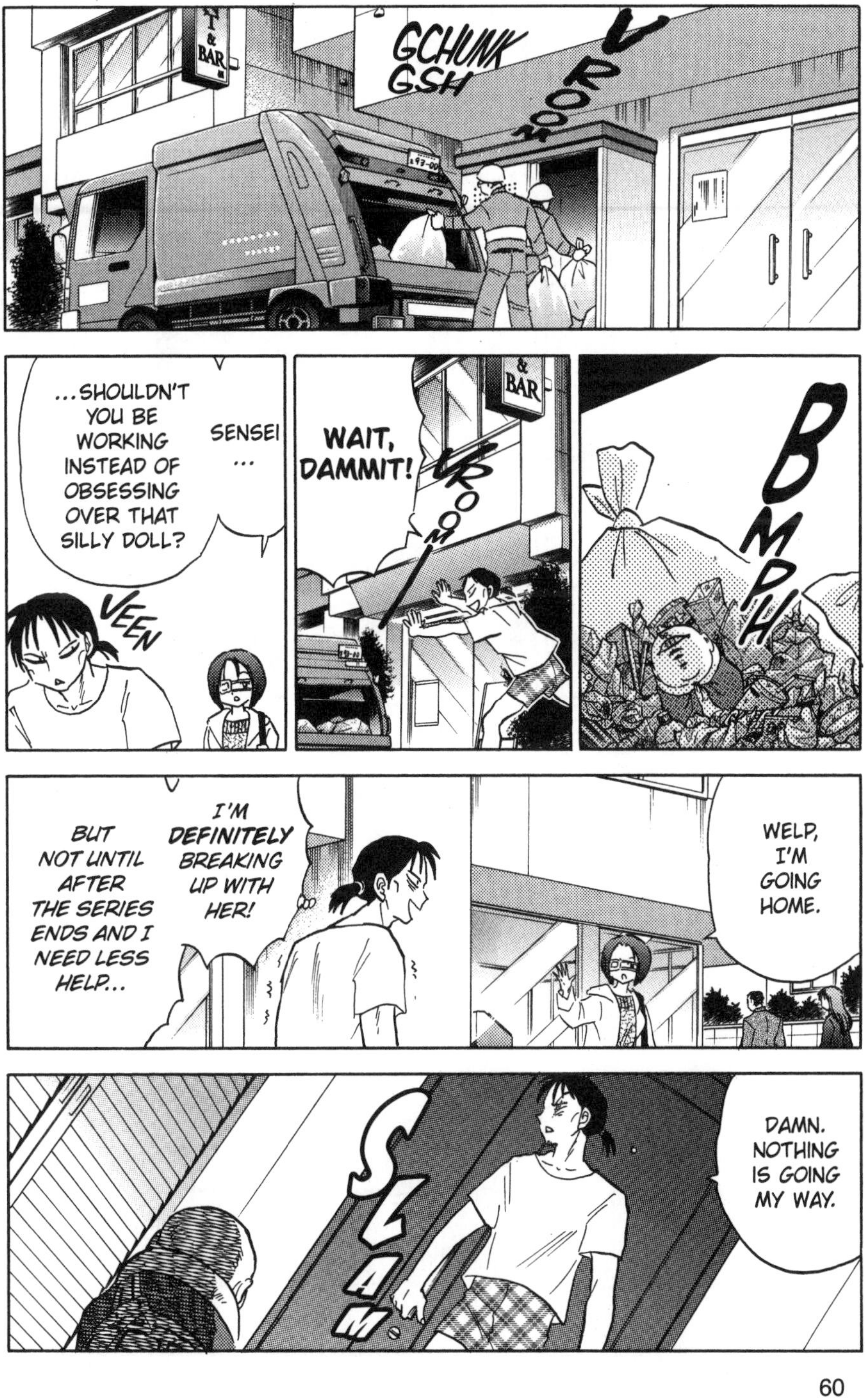
VROOM
GCHUNK
GSH
BMPH
WAIT, DAMMIT!
VROOM
SENSEI...
...SHOULDN'T YOU BE WORKING INSTEAD OF OBSESSING OVER THAT SILLY DOLL?
VEEN
WELP, I'M GOING HOME.
I'M *DEFINITELY* BREAKING UP WITH HER!
BUT NOT UNTIL AFTER THE SERIES ENDS AND I NEED LESS HELP...
DAMN. NOTHING IS GOING MY WAY.
SLAM

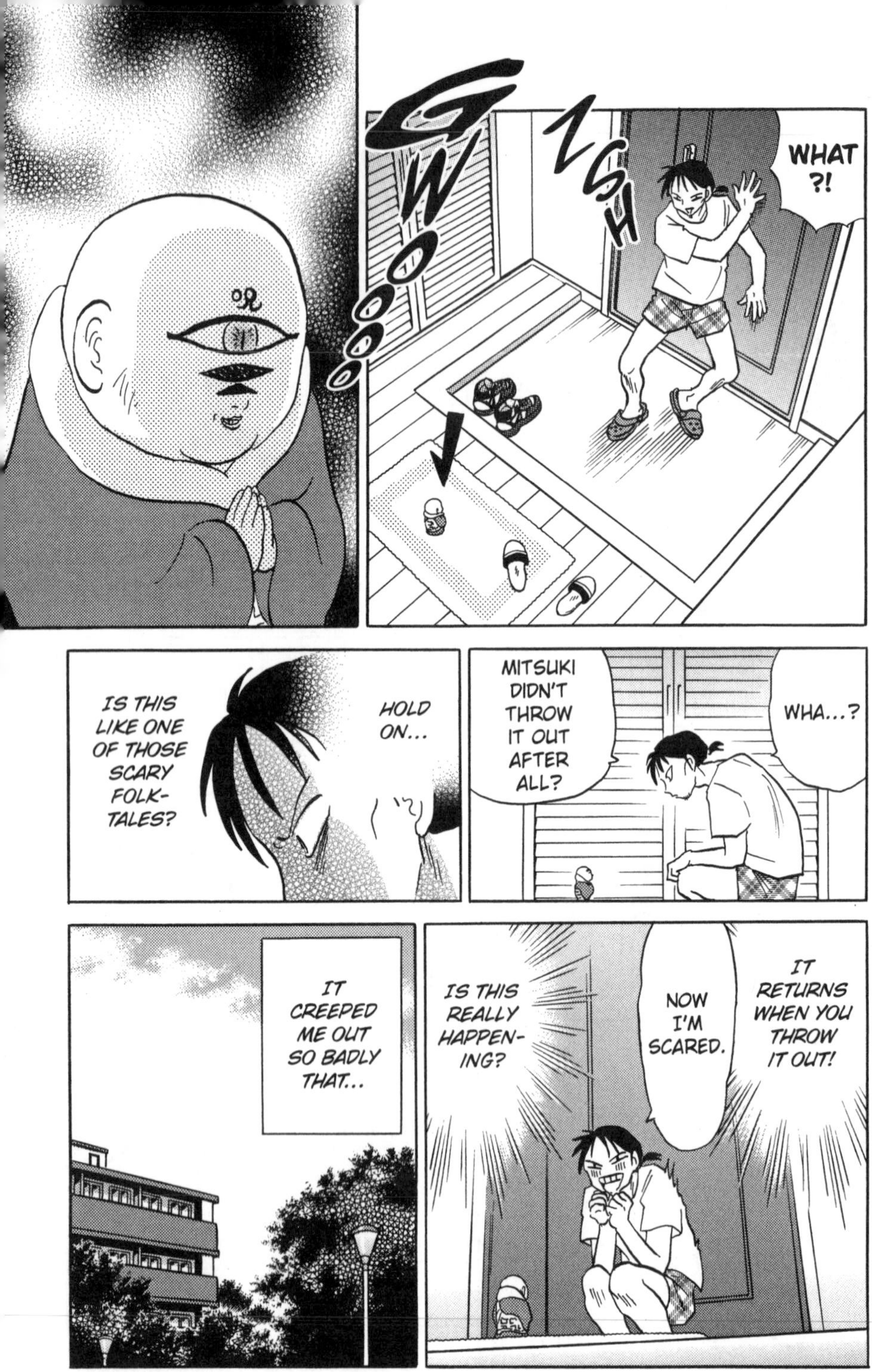
GWOOOOO
ZSH
WHAT ?!
WHA...?
MITSUKI DIDN'T THROW IT OUT AFTER ALL?
HOLD ON...
IS THIS LIKE ONE OF THOSE SCARY FOLK-TALES?
IT RETURNS WHEN YOU THROW IT OUT!
NOW I'M SCARED.
IS THIS REALLY HAPPEN-ING?
IT CREEPED ME OUT SO BADLY THAT...

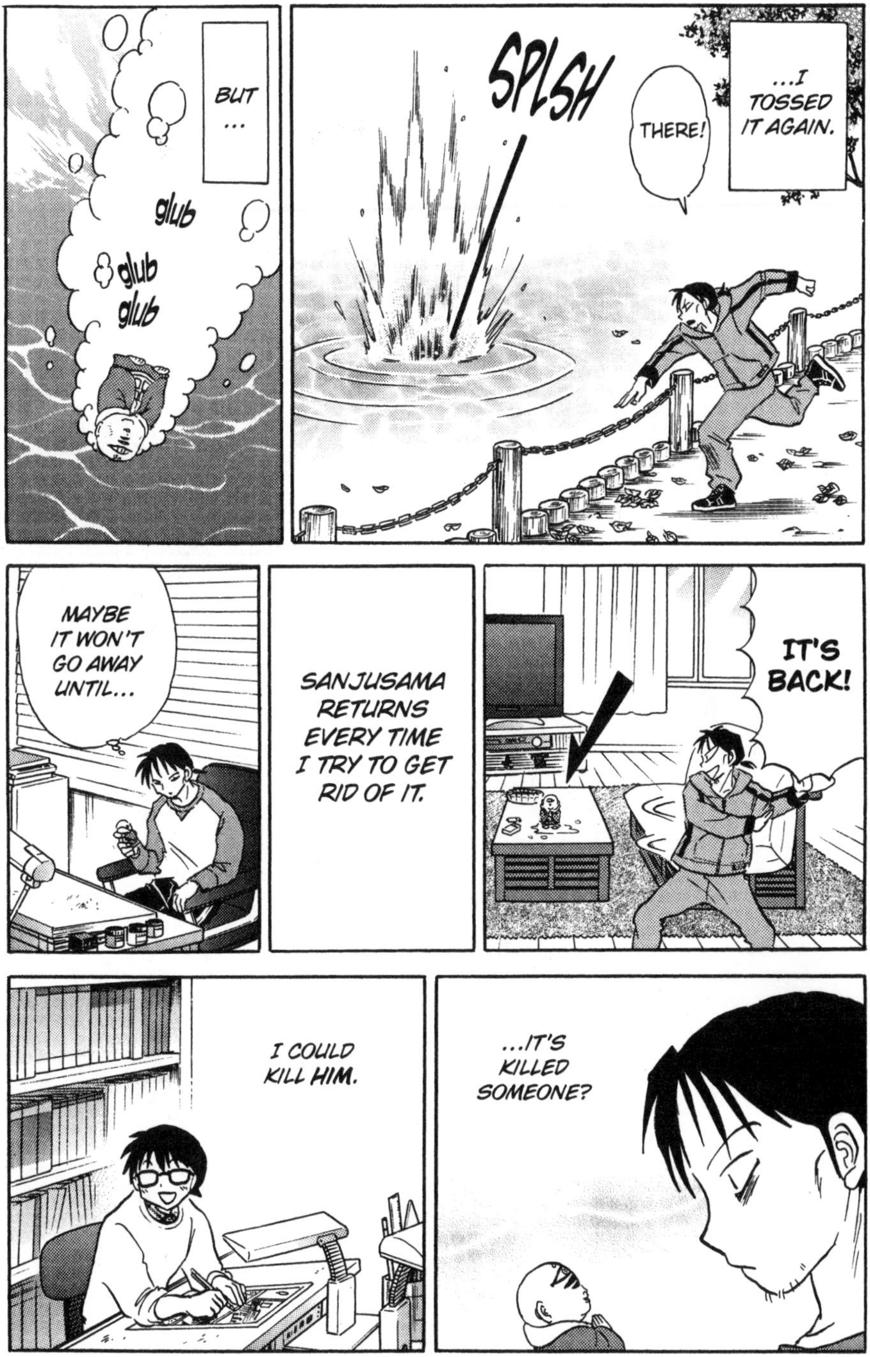
...I TOSSED IT AGAIN.
THERE!
SPLSH
BUT ...
glub
glub
glub
IT'S BACK!
SANJUSAMA RETURNS EVERY TIME I TRY TO GET RID OF IT.
MAYBE IT WON'T GO AWAY UNTIL...
...IT'S KILLED SOMEONE?
I COULD KILL HIM.

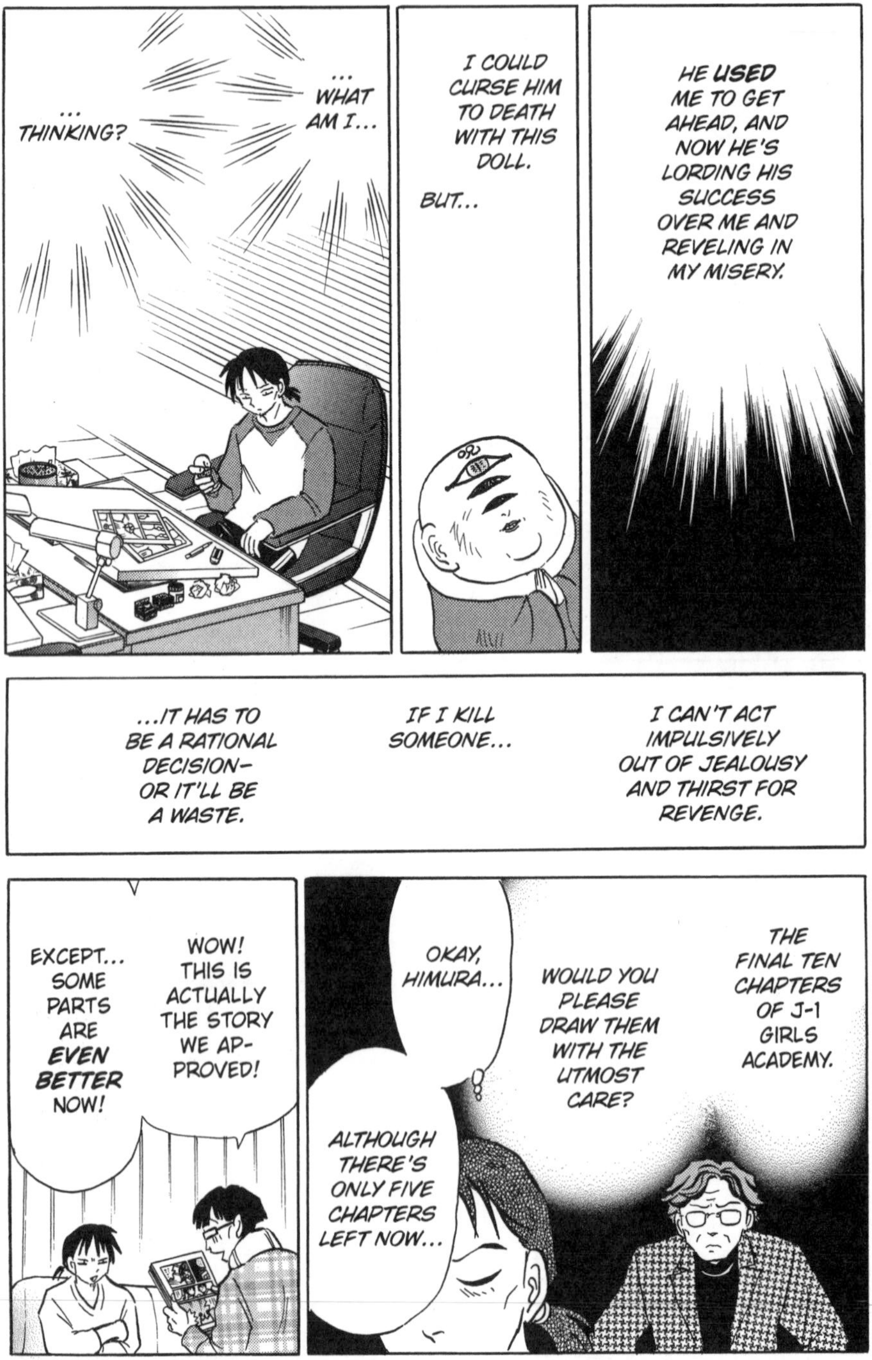
HE **USED** ME TO GET AHEAD, AND NOW HE'S LORDING HIS SUCCESS OVER ME AND REVELING IN MY MISERY.
I COULD CURSE HIM TO DEATH WITH THIS DOLL.
BUT...
... WHAT AM I...
... THINKING?
I CAN'T ACT IMPULSIVELY OUT OF JEALOUSY AND THIRST FOR REVENGE.
IF I KILL SOMEONE...
...IT HAS TO BE A RATIONAL DECISION— OR IT'LL BE A WASTE.
THE FINAL TEN CHAPTERS OF J-1 GIRLS ACADEMY.
WOULD YOU PLEASE DRAW THEM WITH THE UTMOST CARE?
OKAY, HIMURA...
ALTHOUGH THERE'S ONLY FIVE CHAPTERS LEFT NOW...
WOW! THIS IS ACTUALLY THE STORY WE AP-PROVED!
EXCEPT... SOME PARTS ARE **EVEN BETTER** NOW!

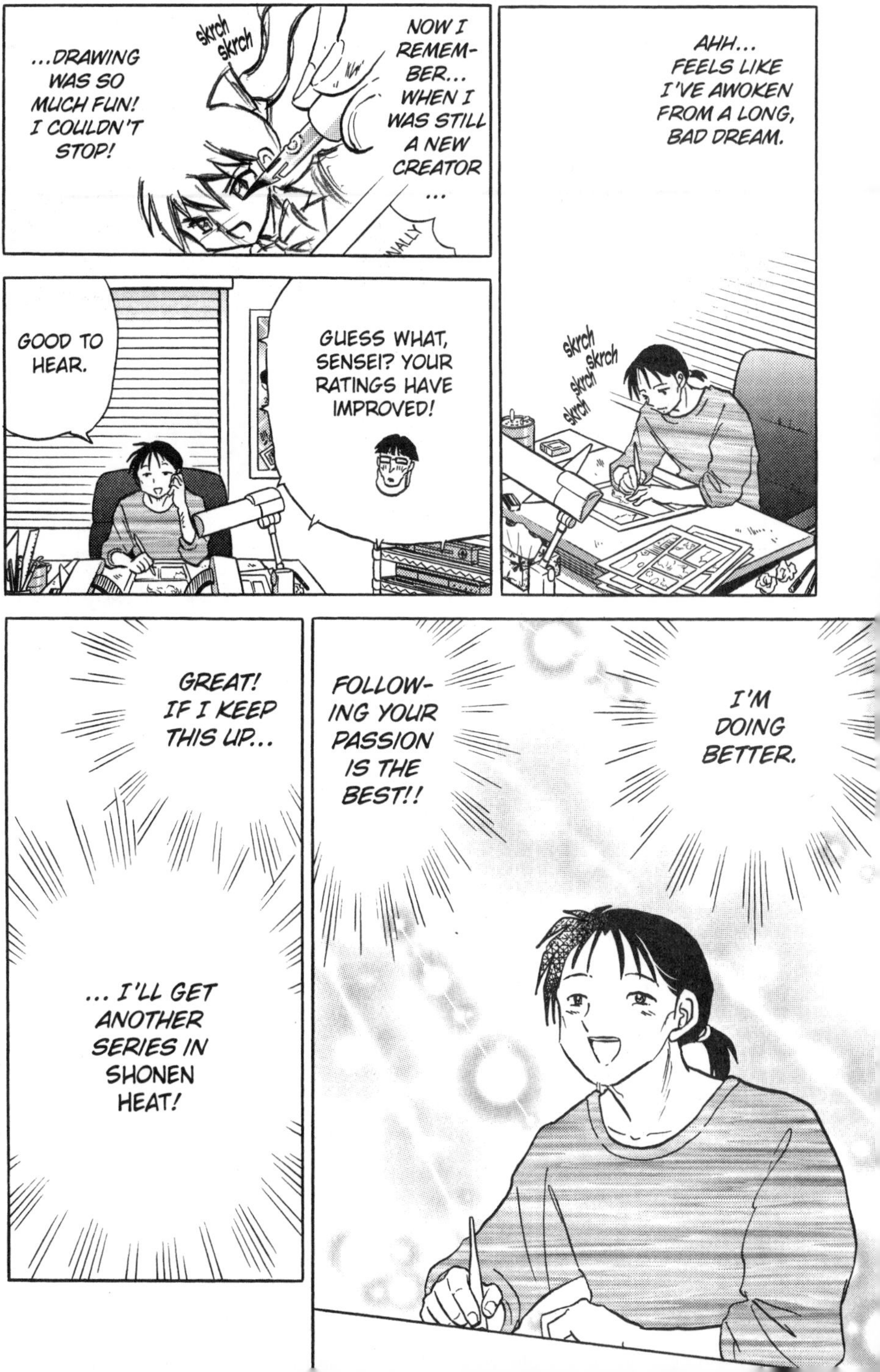
AHH... FEELS LIKE I'VE AWOKEN FROM A LONG, BAD DREAM.
skrch skrch skrch skrch
NOW I REMEM-BER... WHEN I WAS STILL A NEW CREATOR ...
skrch skrch
...DRAWING WAS SO MUCH FUN! I COULDN'T STOP!
GUESS WHAT, SENSEI? YOUR RATINGS HAVE IMPROVED!
GOOD TO HEAR.
I'M DOING BETTER.
FOLLOW-ING YOUR PASSION IS THE BEST!!
GREAT! IF I KEEP THIS UP...
... I'LL GET ANOTHER SERIES IN SHONEN HEAT!

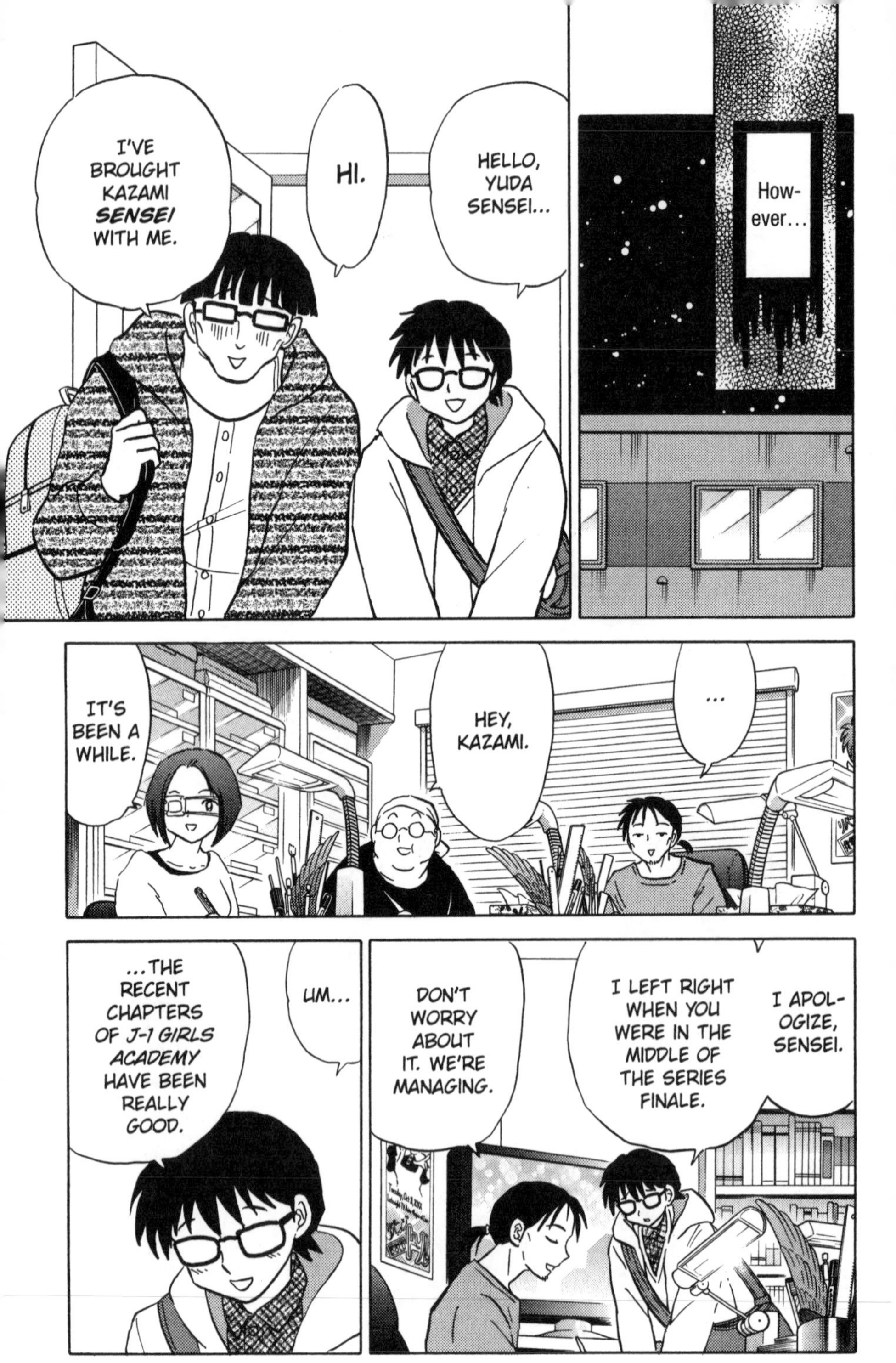
How-ever…
HELLO, YUDA SENSEI…
HI.
I'VE BROUGHT KAZAMI *SENSEI* WITH ME.
…
HEY, KAZAMI.
IT'S BEEN A WHILE.
I APOLOGIZE, SENSEI.
I LEFT RIGHT WHEN YOU WERE IN THE MIDDLE OF THE SERIES FINALE.
DON'T WORRY ABOUT IT. WE'RE MANAGING.
UM…
…THE RECENT CHAPTERS OF *J-1 GIRLS ACADEMY* HAVE BEEN REALLY GOOD.

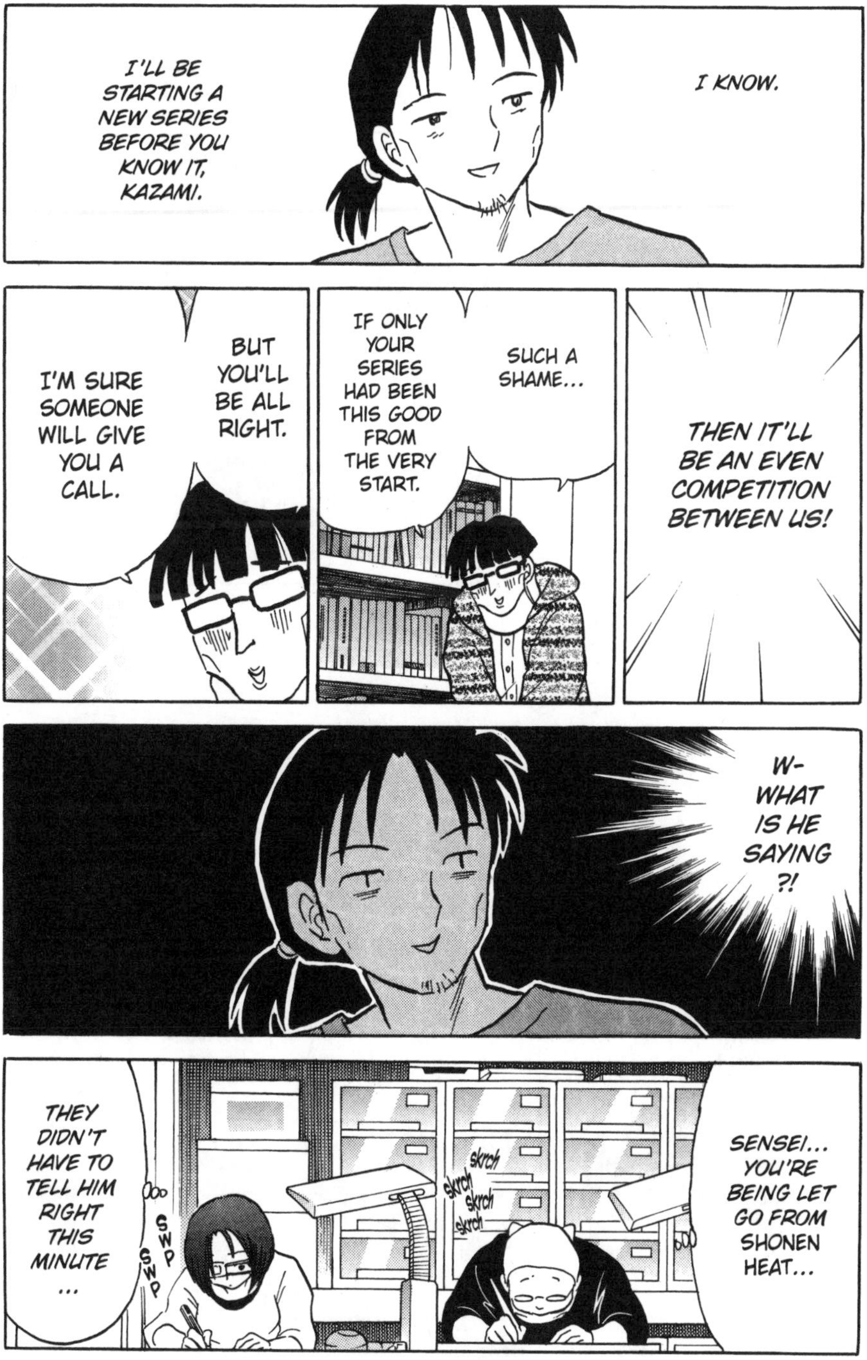
I KNOW.
I'LL BE STARTING A NEW SERIES BEFORE YOU KNOW IT, KAZAMI.
THEN IT'LL BE AN EVEN COMPETITION BETWEEN US!
SUCH A SHAME...
IF ONLY YOUR SERIES HAD BEEN THIS GOOD FROM THE VERY START.
BUT YOU'LL BE ALL RIGHT.
I'M SURE SOMEONE WILL GIVE YOU A CALL.
W-WHAT IS HE SAYING?!
SENSEI... YOU'RE BEING LET GO FROM SHONEN HEAT...
skrch skrch skrch skrch
SWP SWP
THEY DIDN'T HAVE TO TELL HIM RIGHT THIS MINUTE...

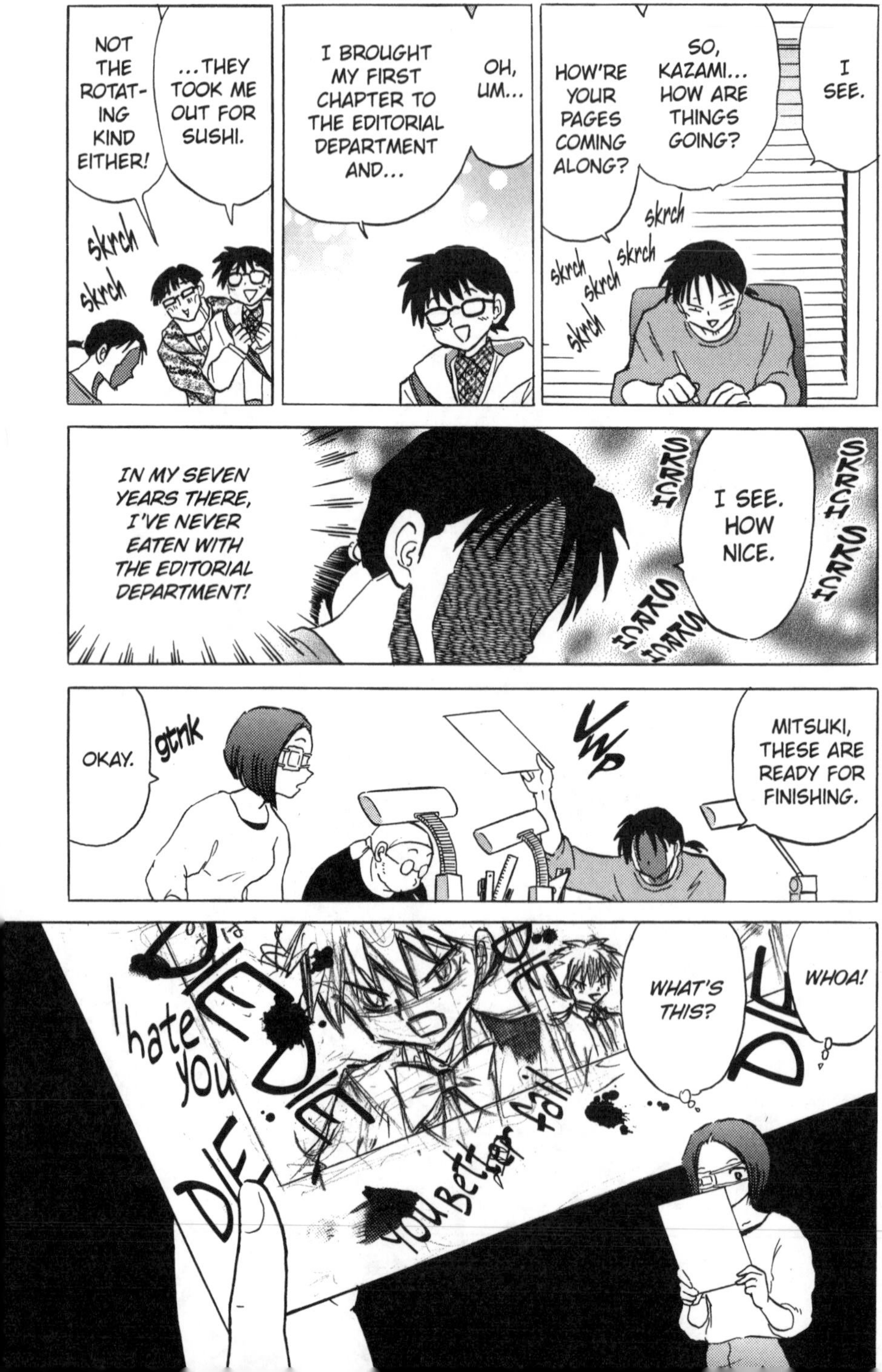
I SEE.
SO, KAZAMI... HOW ARE THINGS GOING?
HOW'RE YOUR PAGES COMING ALONG?
skrch
skrch
skrch
skrch
skrch
OH, UM...
I BROUGHT MY FIRST CHAPTER TO THE EDITORIAL DEPARTMENT AND...
...THEY TOOK ME OUT FOR SUSHI.
NOT THE ROTATING KIND EITHER!
skrch
skrch
SKRCH SKRCH
I SEE. HOW NICE.
SKRCH
SKRCH
SKRCH
IN MY SEVEN YEARS THERE, I'VE NEVER EATEN WITH THE EDITORIAL DEPARTMENT!
MITSUKI, THESE ARE READY FOR FINISHING.
VWP
gtnk
OKAY.
WHOA!
WHAT'S THIS?
DIE
DIE
I hate you
DIE
DIE

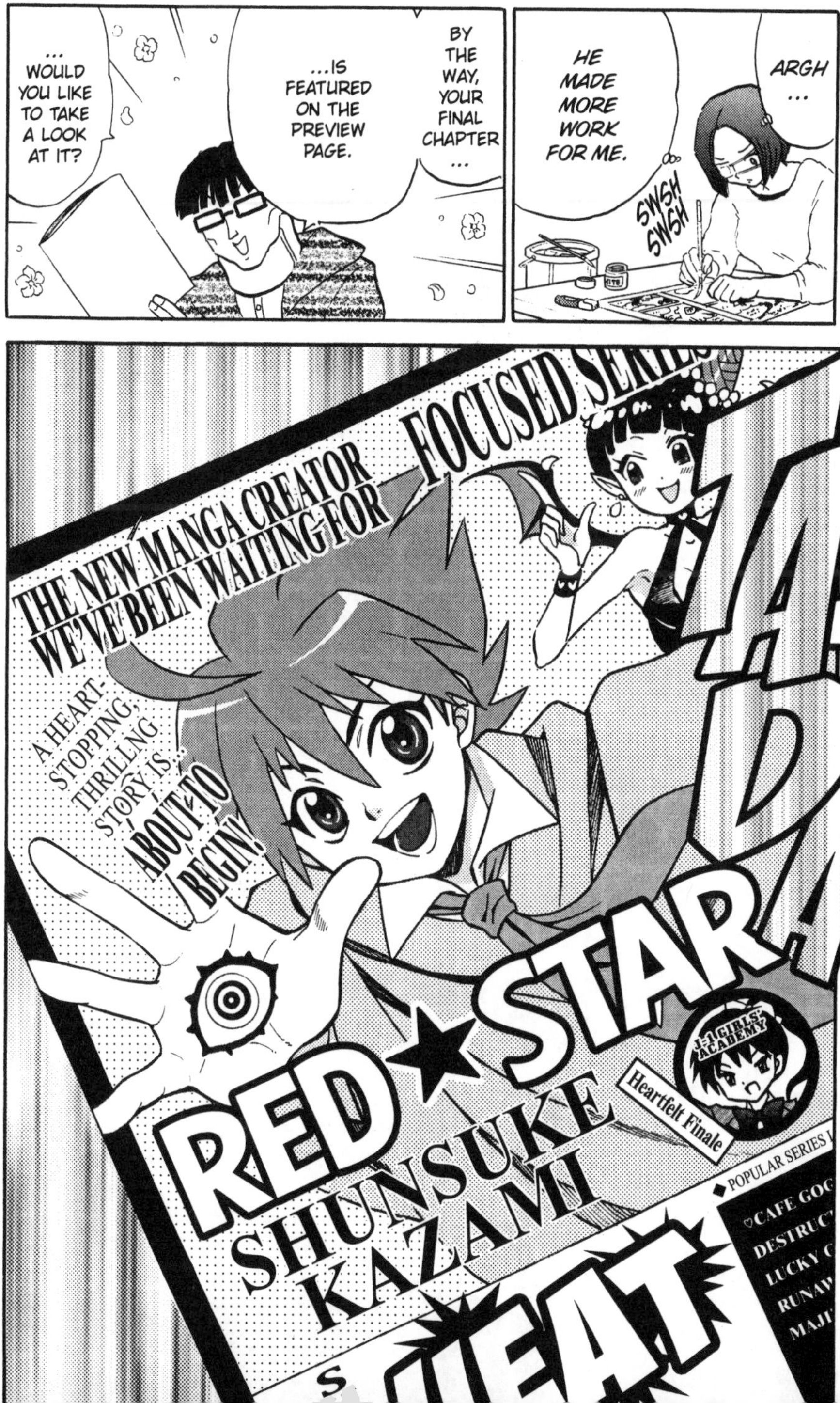
ARGH ...
HE MADE MORE WORK FOR ME.
SWSH SWSH
BY THE WAY, YOUR FINAL CHAPTER ...
...IS FEATURED ON THE PREVIEW PAGE.
... WOULD YOU LIKE TO TAKE A LOOK AT IT?
FOCUSED SERIES
THE NEW MANGA CREATOR WE'VE BEEN WAITING FOR
A HEART-STOPPING, THRILLNG STORY IS... ABOUT TO BEGIN!
RED★STAR
SHUNSUKE KAZAMI
J-1 GIRLS' ACADEMY
Heartfelt Finale
POPULAR SERIES

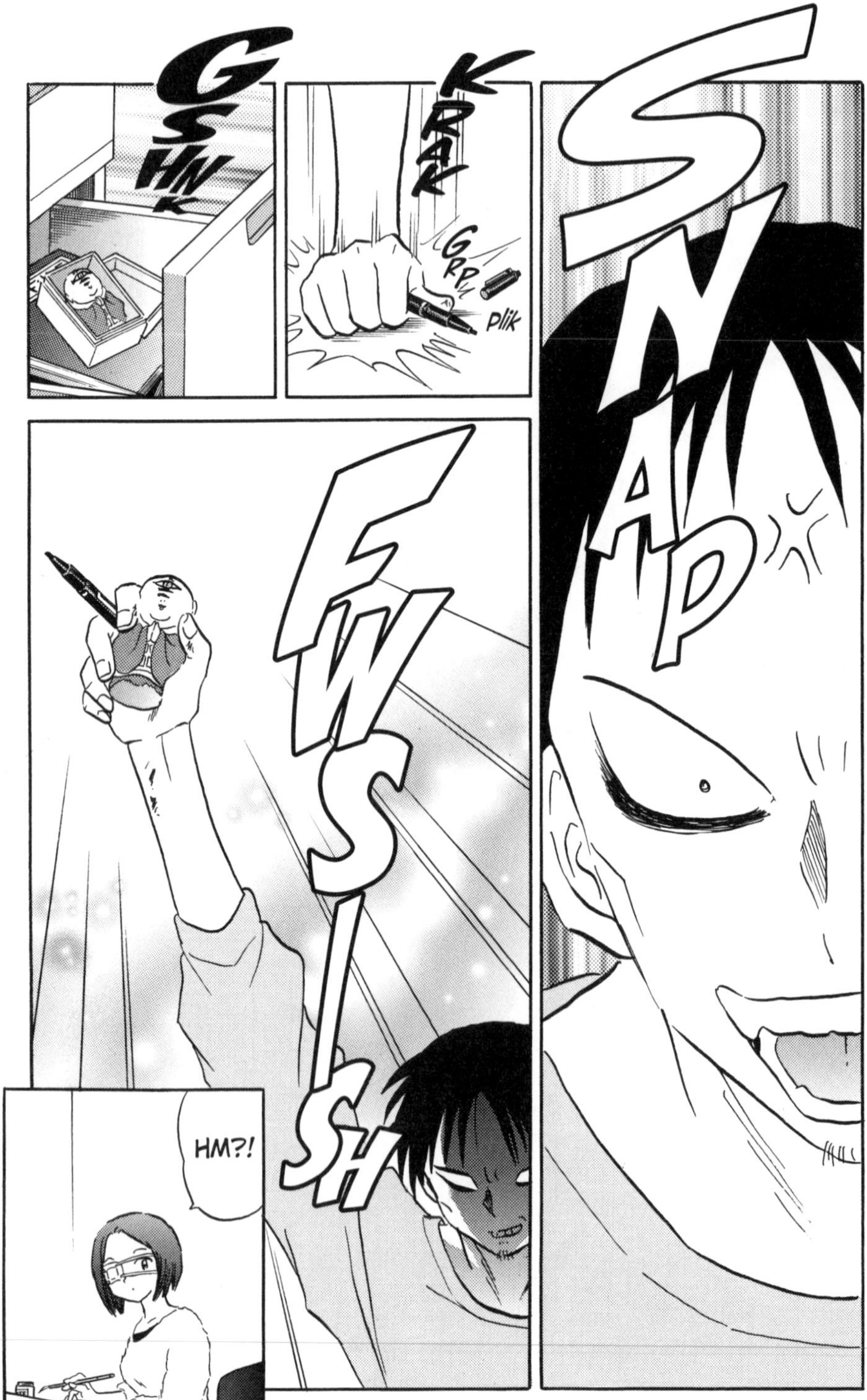
SNAP
KRAK
GRP
plik
GSHNK
FWSSH
HM?!

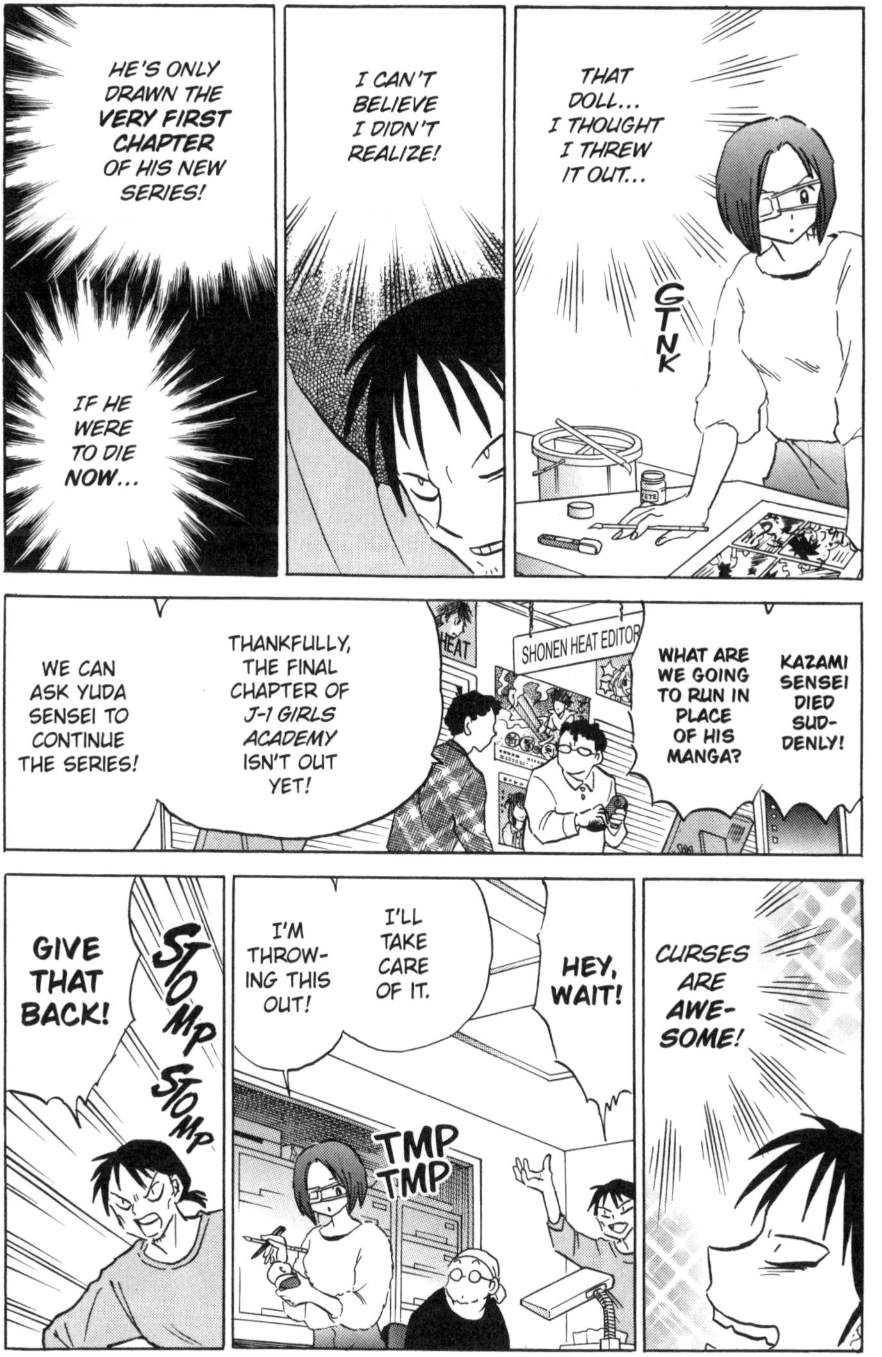
THAT DOLL... I THOUGHT I THREW IT OUT...
GTNK
I CAN'T BELIEVE I DIDN'T REALIZE!
HE'S ONLY DRAWN THE VERY FIRST CHAPTER OF HIS NEW SERIES!
IF HE WERE TO DIE NOW...
KAZAMI SENSEI DIED SUD-DENLY!
WHAT ARE WE GOING TO RUN IN PLACE OF HIS MANGA?
SHONEN HEAT EDITOR
THANKFULLY, THE FINAL CHAPTER OF J-1 GIRLS ACADEMY ISN'T OUT YET!
WE CAN ASK YUDA SENSEI TO CONTINUE THE SERIES!
CURSES ARE AWE-SOME!
HEY, WAIT!
I'LL TAKE CARE OF IT.
I'M THROW-ING THIS OUT!
TMP TMP
GIVE THAT BACK!
STOMP STOMP

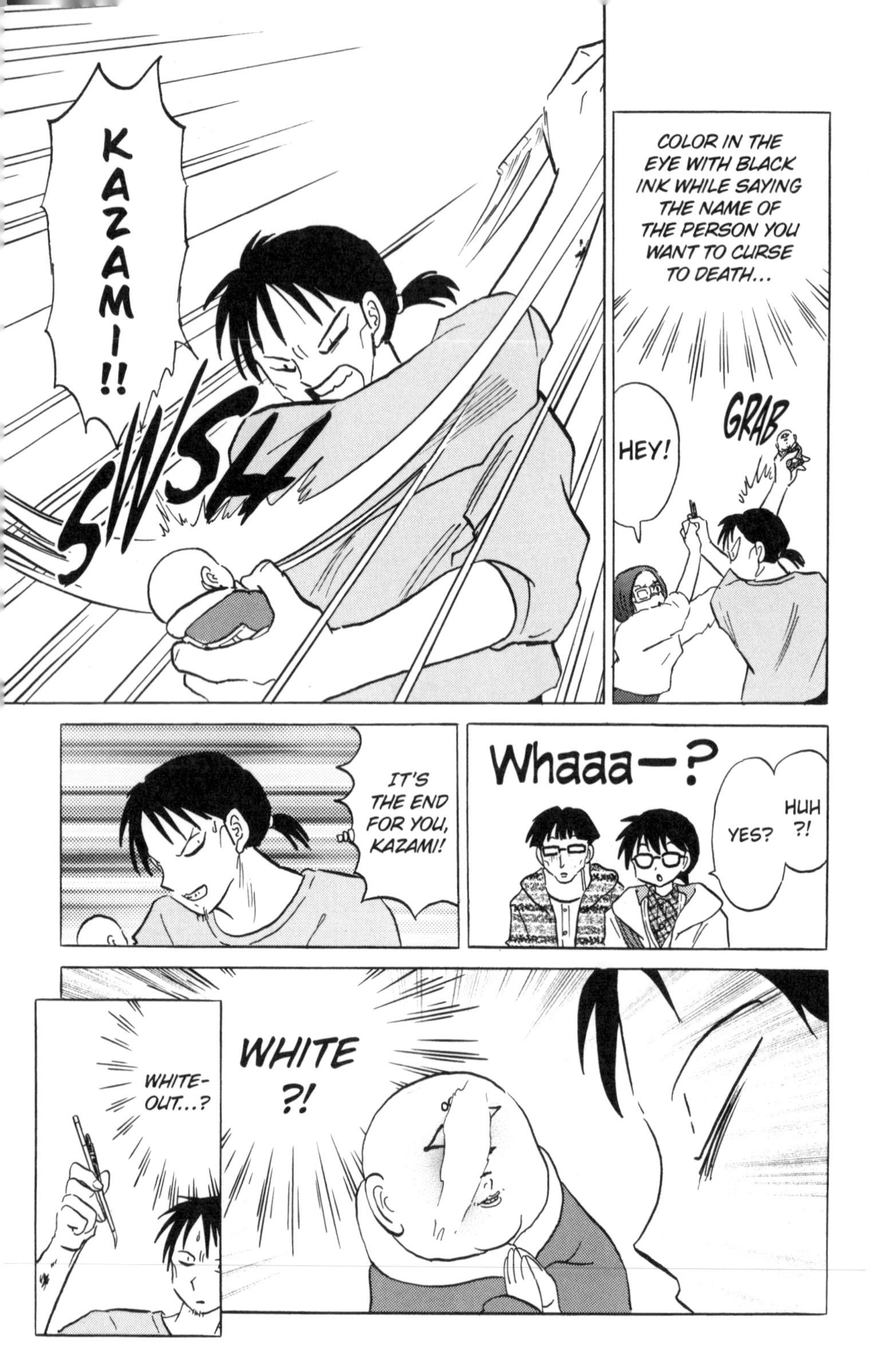
COLOR IN THE EYE WITH BLACK INK WHILE SAYING THE NAME OF THE PERSON YOU WANT TO CURSE TO DEATH...
GRAB
HEY!
KAZAMI!!
SWSH
Whaaa-?
HUH ?!
YES?
IT'S THE END FOR YOU, KAZAMI!
WHITE ?!
WHITE-OUT...?

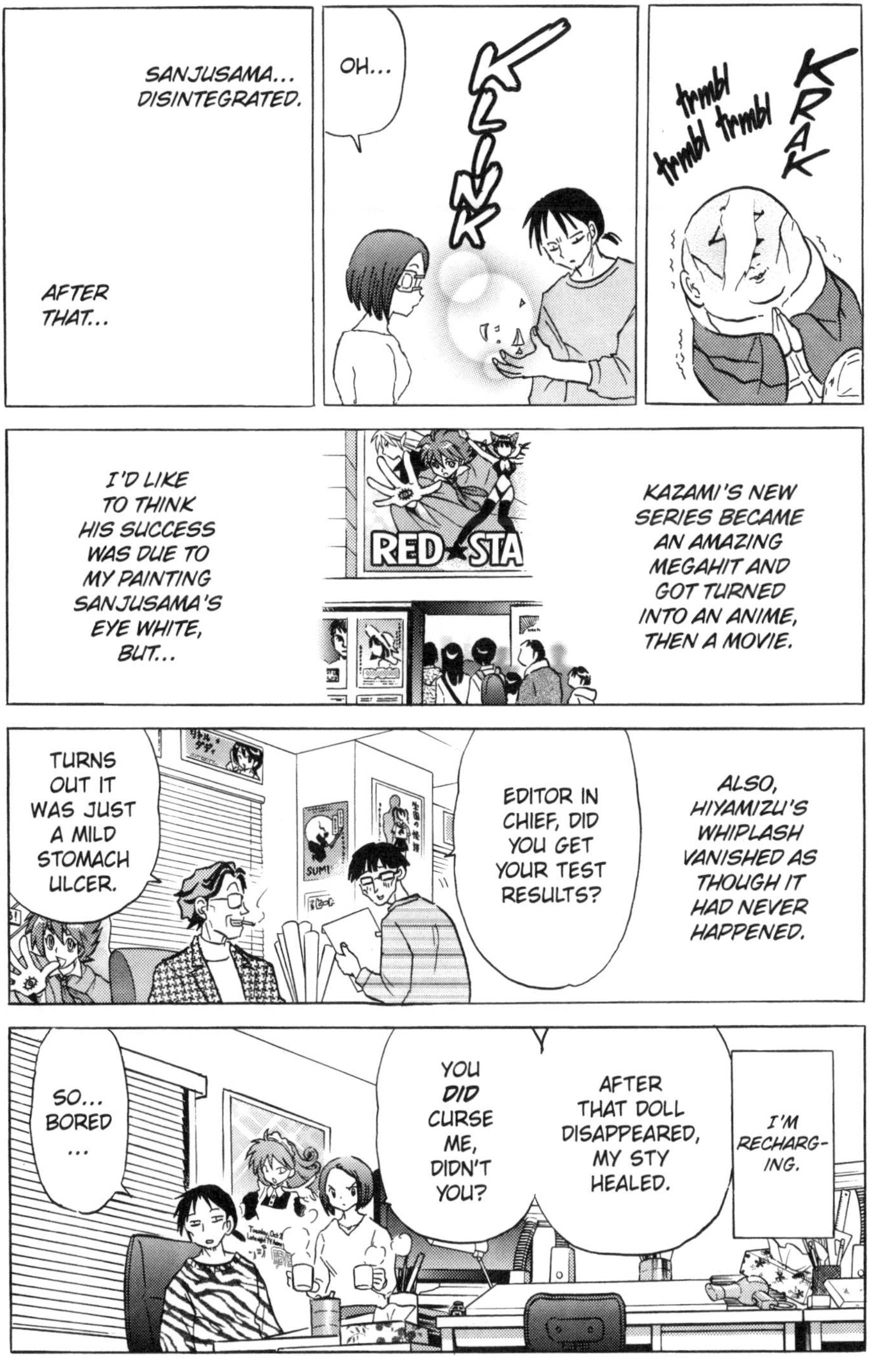
trmbl trmbl trmbl
KRAK
KLINK
OH...
SANJUSAMA... DISINTEGRATED.
AFTER THAT...
KAZAMI'S NEW SERIES BECAME AN AMAZING MEGAHIT AND GOT TURNED INTO AN ANIME, THEN A MOVIE.
RED★STA
I'D LIKE TO THINK HIS SUCCESS WAS DUE TO MY PAINTING SANJUSAMA'S EYE WHITE, BUT...
ALSO, HIYAMIZU'S WHIPLASH VANISHED AS THOUGH IT HAD NEVER HAPPENED.
EDITOR IN CHIEF, DID YOU GET YOUR TEST RESULTS?
TURNS OUT IT WAS JUST A MILD STOMACH ULCER.
SUMI
I'M RECHARG-ING.
AFTER THAT DOLL DISAPPEARED, MY STY HEALED.
YOU *DID* CURSE ME, DIDN'T YOU?
SO... BORED...

The Star Has a Thousand Faces

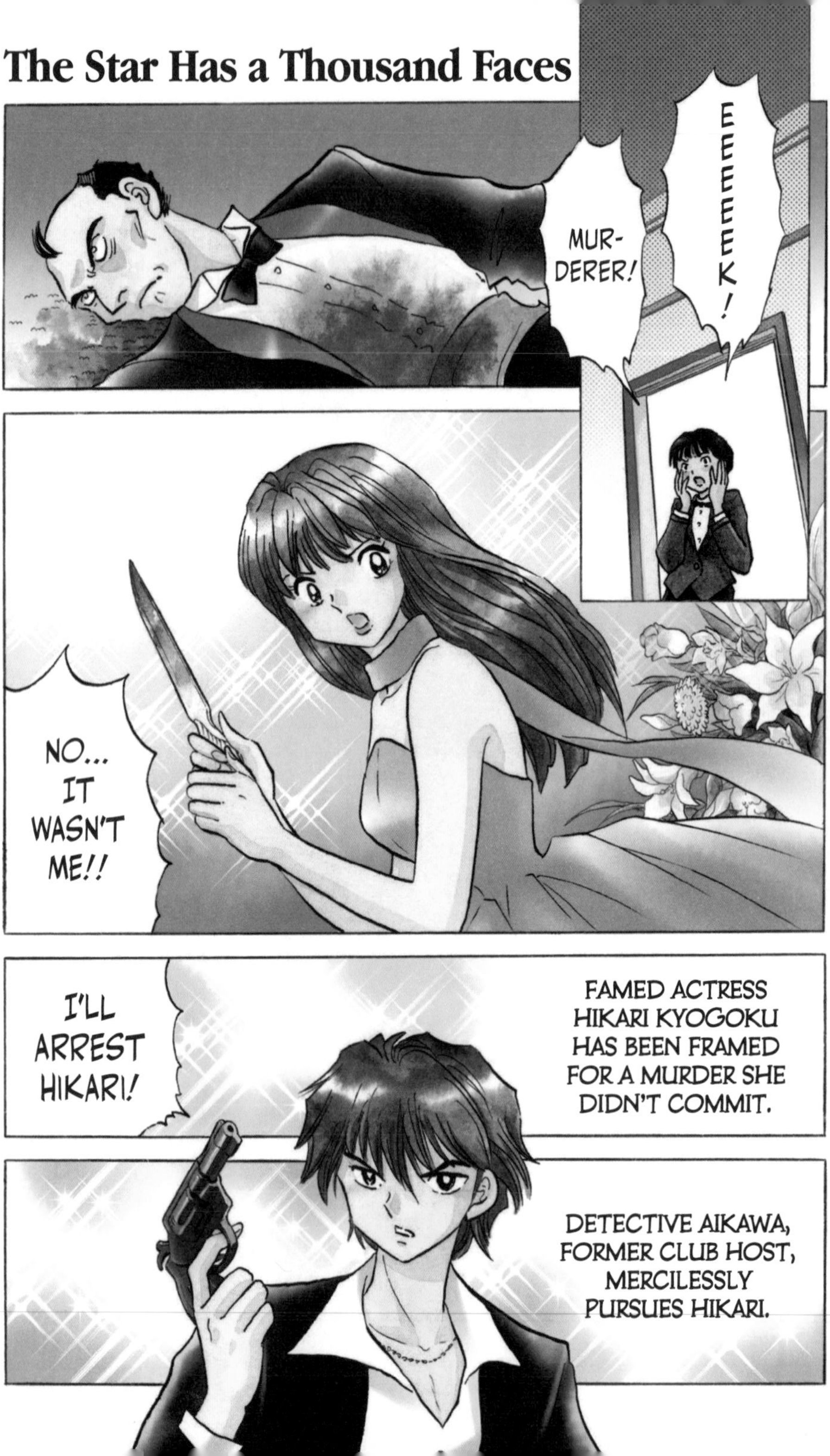
EEEEEEK!
MUR-DERER!
NO... IT WASN'T ME!!
FAMED ACTRESS HIKARI KYOGOKU HAS BEEN FRAMED FOR A MURDER SHE DIDN'T COMMIT.
I'LL ARREST HIKARI!
DETECTIVE AIKAWA, FORMER CLUB HOST, MERCILESSLY PURSUES HIKARI.

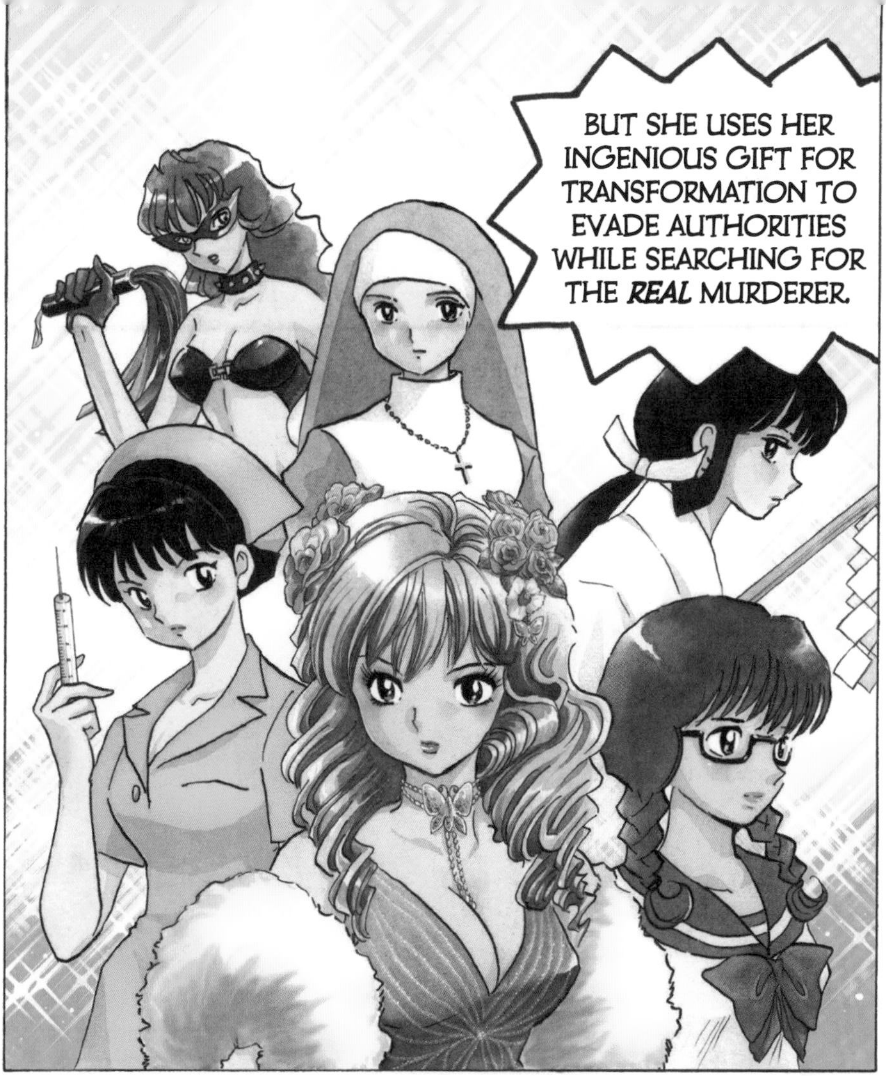
BUT SHE USES HER INGENIOUS GIFT FOR TRANSFORMATION TO EVADE AUTHORITIES WHILE SEARCHING FOR THE *REAL* MURDERER.

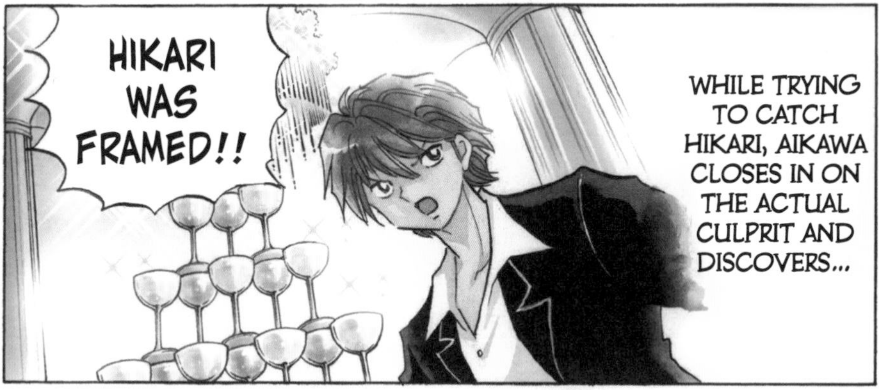
WHILE TRYING TO CATCH HIKARI, AIKAWA CLOSES IN ON THE ACTUAL CULPRIT AND DISCOVERS...
HIKARI WAS FRAMED!!

The Star Has a Thousand Faces

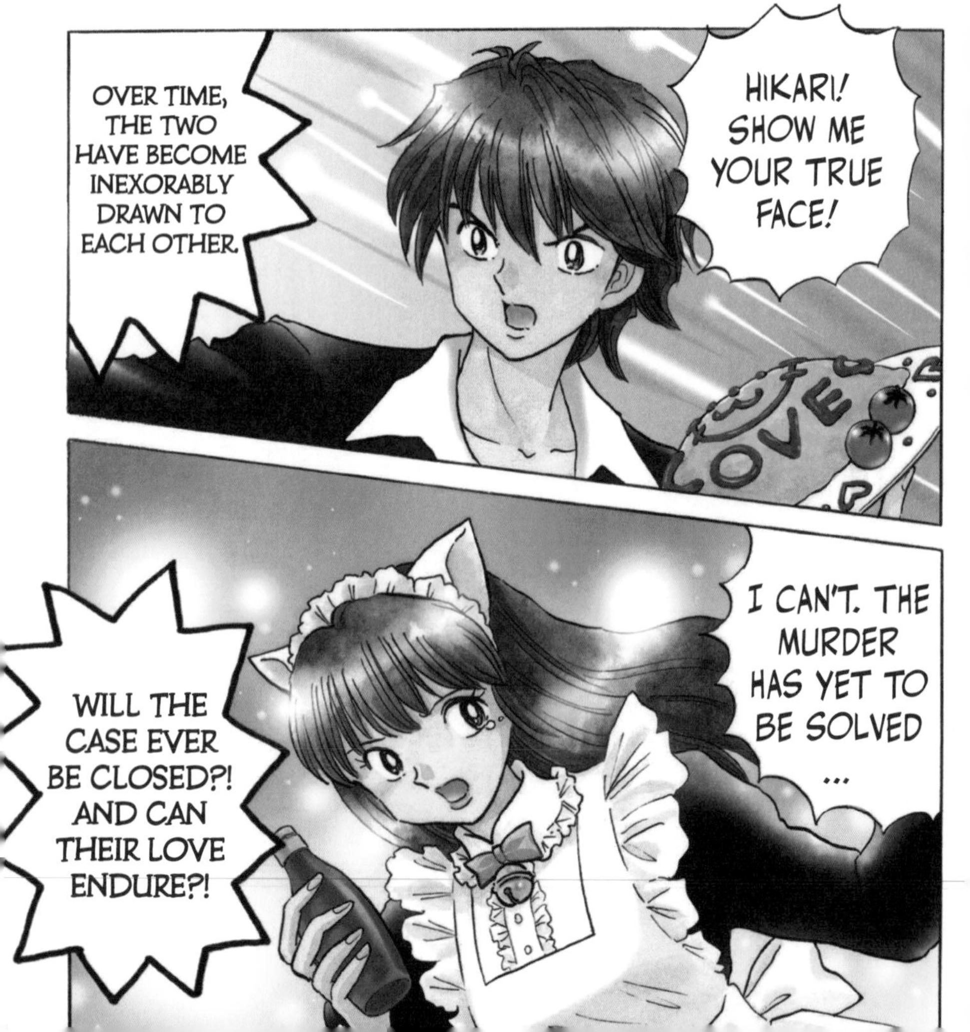
HIKARI! SHOW ME YOUR TRUE FACE!
LOVE
OVER TIME, THE TWO HAVE BECOME INEXORABLY DRAWN TO EACH OTHER.
I CAN'T. THE MURDER HAS YET TO BE SOLVED ...
WILL THE CASE EVER BE CLOSED?! AND CAN THEIR LOVE ENDURE?!

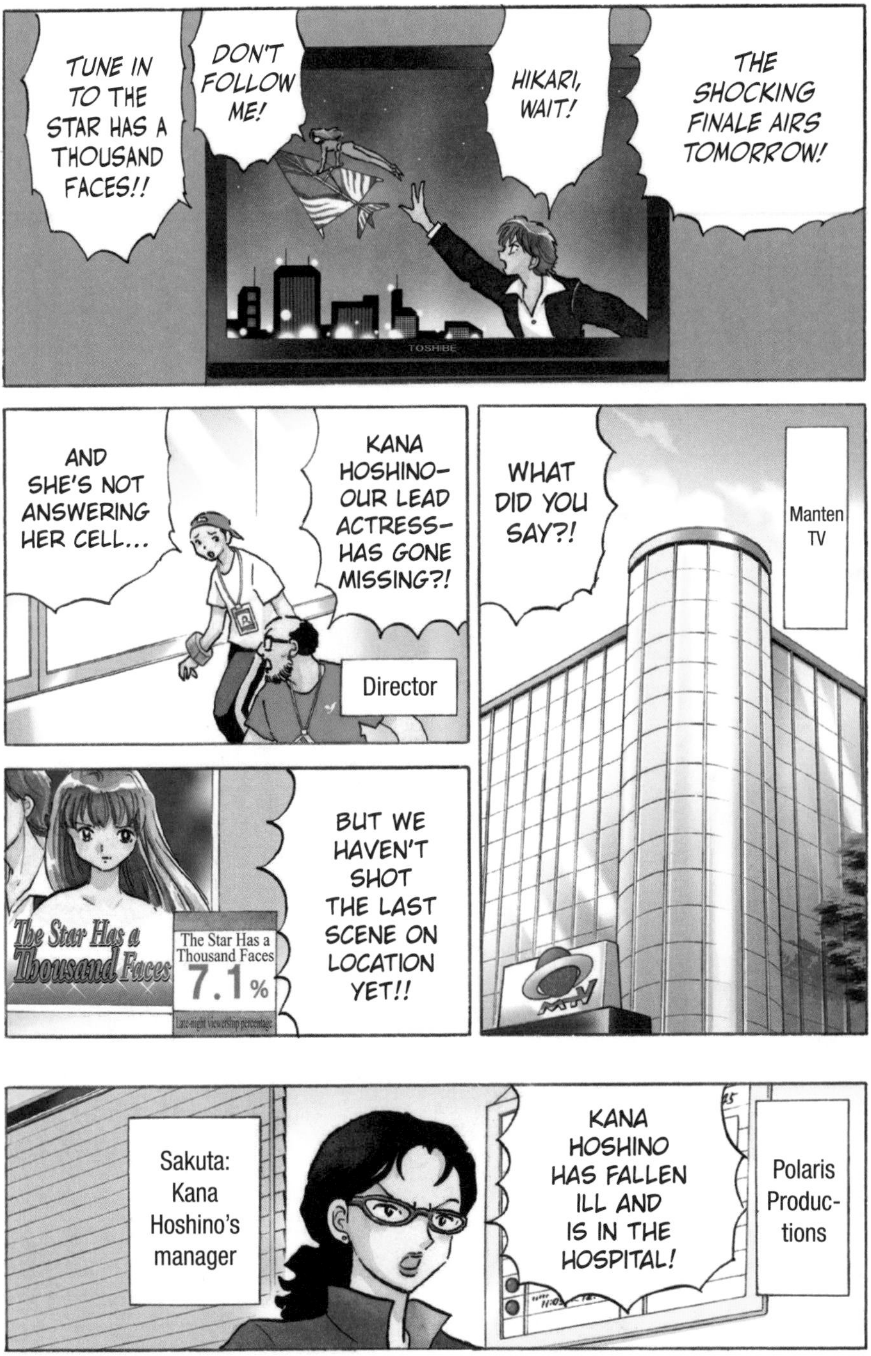
THE SHOCKING FINALE AIRS TOMORROW!
HIKARI, WAIT!
DON'T FOLLOW ME!
TUNE IN TO THE STAR HAS A THOUSAND FACES!!
TOSHIBE
Manten TV
WHAT DID YOU SAY?!
KANA HOSHINO—OUR LEAD ACTRESS—HAS GONE MISSING?!
Director
AND SHE'S NOT ANSWERING HER CELL...
BUT WE HAVEN'T SHOT THE LAST SCENE ON LOCATION YET!!
The Star Has a Thousand Faces
The Star Has a Thousand Faces 7.1%
Late-night viewership percentage
Polaris Productions
KANA HOSHINO HAS FALLEN ILL AND IS IN THE HOSPITAL!
Sakuta: Kana Hoshino's manager

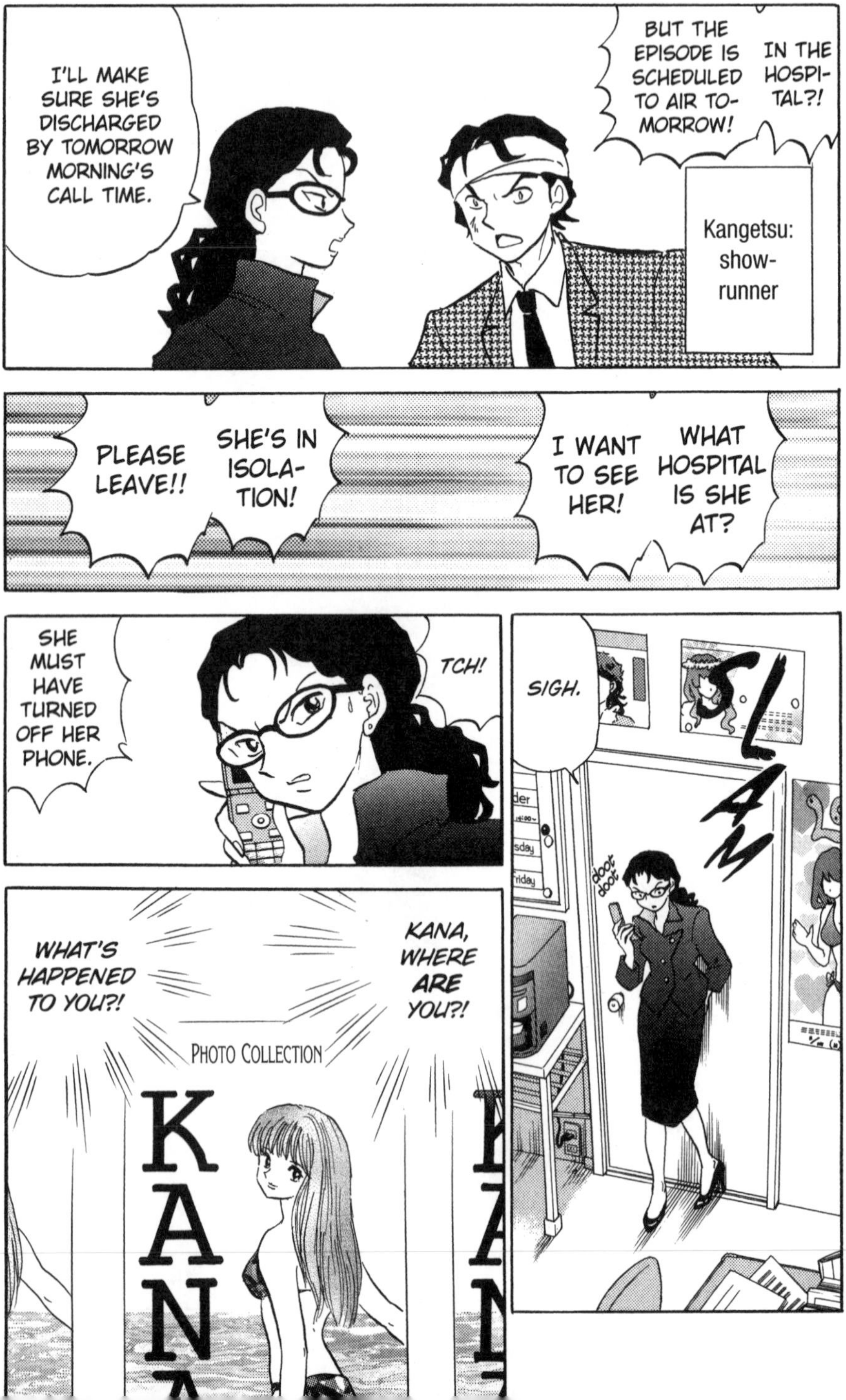
IN THE HOSPITAL?!
BUT THE EPISODE IS SCHEDULED TO AIR TOMORROW!
Kangetsu: showrunner
I'LL MAKE SURE SHE'S DISCHARGED BY TOMORROW MORNING'S CALL TIME.
WHAT HOSPITAL IS SHE AT?
I WANT TO SEE HER!
SHE'S IN ISOLATION!
PLEASE LEAVE!!
SLAM
SIGH.
doot doot
TCH!
SHE MUST HAVE TURNED OFF HER PHONE.
KANA, WHERE ARE YOU?!
WHAT'S HAPPENED TO YOU?!
PHOTO COLLECTION
KANA

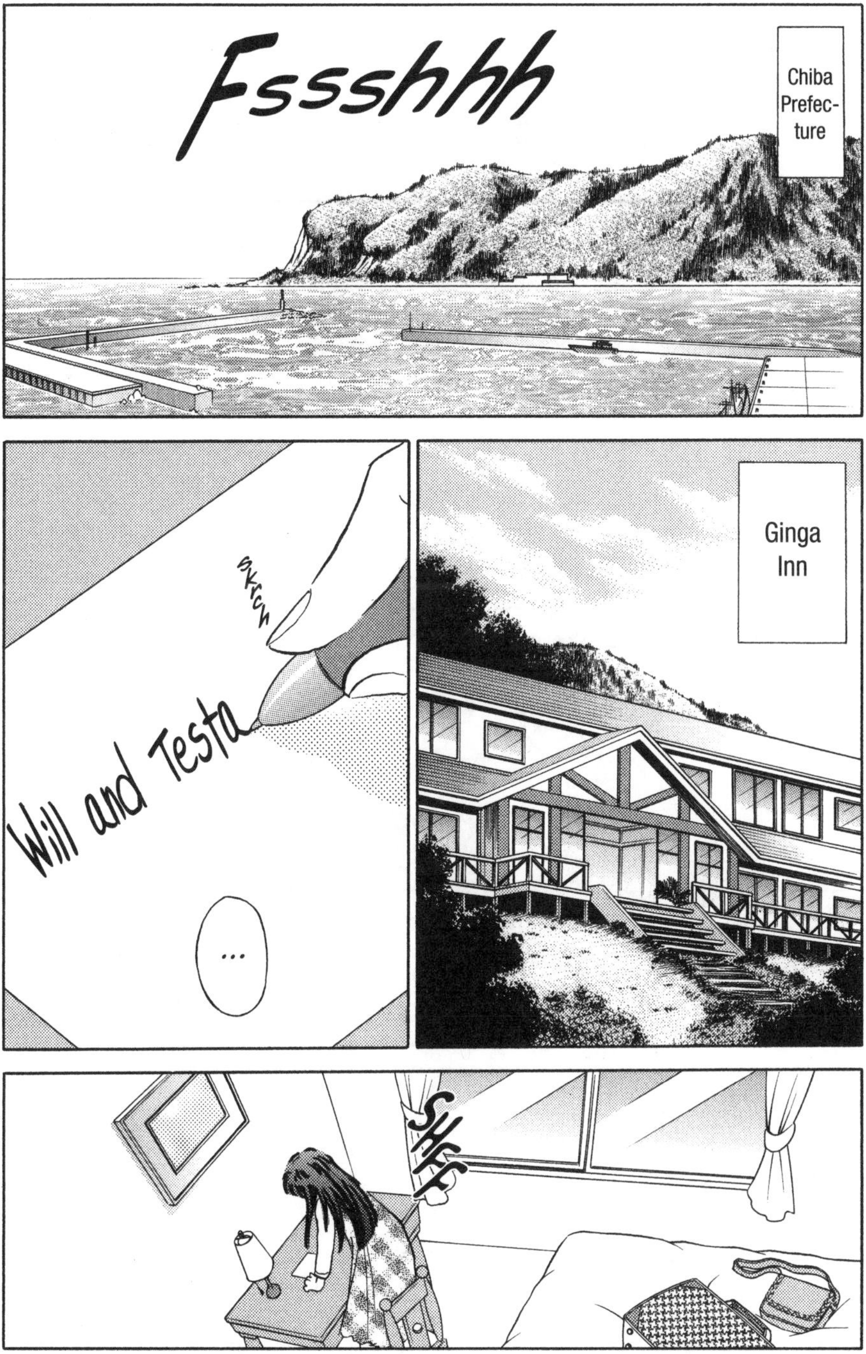
Fssshhh
Chiba Prefec-ture
Ginga Inn
skrch
Will and Testa
...
SHFF

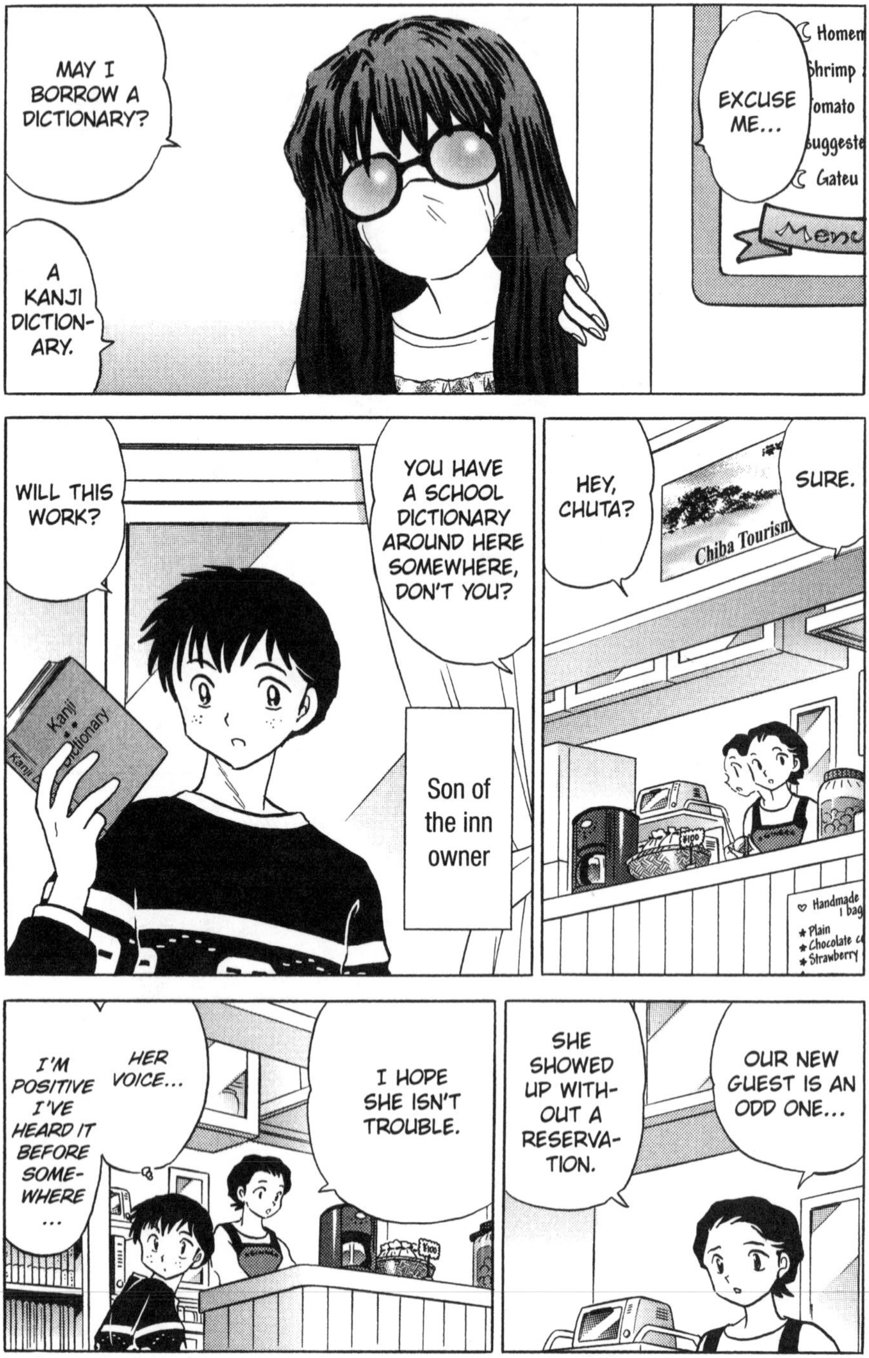
EXCUSE ME...
MAY I BORROW A DICTIONARY?
A KANJI DICTIONARY.
SURE.
HEY, CHUTA?
Chiba Tourism
YOU HAVE A SCHOOL DICTIONARY AROUND HERE SOMEWHERE, DON'T YOU?
Son of the inn owner
WILL THIS WORK?
Kanji Dictionary
OUR NEW GUEST IS AN ODD ONE...
SHE SHOWED UP WITHOUT A RESERVATION.
I HOPE SHE ISN'T TROUBLE.
HER VOICE...
I'M POSITIVE I'VE HEARD IT BEFORE SOMEWHERE...

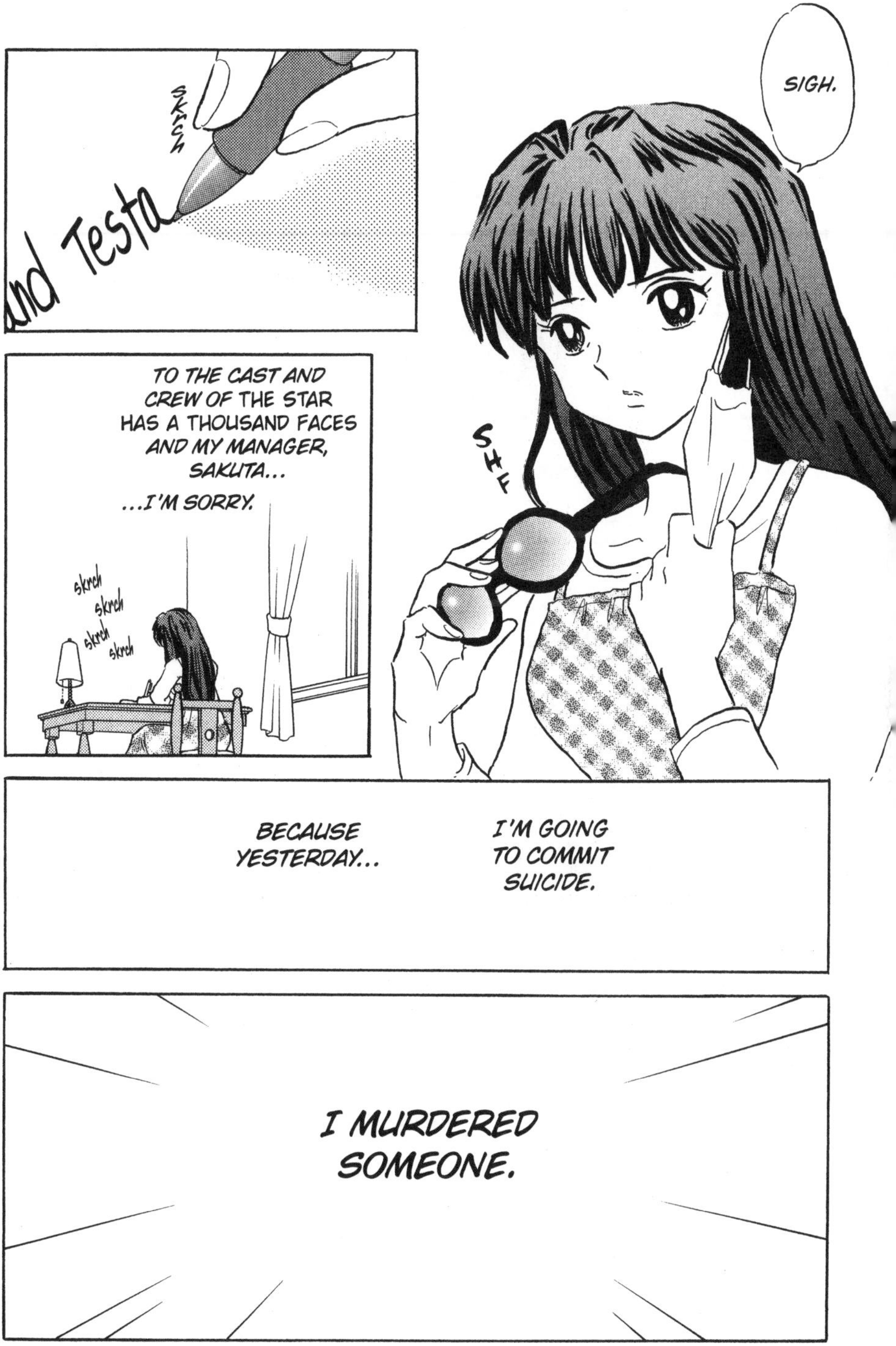
SIGH.
SHF
skrch
and Testa
TO THE CAST AND CREW OF THE STAR HAS A THOUSAND FACES AND MY MANAGER, SAKUTA...
...I'M SORRY.
skrch skrch skrch skrch
I'M GOING TO COMMIT SUICIDE.
BECAUSE YESTERDAY...
I MURDERED SOMEONE.

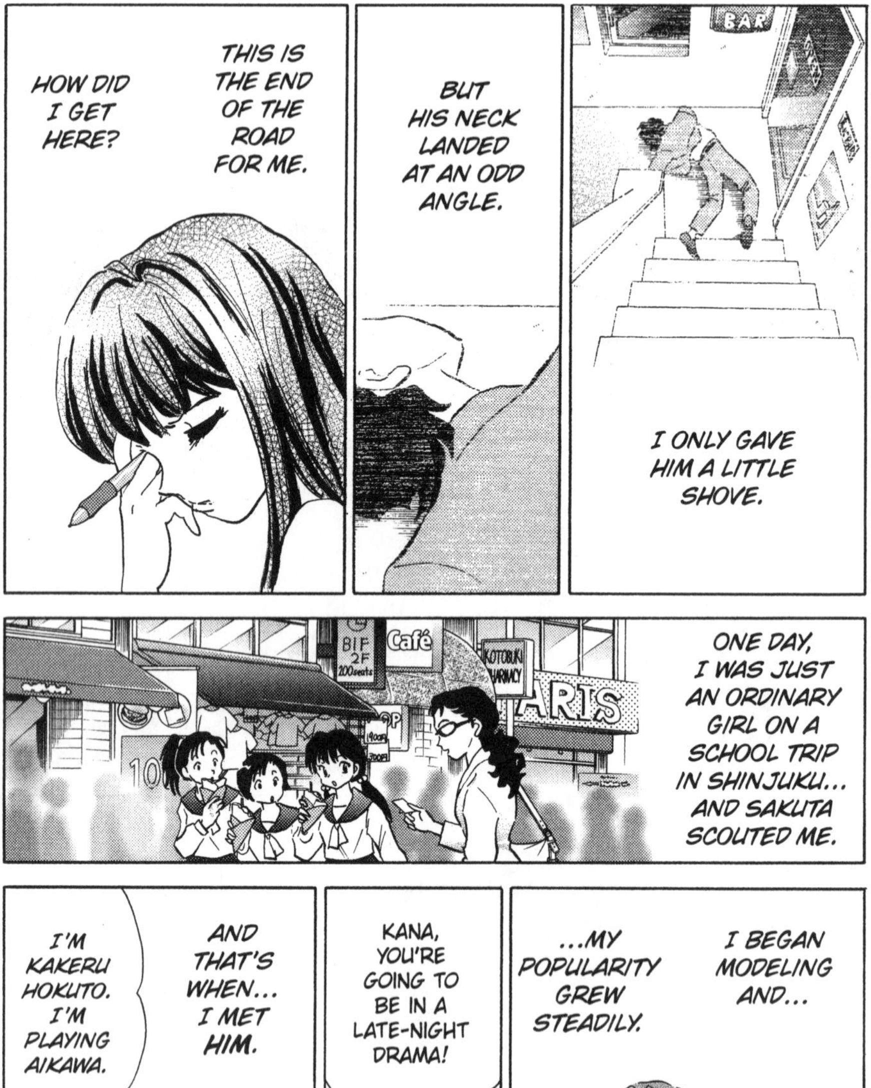
BAR
I ONLY GAVE HIM A LITTLE SHOVE.
BUT HIS NECK LANDED AT AN ODD ANGLE.
THIS IS THE END OF THE ROAD FOR ME.
HOW DID I GET HERE?
ONE DAY, I WAS JUST AN ORDINARY GIRL ON A SCHOOL TRIP IN SHINJUKU... AND SAKUTA SCOUTED ME.
Café
I BEGAN MODELING AND...
...MY POPULARITY GREW STEADILY.
KANA, YOU'RE GOING TO BE IN A LATE-NIGHT DRAMA!
AND THAT'S WHEN... I MET HIM.
I'M KAKERU HOKUTO. I'M PLAYING AIKAWA.

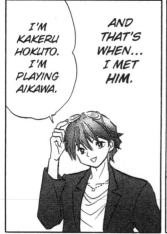

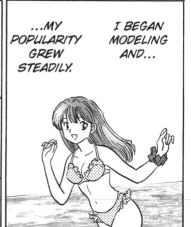

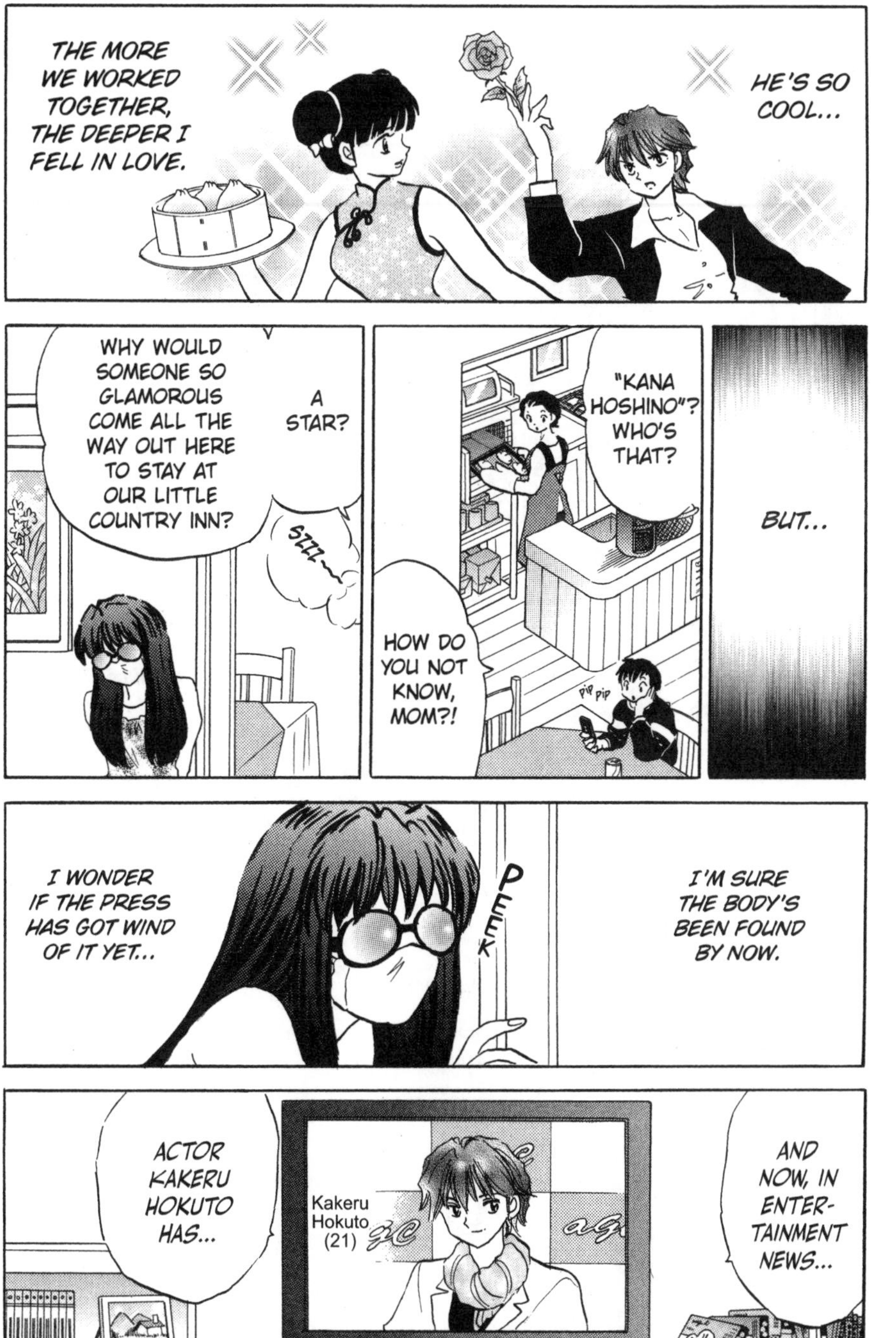
HE'S SO COOL...
THE MORE WE WORKED TOGETHER, THE DEEPER I FELL IN LOVE.
BUT...
"KANA HOSHINO"? WHO'S THAT?
pip pip
HOW DO YOU NOT KNOW, MOM?!
A STAR?
WHY WOULD SOMEONE SO GLAMOROUS COME ALL THE WAY OUT HERE TO STAY AT OUR LITTLE COUNTRY INN?
SZZZ~
I'M SURE THE BODY'S BEEN FOUND BY NOW.
PEEK
I WONDER IF THE PRESS HAS GOT WIND OF IT YET...
AND NOW, IN ENTER-TAINMENT NEWS...
Kakeru Hokuto (21)
ACTOR KAKERU HOKUTO HAS...

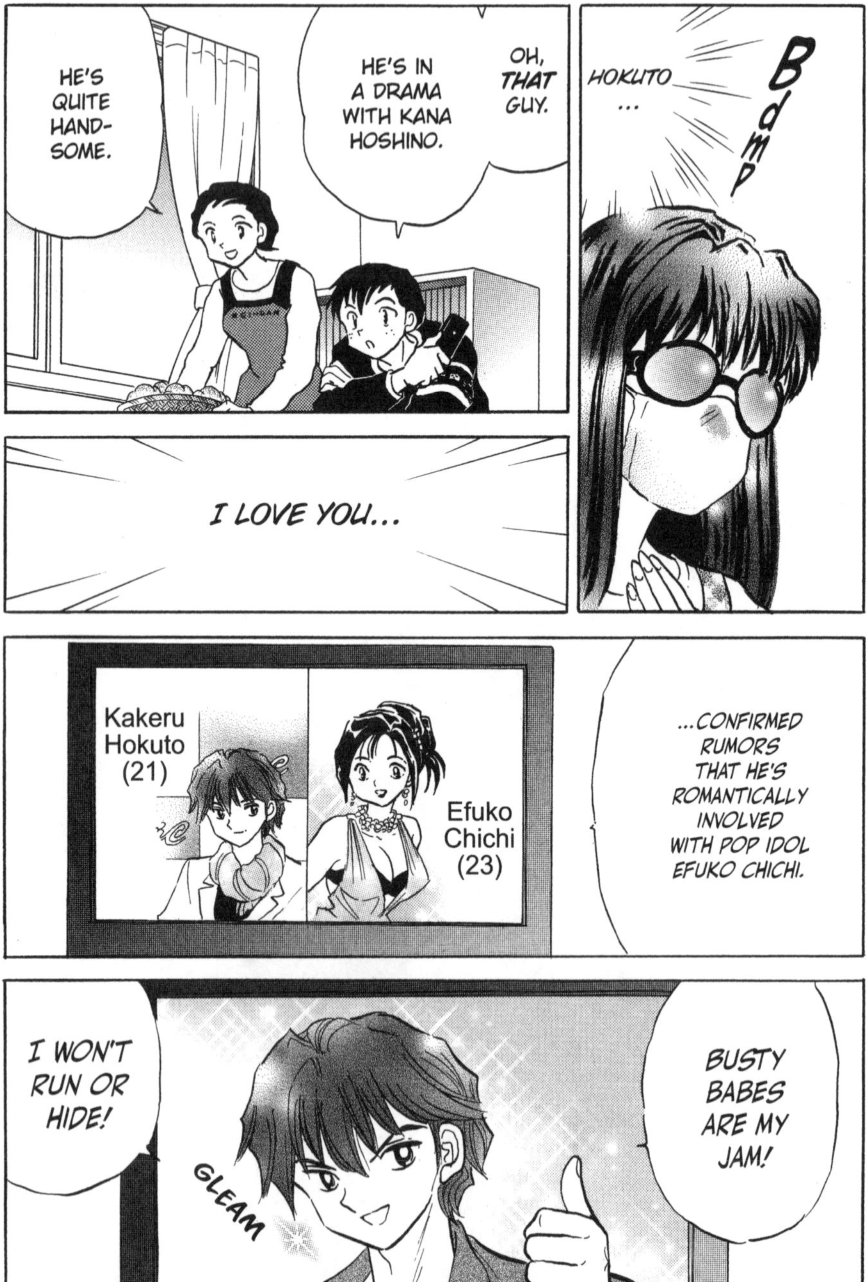
HOKUTO ...
Bdmp
OH, *THAT* GUY.
HE'S IN A DRAMA WITH KANA HOSHINO.
HE'S QUITE HAND-SOME.
I LOVE YOU...
...CONFIRMED RUMORS THAT HE'S ROMANTICALLY INVOLVED WITH POP IDOL EFUKO CHICHI.
Efuko Chichi (23)
Kakeru Hokuto (21)
BUSTY BABES ARE MY JAM!
GLEAM
I WON'T RUN OR HIDE!

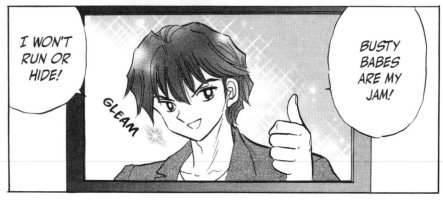

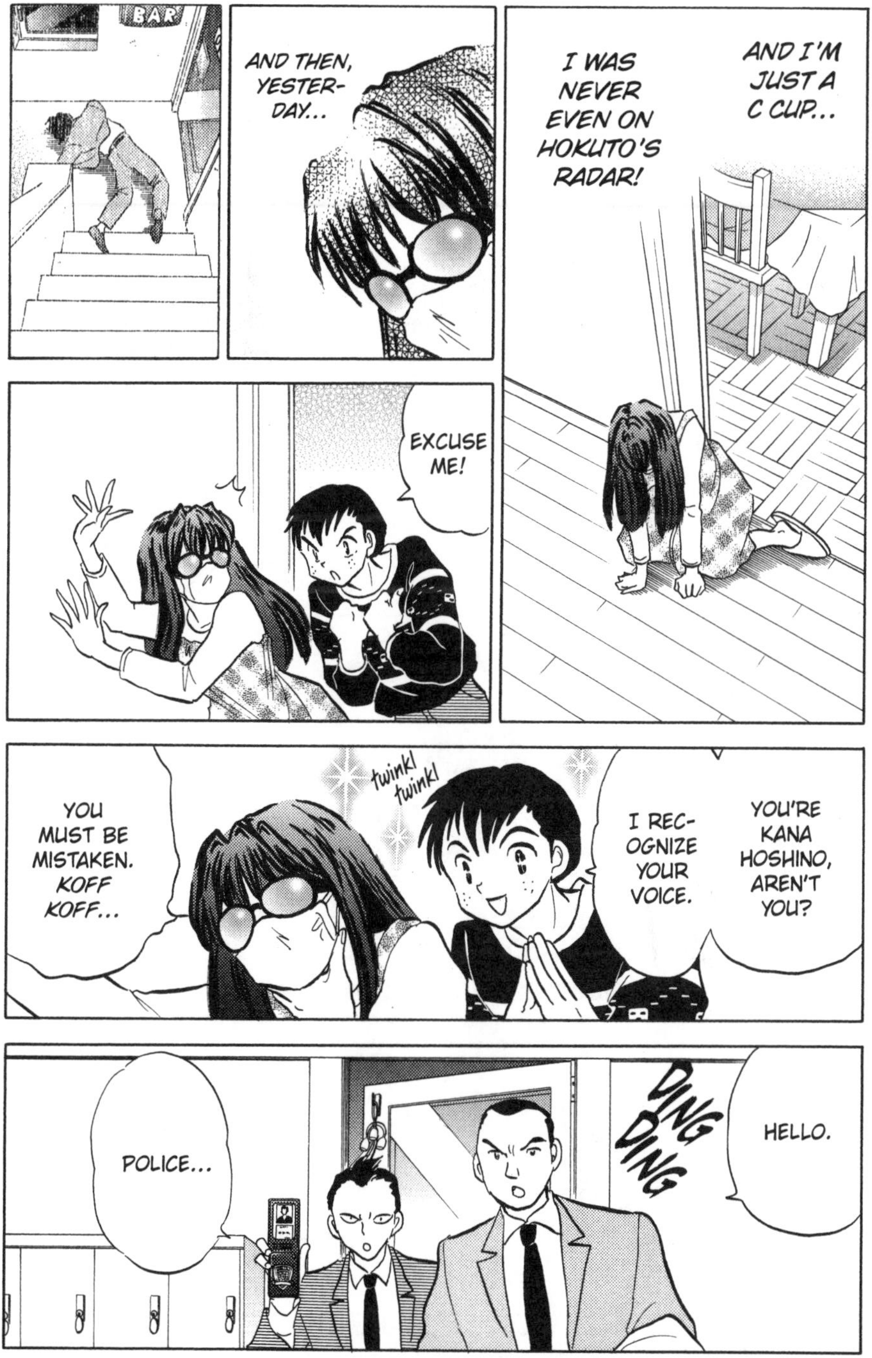
AND I'M JUST A C CUP...
I WAS NEVER EVEN ON HOKUTO'S RADAR!
AND THEN, YESTERDAY...
BAR
EXCUSE ME!
YOU'RE KANA HOSHINO, AREN'T YOU?
I RECOGNIZE YOUR VOICE.
twinkl twinkl
YOU MUST BE MISTAKEN. KOFF KOFF...
HELLO.
DING DING
POLICE...

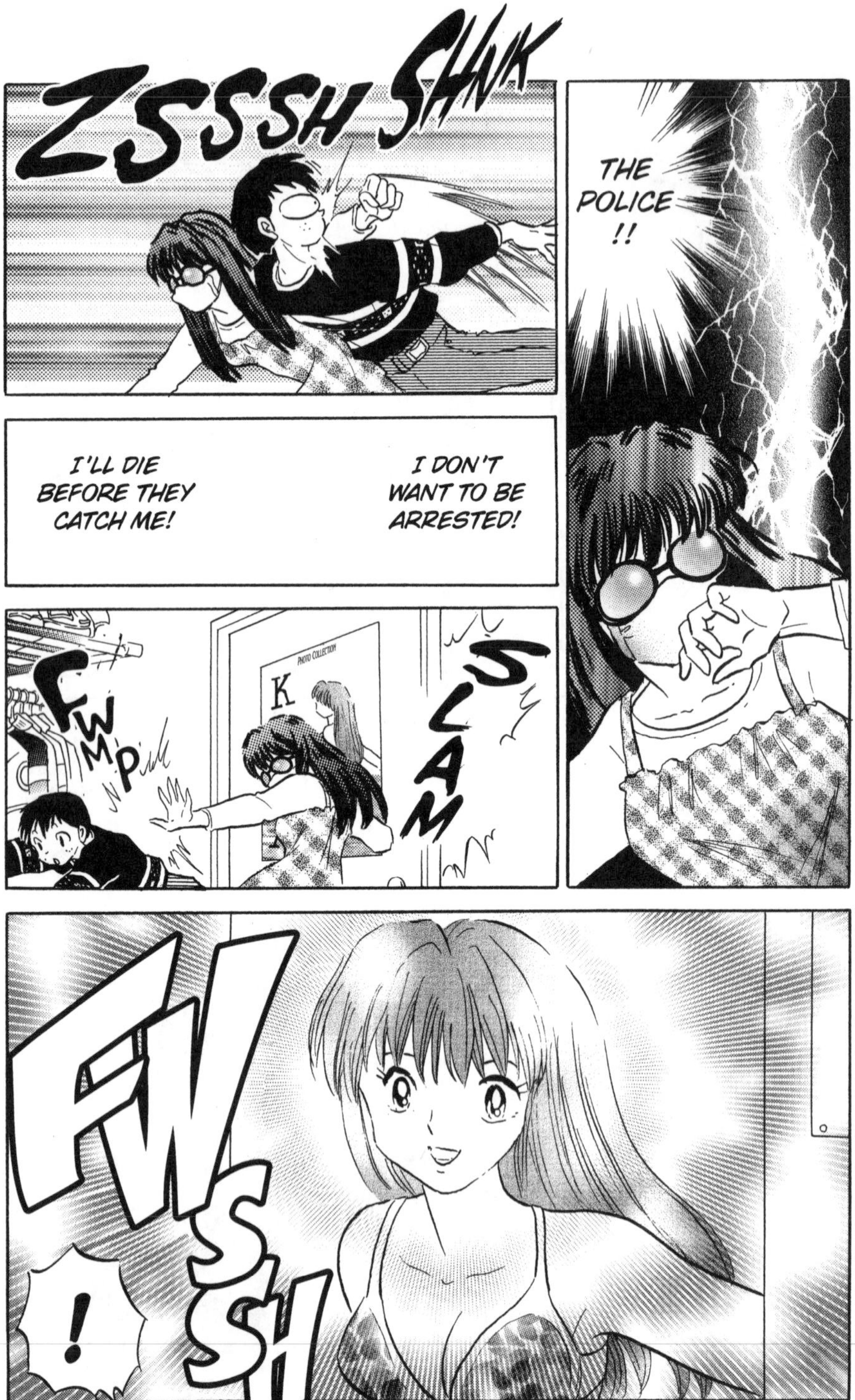
THE POLICE !!
ZSSSH SHNK
I DON'T WANT TO BE ARRESTED!
I'LL DIE BEFORE THEY CATCH ME!
SLAM
FWMP
PHOTO COLLECTION
K
FWSSH
!

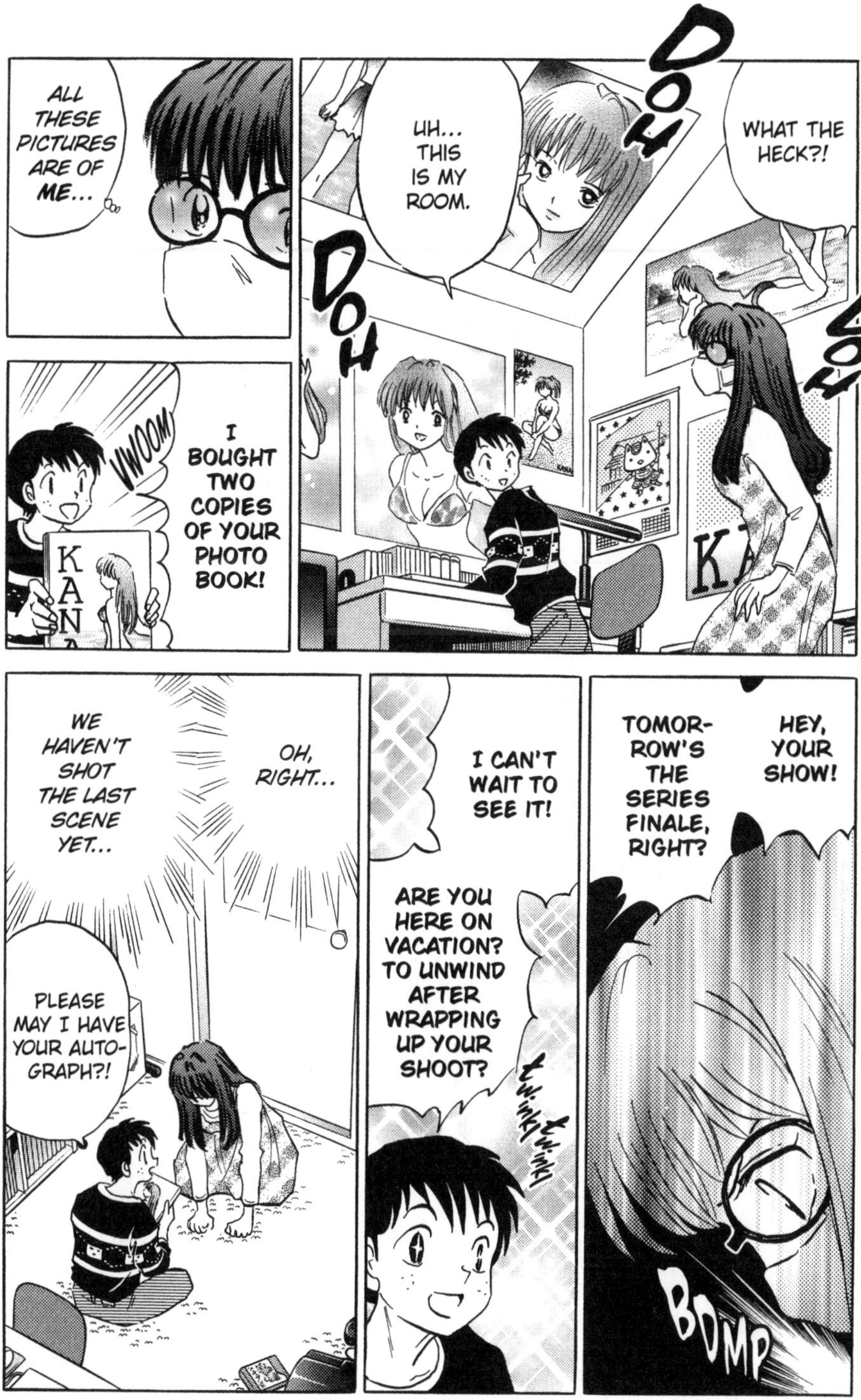
DOH
WHAT THE HECK?!
UH... THIS IS MY ROOM.
DOH
DOH
ALL THESE PICTURES ARE OF ME...
VWOOM
I BOUGHT TWO COPIES OF YOUR PHOTO BOOK!
HEY, YOUR SHOW!
TOMOR-ROW'S THE SERIES FINALE, RIGHT?
BOMP
I CAN'T WAIT TO SEE IT!
ARE YOU HERE ON VACATION? TO UNWIND AFTER WRAPPING UP YOUR SHOOT?
twinkl twinkl
OH, RIGHT...
WE HAVEN'T SHOT THE LAST SCENE YET...
PLEASE MAY I HAVE YOUR AUTO-GRAPH?!

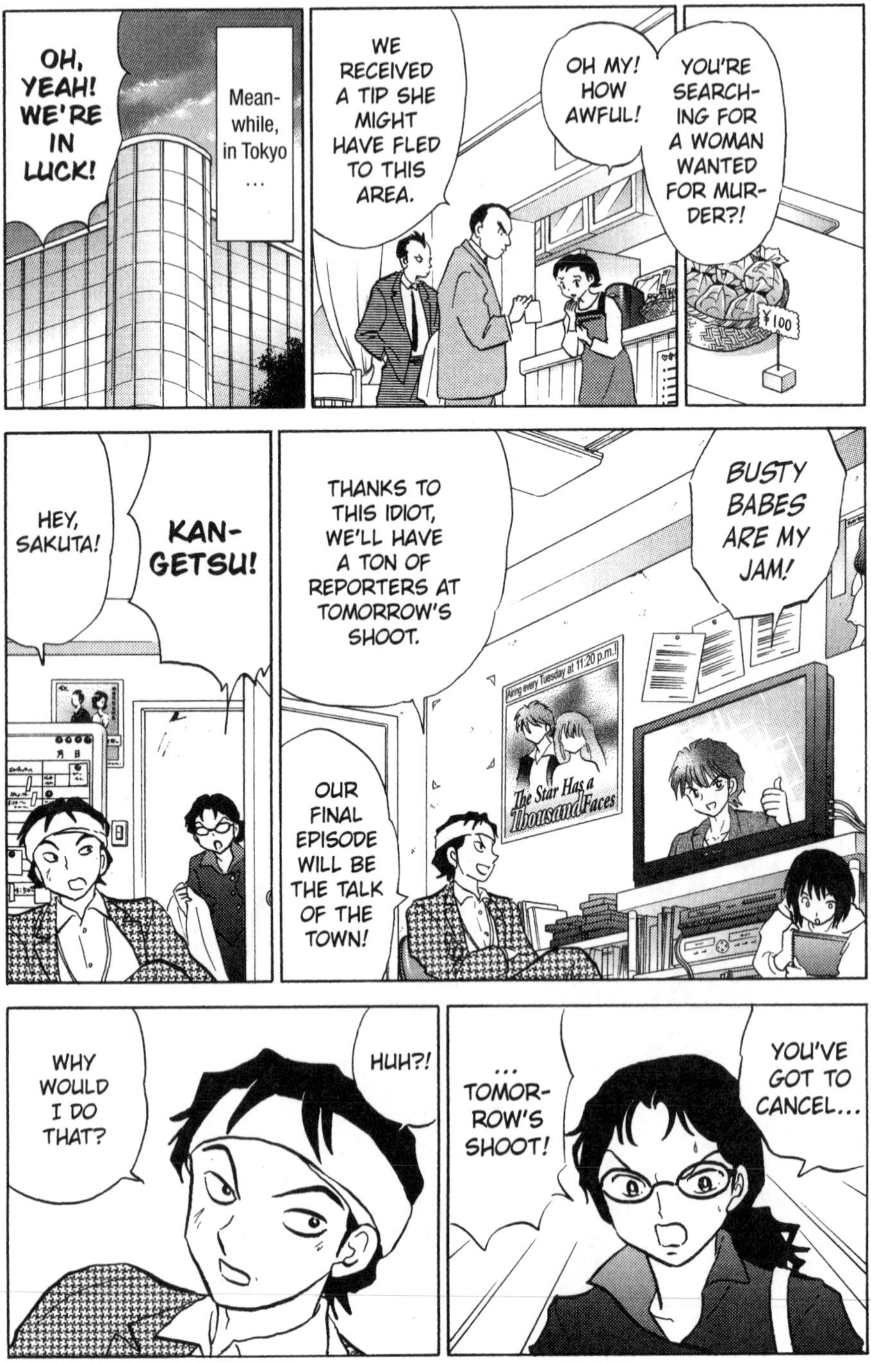
YOU'RE SEARCHING FOR A WOMAN WANTED FOR MURDER?!
¥100
OH MY! HOW AWFUL!
WE RECEIVED A TIP SHE MIGHT HAVE FLED TO THIS AREA.
Meanwhile, in Tokyo…
OH, YEAH! WE'RE IN LUCK!
BUSTY BABES ARE MY JAM!
THANKS TO THIS IDIOT, WE'LL HAVE A TON OF REPORTERS AT TOMORROW'S SHOOT.
Airing every Tuesday at 11:20 p.m.!
The Star Has a Thousand Faces
OUR FINAL EPISODE WILL BE THE TALK OF THE TOWN!
KAN-GETSU!
HEY, SAKUTA!
YOU'VE GOT TO CANCEL…
… TOMORROW'S SHOOT!
HUH?!
WHY WOULD I DO THAT?

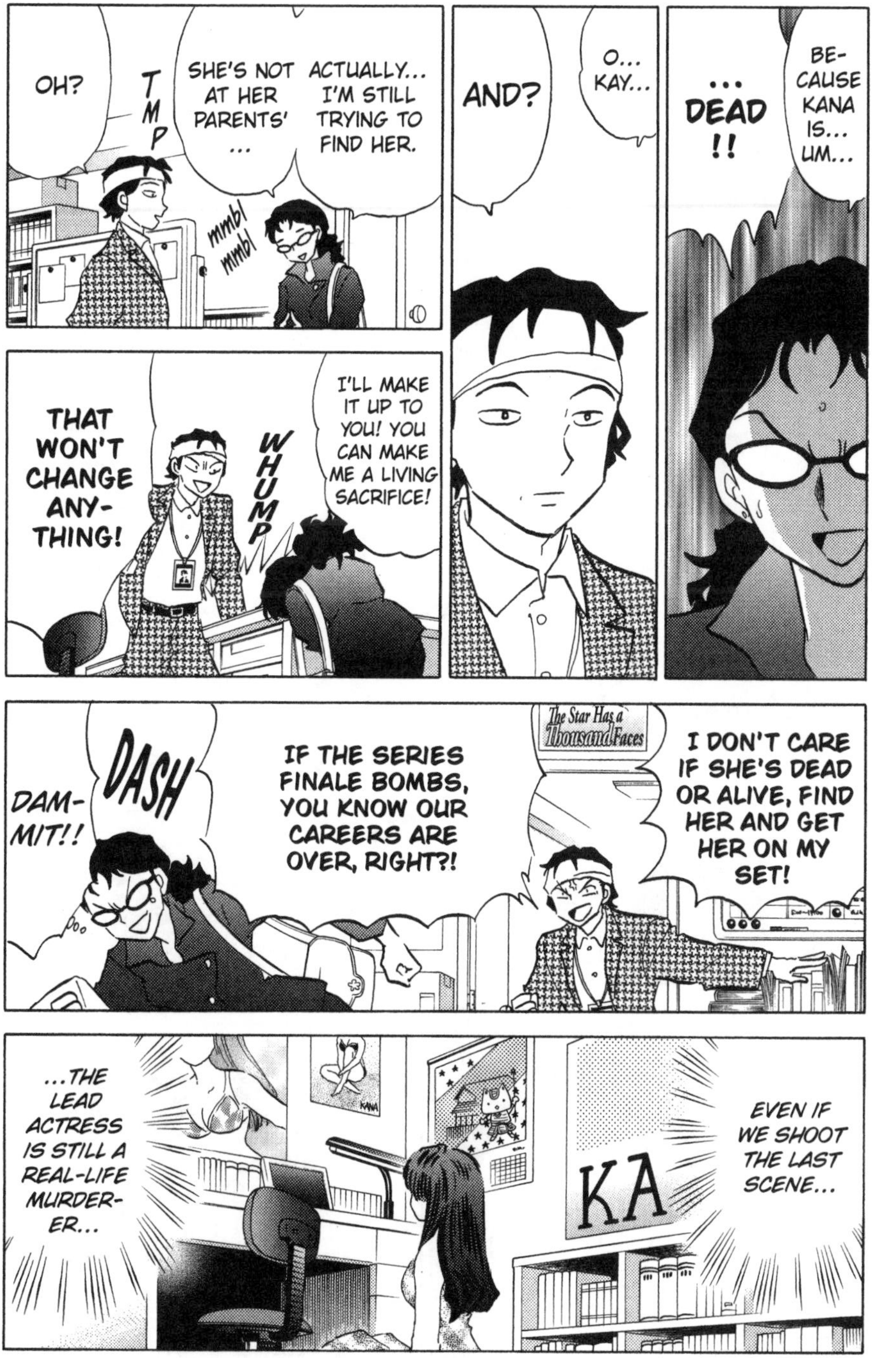
BE-CAUSE KANA IS... UM...
...DEAD!!
O... KAY...
AND?
ACTUALLY... I'M STILL TRYING TO FIND HER.
SHE'S NOT AT HER PARENTS'...
TMP
OH?
mmbl mmbl
I'LL MAKE IT UP TO YOU! YOU CAN MAKE ME A LIVING SACRIFICE!
WHUMP
THAT WON'T CHANGE ANYTHING!
I DON'T CARE IF SHE'S DEAD OR ALIVE, FIND HER AND GET HER ON MY SET!
The Star Has a Thousand Faces
IF THE SERIES FINALE BOMBS, YOU KNOW OUR CAREERS ARE OVER, RIGHT?!
DASH
DAM-MIT!!
EVEN IF WE SHOOT THE LAST SCENE...
KA
...THE LEAD ACTRESS IS STILL A REAL-LIFE MURDERER...

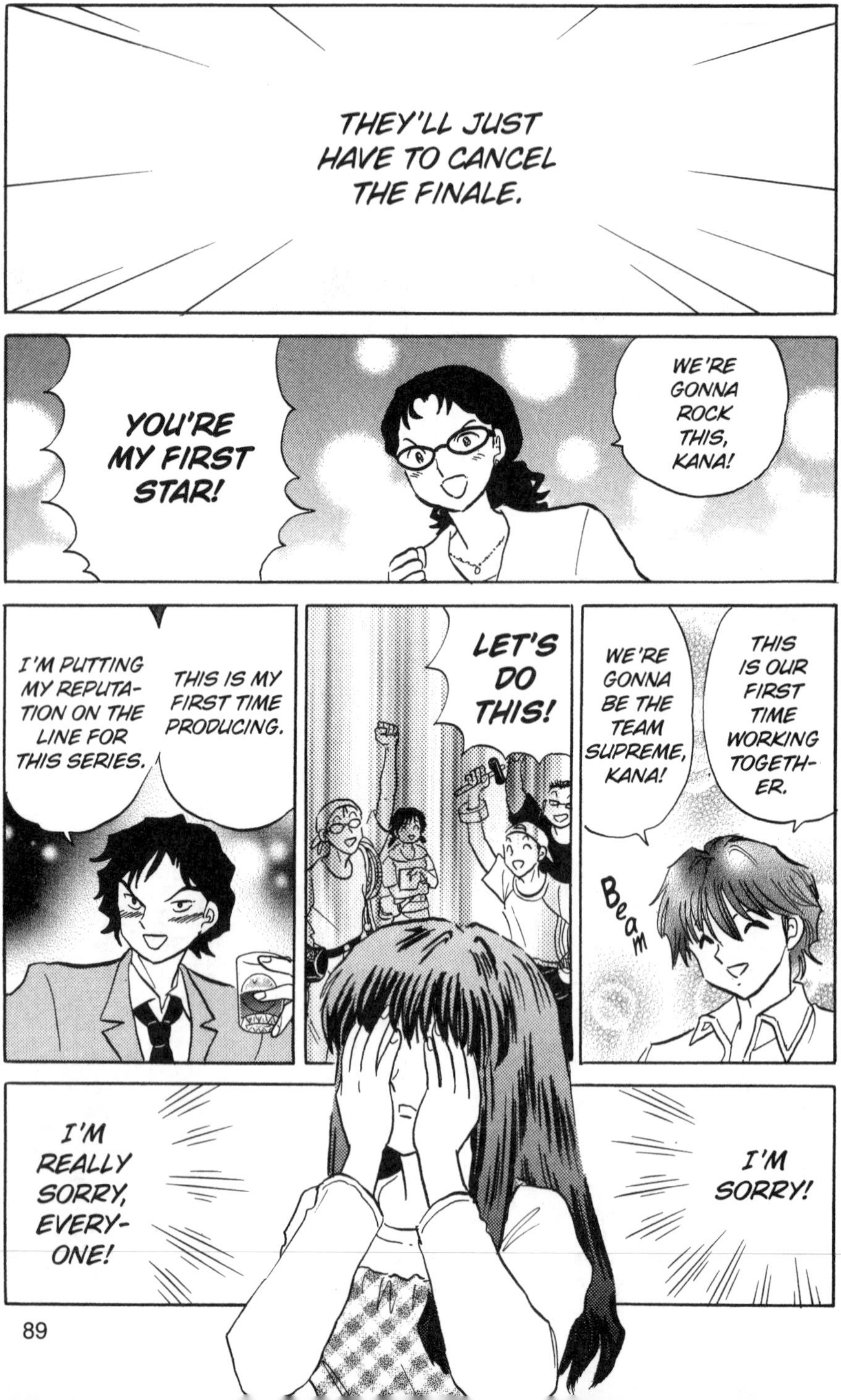
THEY'LL JUST HAVE TO CANCEL THE FINALE.
WE'RE GONNA ROCK THIS, KANA!
YOU'RE MY FIRST STAR!
THIS IS OUR FIRST TIME WORKING TOGETH-ER.
WE'RE GONNA BE THE TEAM SUPREME, KANA!
Beam
LET'S DO THIS!
THIS IS MY FIRST TIME PRODUCING.
I'M PUTTING MY REPUTA-TION ON THE LINE FOR THIS SERIES.
I'M SORRY!
I'M REALLY SORRY, EVERY-ONE!

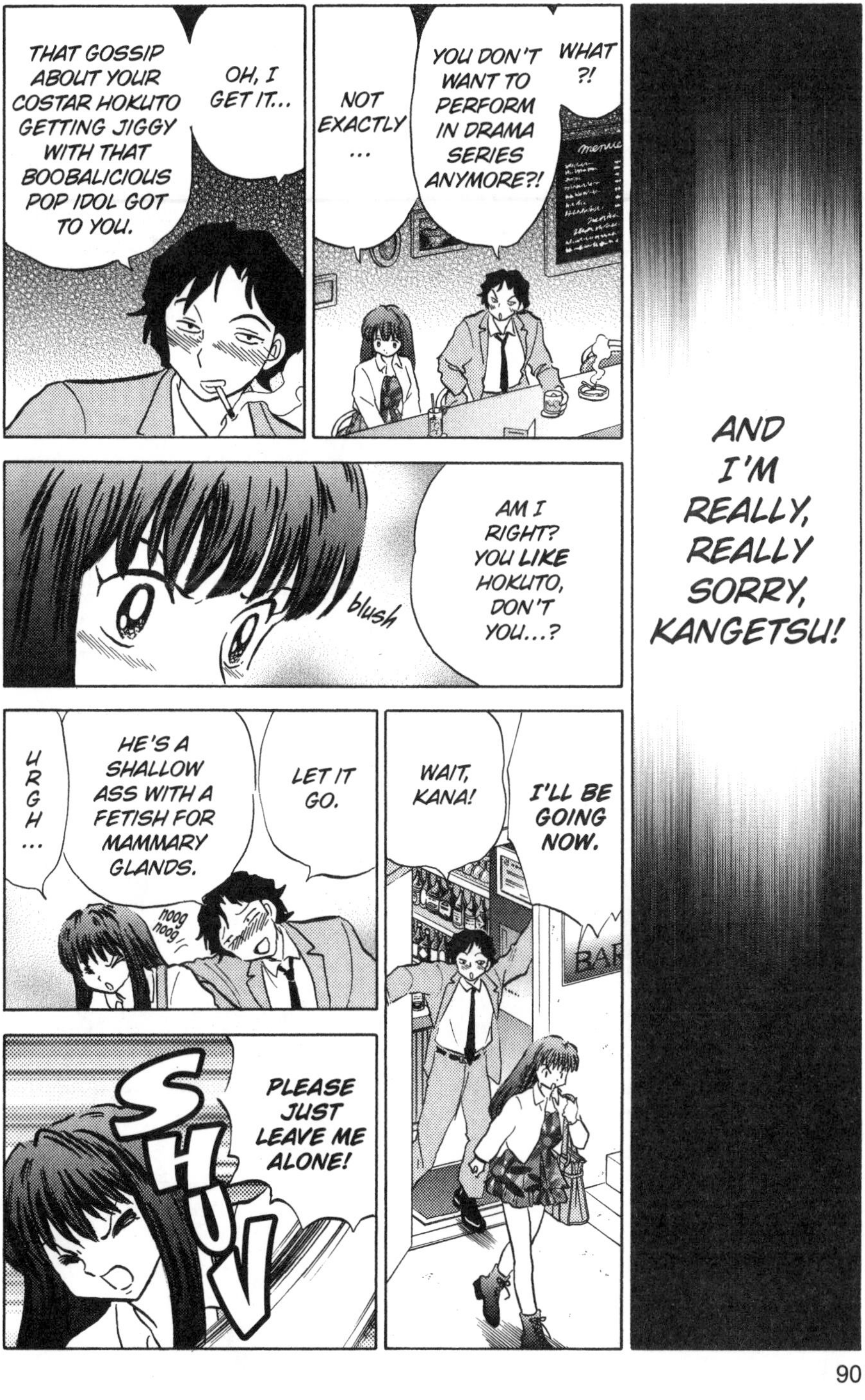
AND I'M REALLY, REALLY SORRY, KANGETSU!
WHAT ?!
YOU DON'T WANT TO PERFORM IN DRAMA SERIES ANYMORE?!
NOT EXACTLY ...
OH, I GET IT...
THAT GOSSIP ABOUT YOUR COSTAR HOKUTO GETTING JIGGY WITH THAT BOOBALICIOUS POP IDOL GOT TO YOU.
AM I RIGHT? YOU LIKE HOKUTO, DON'T YOU...?
blush
I'LL BE GOING NOW.
WAIT, KANA!
BAR
LET IT GO.
HE'S A SHALLOW ASS WITH A FETISH FOR MAMMARY GLANDS.
URGH...
noog noog
PLEASE JUST LEAVE ME ALONE!
SHUV

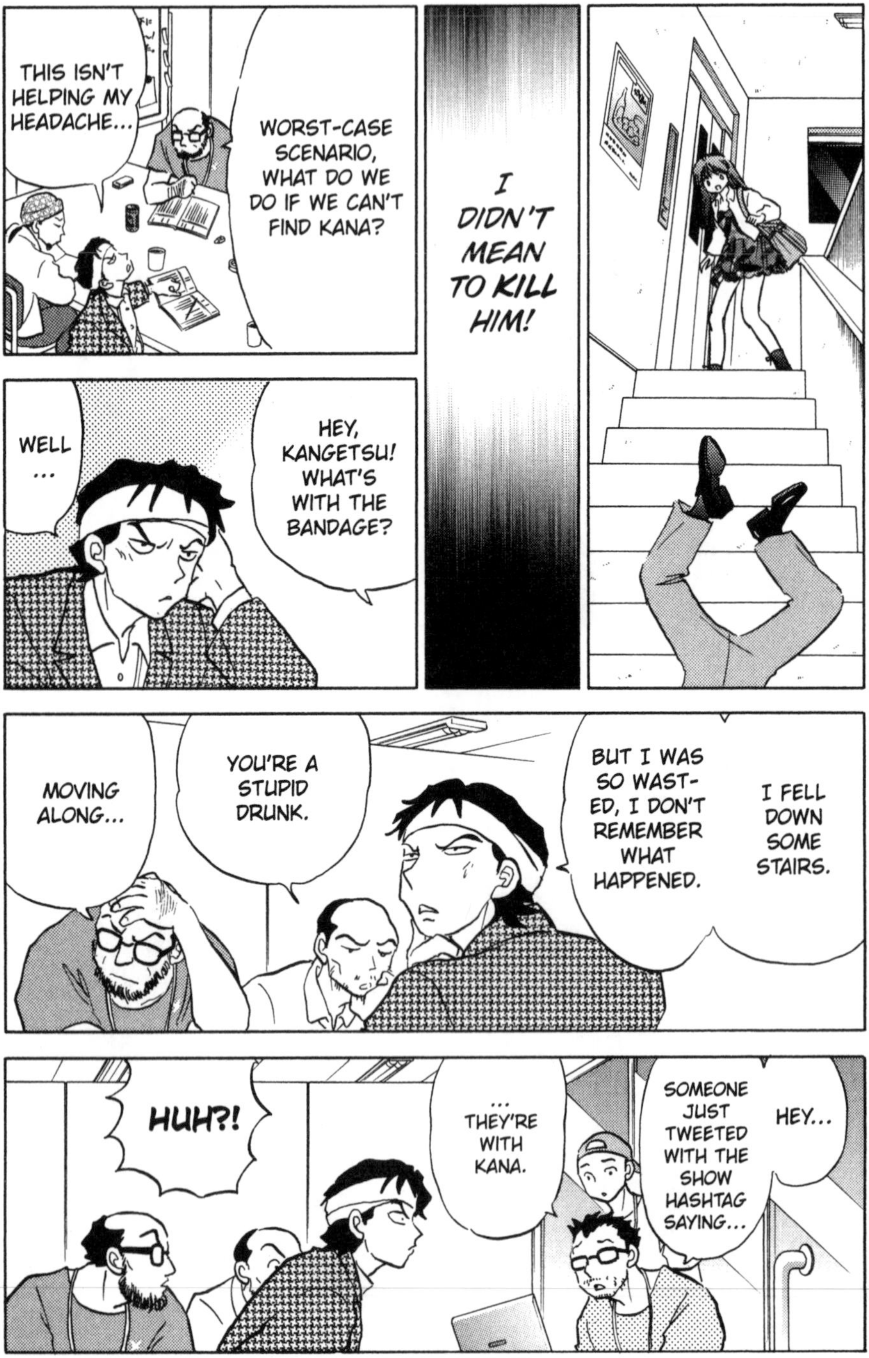
I DIDN'T MEAN TO KILL HIM!
WORST-CASE SCENARIO, WHAT DO WE DO IF WE CAN'T FIND KANA?
THIS ISN'T HELPING MY HEADACHE...
HEY, KANGETSU! WHAT'S WITH THE BANDAGE?
WELL ...
I FELL DOWN SOME STAIRS.
BUT I WAS SO WAST-ED, I DON'T REMEMBER WHAT HAPPENED.
YOU'RE A STUPID DRUNK.
MOVING ALONG...
HEY...
SOMEONE JUST TWEETED WITH THE SHOW HASHTAG SAYING...
... THEY'RE WITH KANA.
HUH?!

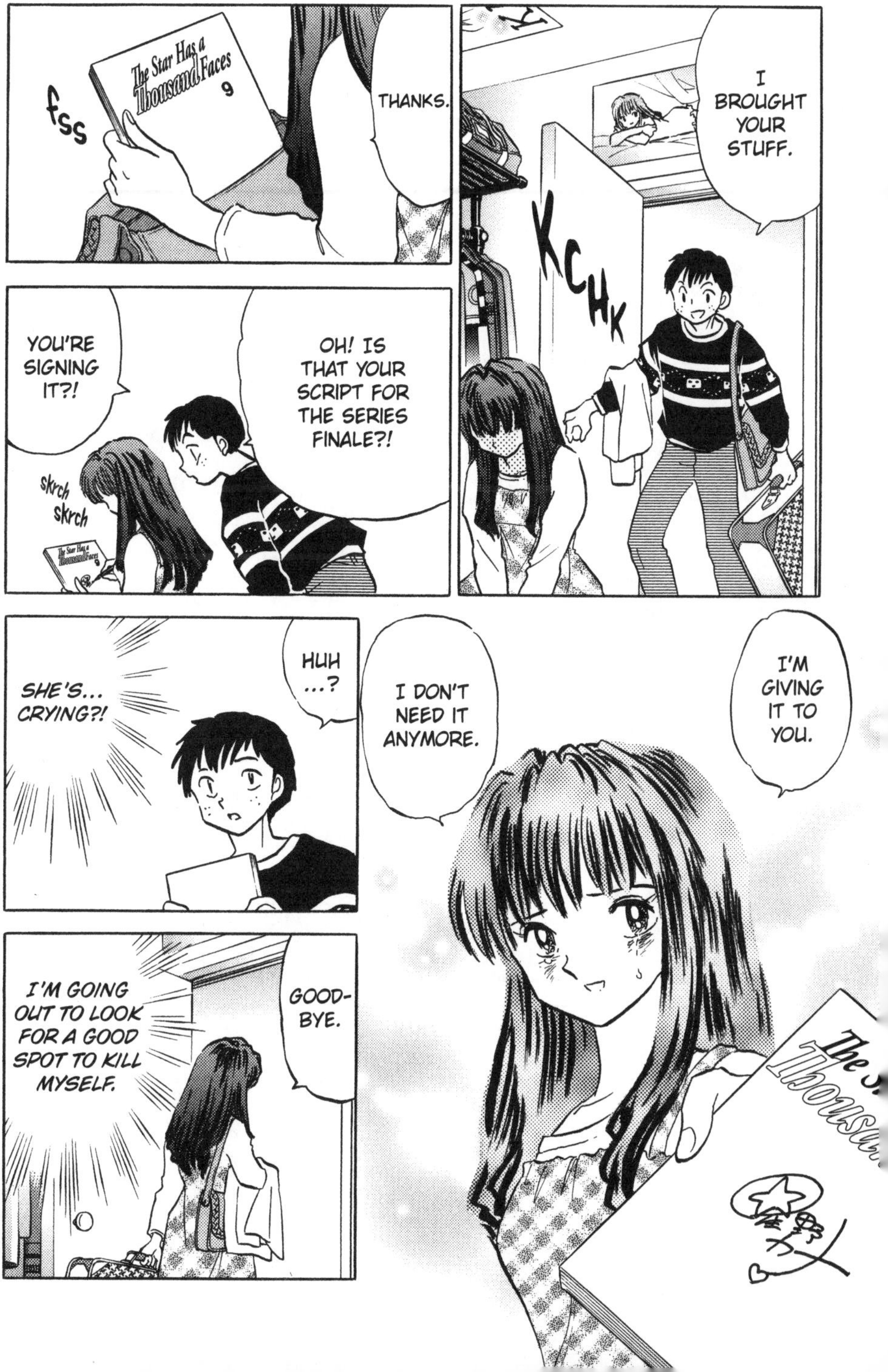
I BROUGHT YOUR STUFF.
KCHK
The Star Has a Thousand Faces 9
fss
THANKS.
OH! IS THAT YOUR SCRIPT FOR THE SERIES FINALE?!
YOU'RE SIGNING IT?!
skrch skrch
The Star Has a Thousand Faces
I'M GIVING IT TO YOU.
I DON'T NEED IT ANYMORE.
HUH ...?
SHE'S... CRYING?!
GOOD-BYE.
I'M GOING OUT TO LOOK FOR A GOOD SPOT TO KILL MYSELF.

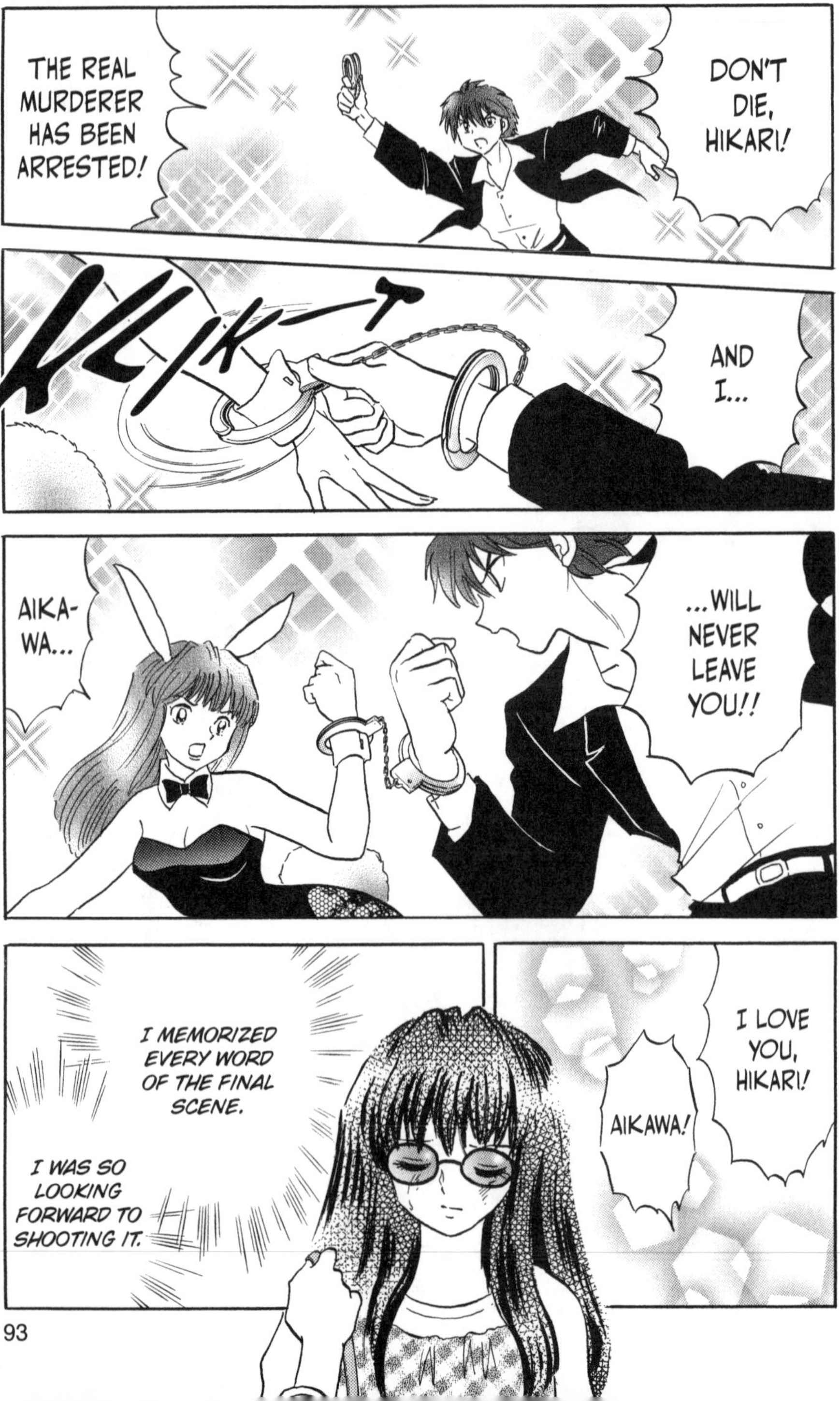
DON'T DIE, HIKARI!
THE REAL MURDERER HAS BEEN ARRESTED!
KLIK—T
AND I...
...WILL NEVER LEAVE YOU!!
AIKAWA...
I LOVE YOU, HIKARI!
AIKAWA!
I MEMORIZED EVERY WORD OF THE FINAL SCENE.
I WAS SO LOOKING FORWARD TO SHOOTING IT.

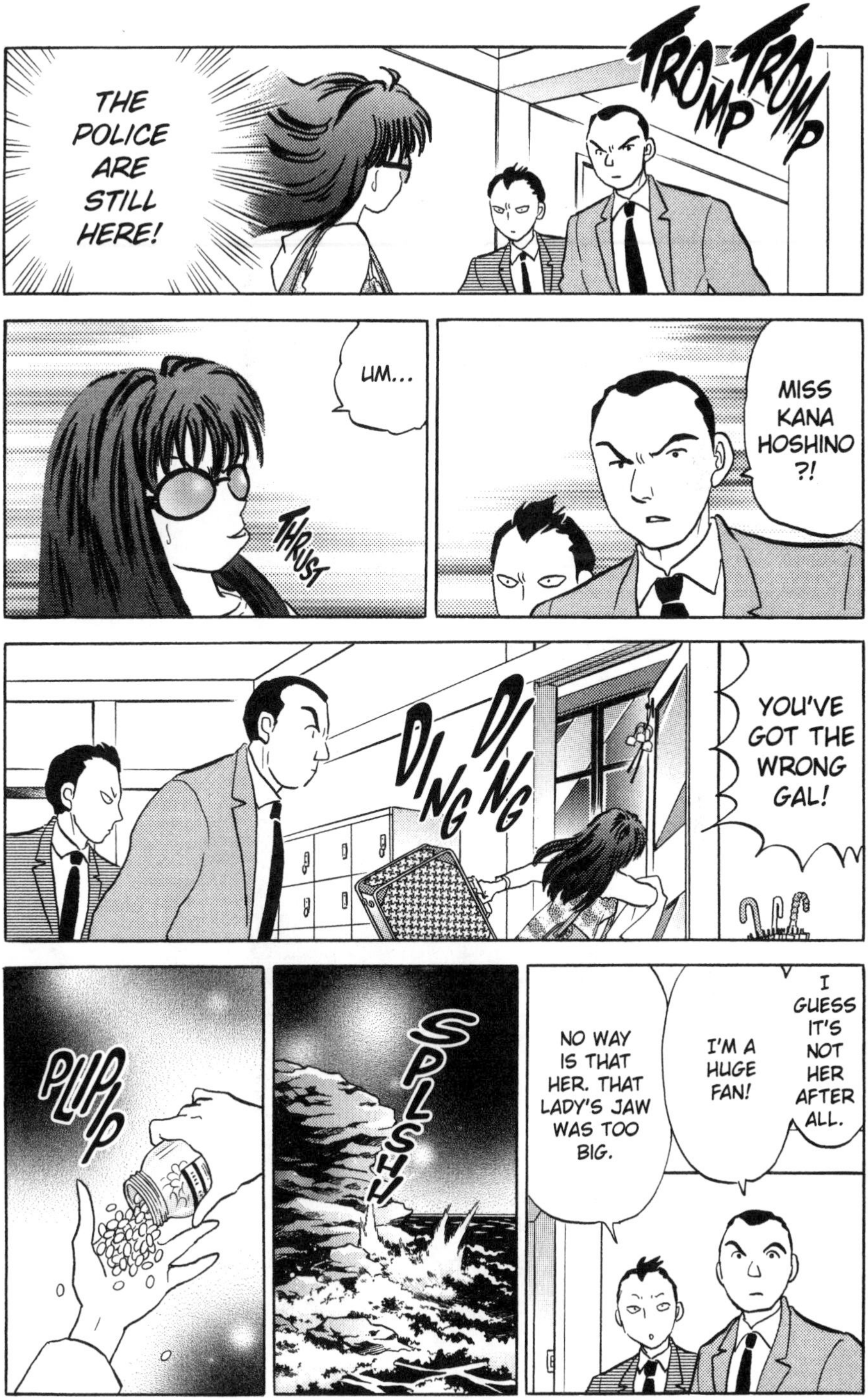
TROMP TROMP
THE POLICE ARE STILL HERE!
MISS KANA HOSHINO ?!
UM...
THRUST
YOU'VE GOT THE WRONG GAL!
DING DING
I GUESS IT'S NOT HER AFTER ALL.
I'M A HUGE FAN!
NO WAY IS THAT HER. THAT LADY'S JAW WAS TOO BIG.
SPLSHH
PLUPP

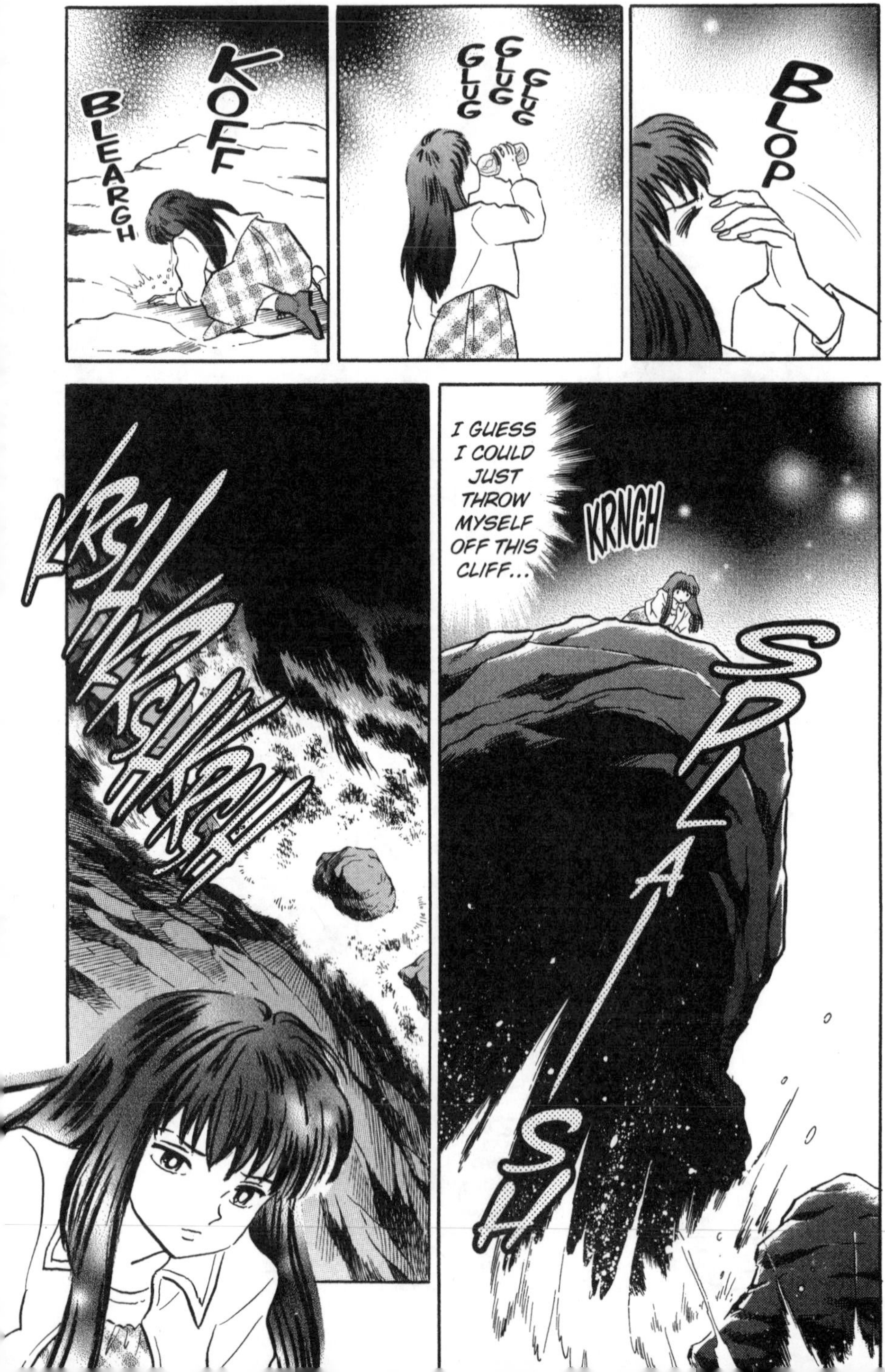
BLOP
GLUG GLUG GLUG
KOFF
BLEARGH
I GUESS I COULD JUST THROW MYSELF OFF THIS CLIFF...
KRNCH
SPLASH

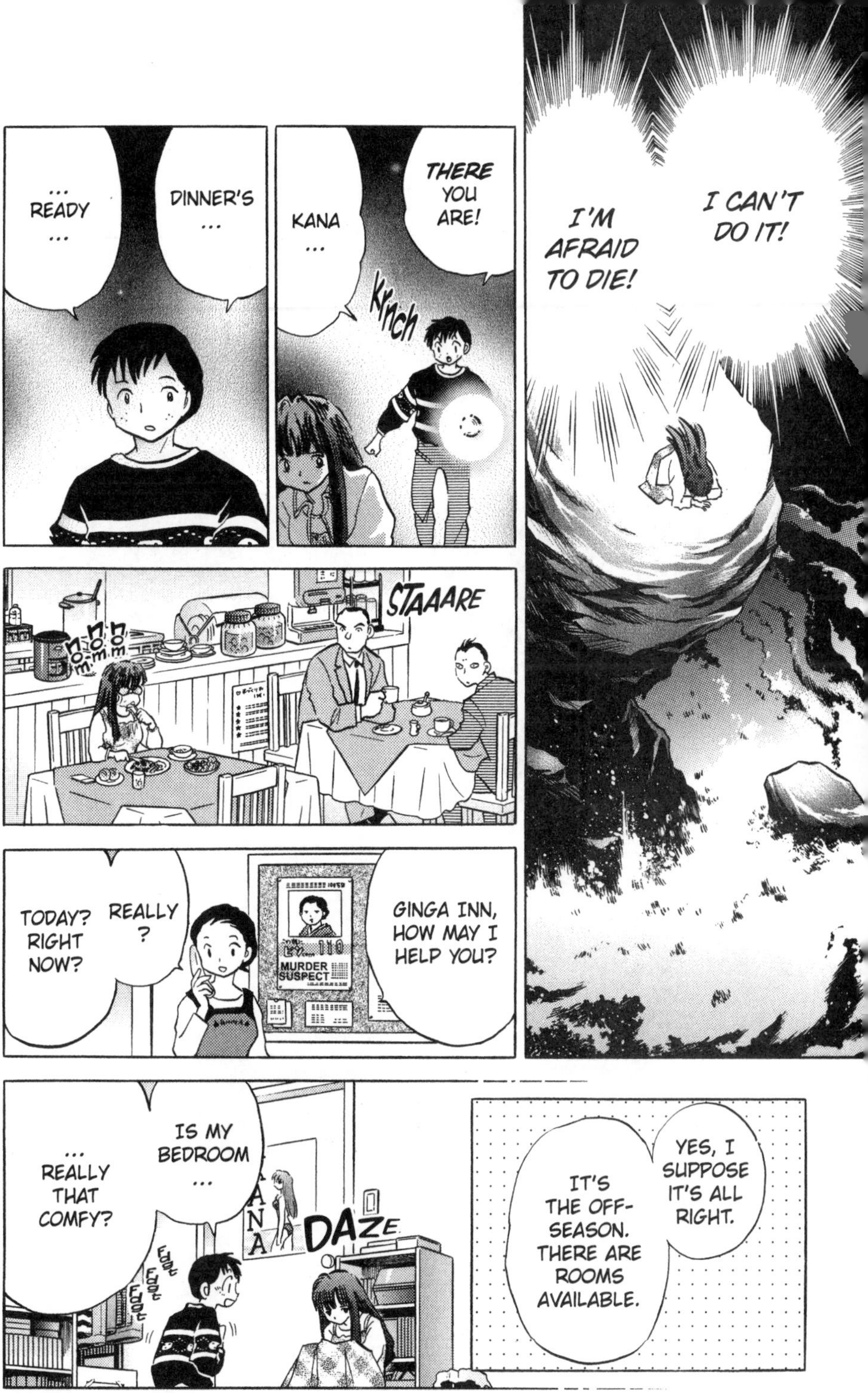

I CAN'T DO IT!
I'M AFRAID TO DIE!
THERE YOU ARE!
KANA ...
Krnch
DINNER'S ...
... READY ...
STAAARE
GINGA INN, HOW MAY I HELP YOU?
MURDER SUSPECT
110
REALLY ?
TODAY? RIGHT NOW?
YES, I SUPPOSE IT'S ALL RIGHT.
IT'S THE OFF-SEASON. THERE ARE ROOMS AVAILABLE.
IS MY BEDROOM ...
... REALLY THAT COMFY?
KANA
DAZE
Fdot Fdot Fdot

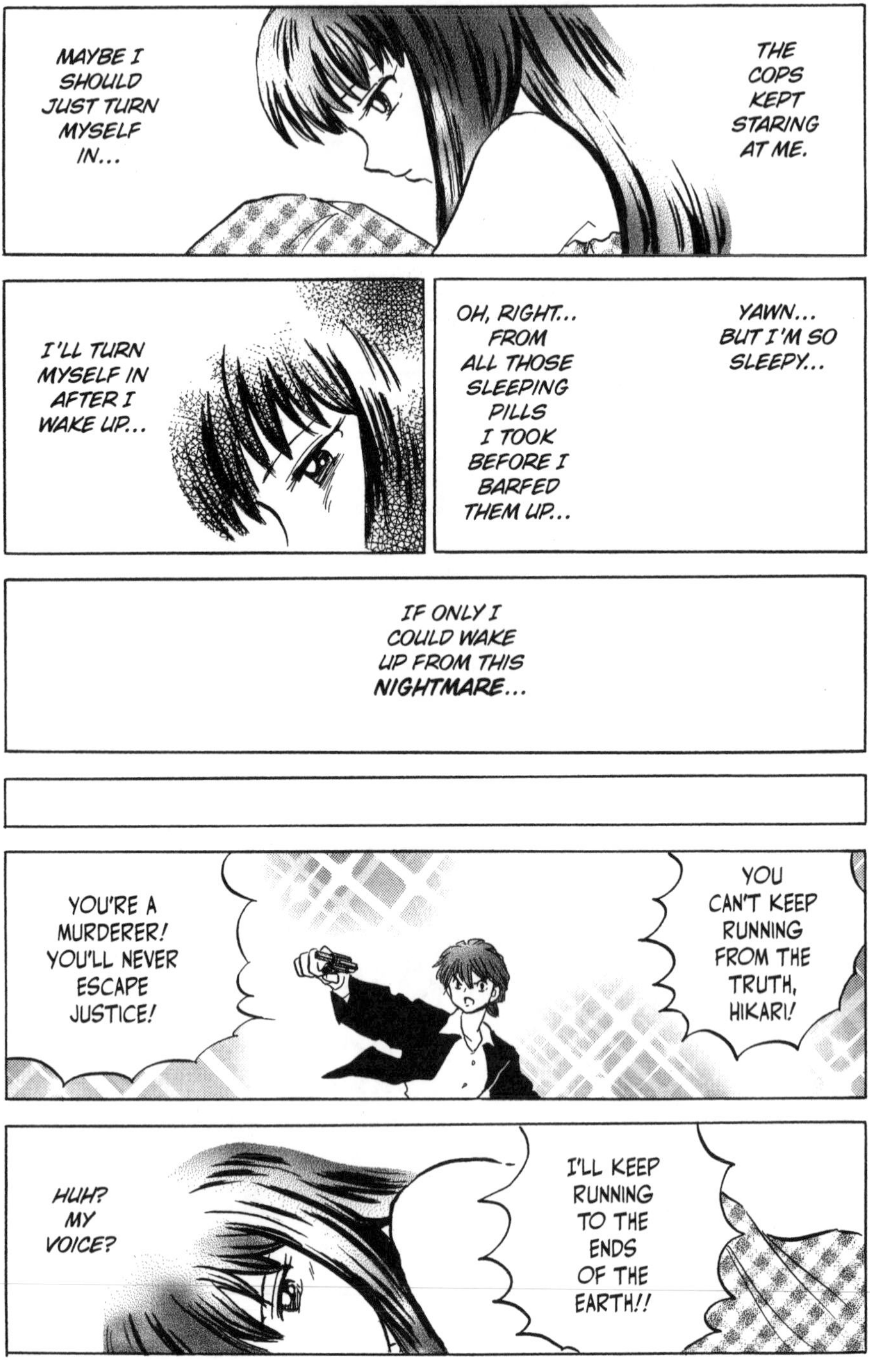
THE COPS KEPT STARING AT ME.
MAYBE I SHOULD JUST TURN MYSELF IN...
YAWN... BUT I'M SO SLEEPY...
OH, RIGHT... FROM ALL THOSE SLEEPING PILLS I TOOK BEFORE I BARFED THEM UP...
I'LL TURN MYSELF IN AFTER I WAKE UP...
IF ONLY I COULD WAKE UP FROM THIS **NIGHTMARE**...
YOU CAN'T KEEP RUNNING FROM THE TRUTH, HIKARI!
YOU'RE A MURDERER! YOU'LL NEVER ESCAPE JUSTICE!
I'LL KEEP RUNNING TO THE ENDS OF THE EARTH!!
HUH? MY VOICE?

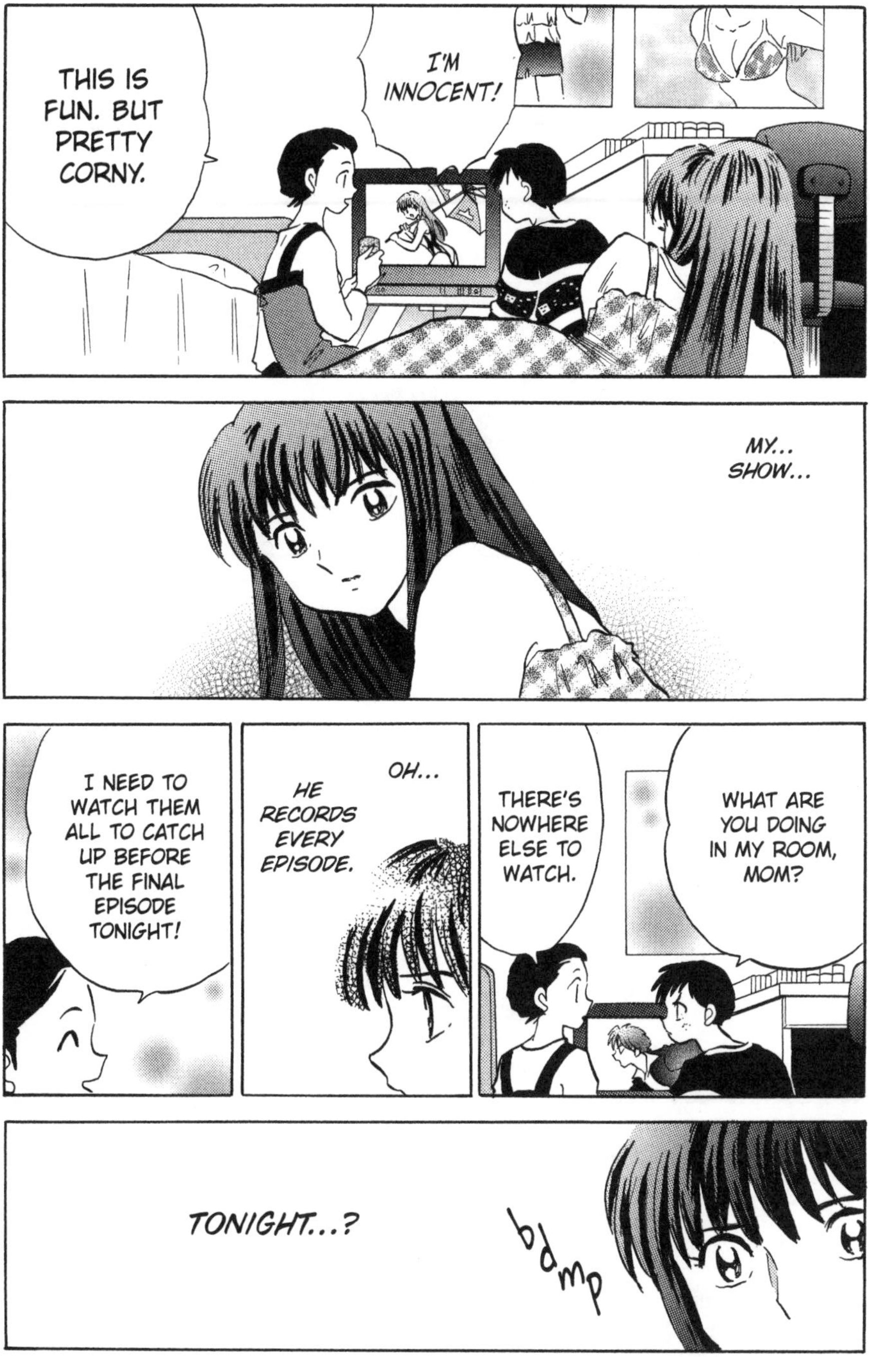
I'M INNOCENT!
THIS IS FUN. BUT PRETTY CORNY.
MY... SHOW...
WHAT ARE YOU DOING IN MY ROOM, MOM?
THERE'S NOWHERE ELSE TO WATCH.
OH...
HE RECORDS EVERY EPISODE.
I NEED TO WATCH THEM ALL TO CATCH UP BEFORE THE FINAL EPISODE TONIGHT!
bdmp
TONIGHT...?

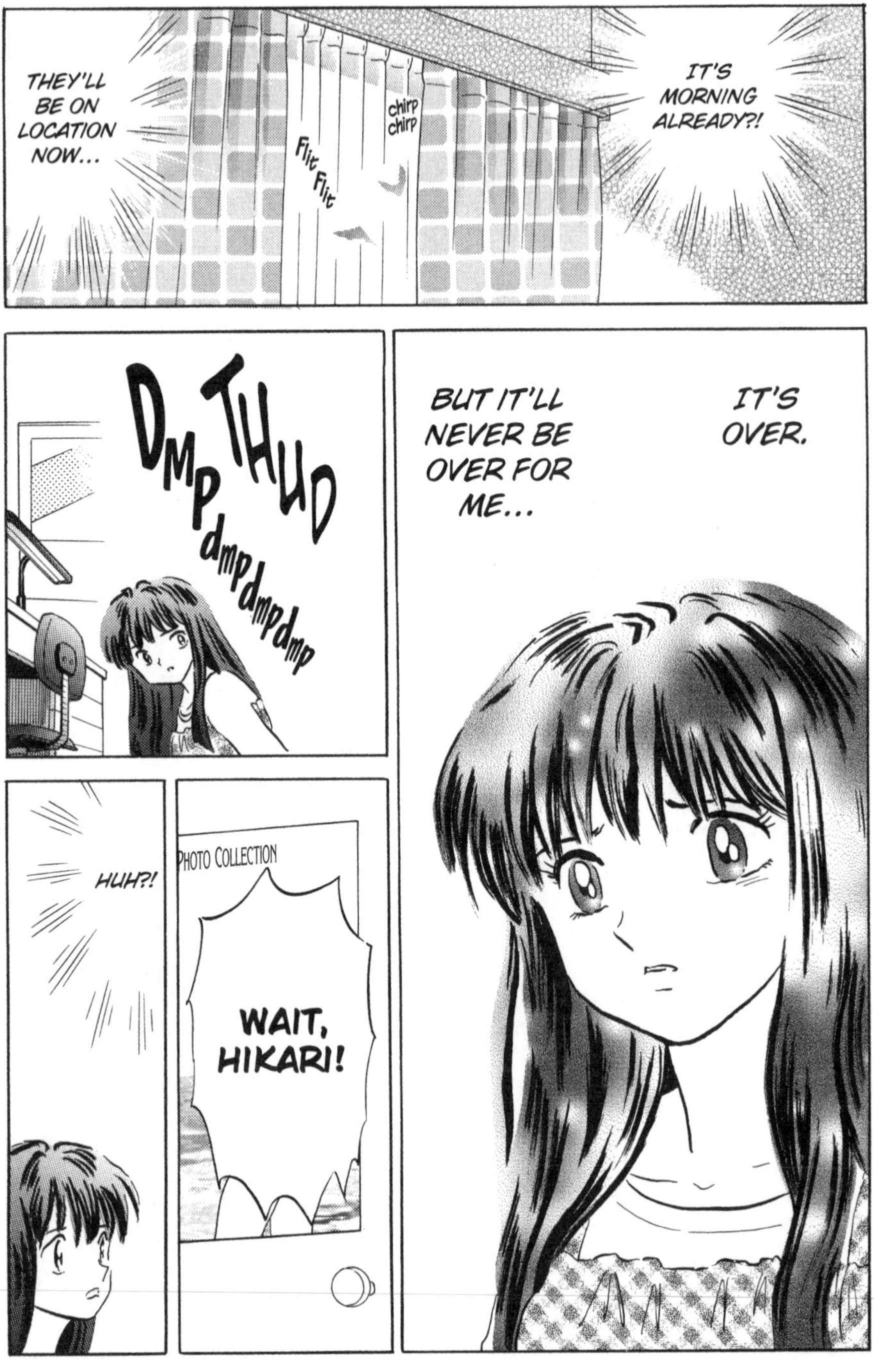
IT'S MORNING ALREADY?!
chirp chirp
Flit Flit
THEY'LL BE ON LOCATION NOW...
IT'S OVER.
BUT IT'LL NEVER BE OVER FOR ME...
THUD
DMP
dmp dmp dmp
PHOTO COLLECTION
WAIT, HIKARI!
HUH?!

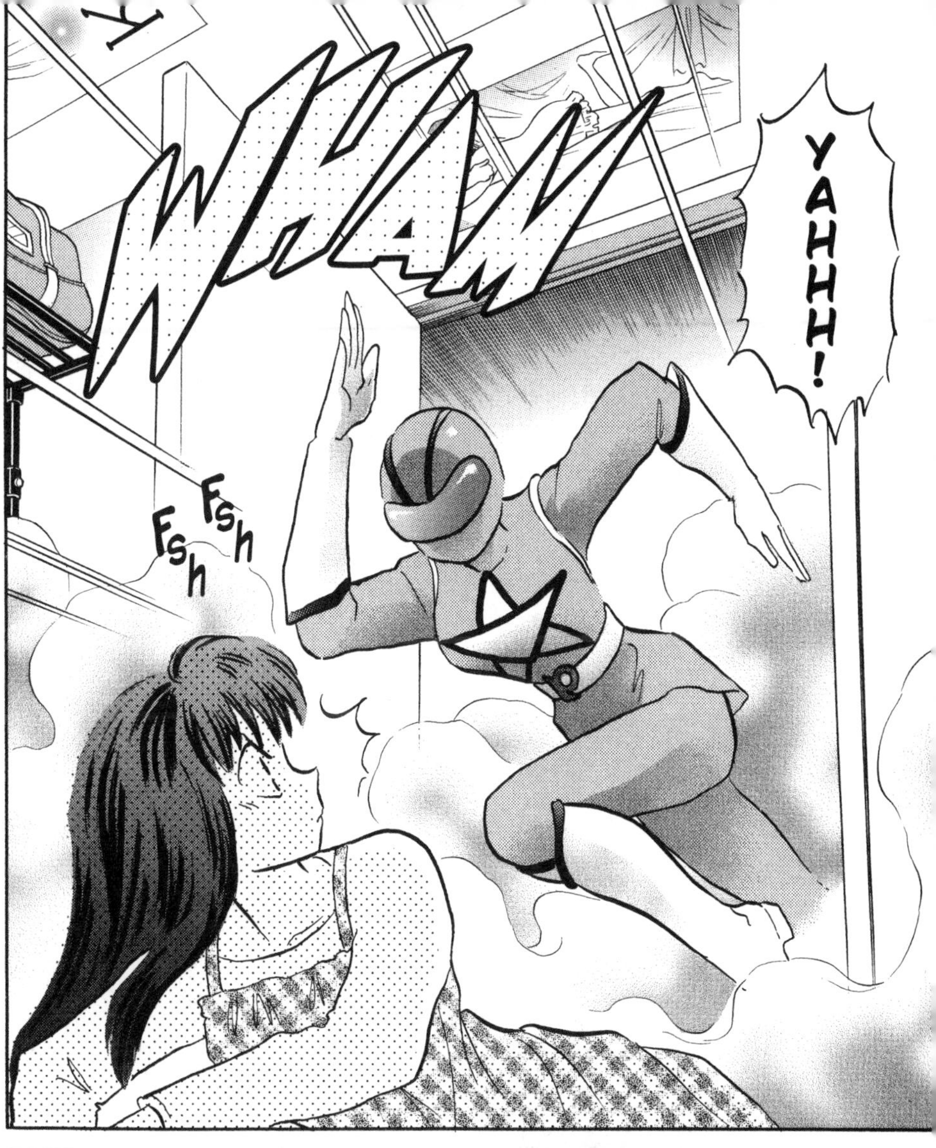
YAHHH!
WHAM
Fsh Fsh

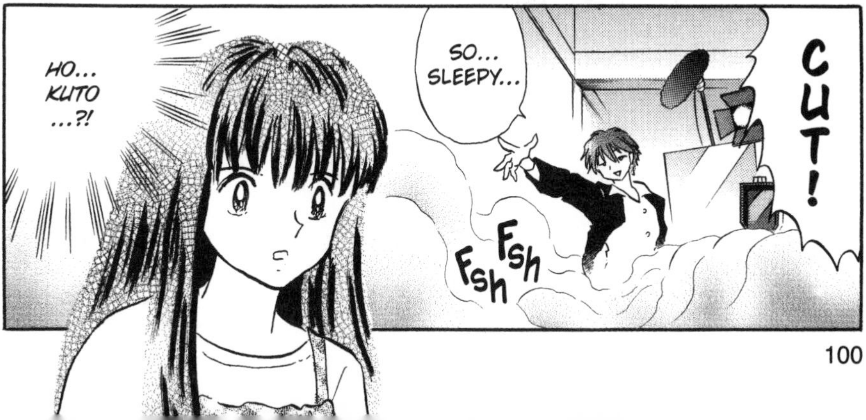
CUT!
SO... SLEEPY...
Fsh Fsh
HO... KUTO ...?!

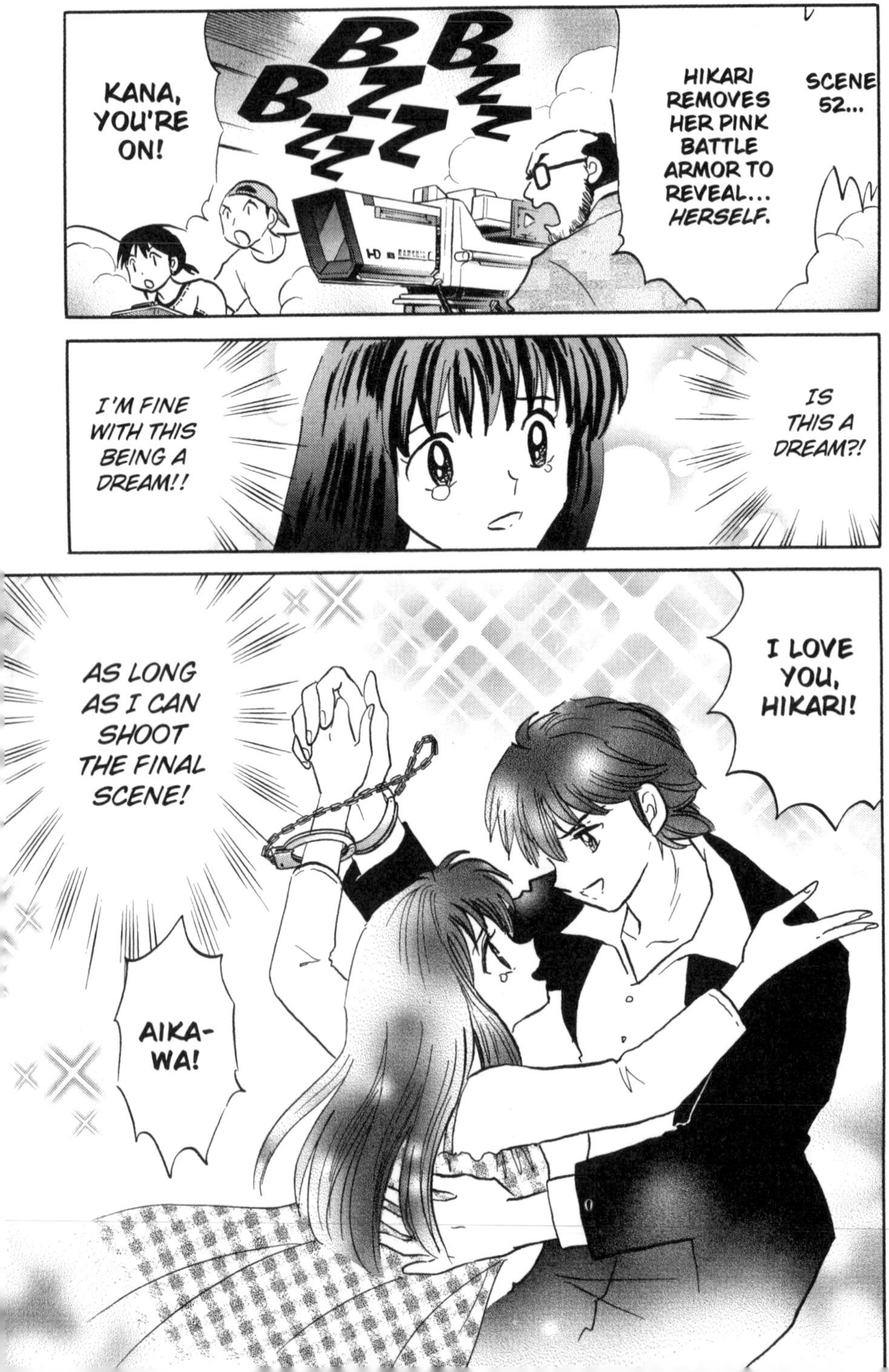
SCENE 52...
HIKARI REMOVES HER PINK BATTLE ARMOR TO REVEAL... HERSELF.
BZZZ BZZZ
KANA, YOU'RE ON!
IS THIS A DREAM?!
I'M FINE WITH THIS BEING A DREAM!!
I LOVE YOU, HIKARI!
AS LONG AS I CAN SHOOT THE FINAL SCENE!
AIKA-WA!

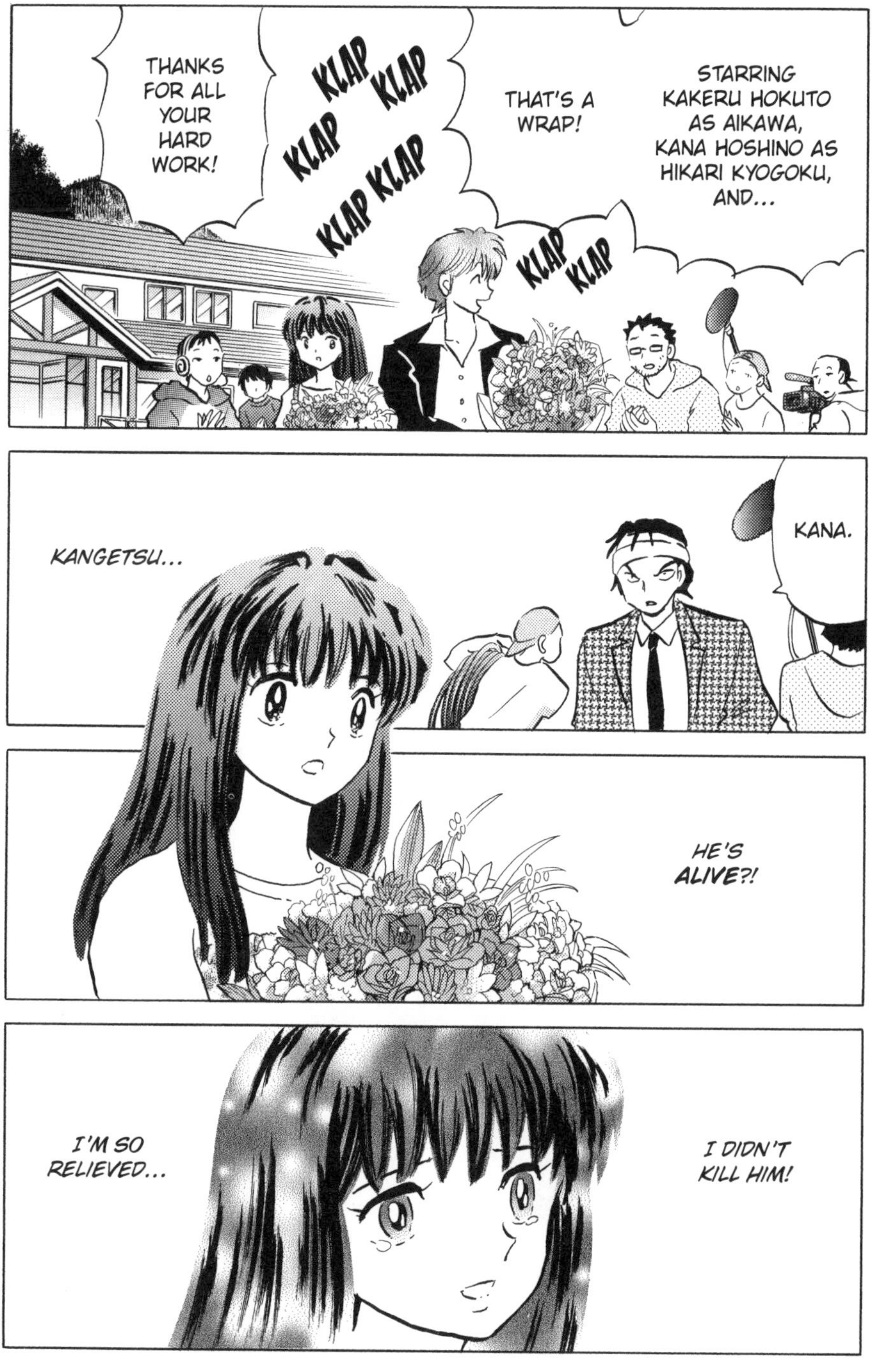
STARRING KAKERU HOKUTO AS AIKAWA, KANA HOSHINO AS HIKARI KYOGOKU, AND...
KLAP KLAP
THAT'S A WRAP!
KLAP KLAP KLAP KLAP KLAP KLAP
THANKS FOR ALL YOUR HARD WORK!
KANA.
KANGETSU...
HE'S ALIVE?!
I DIDN'T KILL HIM!
I'M SO RELIEVED...

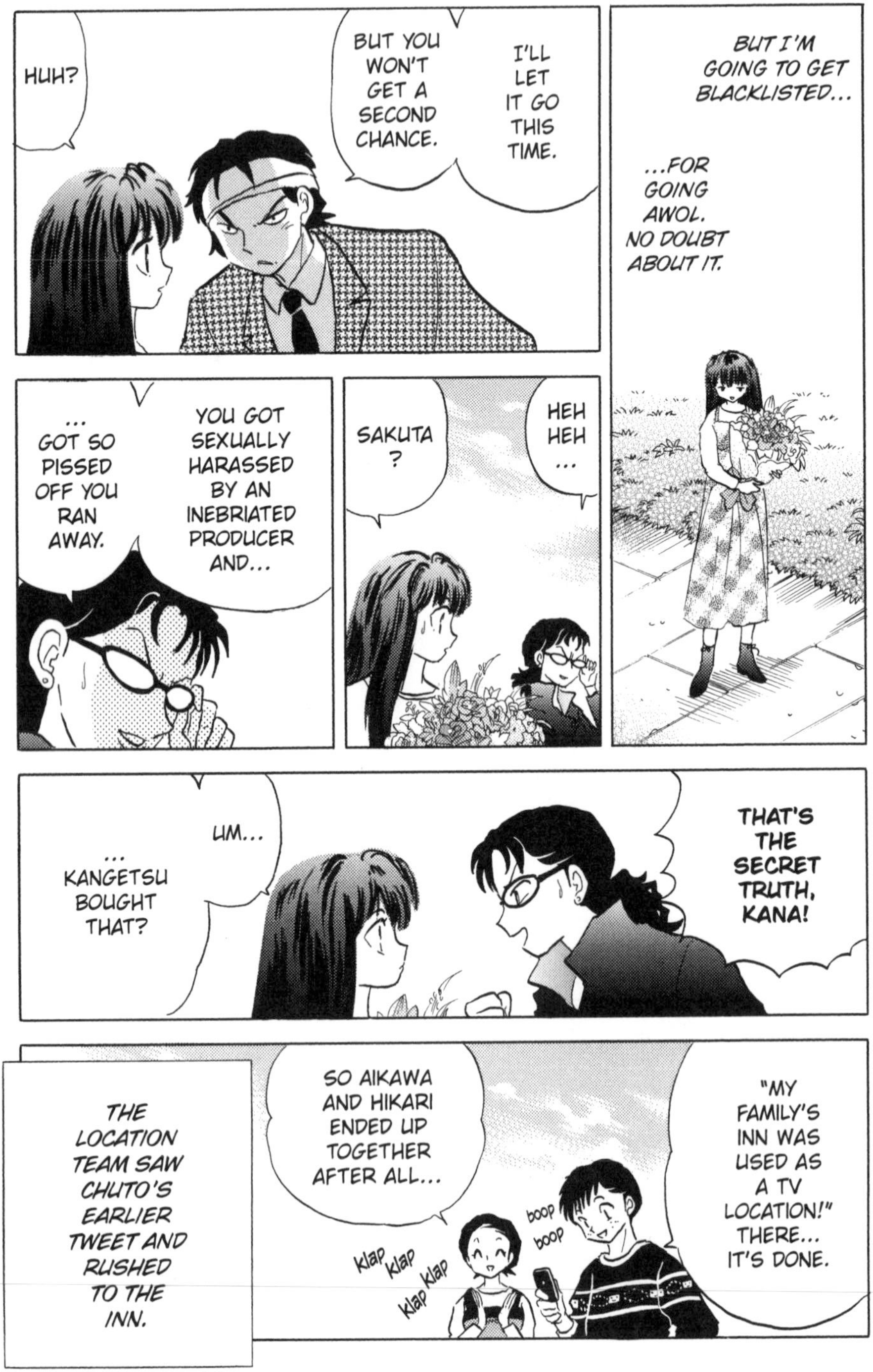
BUT I'M GOING TO GET BLACKLISTED...
...FOR GOING AWOL. NO DOUBT ABOUT IT.
I'LL LET IT GO THIS TIME.
BUT YOU WON'T GET A SECOND CHANCE.
HUH?
HEH HEH ...
SAKUTA ?
YOU GOT SEXUALLY HARASSED BY AN INEBRIATED PRODUCER AND...
...GOT SO PISSED OFF YOU RAN AWAY.
THAT'S THE SECRET TRUTH, KANA!
UM...
...KANGETSU BOUGHT THAT?
"MY FAMILY'S INN WAS USED AS A TV LOCATION!" THERE... IT'S DONE.
boop boop
SO AIKAWA AND HIKARI ENDED UP TOGETHER AFTER ALL...
klap klap klap klap
THE LOCATION TEAM SAW CHUTO'S EARLIER TWEET AND RUSHED TO THE INN.

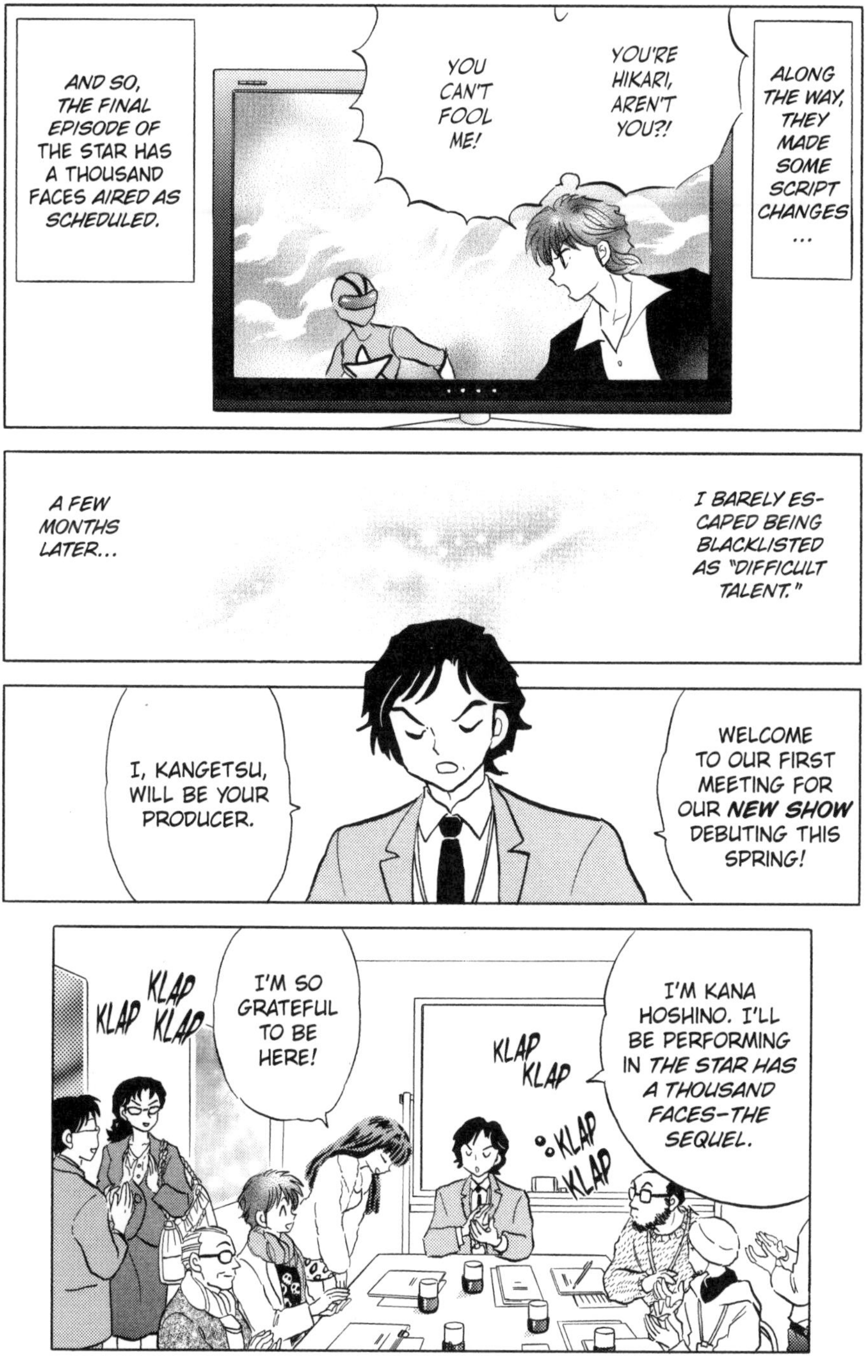
ALONG THE WAY, THEY MADE SOME SCRIPT CHANGES...
YOU'RE HIKARI, AREN'T YOU?!
YOU CAN'T FOOL ME!
AND SO, THE FINAL EPISODE OF THE STAR HAS A THOUSAND FACES AIRED AS SCHEDULED.
I BARELY ES-CAPED BEING BLACKLISTED AS "DIFFICULT TALENT."
A FEW MONTHS LATER...
WELCOME TO OUR FIRST MEETING FOR OUR **NEW SHOW** DEBUTING THIS SPRING!
I, KANGETSU, WILL BE YOUR PRODUCER.
I'M KANA HOSHINO. I'LL BE PERFORMING IN *THE STAR HAS A THOUSAND FACES—THE SEQUEL.*
KLAP KLAP
KLAP KLAP
I'M SO GRATEFUL TO BE HERE!
KLAP KLAP
KLAP

Lovely Flower

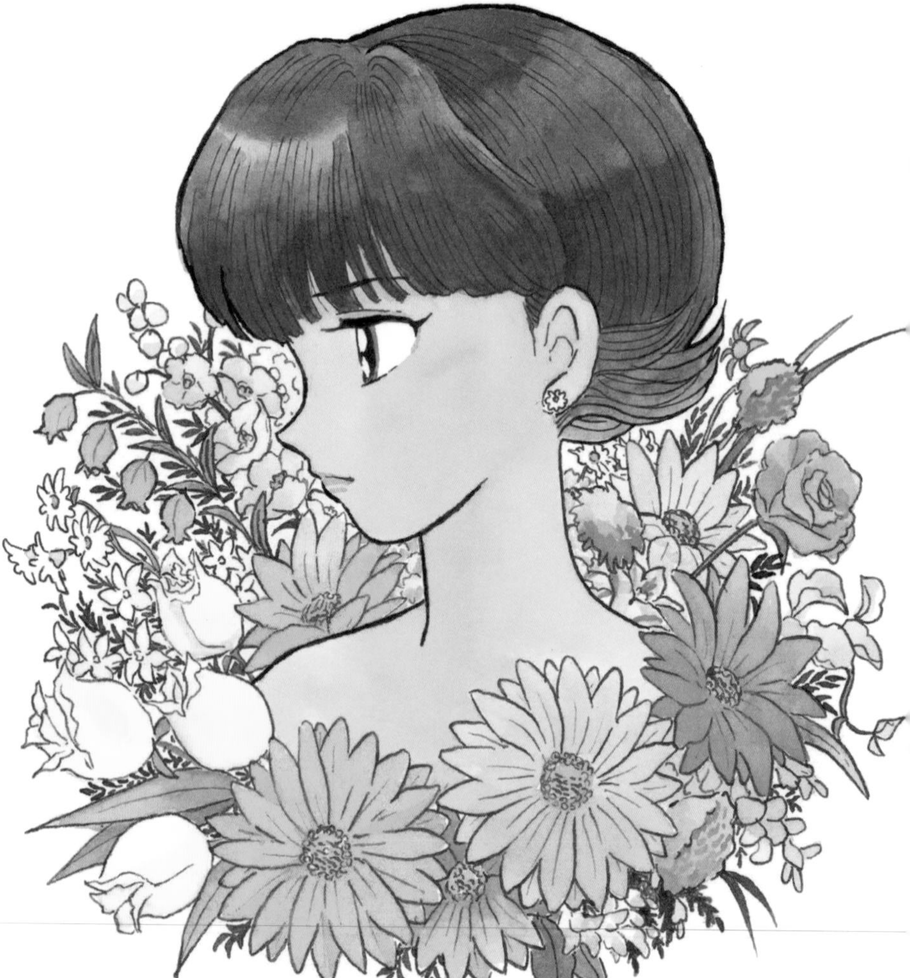

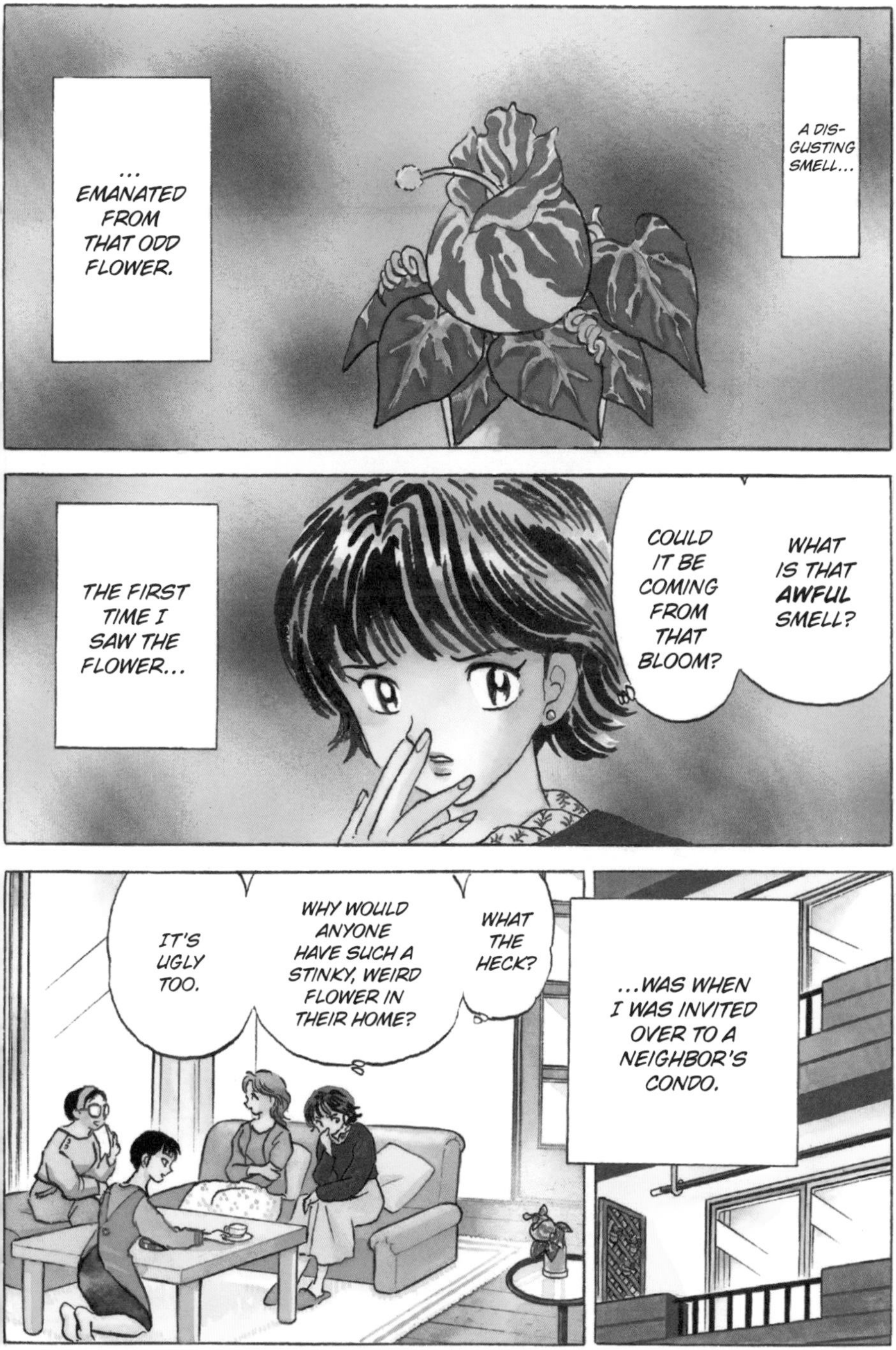
A DIS-GUSTING SMELL...
...EMANATED FROM THAT ODD FLOWER.
WHAT IS THAT AWFUL SMELL?
COULD IT BE COMING FROM THAT BLOOM?
THE FIRST TIME I SAW THE FLOWER...
...WAS WHEN I WAS INVITED OVER TO A NEIGHBOR'S CONDO.
WHAT THE HECK?
WHY WOULD ANYONE HAVE SUCH A STINKY, WEIRD FLOWER IN THEIR HOME?
IT'S UGLY TOO.

Research contributor: "Japan Flavor and Fragrance School"
TEL: 03-3257-0710

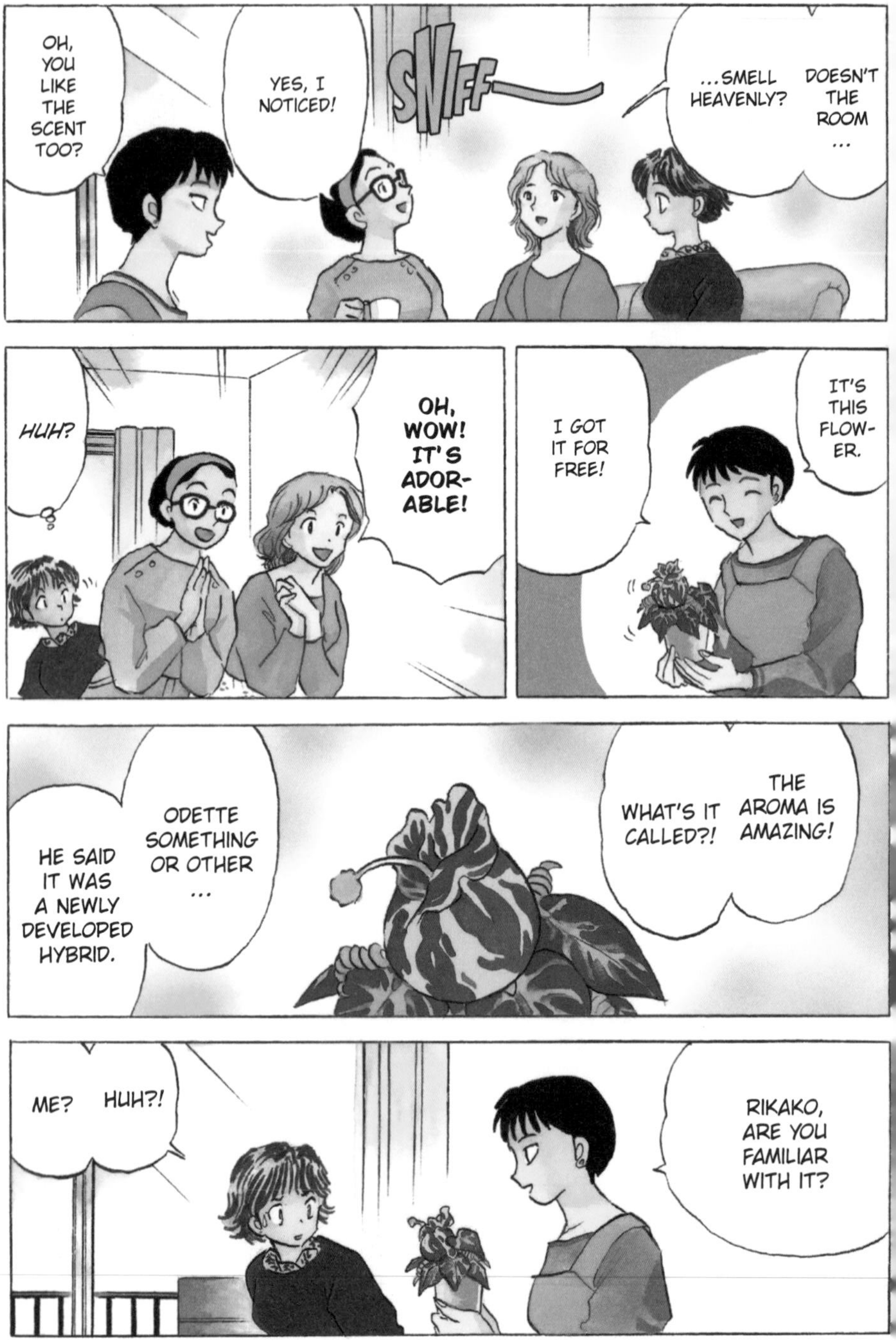
DOESN'T THE ROOM ...
...SMELL HEAVENLY?
SNIFF
YES, I NOTICED!
OH, YOU LIKE THE SCENT TOO?
IT'S THIS FLOWER.
I GOT IT FOR FREE!
OH, WOW! IT'S ADORABLE!
HUH?
THE AROMA IS AMAZING!
WHAT'S IT CALLED?!
ODETTE SOMETHING OR OTHER ...
HE SAID IT WAS A NEWLY DEVELOPED HYBRID.
RIKAKO, ARE YOU FAMILIAR WITH IT?
HUH?!
ME?

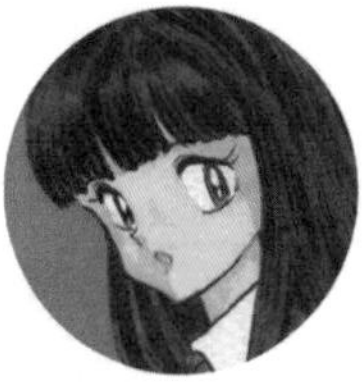
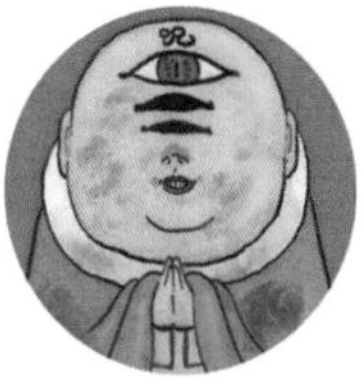
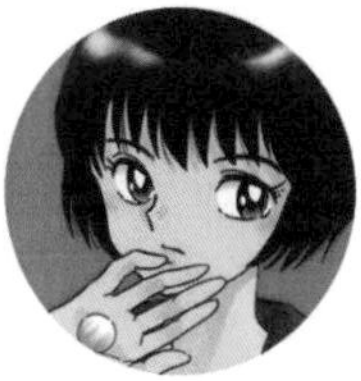
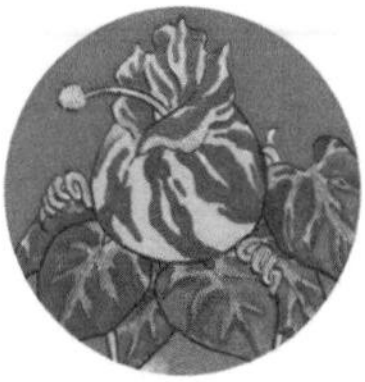
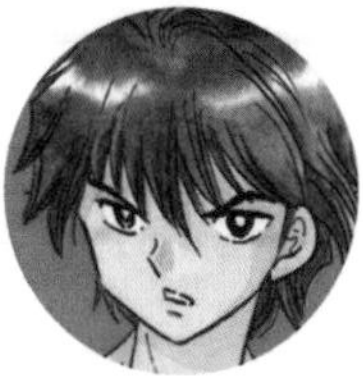

RUMIC WORLD

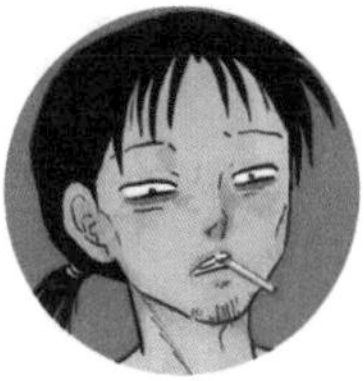
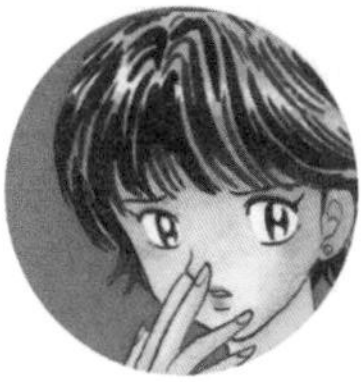
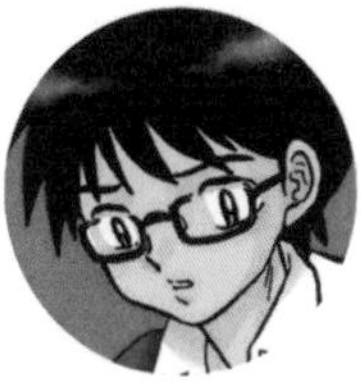
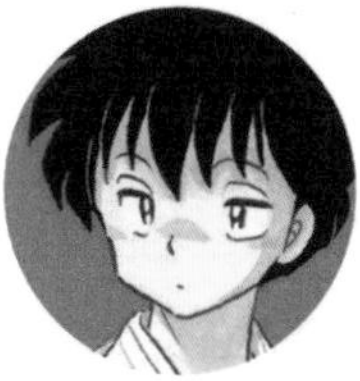
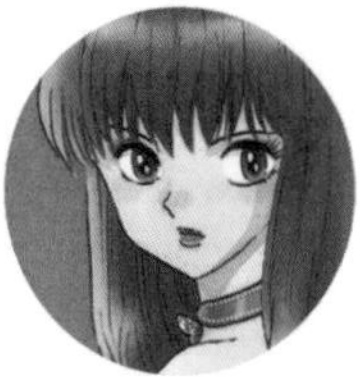

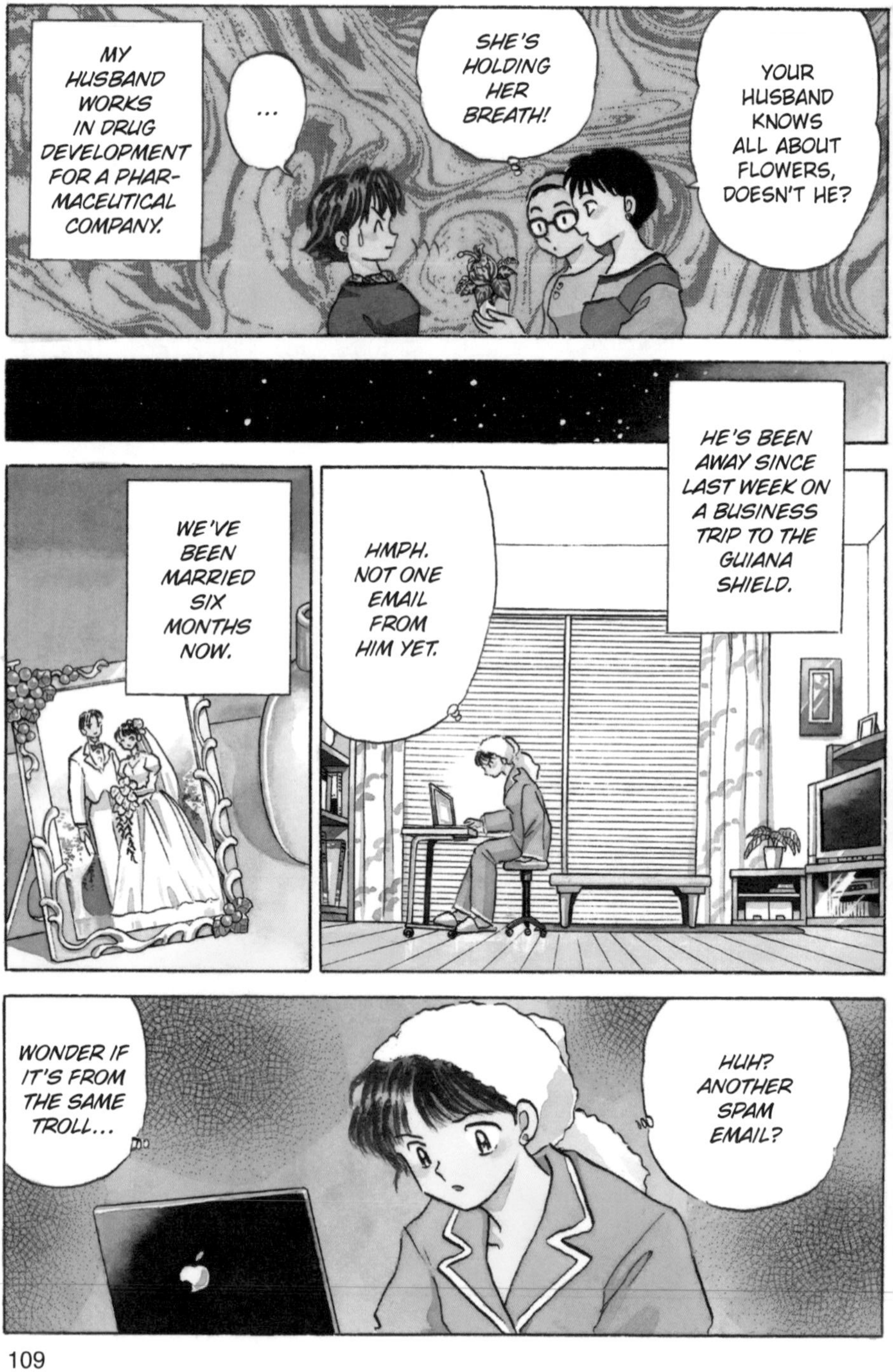
YOUR HUSBAND KNOWS ALL ABOUT FLOWERS, DOESN'T HE?
SHE'S HOLDING HER BREATH!
...
MY HUSBAND WORKS IN DRUG DEVELOPMENT FOR A PHAR-MACEUTICAL COMPANY.
HE'S BEEN AWAY SINCE LAST WEEK ON A BUSINESS TRIP TO THE GUIANA SHIELD.
HMPH. NOT ONE EMAIL FROM HIM YET.
WE'VE BEEN MARRIED SIX MONTHS NOW.
HUH? ANOTHER SPAM EMAIL?
WONDER IF IT'S FROM THE SAME TROLL...

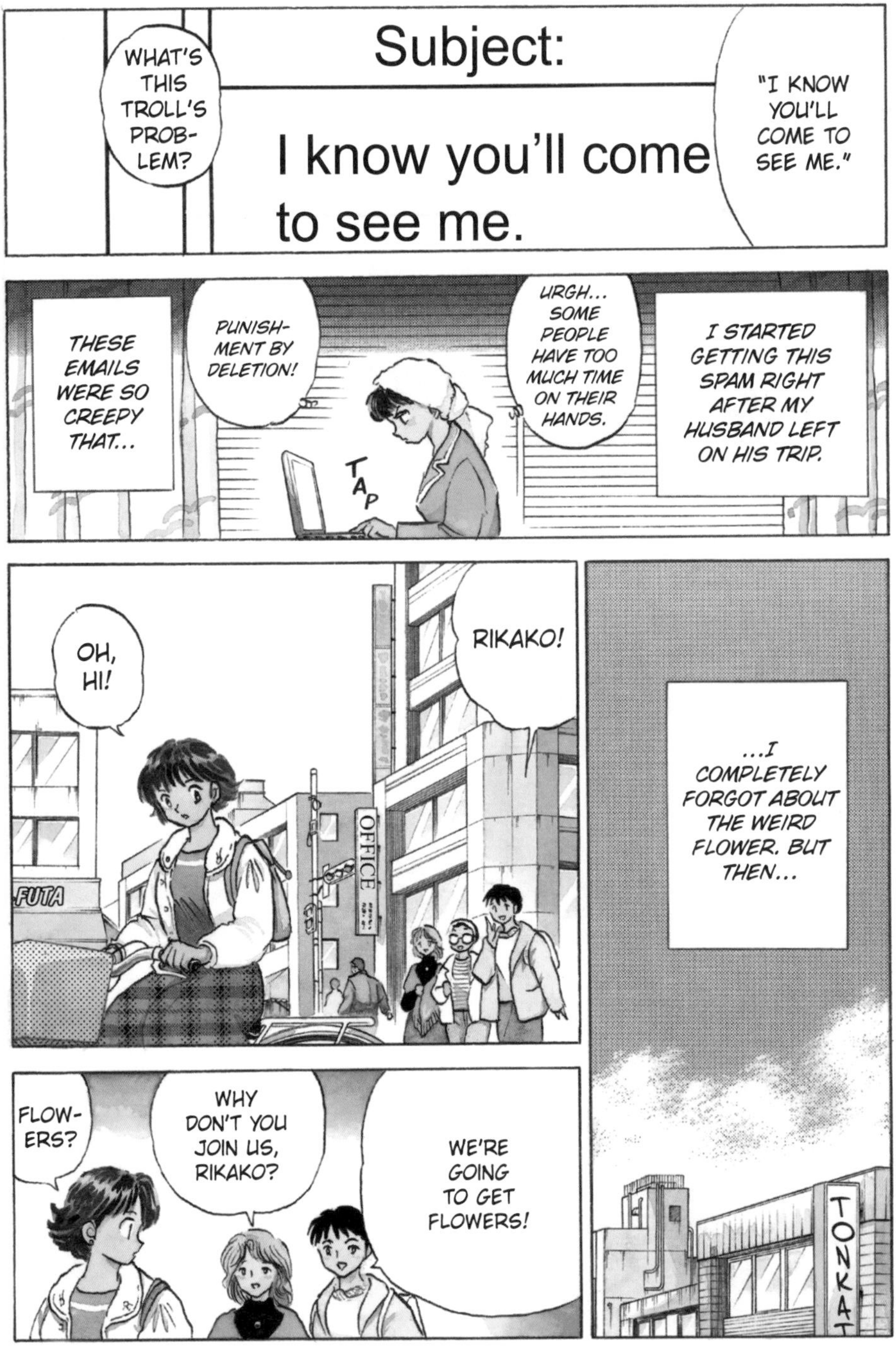
"I KNOW YOU'LL COME TO SEE ME."
Subject:
I know you'll come to see me.
WHAT'S THIS TROLL'S PROB-LEM?
I STARTED GETTING THIS SPAM RIGHT AFTER MY HUSBAND LEFT ON HIS TRIP.
URGH... SOME PEOPLE HAVE TOO MUCH TIME ON THEIR HANDS.
PUNISH-MENT BY DELETION!
TAP
THESE EMAILS WERE SO CREEPY THAT...
...I COMPLETELY FORGOT ABOUT THE WEIRD FLOWER. BUT THEN...
TONKAT
RIKAKO!
OFFICE
OH, HI!
FUTA
WE'RE GOING TO GET FLOWERS!
WHY DON'T YOU JOIN US, RIKAKO?
FLOW-ERS?

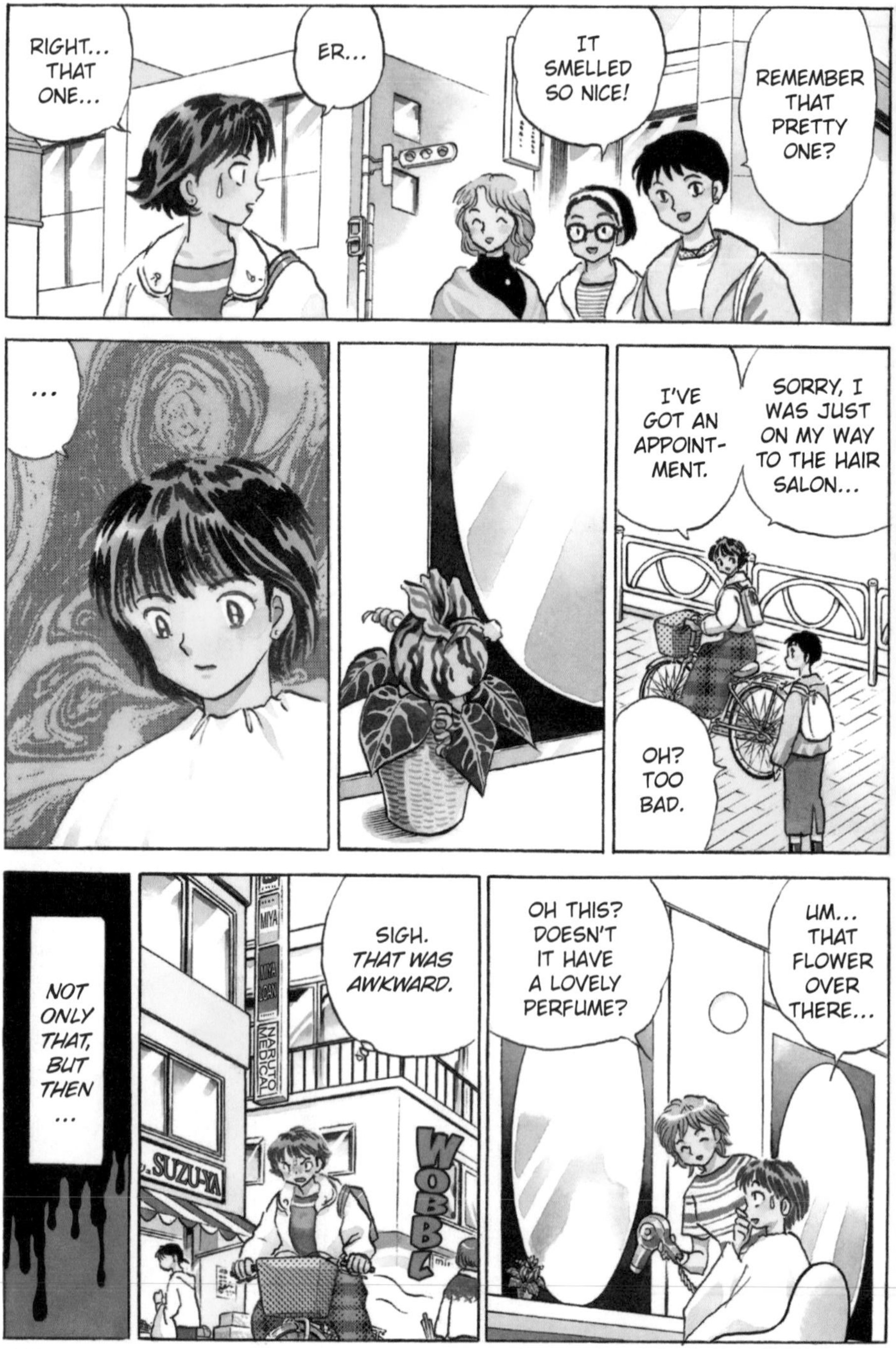
REMEMBER THAT PRETTY ONE?
IT SMELLED SO NICE!
ER...
RIGHT... THAT ONE...
SORRY, I WAS JUST ON MY WAY TO THE HAIR SALON...
I'VE GOT AN APPOINTMENT.
OH? TOO BAD.
...
UM... THAT FLOWER OVER THERE...
OH THIS? DOESN'T IT HAVE A LOVELY PERFUME?
SIGH. *THAT WAS AWKWARD.*
MIYA
MIYA LOAN
NARUTO MEDICAL
SUZU-YA
WOBBL
NOT ONLY THAT, BUT THEN ...

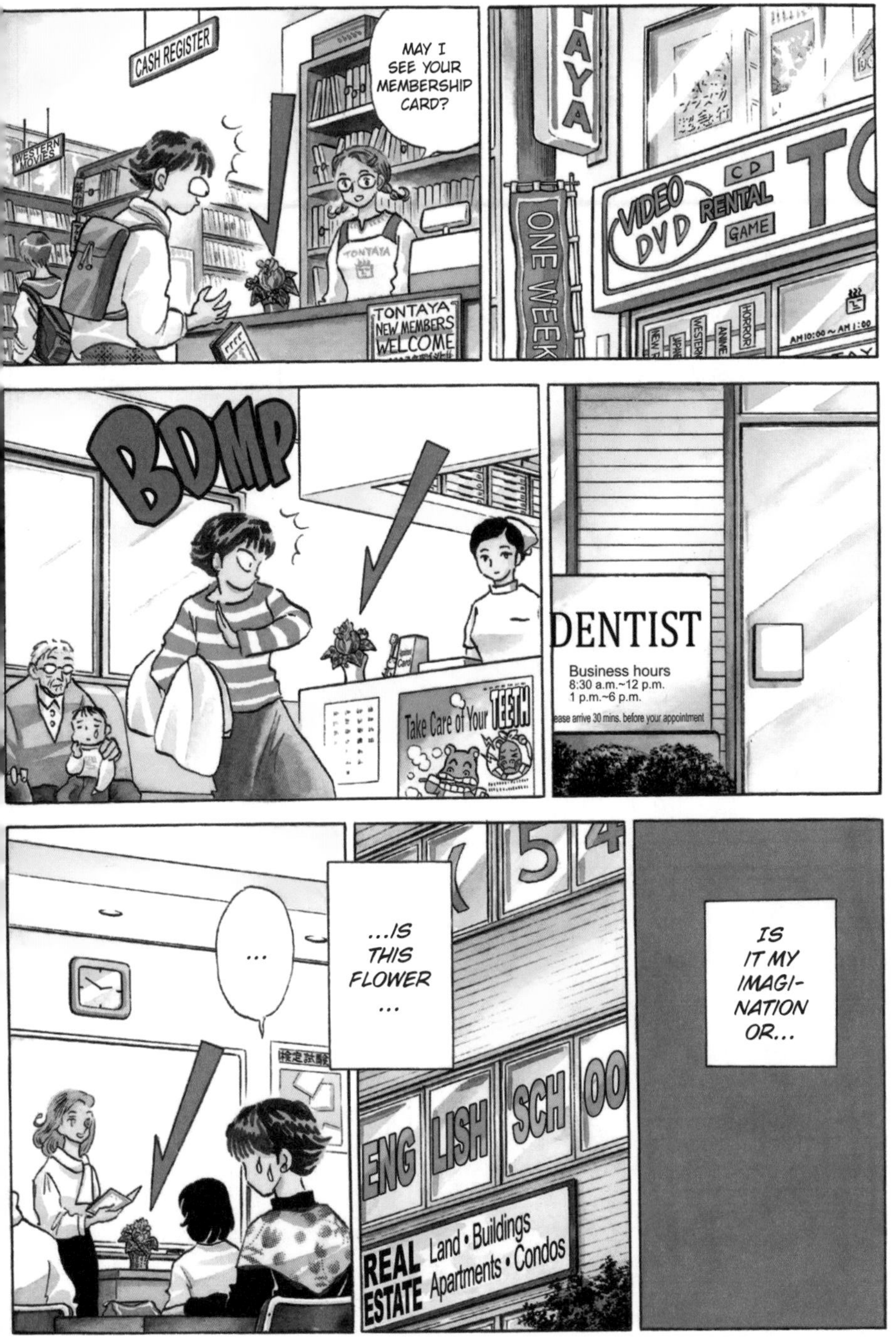

TAYA
VIDEO DVD
CD
RENTAL
GAME
TO
ONE WEEK
NEW
WESTERN
ANIME
HORROR
AM10:00 ~ AM1:00
CASH REGISTER
MAY I SEE YOUR MEMBERSHIP CARD?
WESTERN MOVIES
TONTAYA
TONTAYA NEW MEMBERS WELCOME
DENTIST
Business hours
8:30 a.m.~12 p.m.
1 p.m.~6 p.m.
ease arrive 30 mins. before your appointment
BDMP
Take Care of Your TEETH
IS IT MY IMAGI- NATION OR...
...IS THIS FLOWER ...
ENG LISH SCH OO
REAL ESTATE
Land • Buildings
Apartments • Condos
...

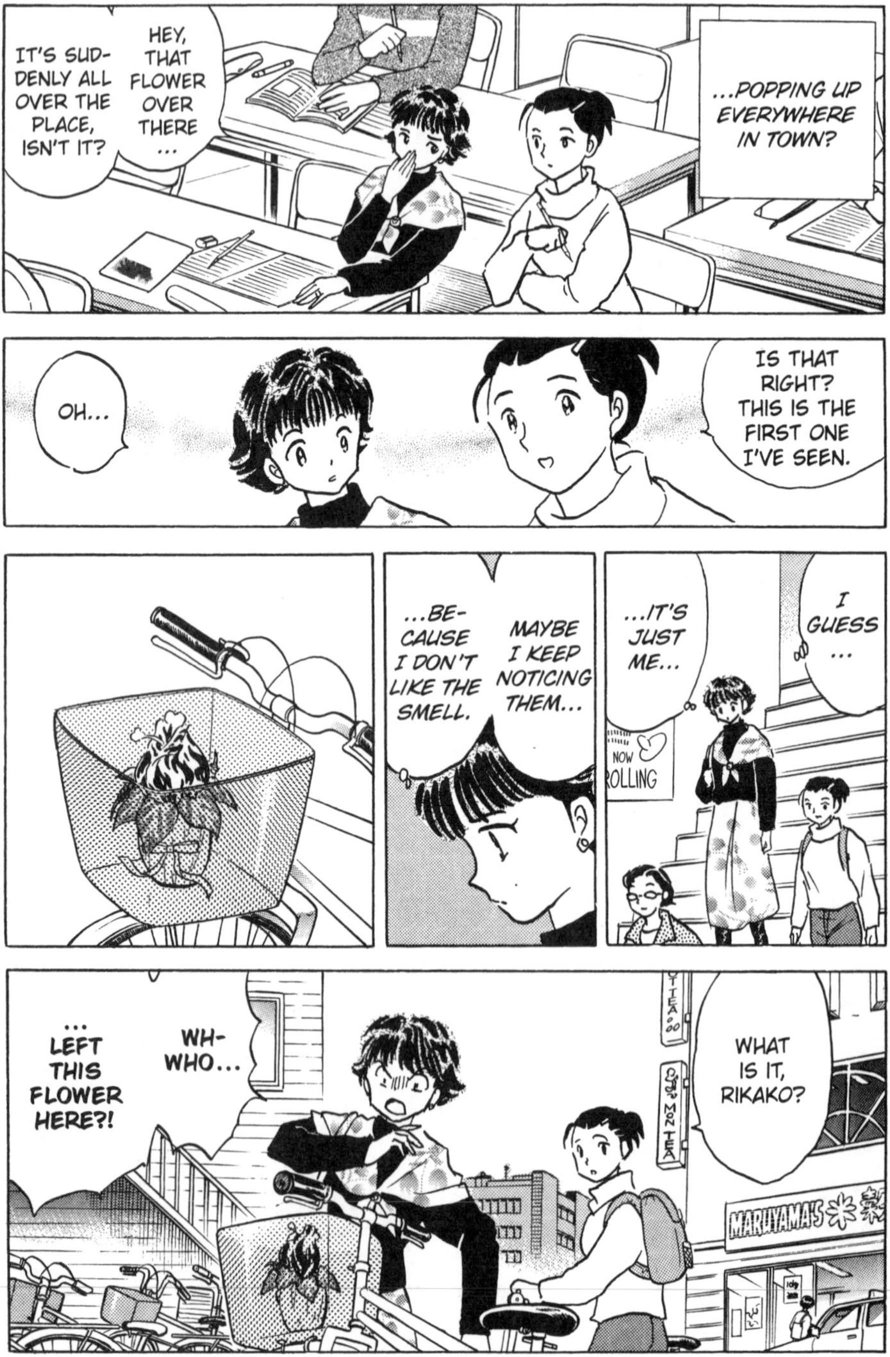
...POPPING UP EVERYWHERE IN TOWN?
HEY, THAT FLOWER OVER THERE...
IT'S SUDDENLY ALL OVER THE PLACE, ISN'T IT?
IS THAT RIGHT? THIS IS THE FIRST ONE I'VE SEEN.
OH...
I GUESS...
...IT'S JUST ME...
NOW ROLLING
MAYBE I KEEP NOTICING THEM...
...BECAUSE I DON'T LIKE THE SMELL.
WHAT IS IT, RIKAKO?
MARUYAMA'S
WH-WHO...
...LEFT THIS FLOWER HERE?!

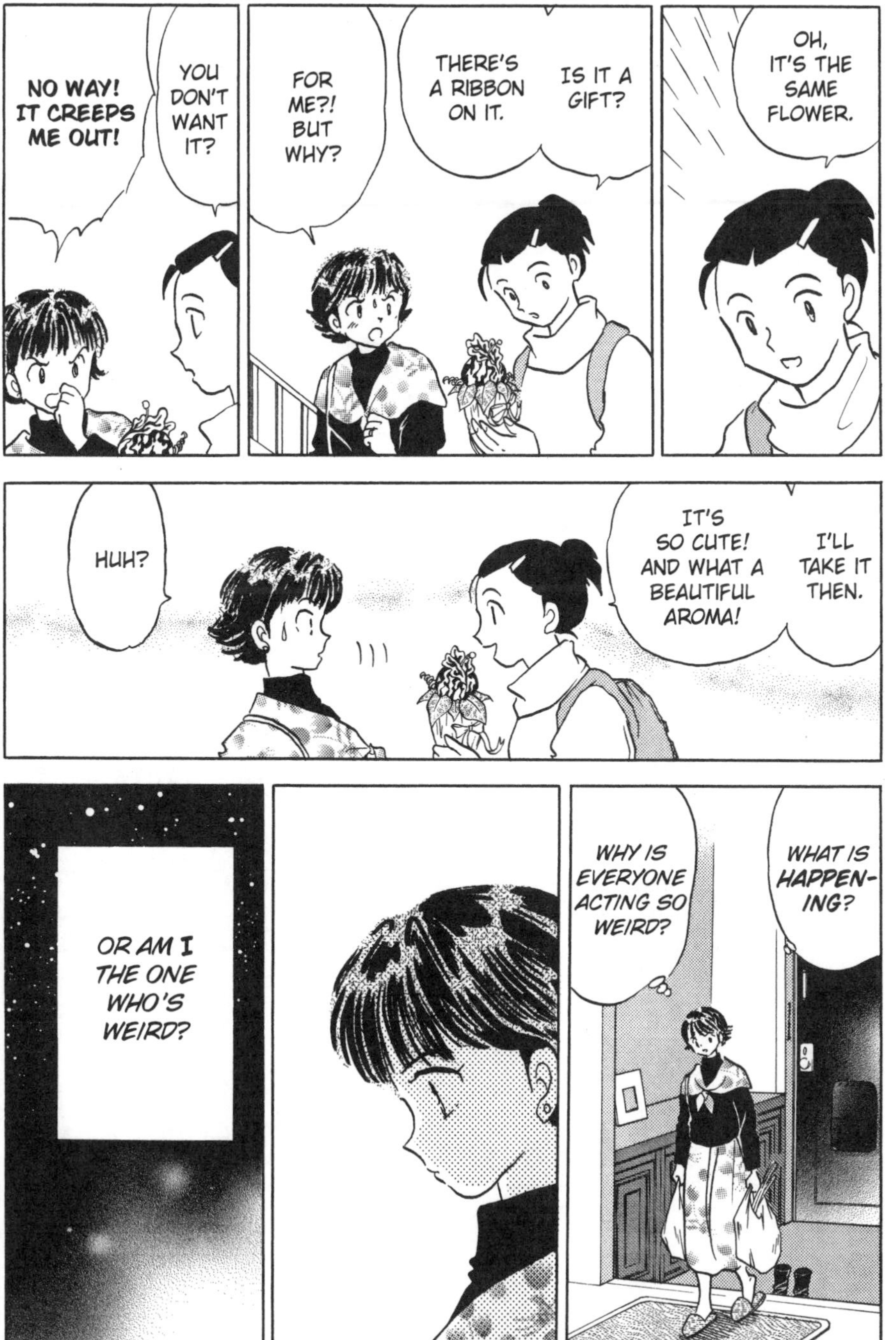
OH, IT'S THE SAME FLOWER.
IS IT A GIFT?
THERE'S A RIBBON ON IT.
FOR ME?! BUT WHY?
YOU DON'T WANT IT?
NO WAY! IT CREEPS ME OUT!
I'LL TAKE IT THEN.
IT'S SO CUTE! AND WHAT A BEAUTIFUL AROMA!
HUH?
WHAT IS HAPPENING?
WHY IS EVERYONE ACTING SO WEIRD?
OR AM I THE ONE WHO'S WEIRD?

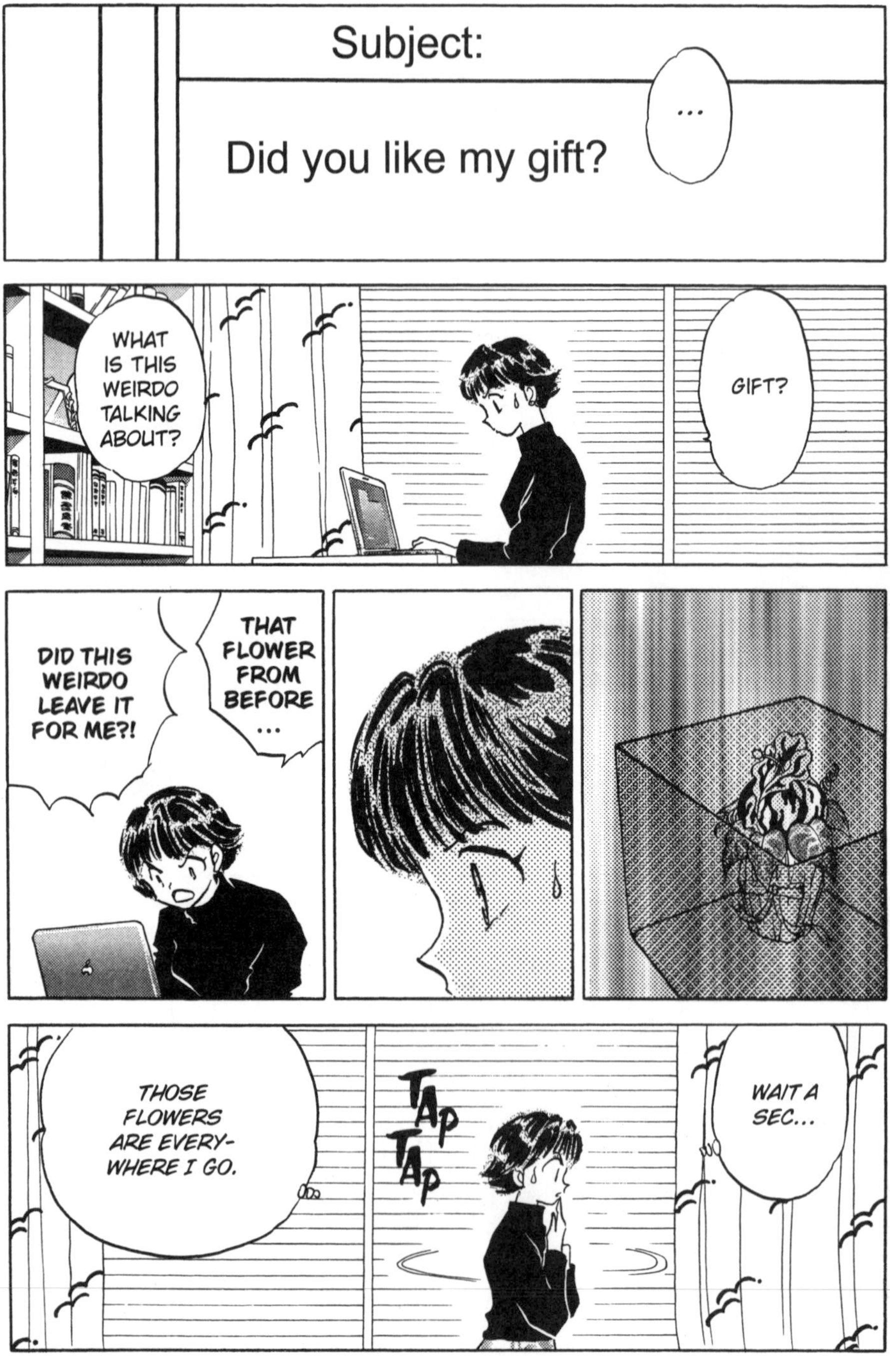
Subject:
Did you like my gift?
...
GIFT?
WHAT IS THIS WEIRDO TALKING ABOUT?
THAT FLOWER FROM BEFORE ...
DID THIS WEIRDO LEAVE IT FOR ME?!
WAIT A SEC...
TAP TAP
THOSE FLOWERS ARE EVERY-WHERE I GO.

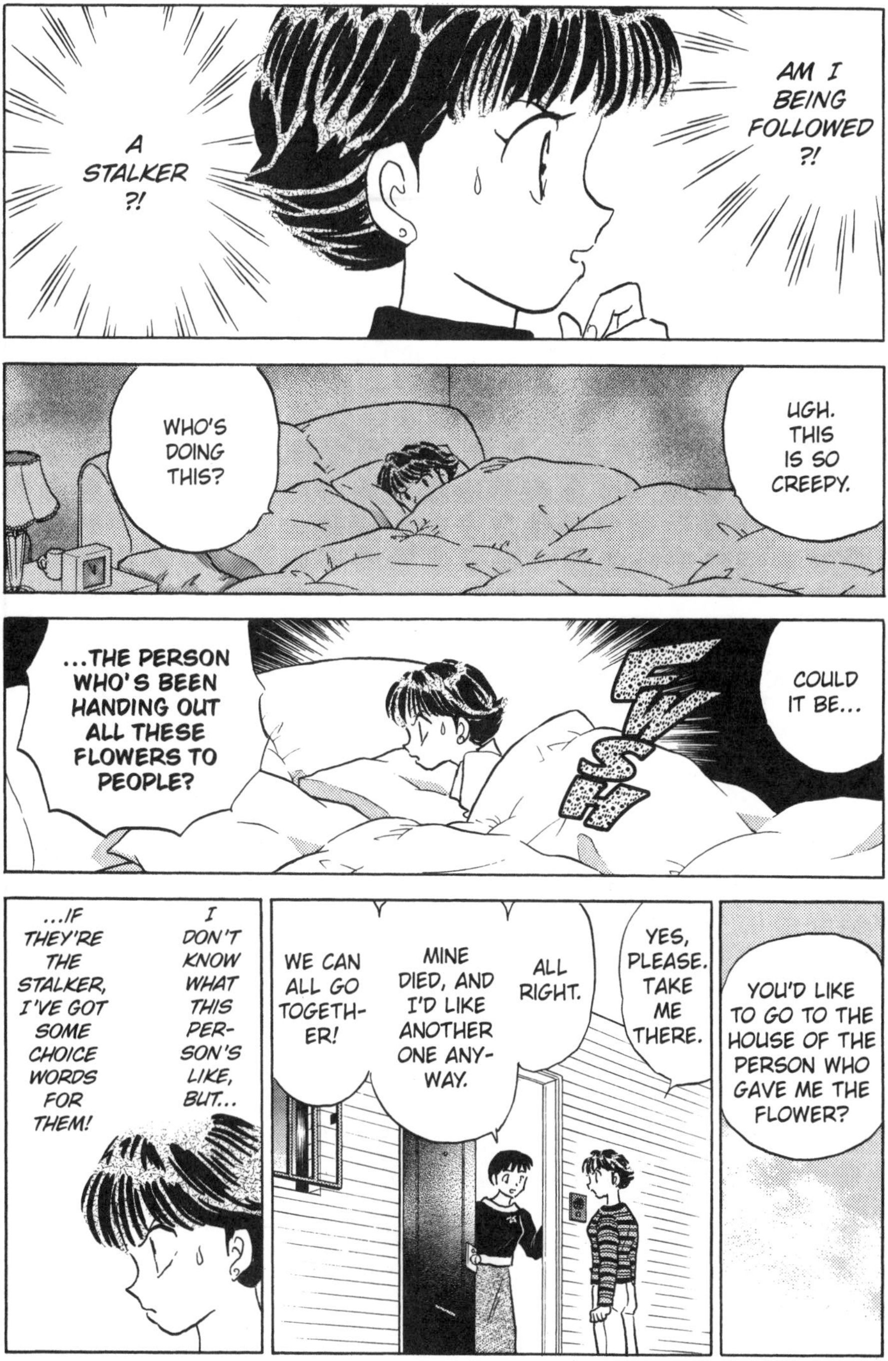
AM I BEING FOLLOWED ?!
A STALKER ?!
UGH. THIS IS SO CREEPY.
WHO'S DOING THIS?
COULD IT BE...
...THE PERSON WHO'S BEEN HANDING OUT ALL THESE FLOWERS TO PEOPLE?
YOU'D LIKE TO GO TO THE HOUSE OF THE PERSON WHO GAVE ME THE FLOWER?
YES, PLEASE. TAKE ME THERE.
ALL RIGHT.
MINE DIED, AND I'D LIKE ANOTHER ONE ANYWAY.
WE CAN ALL GO TOGETHER!
I DON'T KNOW WHAT THIS PERSON'S LIKE, BUT...
...IF THEY'RE THE STALKER, I'VE GOT SOME CHOICE WORDS FOR THEM!

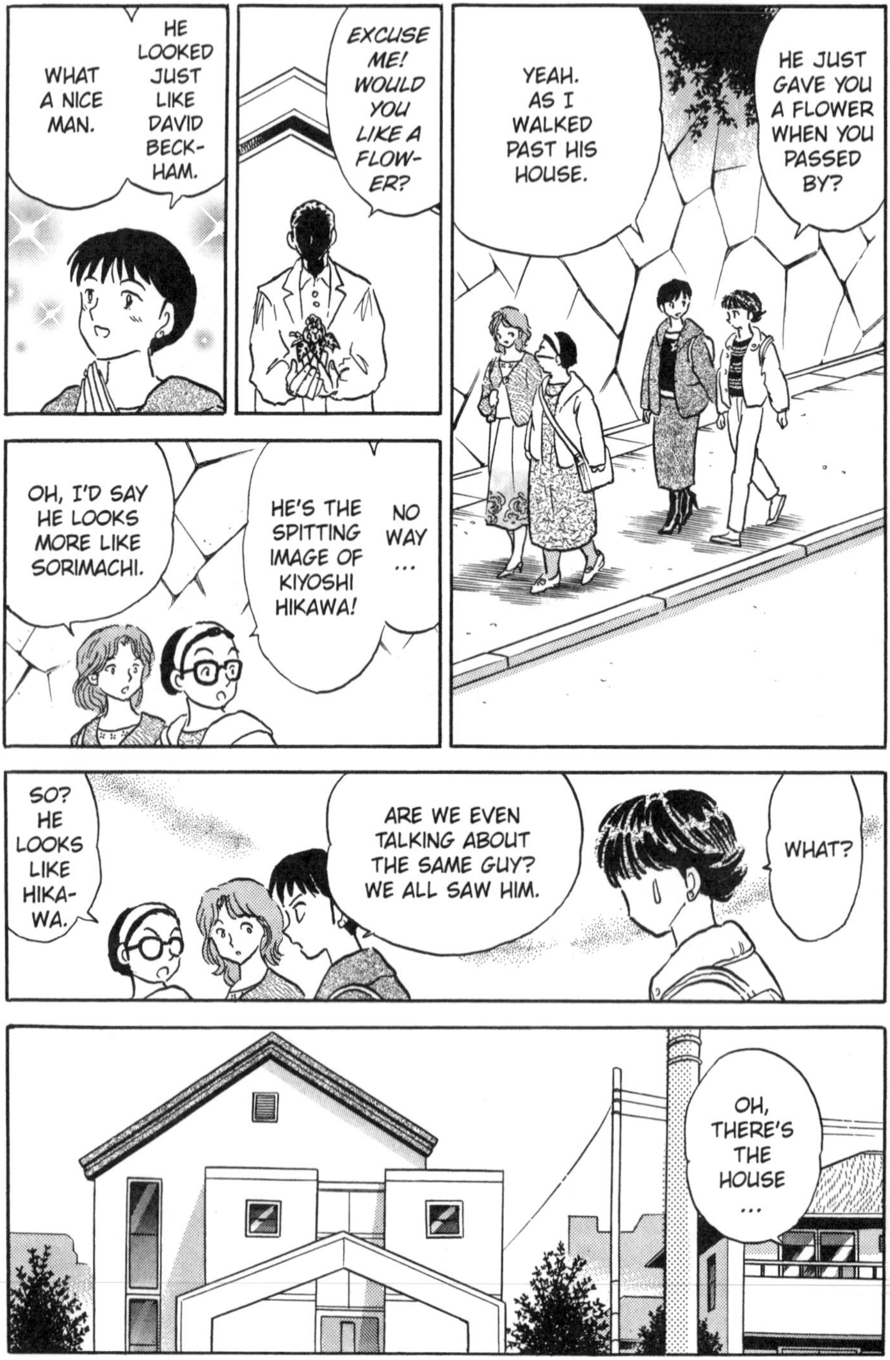
HE JUST GAVE YOU A FLOWER WHEN YOU PASSED BY?
YEAH. AS I WALKED PAST HIS HOUSE.
EXCUSE ME! WOULD YOU LIKE A FLOWER?
HE LOOKED JUST LIKE DAVID BECKHAM.
WHAT A NICE MAN.
NO WAY...
HE'S THE SPITTING IMAGE OF KIYOSHI HIKAWA!
OH, I'D SAY HE LOOKS MORE LIKE SORIMACHI.
WHAT?
ARE WE EVEN TALKING ABOUT THE SAME GUY? WE ALL SAW HIM.
SO? HE LOOKS LIKE HIKAWA.
OH, THERE'S THE HOUSE...

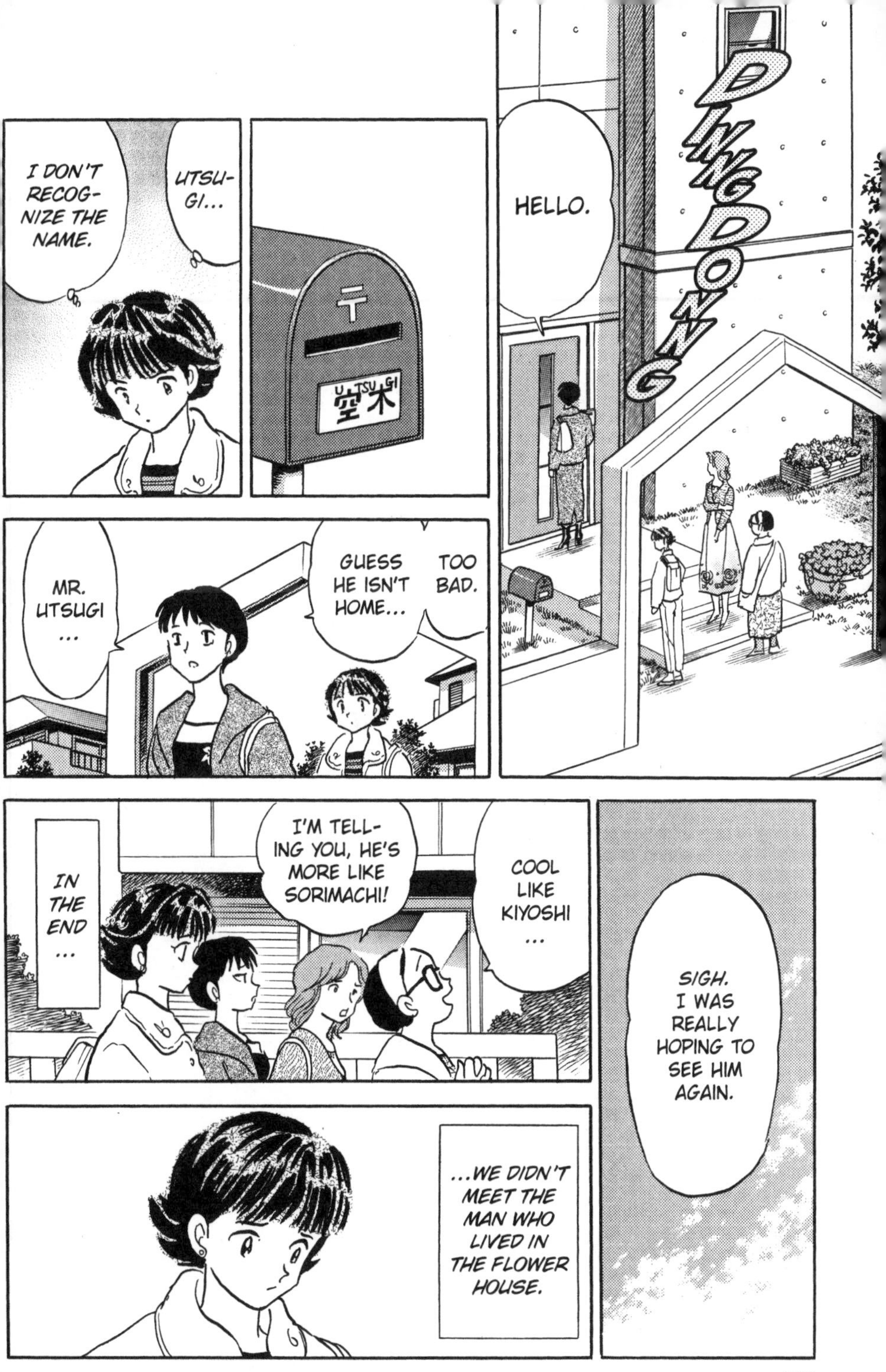
DING DONG
HELLO.
UTSUGI 空木
UTSU-GI...
I DON'T RECOG-NIZE THE NAME.
TOO BAD.
GUESS HE ISN'T HOME...
MR. UTSUGI...
SIGH. I WAS REALLY HOPING TO SEE HIM AGAIN.
COOL LIKE KIYOSHI...
I'M TELL-ING YOU, HE'S MORE LIKE SORIMACHI!
IN THE END...
...WE DIDN'T MEET THE MAN WHO LIVED IN THE FLOWER HOUSE.

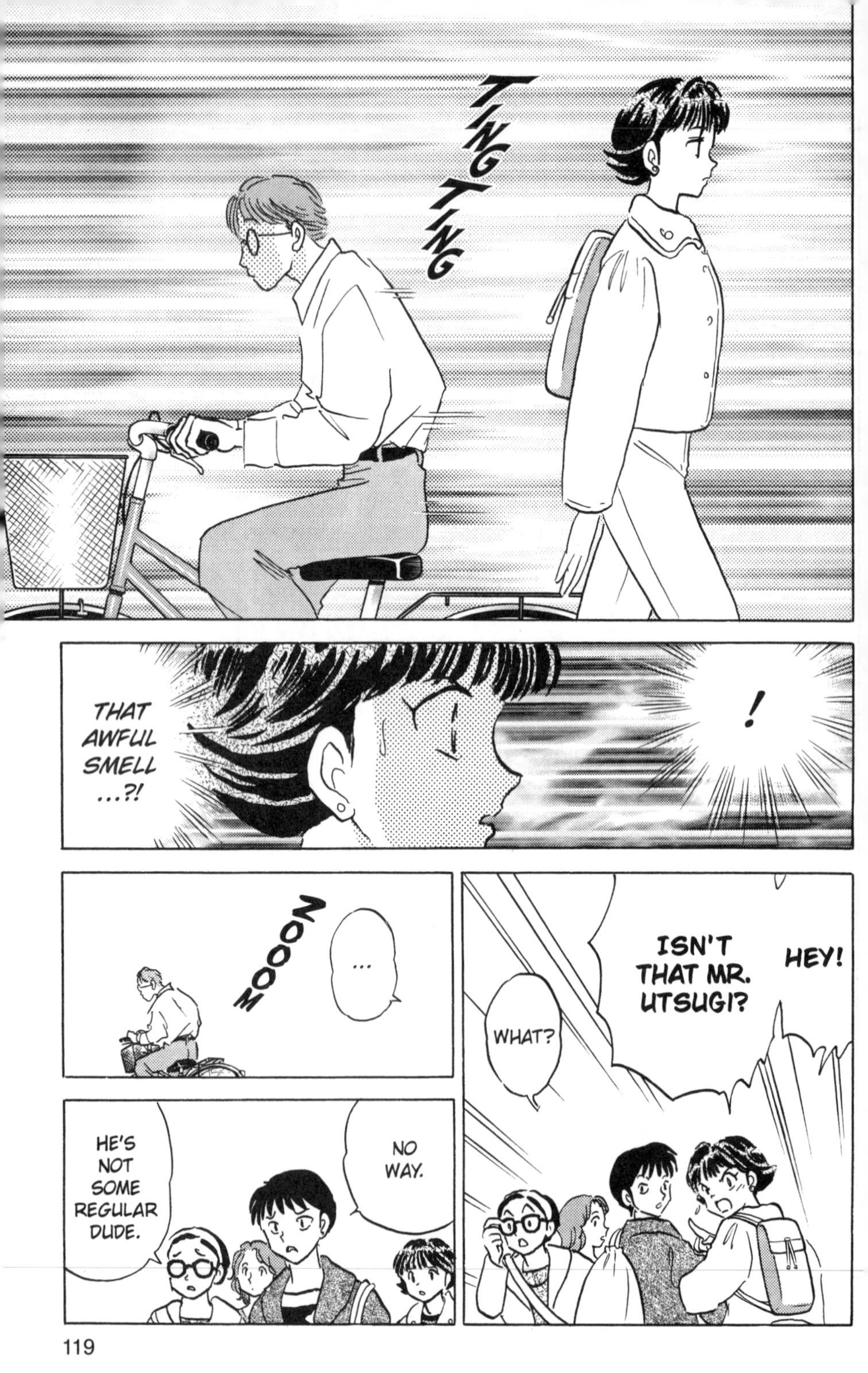
TING TING TING
!
THAT AWFUL SMELL ...?!
HEY!
ISN'T THAT MR. UTSUGI?
WHAT?
...
ZOOOOM
NO WAY.
HE'S NOT SOME REGULAR DUDE.

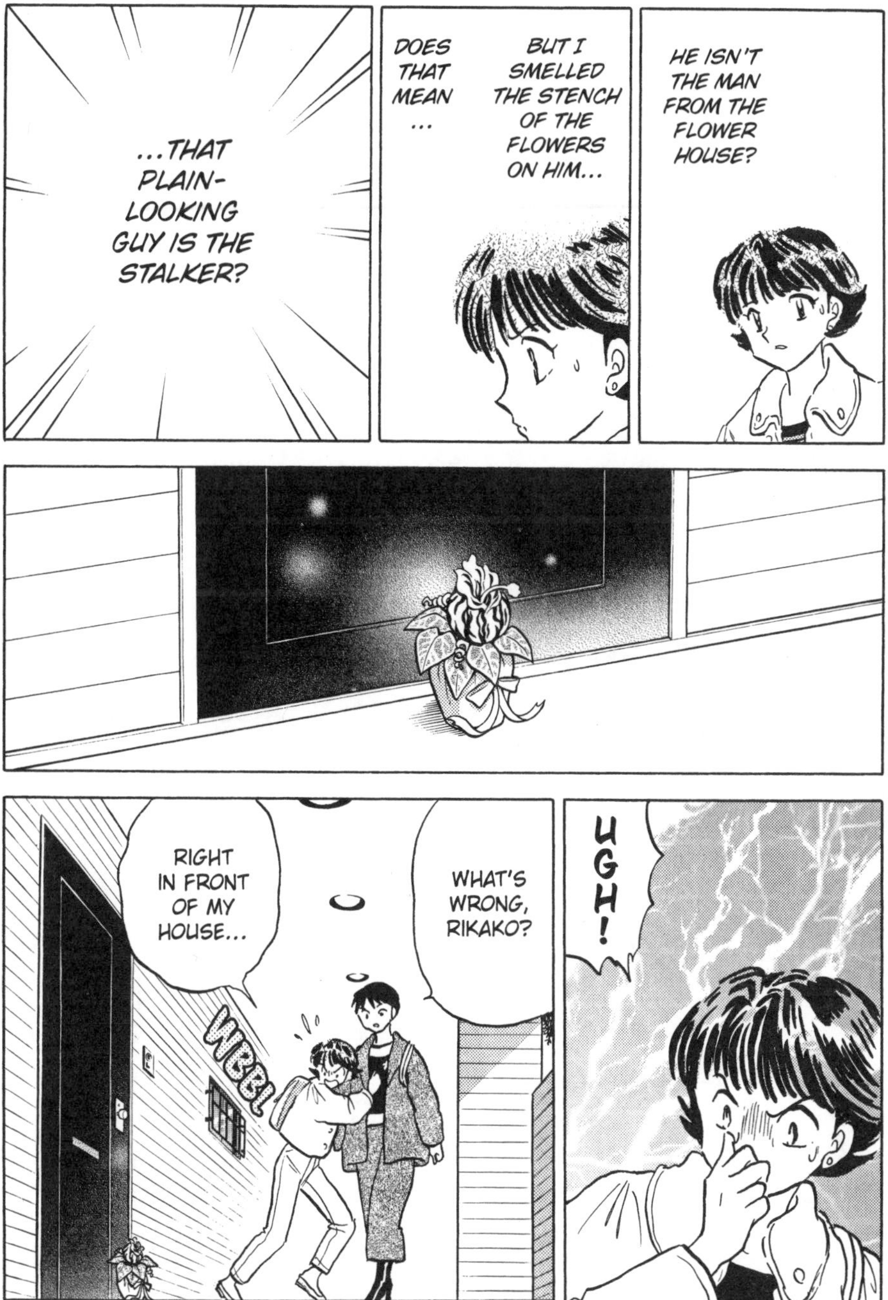
HE ISN'T THE MAN FROM THE FLOWER HOUSE?
BUT I SMELLED THE STENCH OF THE FLOWERS ON HIM...
DOES THAT MEAN ...
...THAT PLAIN-LOOKING GUY IS THE STALKER?
UGH!
WHAT'S WRONG, RIKAKO?
RIGHT IN FRONT OF MY HOUSE...
WBBL

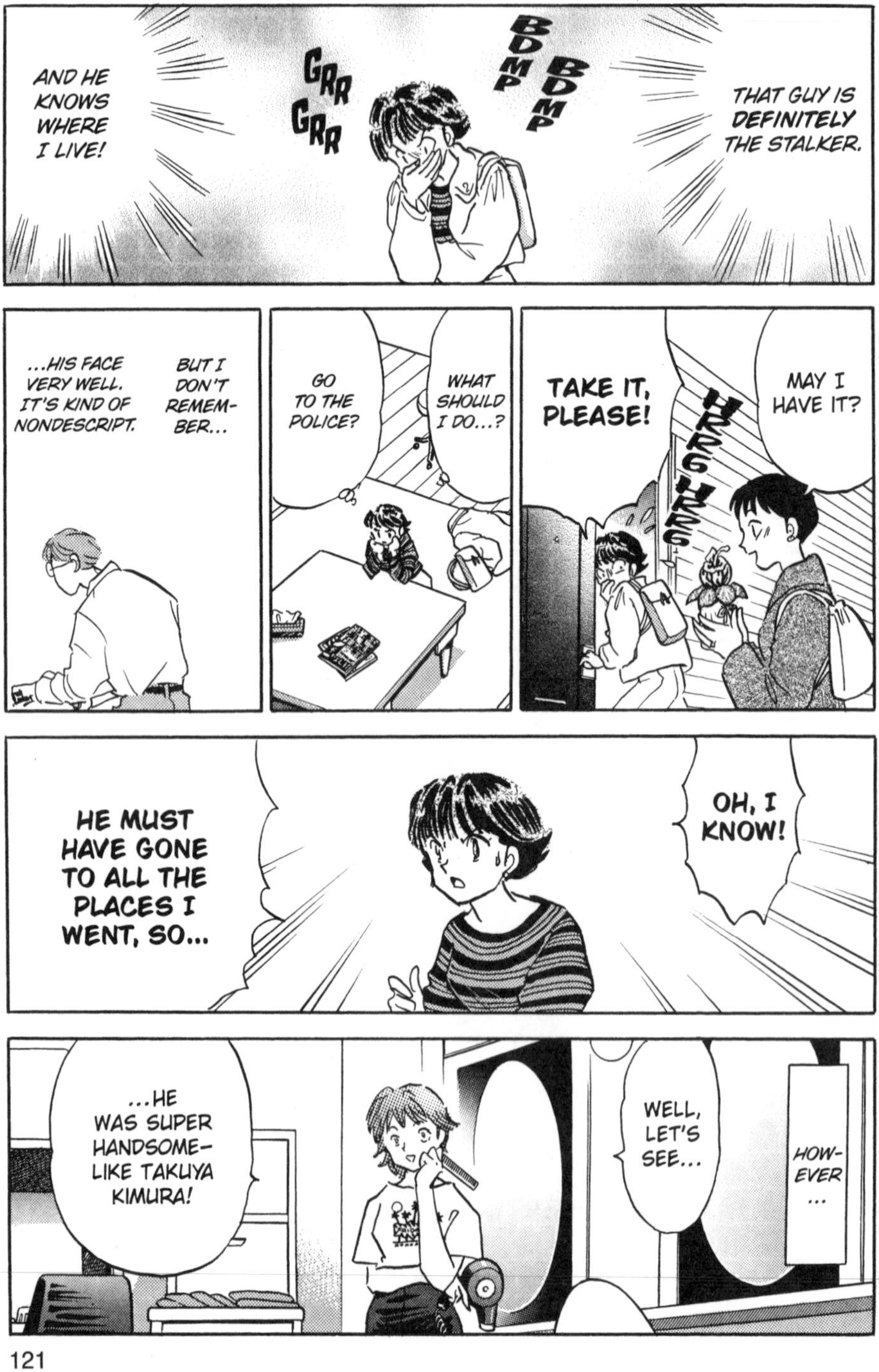
THAT GUY IS DEFINITELY THE STALKER.
BDMP BDMP
GRR GRR
AND HE KNOWS WHERE I LIVE!
MAY I HAVE IT?
HRRG HRRG
TAKE IT, PLEASE!
WHAT SHOULD I DO...?
GO TO THE POLICE?
BUT I DON'T REMEM-BER...
...HIS FACE VERY WELL. IT'S KIND OF NONDESCRIPT.
OH, I KNOW!
HE MUST HAVE GONE TO ALL THE PLACES I WENT, SO...
HOW-EVER...
WELL, LET'S SEE...
...HE WAS SUPER HANDSOME-LIKE TAKUYA KIMURA!

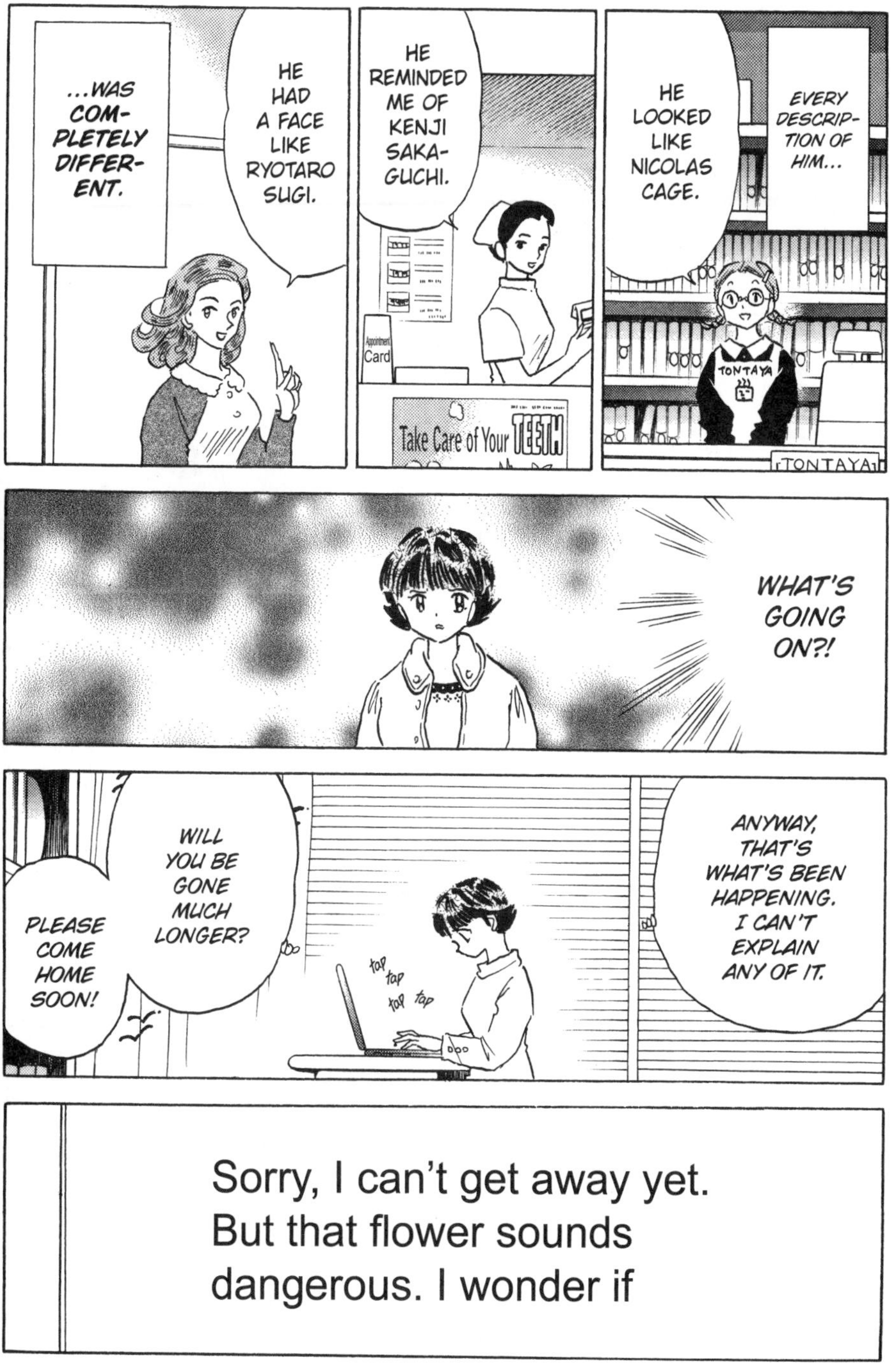
EVERY DESCRIPTION OF HIM...
HE LOOKED LIKE NICOLAS CAGE.
TONTAYA
TONTAYA
HE REMINDED ME OF KENJI SAKAGUCHI.
Appointment Card
Take Care of Your TEETH
HE HAD A FACE LIKE RYOTARO SUGI.
...WAS COMPLETELY DIFFERENT.
WHAT'S GOING ON?!
ANYWAY, THAT'S WHAT'S BEEN HAPPENING. I CAN'T EXPLAIN ANY OF IT.
WILL YOU BE GONE MUCH LONGER?
PLEASE COME HOME SOON!
tap tap tap tap
Sorry, I can't get away yet.
But that flower sounds
dangerous. I wonder if

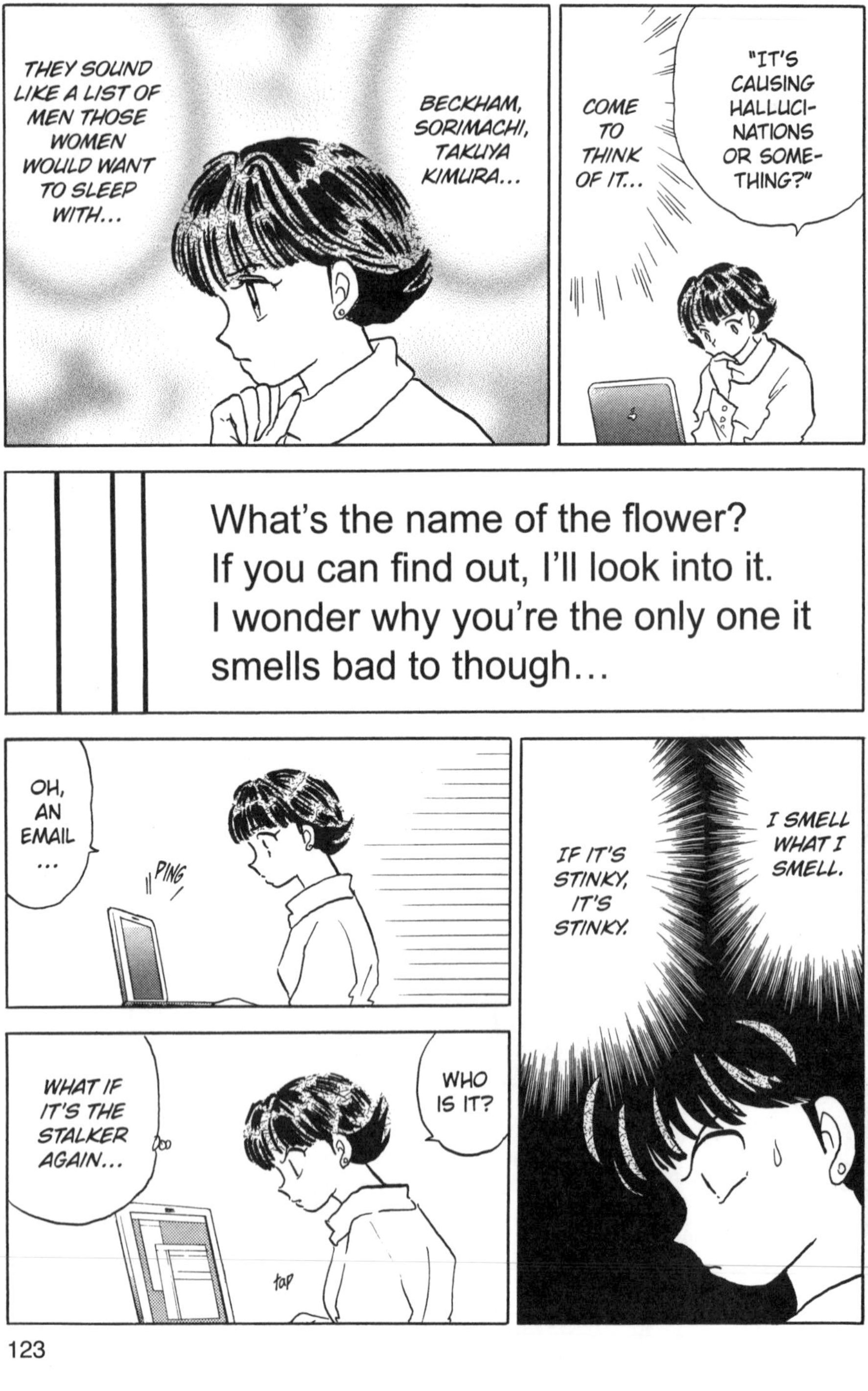
"IT'S CAUSING HALLUCI-NATIONS OR SOME-THING?"
COME TO THINK OF IT...
BECKHAM, SORIMACHI, TAKUYA KIMURA...
THEY SOUND LIKE A LIST OF MEN THOSE WOMEN WOULD WANT TO SLEEP WITH...
What's the name of the flower?
If you can find out, I'll look into it.
I wonder why you're the only one it smells bad to though…
I SMELL WHAT I SMELL.
IF IT'S STINKY, IT'S STINKY.
OH, AN EMAIL...
PING
WHO IS IT?
WHAT IF IT'S THE STALKER AGAIN...
tap

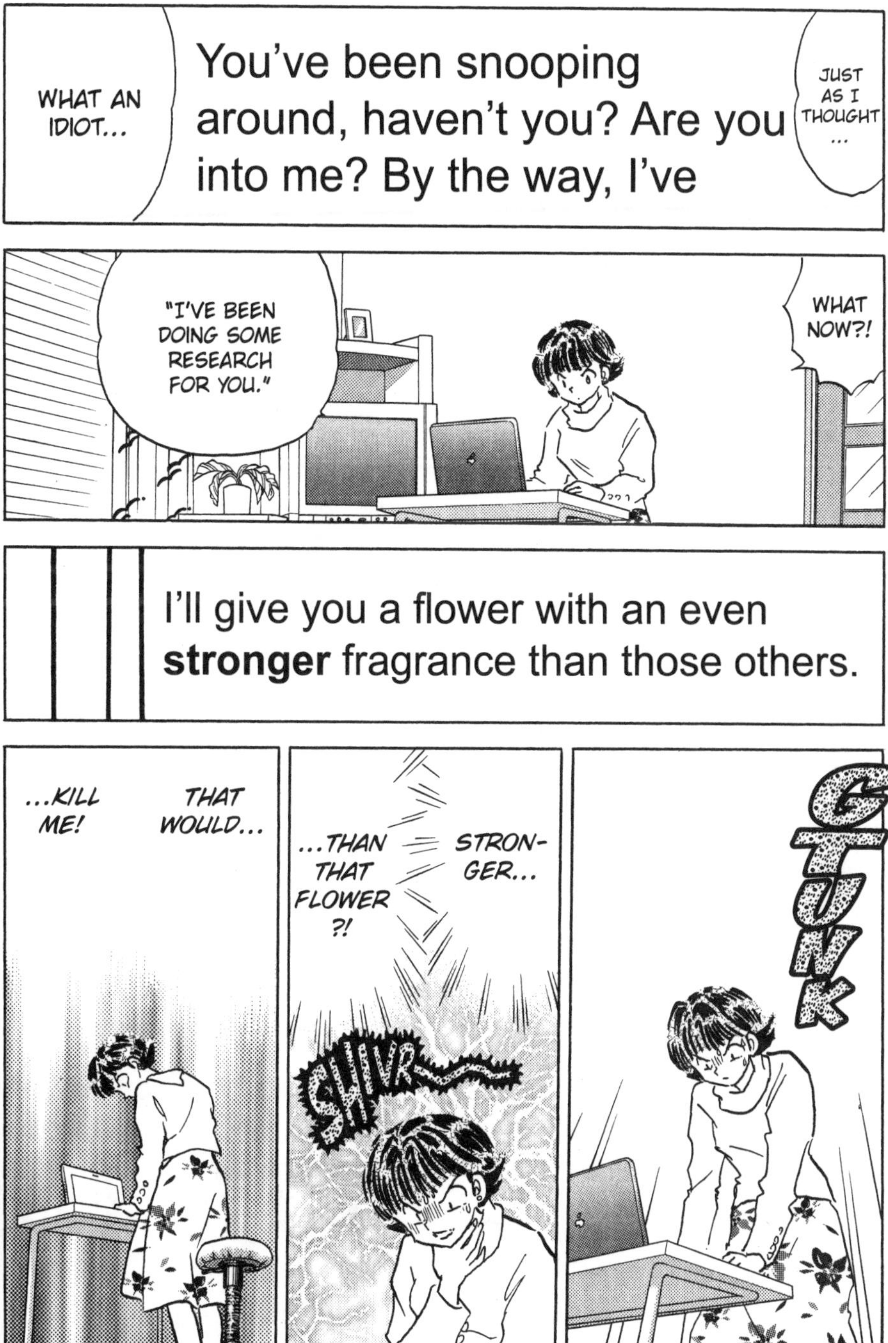
JUST AS I THOUGHT...
You've been snooping around, haven't you? Are you into me? By the way, I've
WHAT AN IDIOT...
WHAT NOW?!
"I'VE BEEN DOING SOME RESEARCH FOR YOU."
I'll give you a flower with an even **stronger** fragrance than those others.
GTUNK
STRONGER...
...THAN THAT FLOWER?!
SHIVR
THAT WOULD...
...KILL ME!

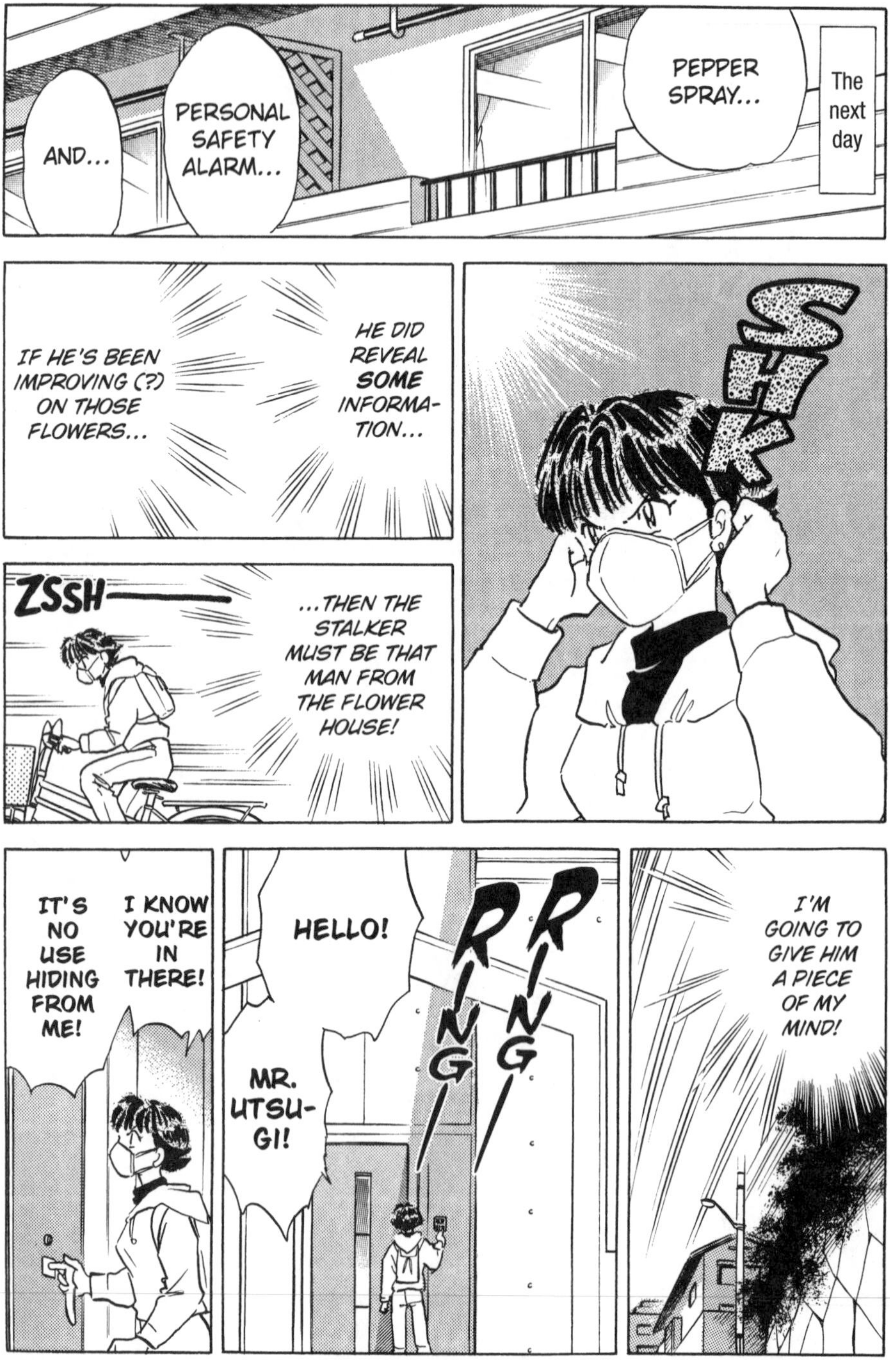
The next day
PEPPER SPRAY...
PERSONAL SAFETY ALARM...
AND...
SHK
HE DID REVEAL **SOME** INFORMATION...
IF HE'S BEEN IMPROVING (?) ON THOSE FLOWERS...
...THEN THE STALKER MUST BE THAT MAN FROM THE FLOWER HOUSE!
ZSSH
I'M GOING TO GIVE HIM A PIECE OF MY MIND!
RRING
RRING
HELLO!
MR. UTSUGI!
I KNOW YOU'RE IN THERE!
IT'S NO USE HIDING FROM ME!

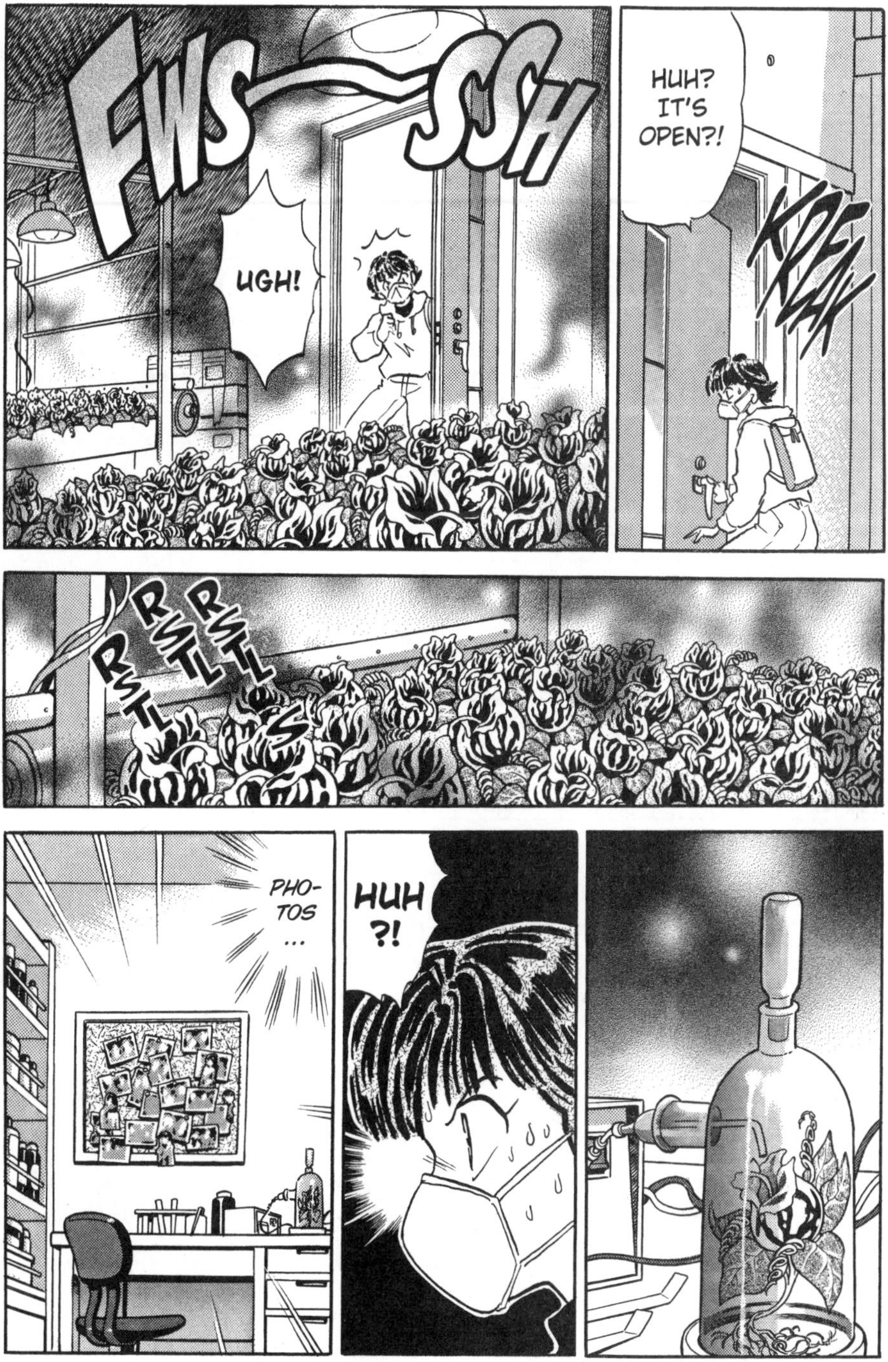
HUH? IT'S OPEN?!
KREAK
FWS-SSH
UGH!
RSTL RSTL RSTL
HUH ?!
PHO-TOS ...

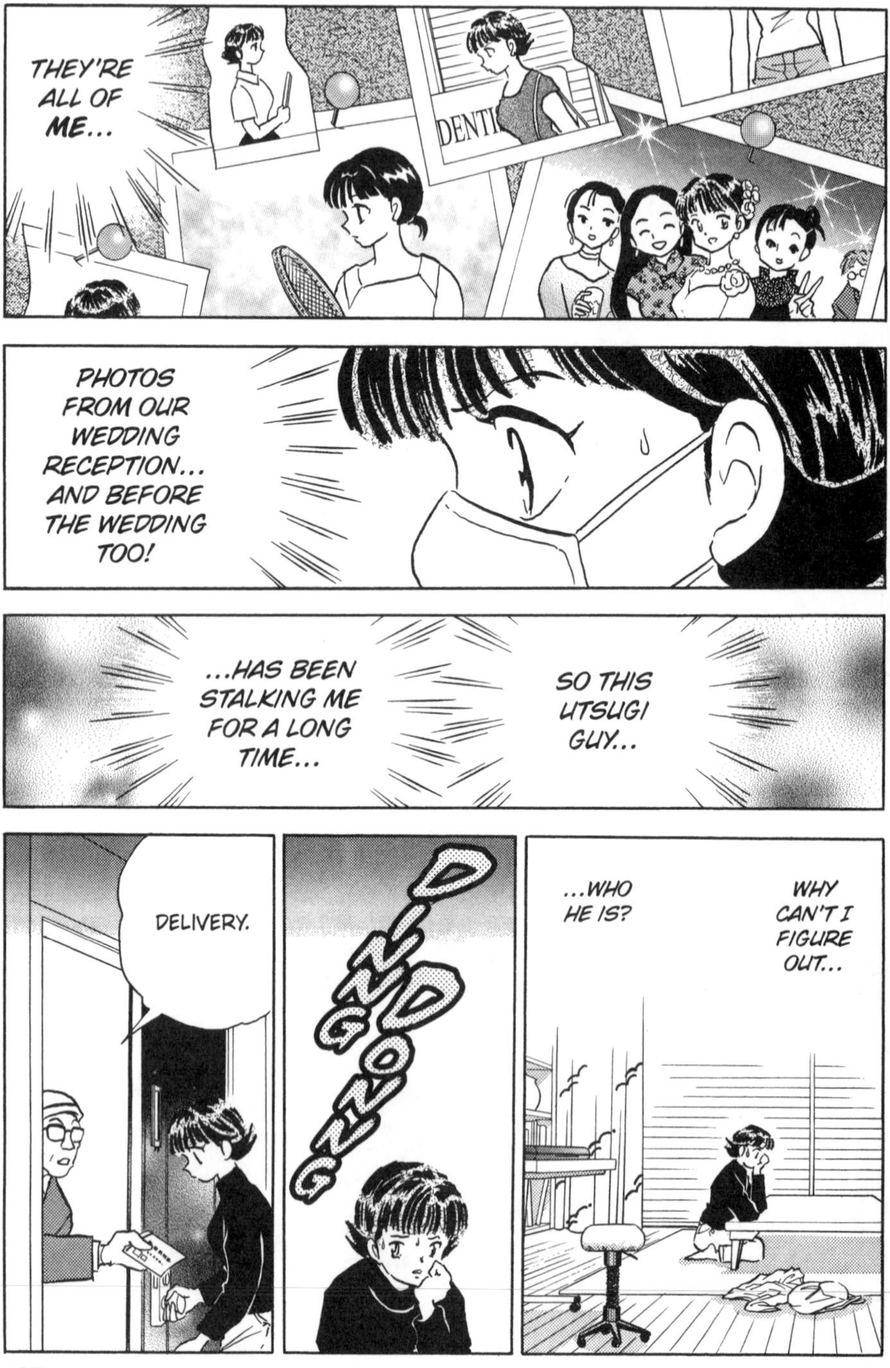
THEY'RE ALL OF ME...
PHOTOS FROM OUR WEDDING RECEPTION... AND BEFORE THE WEDDING TOO!
SO THIS UTSUGI GUY...
...HAS BEEN STALKING ME FOR A LONG TIME...
WHY CAN'T I FIGURE OUT...
...WHO HE IS?
DING DONG
DELIVERY.

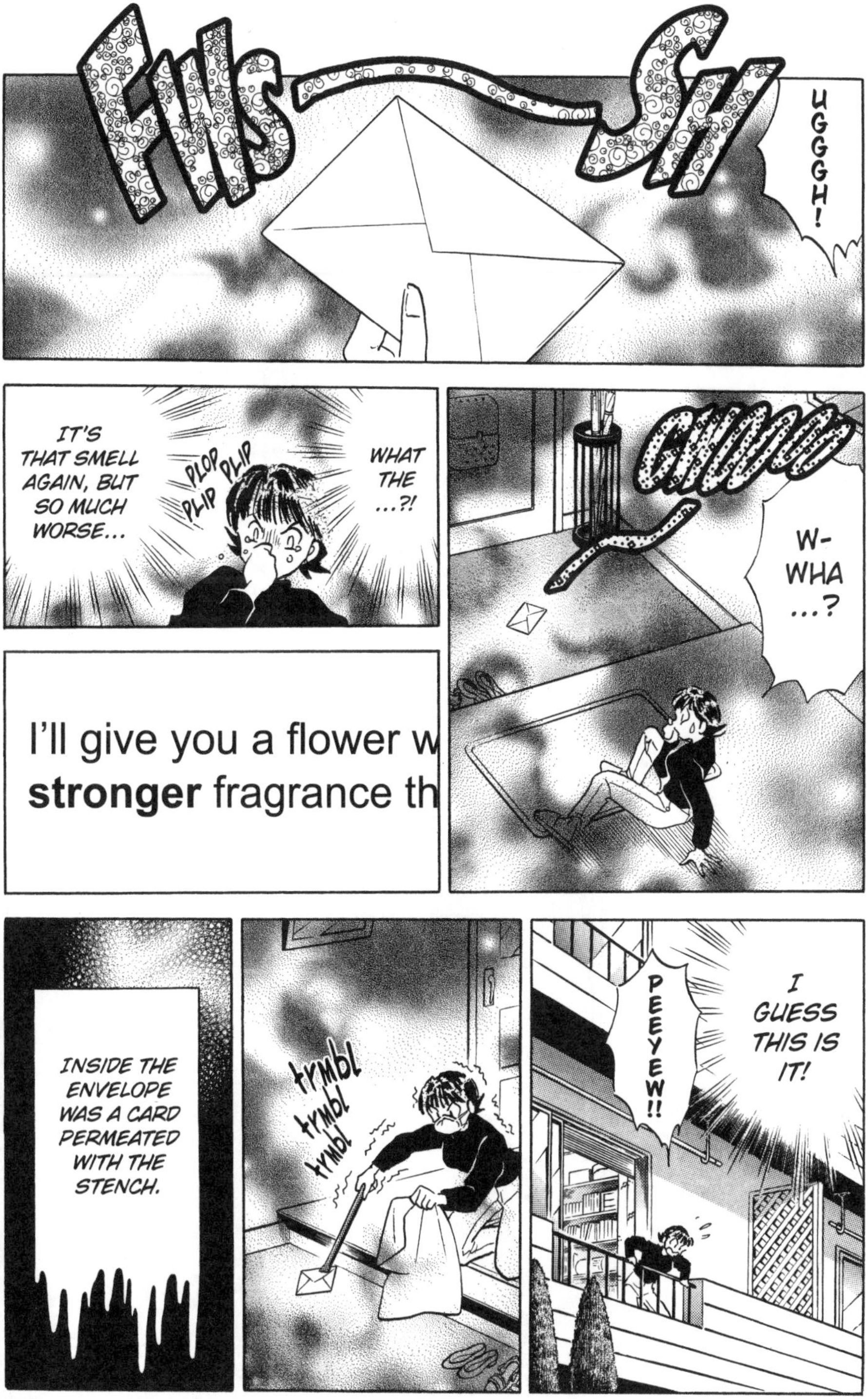
FHS—SH
UGGGH!
W-WHA ...?
WHAT THE ...?!
PLOP PLIP PLIP
IT'S THAT SMELL AGAIN, BUT SO MUCH WORSE...
I'll give you a flower w
stronger fragrance th
I GUESS THIS IS IT!
PEEYEW!!
trmbl trmbl trmbl
INSIDE THE ENVELOPE WAS A CARD PERMEATED WITH THE STENCH.

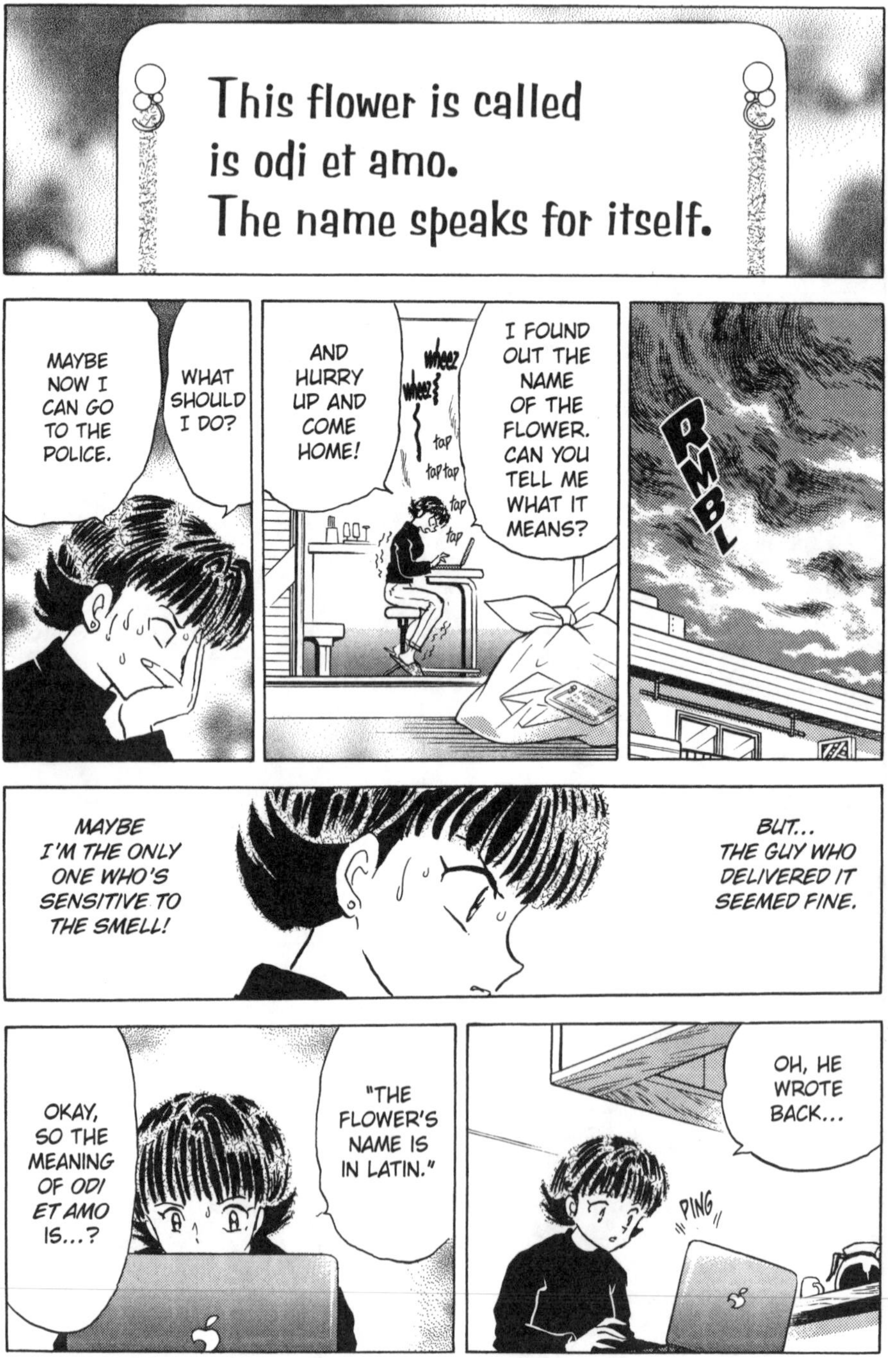
This flower is called is odi et amo. The name speaks for itself.
RMBL
I FOUND OUT THE NAME OF THE FLOWER. CAN YOU TELL ME WHAT IT MEANS?
wheez wheez
tap taptap tap tap
AND HURRY UP AND COME HOME!
WHAT SHOULD I DO?
MAYBE NOW I CAN GO TO THE POLICE.
BUT... THE GUY WHO DELIVERED IT SEEMED FINE.
MAYBE I'M THE ONLY ONE WHO'S SENSITIVE TO THE SMELL!
OH, HE WROTE BACK...
PING
"THE FLOWER'S NAME IS IN LATIN."
OKAY, SO THE MEANING OF ODI ET AMO IS...?

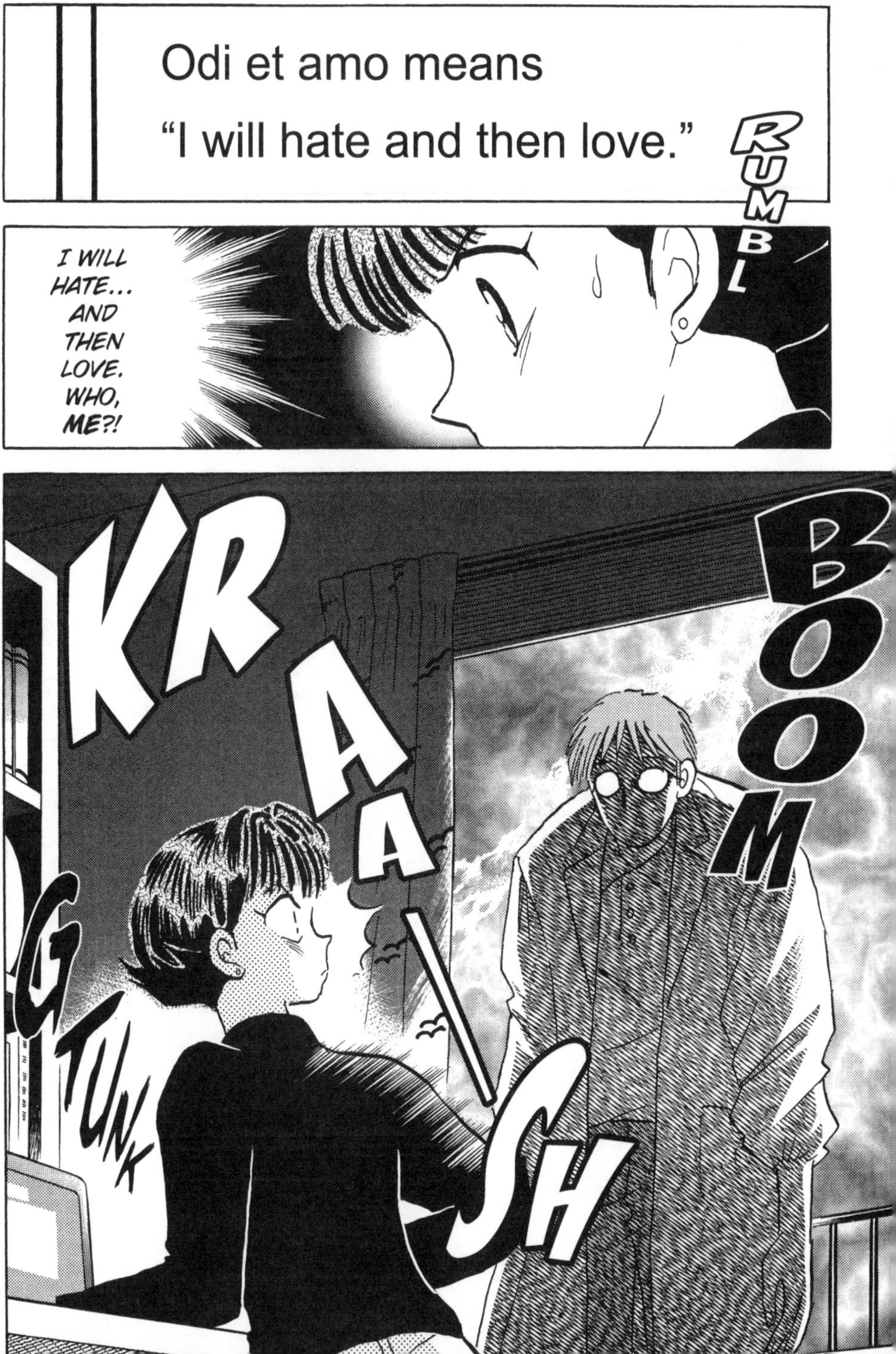
Odi et amo means
“I will hate and then love.”
RUMBL
I WILL HATE... AND THEN LOVE. WHO, ME?!
BOOM
KRAAASH
GTUNK

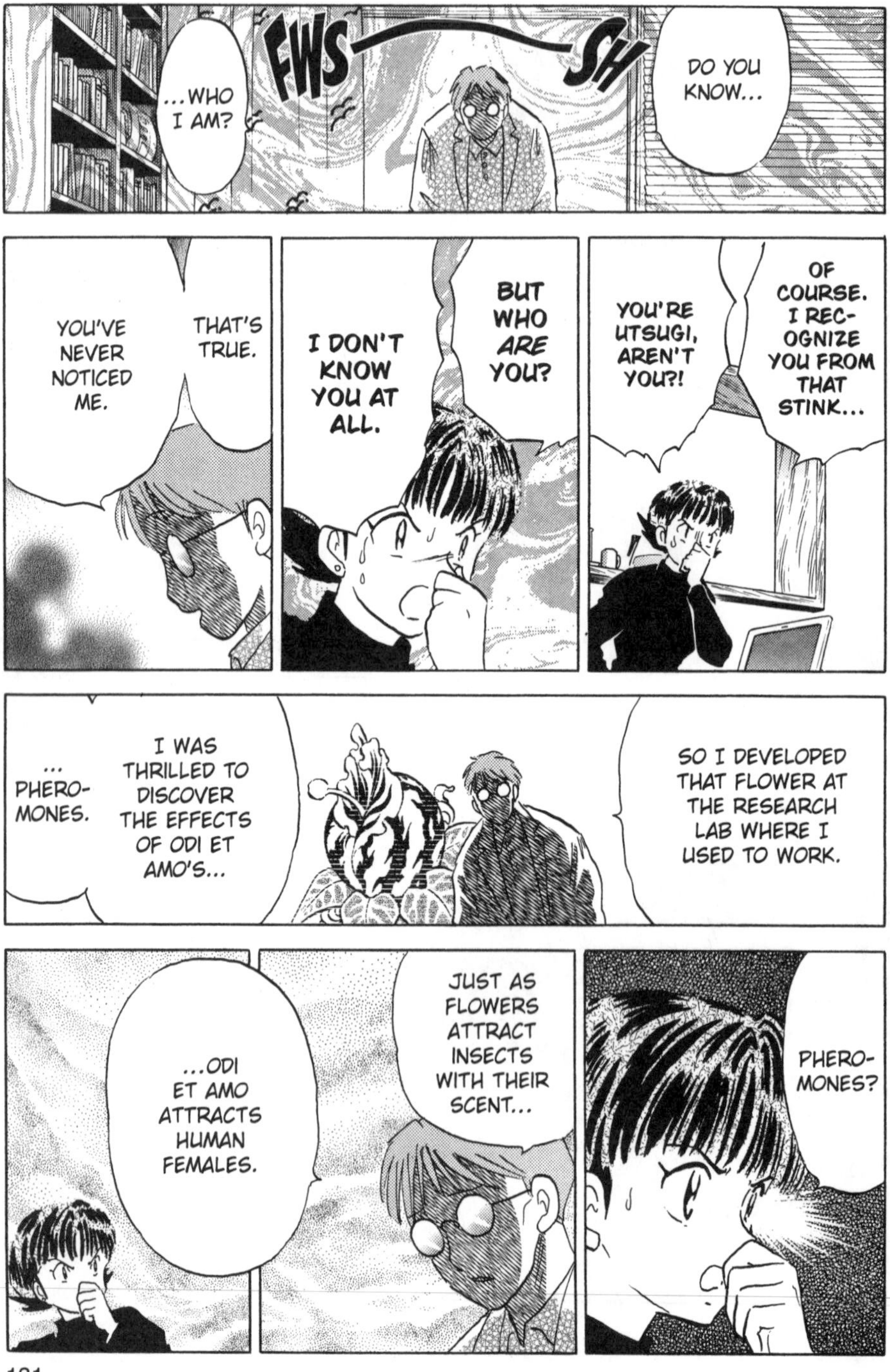
DO YOU KNOW...
FWS—SH
...WHO I AM?
OF COURSE. I RECOGNIZE YOU FROM THAT STINK...
YOU'RE UTSUGI, AREN'T YOU?!
BUT WHO ARE YOU?
I DON'T KNOW YOU AT ALL.
THAT'S TRUE.
YOU'VE NEVER NOTICED ME.
SO I DEVELOPED THAT FLOWER AT THE RESEARCH LAB WHERE I USED TO WORK.
I WAS THRILLED TO DISCOVER THE EFFECTS OF ODI ET AMO'S...
...PHEROMONES.
PHEROMONES?
JUST AS FLOWERS ATTRACT INSECTS WITH THEIR SCENT...
...ODI ET AMO ATTRACTS HUMAN FEMALES.

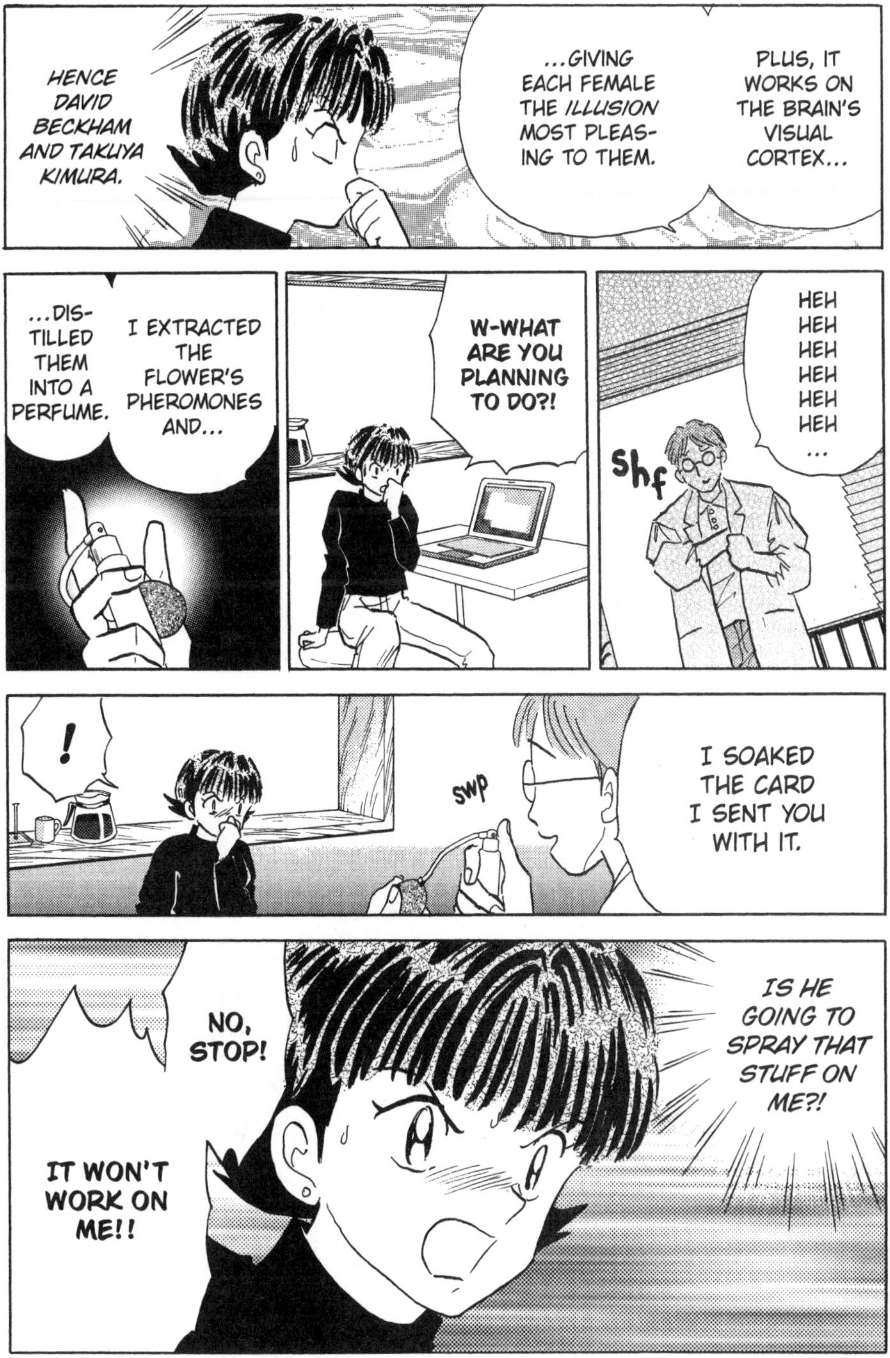
PLUS, IT WORKS ON THE BRAIN'S VISUAL CORTEX...
...GIVING EACH FEMALE THE *ILLUSION* MOST PLEASING TO THEM.
HENCE DAVID BECKHAM AND TAKUYA KIMURA.
HEH HEH HEH HEH HEH HEH ...
shf
W-WHAT ARE YOU PLANNING TO DO?!
I EXTRACTED THE FLOWER'S PHEROMONES AND...
...DISTILLED THEM INTO A PERFUME.
I SOAKED THE CARD I SENT YOU WITH IT.
swp
!
IS HE GOING TO SPRAY THAT STUFF ON ME?!
NO, STOP!
IT WON'T WORK ON ME!!

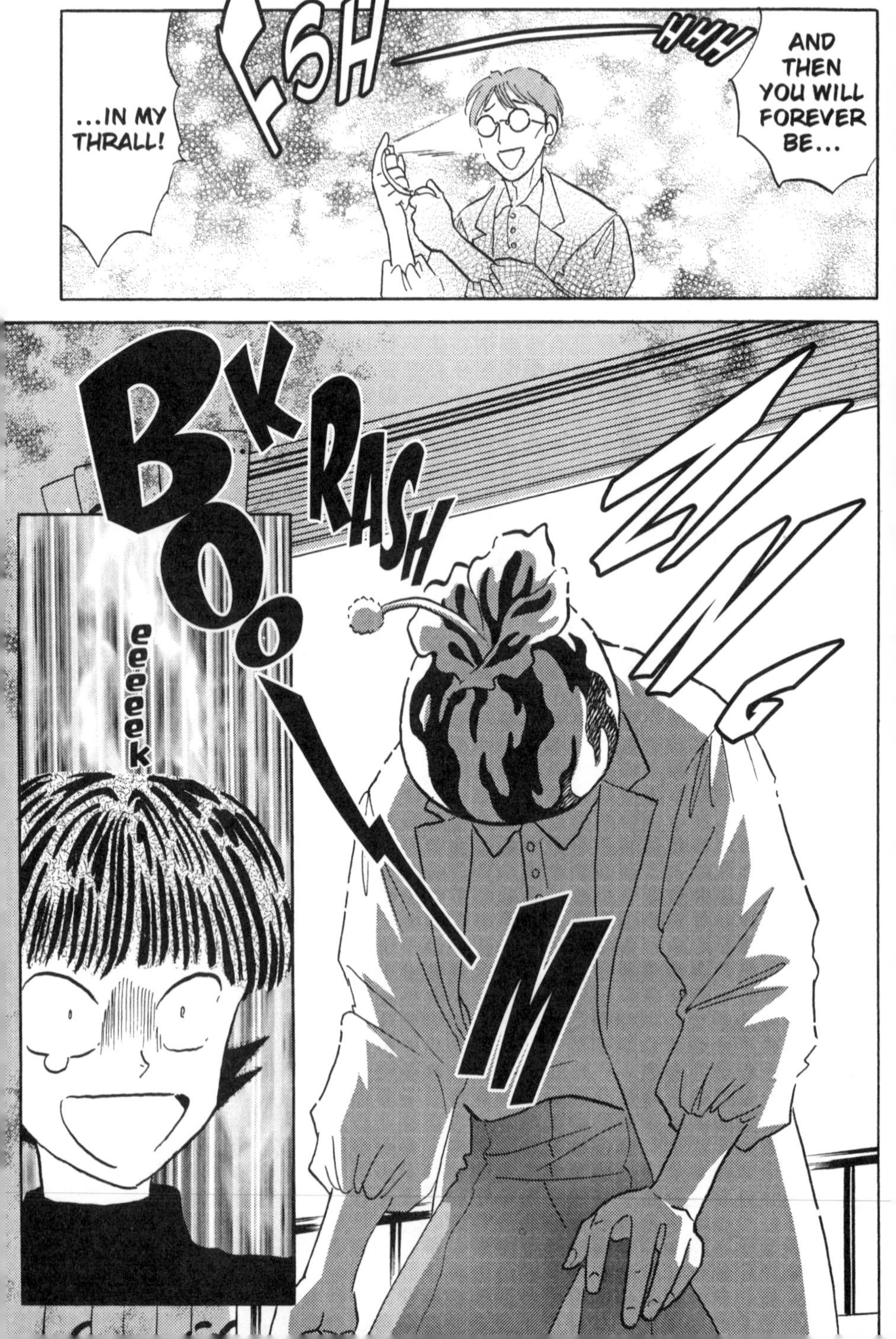
AND THEN YOU WILL FOREVER BE…
FSHHHH
…IN MY THRALL!
BKRASH
BOOOM
eeeeeek

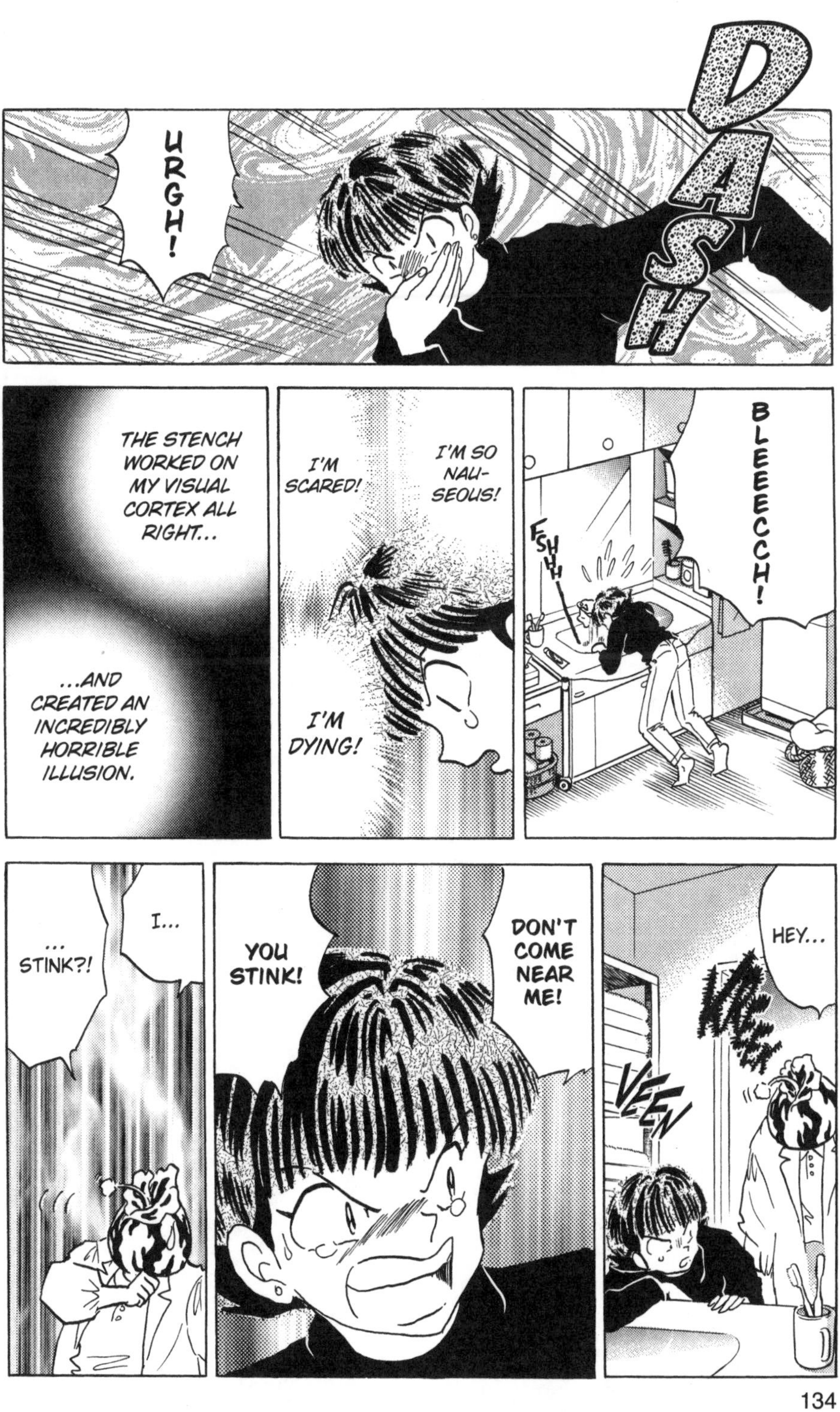
DASH
URGH!
BLEEEECCH!
FSHHH
I'M SO NAUSEOUS!
I'M SCARED!
I'M DYING!
THE STENCH WORKED ON MY VISUAL CORTEX ALL RIGHT...
...AND CREATED AN INCREDIBLY HORRIBLE ILLUSION.
HEY...
VEEN
DON'T COME NEAR ME!
YOU STINK!
I...
... STINK?!

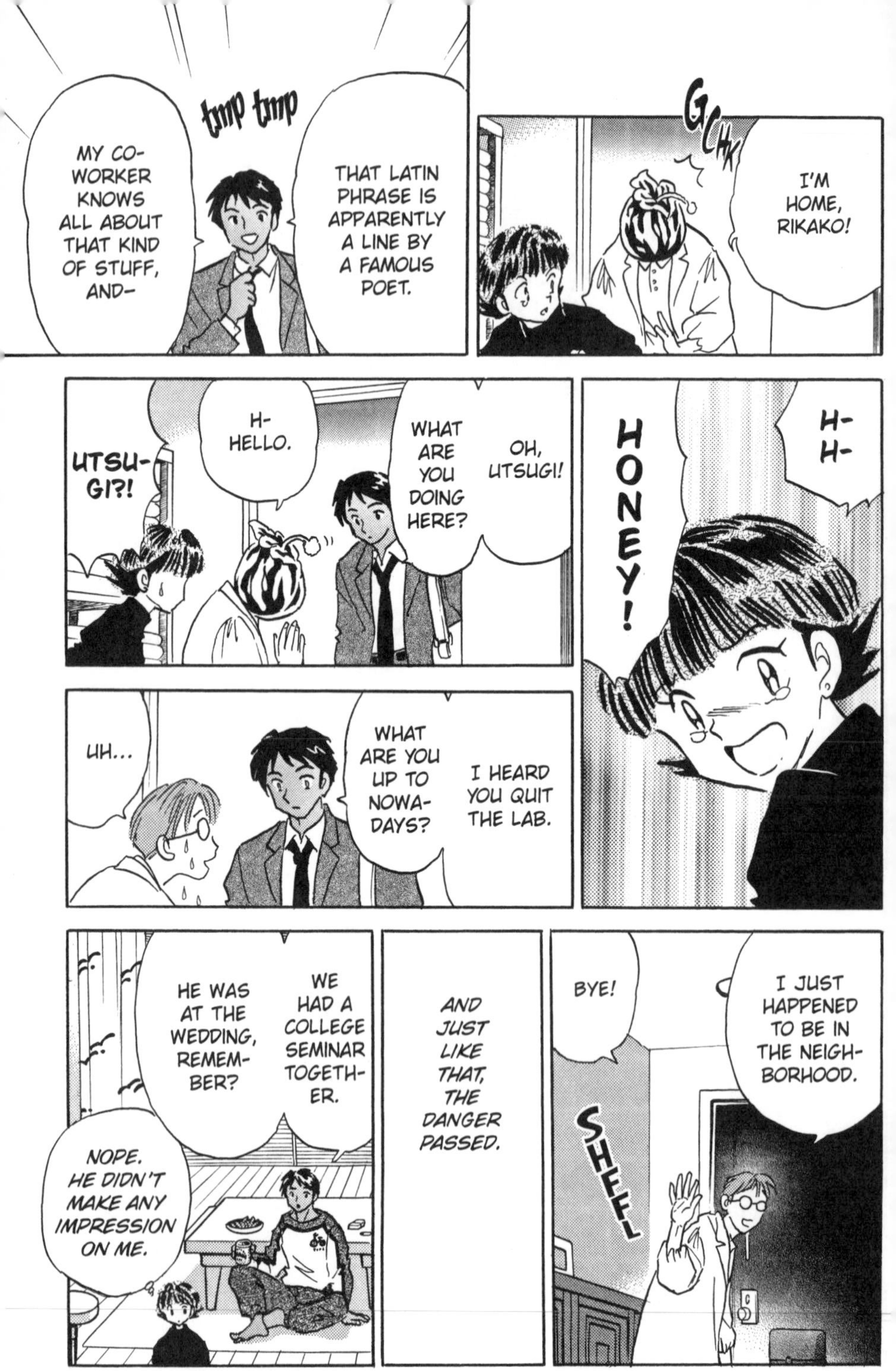
GCHK
I'M HOME, RIKAKO!
THAT LATIN PHRASE IS APPARENTLY A LINE BY A FAMOUS POET.
tmp tmp
MY CO-WORKER KNOWS ALL ABOUT THAT KIND OF STUFF, AND–
H-H-
HONEY!
OH, UTSUGI!
WHAT ARE YOU DOING HERE?
H-HELLO.
UTSUGI?!
I HEARD YOU QUIT THE LAB.
WHAT ARE YOU UP TO NOWADAYS?
UH...
I JUST HAPPENED TO BE IN THE NEIGHBORHOOD.
BYE!
SHEFL
AND JUST LIKE THAT, THE DANGER PASSED.
WE HAD A COLLEGE SEMINAR TOGETHER.
HE WAS AT THE WEDDING, REMEMBER?
NOPE. HE DIDN'T MAKE ANY IMPRESSION ON ME.

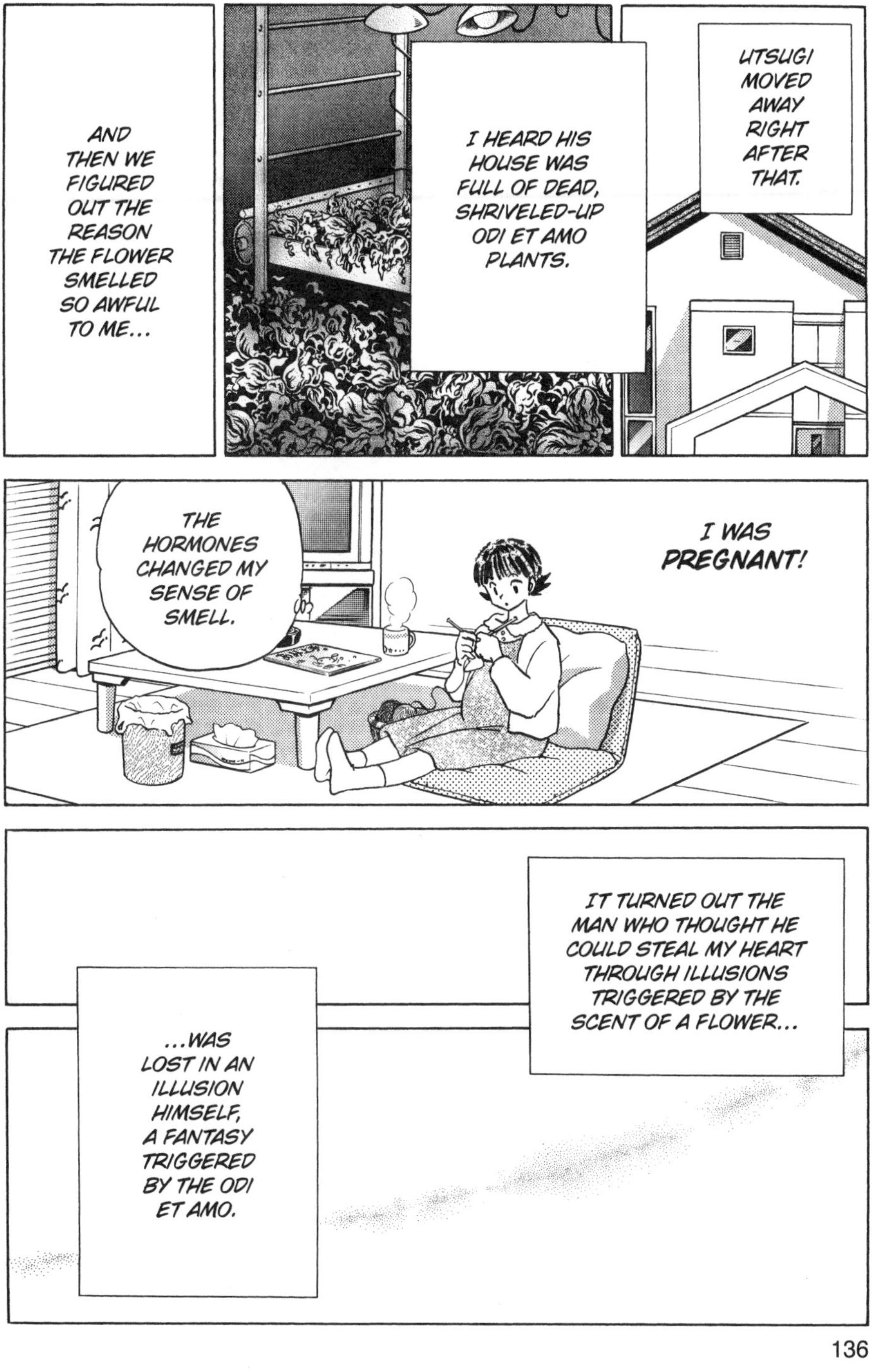
UTSUGI MOVED AWAY RIGHT AFTER THAT.
I HEARD HIS HOUSE WAS FULL OF DEAD, SHRIVELED-UP ODI ET AMO PLANTS.
AND THEN WE FIGURED OUT THE REASON THE FLOWER SMELLED SO AWFUL TO ME...
I WAS **PREGNANT!**
THE HORMONES CHANGED MY SENSE OF SMELL.
IT TURNED OUT THE MAN WHO THOUGHT HE COULD STEAL MY HEART THROUGH ILLUSIONS TRIGGERED BY THE SCENT OF A FLOWER...
...WAS LOST IN AN ILLUSION HIMSELF, A FANTASY TRIGGERED BY THE ODI ET AMO.

With Cat

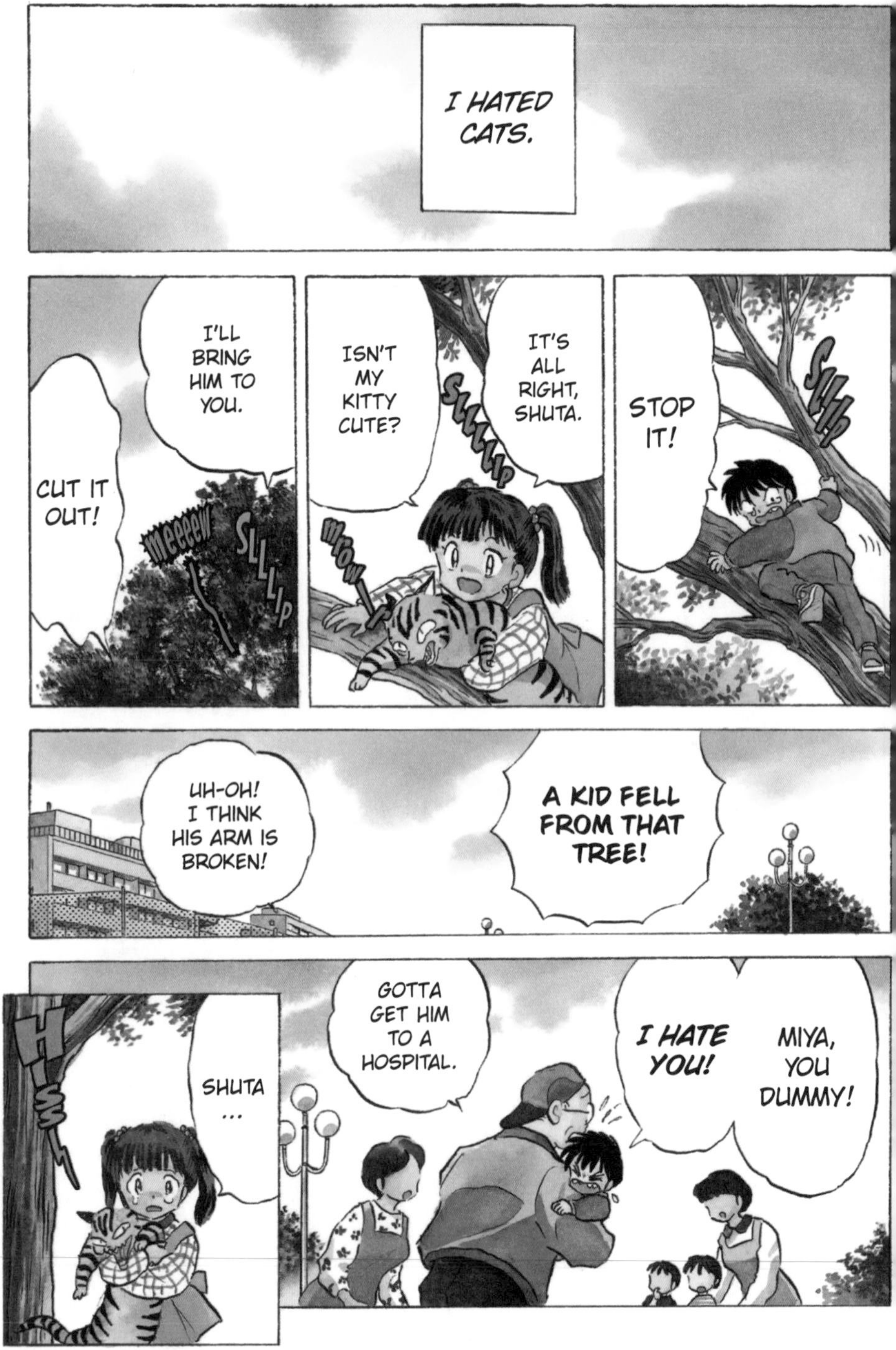
I HATED CATS.
STOP IT!
SLLIP
IT'S ALL RIGHT, SHUTA.
ISN'T MY KITTY CUTE?
SLLLLIP
mrow
I'LL BRING HIM TO YOU.
CUT IT OUT!
meeeew
SLLLLIP
A KID FELL FROM THAT TREE!
UH-OH! I THINK HIS ARM IS BROKEN!
MIYA, YOU DUMMY!
I HATE YOU!
GOTTA GET HIM TO A HOSPITAL.
SHUTA...
HISS

With Cat

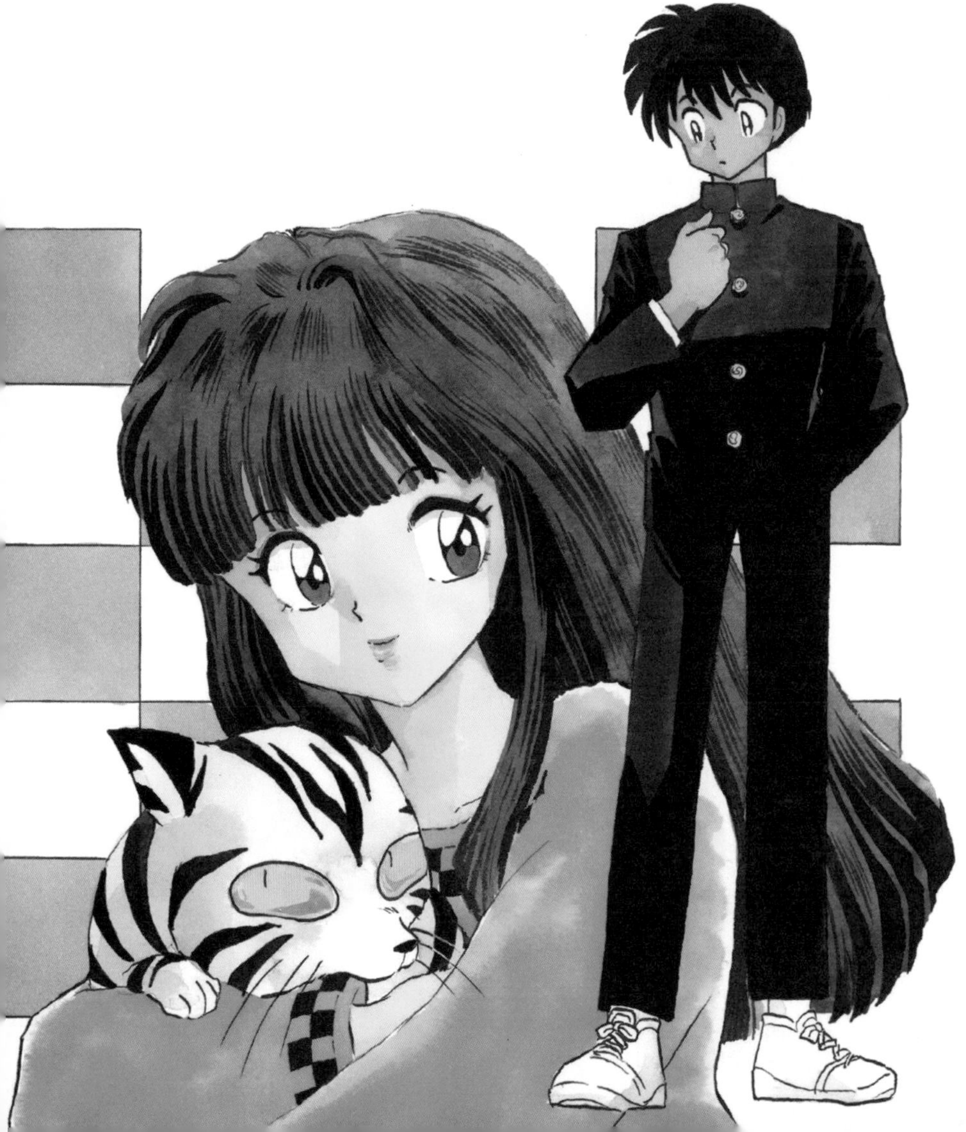

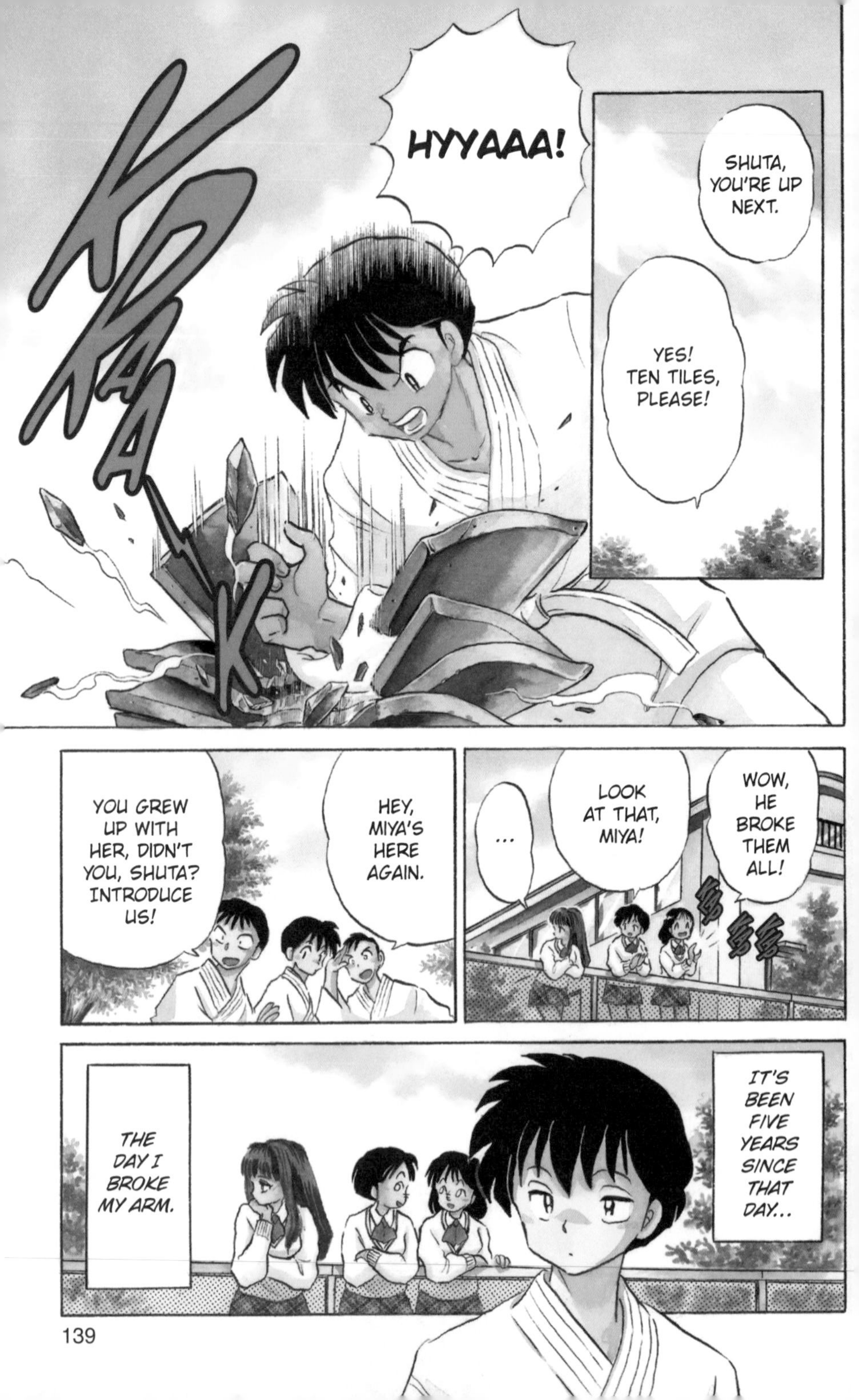
SHUTA, YOU'RE UP NEXT.
YES! TEN TILES, PLEASE!
HYYAAA!
KRAAAK
WOW, HE BROKE THEM ALL!
LOOK AT THAT, MIYA!
...
HEY, MIYA'S HERE AGAIN.
YOU GREW UP WITH HER, DIDN'T YOU, SHUTA? INTRODUCE US!
IT'S BEEN FIVE YEARS SINCE THAT DAY...
THE DAY I BROKE MY ARM.

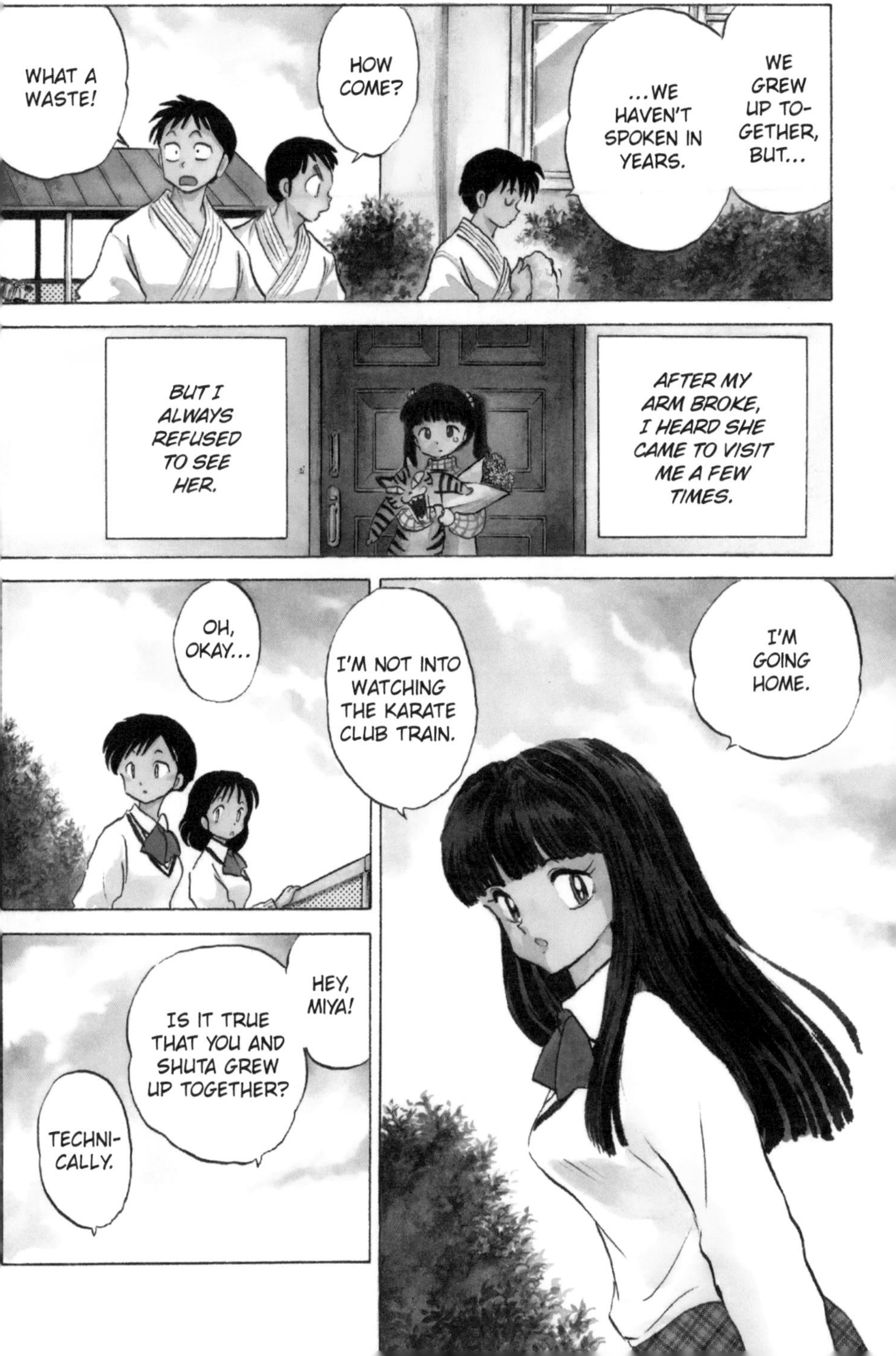
WE GREW UP TO-GETHER, BUT...
...WE HAVEN'T SPOKEN IN YEARS.
HOW COME?
WHAT A WASTE!
AFTER MY ARM BROKE, I HEARD SHE CAME TO VISIT ME A FEW TIMES.
BUT I ALWAYS REFUSED TO SEE HER.
I'M GOING HOME.
I'M NOT INTO WATCHING THE KARATE CLUB TRAIN.
OH, OKAY...
HEY, MIYA!
IS IT TRUE THAT YOU AND SHUTA GREW UP TOGETHER?
TECHNI-CALLY.

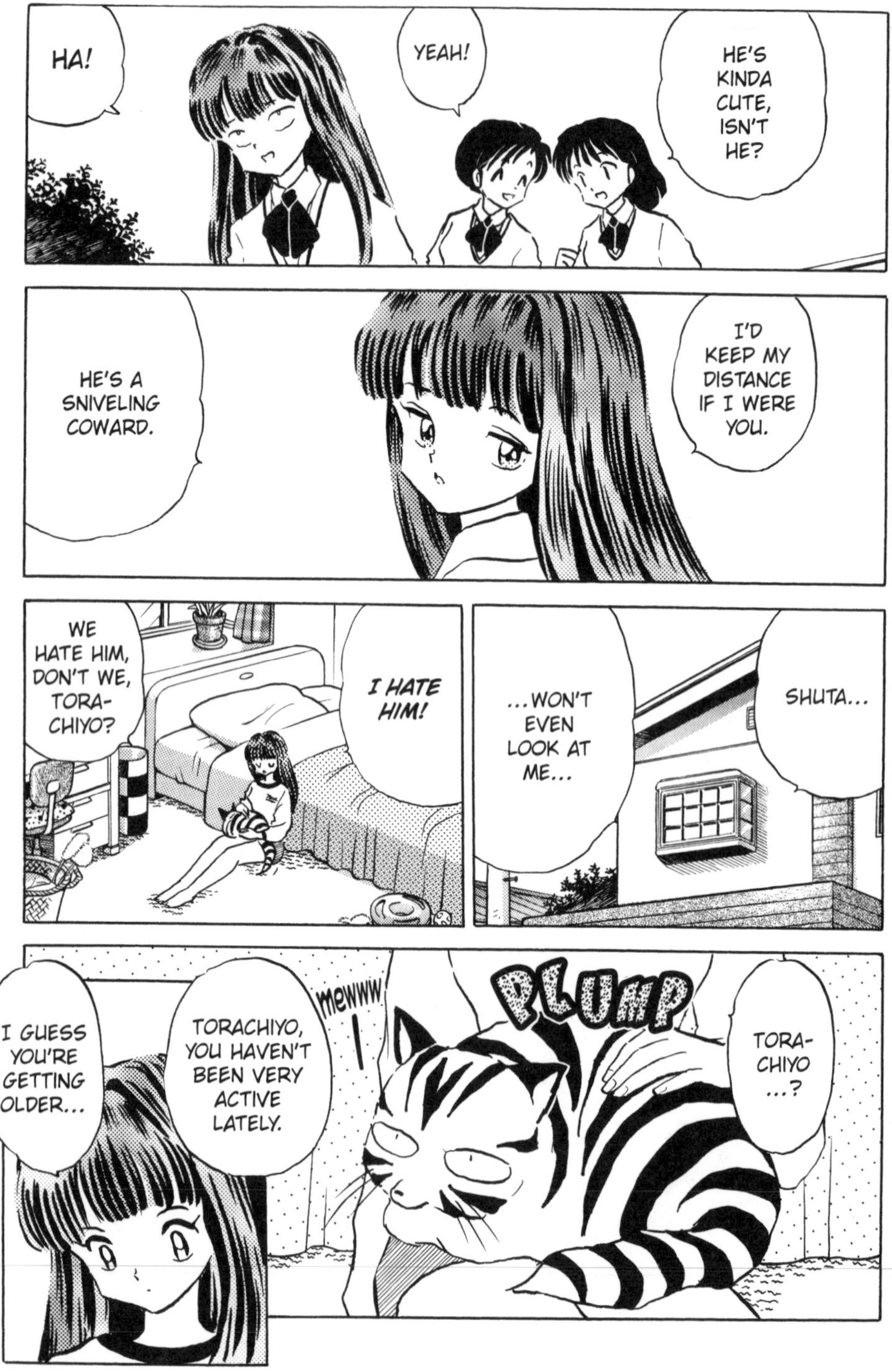
HE'S KINDA CUTE, ISN'T HE?
YEAH!
HA!
I'D KEEP MY DISTANCE IF I WERE YOU.
HE'S A SNIVELING COWARD.
SHUTA...
...WON'T EVEN LOOK AT ME...
I HATE HIM!
WE HATE HIM, DON'T WE, TORA-CHIYO?
TORA-CHIYO ...?
PLUMP
mewww
TORACHIYO, YOU HAVEN'T BEEN VERY ACTIVE LATELY.
I GUESS YOU'RE GETTING OLDER...

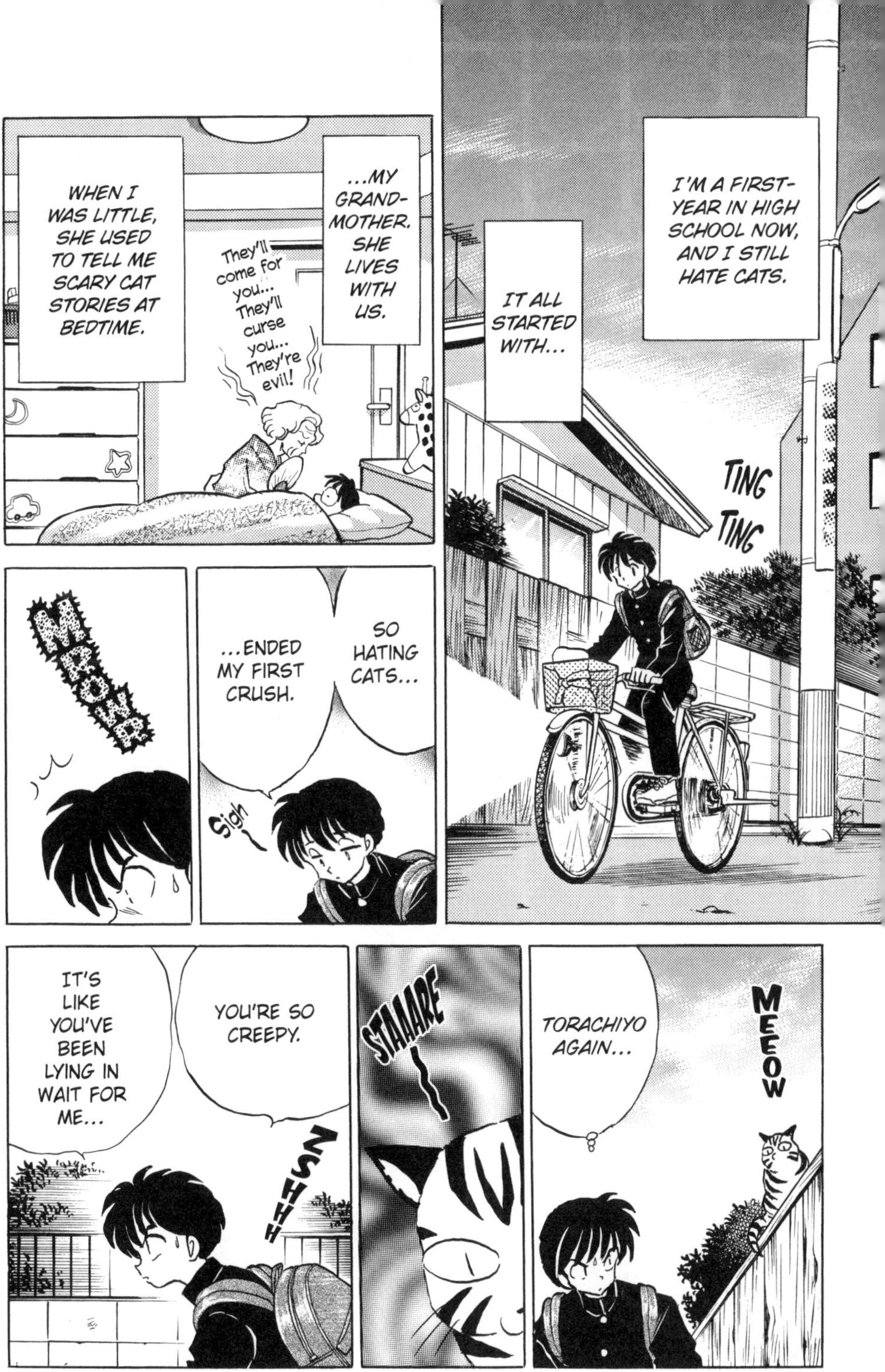
I'M A FIRST-YEAR IN HIGH SCHOOL NOW, AND I STILL HATE CATS.
IT ALL STARTED WITH...
TING
TING
...MY GRANDMOTHER. SHE LIVES WITH US.
WHEN I WAS LITTLE, SHE USED TO TELL ME SCARY CAT STORIES AT BEDTIME.
They'll come for you... They'll curse you... They're evil!
SO HATING CATS...
...ENDED MY FIRST CRUSH.
Sigh
MROWR
MEEOW
TORACHIYO AGAIN...
STAAARE
YOU'RE SO CREEPY.
IT'S LIKE YOU'VE BEEN LYING IN WAIT FOR ME...
NSHHHH

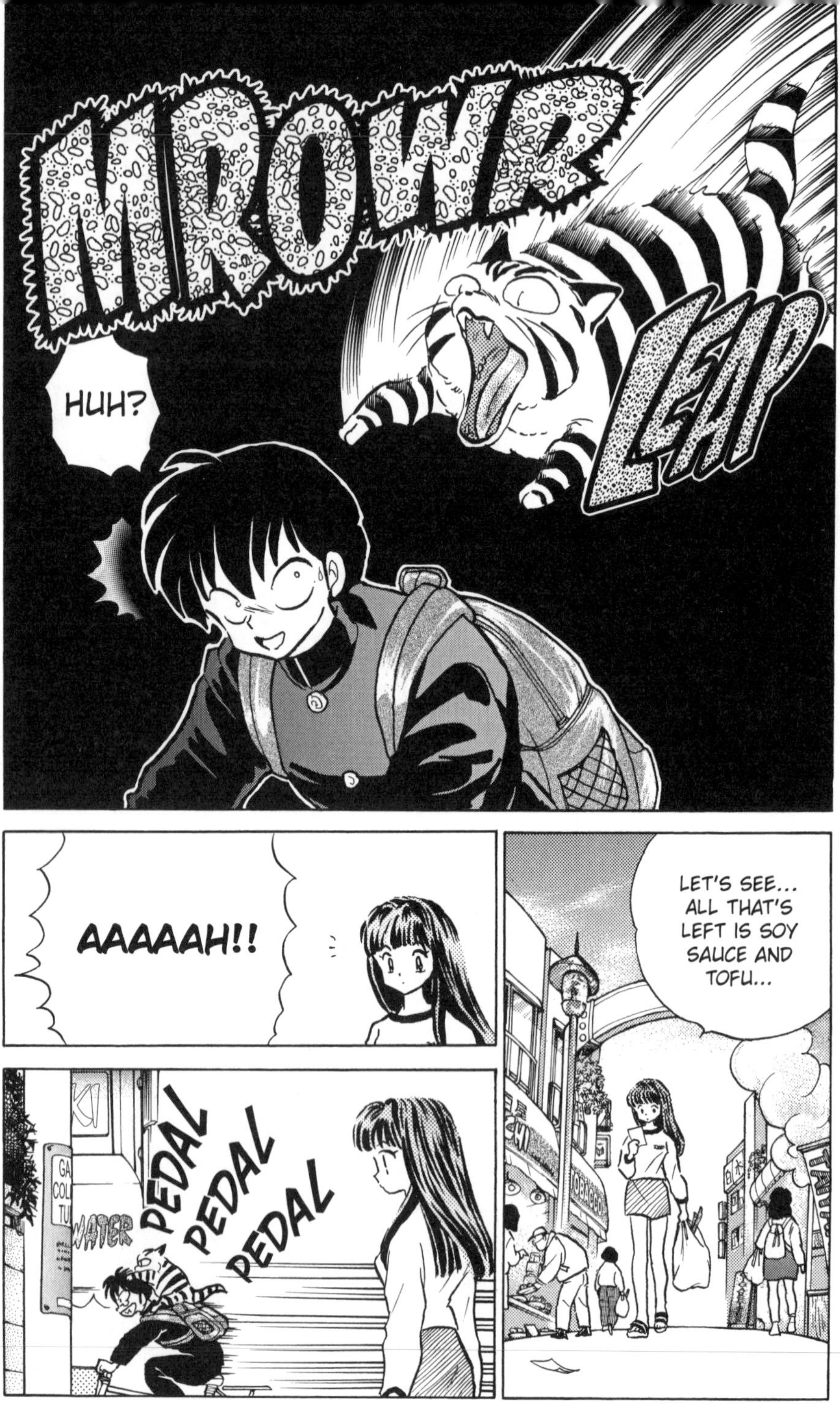
MROWR
LEAP
HUH?
LET'S SEE... ALL THAT'S LEFT IS SOY SAUCE AND TOFU...
AAAAAH!!
PEDAL PEDAL PEDAL

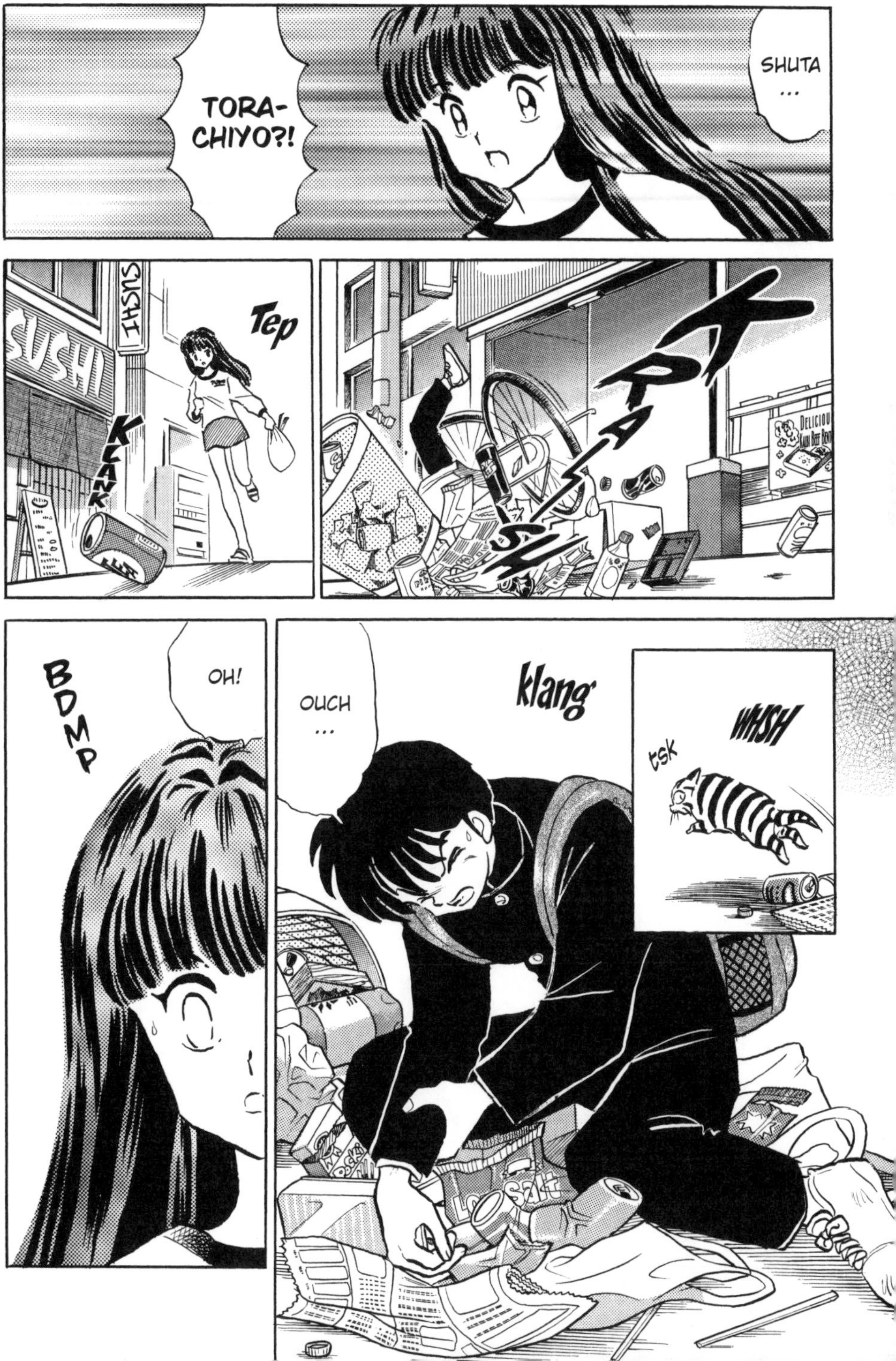
SHUTA ...
TORA-CHIYO?!
KRASH
Tep
SUSHI
SUSHI
KLANK
WHSH
tsk
klang
OUCH ...
OH!
BDMP

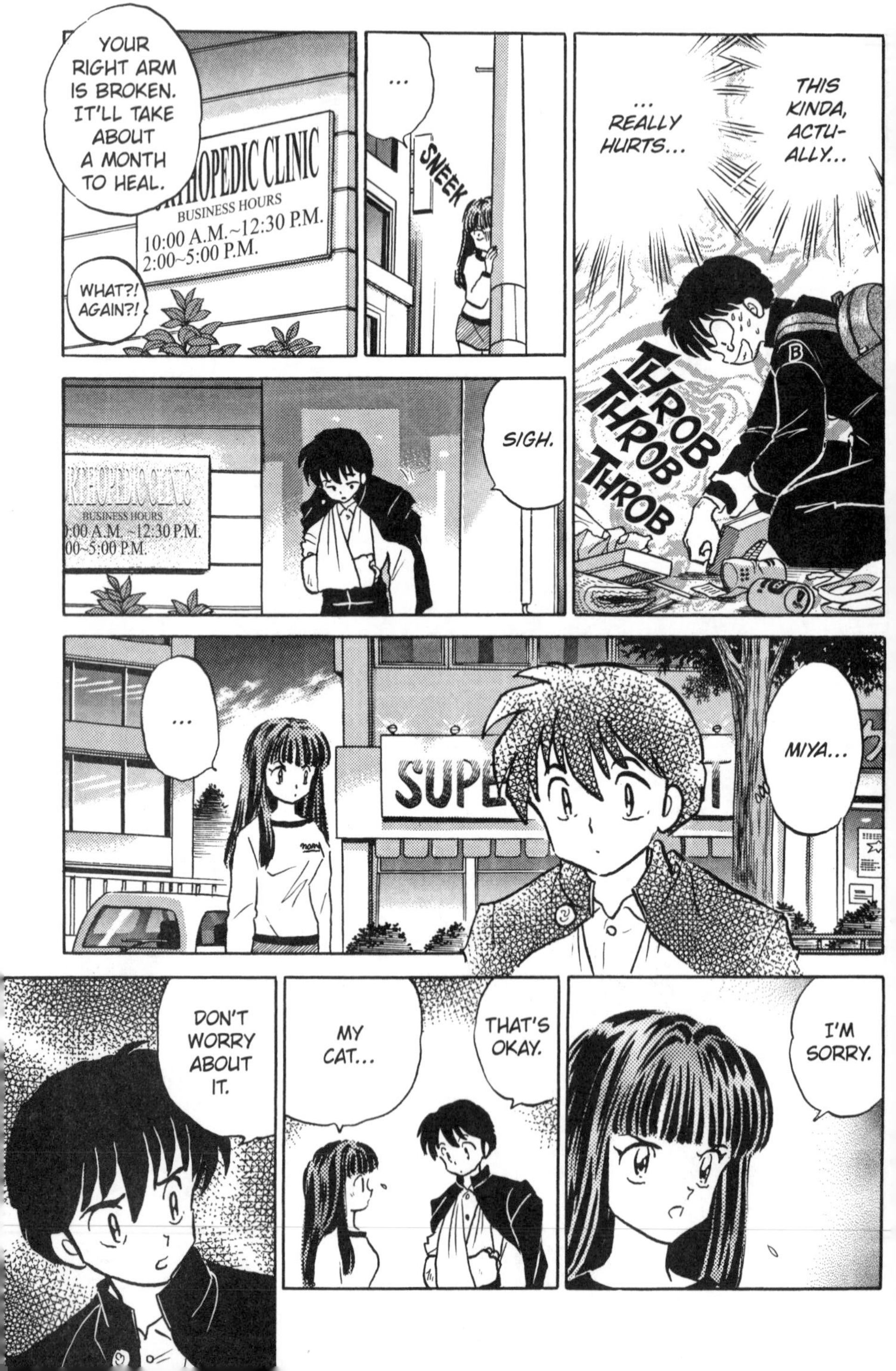
THIS KINDA, ACTUALLY...
... REALLY HURTS...
THROB THROB THROB
...
SNEEK
YOUR RIGHT ARM IS BROKEN. IT'LL TAKE ABOUT A MONTH TO HEAL.
THOPEDIC CLINIC
BUSINESS HOURS
10:00 A.M.~12:30 P.M.
2:00~5:00 P.M.
WHAT?! AGAIN?!
SIGH.
MIYA...
...
I'M SORRY.
THAT'S OKAY.
MY CAT...
DON'T WORRY ABOUT IT.

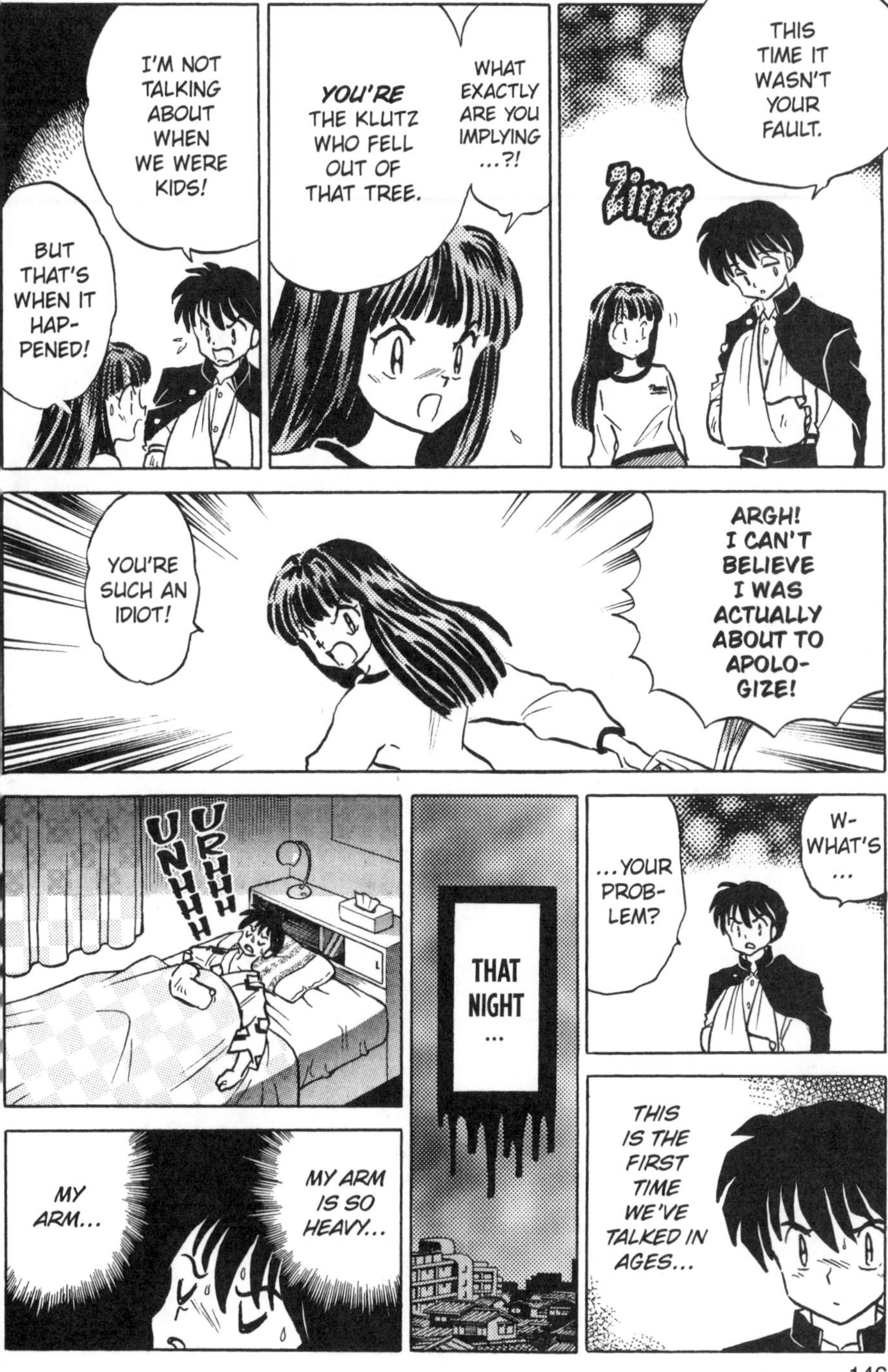
THIS TIME IT WASN'T YOUR FAULT.
Zing
WHAT EXACTLY ARE YOU IMPLYING ...?!
YOU'RE THE KLUTZ WHO FELL OUT OF THAT TREE.
I'M NOT TALKING ABOUT WHEN WE WERE KIDS!
BUT THAT'S WHEN IT HAP-PENED!
ARGH! I CAN'T BELIEVE I WAS ACTUALLY ABOUT TO APOLO-GIZE!
YOU'RE SUCH AN IDIOT!
W-WHAT'S ...
...YOUR PROB-LEM?
THIS IS THE FIRST TIME WE'VE TALKED IN AGES...
THAT NIGHT ...
URHHH
UNHHHH
MY ARM IS SO HEAVY...
MY ARM...

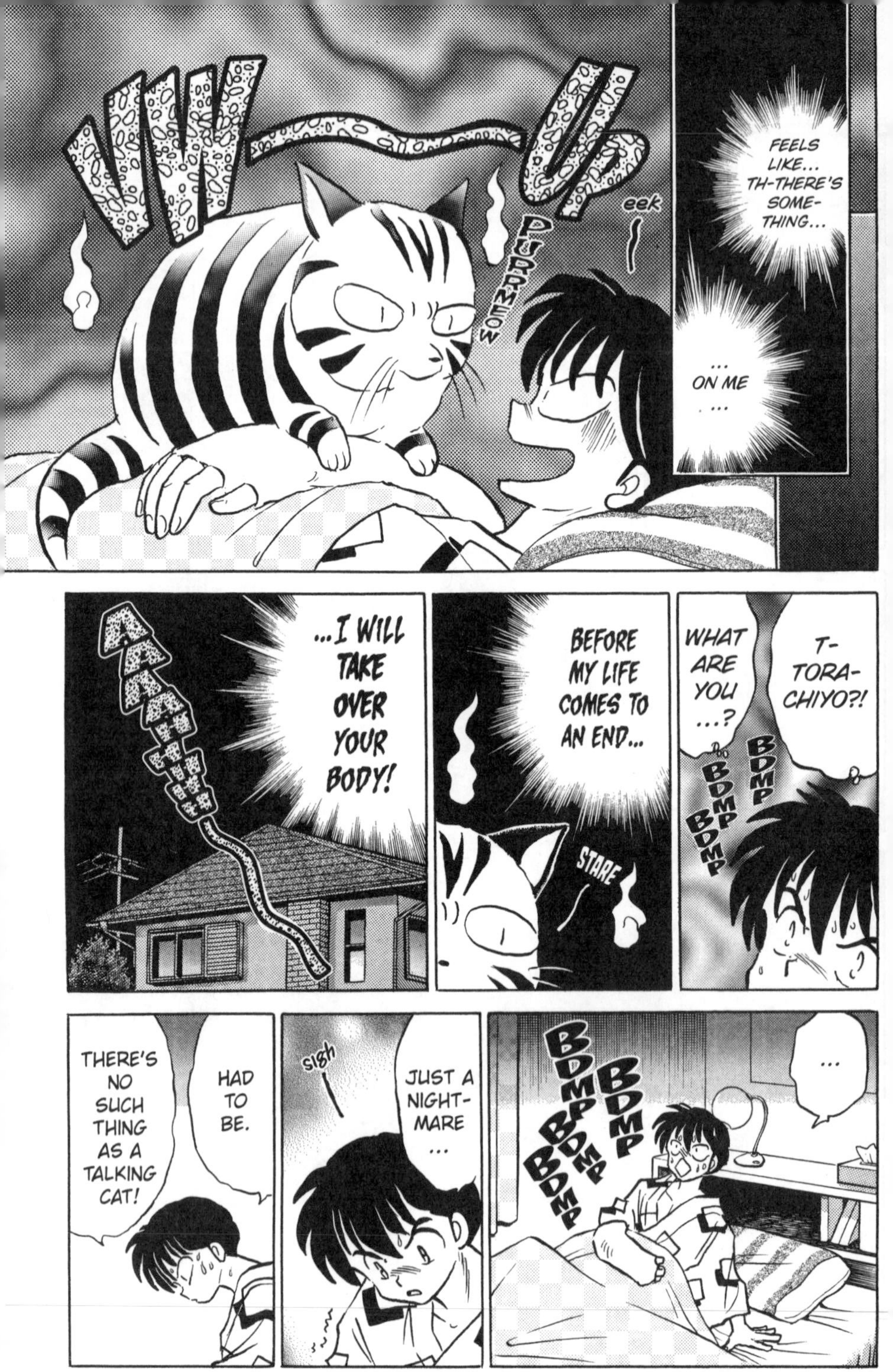
FEELS LIKE... TH-THERE'S SOME-THING...
... ON ME ...
VWW—UP
eek
PURRMEOW
T-TORA-CHIYO?!
WHAT ARE YOU ...?
BDMP BDMP BDMP BDMP
BEFORE MY LIFE COMES TO AN END...
STARE
...I WILL TAKE OVER YOUR BODY!
AAAAH
...
BDMP BDMP BDMP BDMP
JUST A NIGHT-MARE ...
sigh
HAD TO BE.
THERE'S NO SUCH THING AS A TALKING CAT!

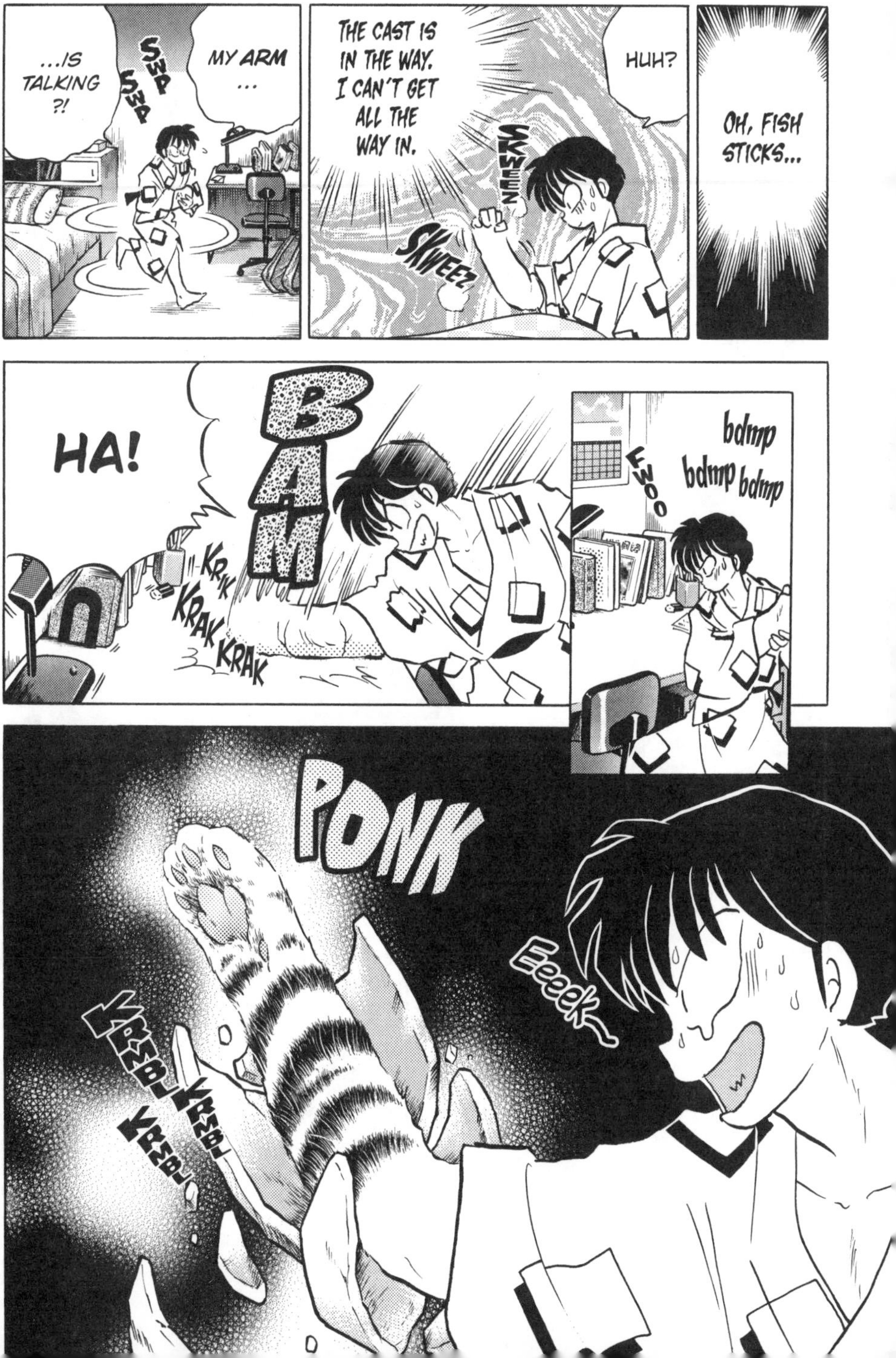
OH, FISH STICKS...
HUH?
THE CAST IS IN THE WAY. I CAN'T GET ALL THE WAY IN.
SKWEEZ
SKWEEZ
MY ARM ...
...IS TALKING ?!
SWP
SWP
bdmp
bdmp bdmp
FWOO
HA!
BAM
KRIK
KRAK
KRAK
PONK
Eeeek~
KRMBL
KRMBL
KRMBL

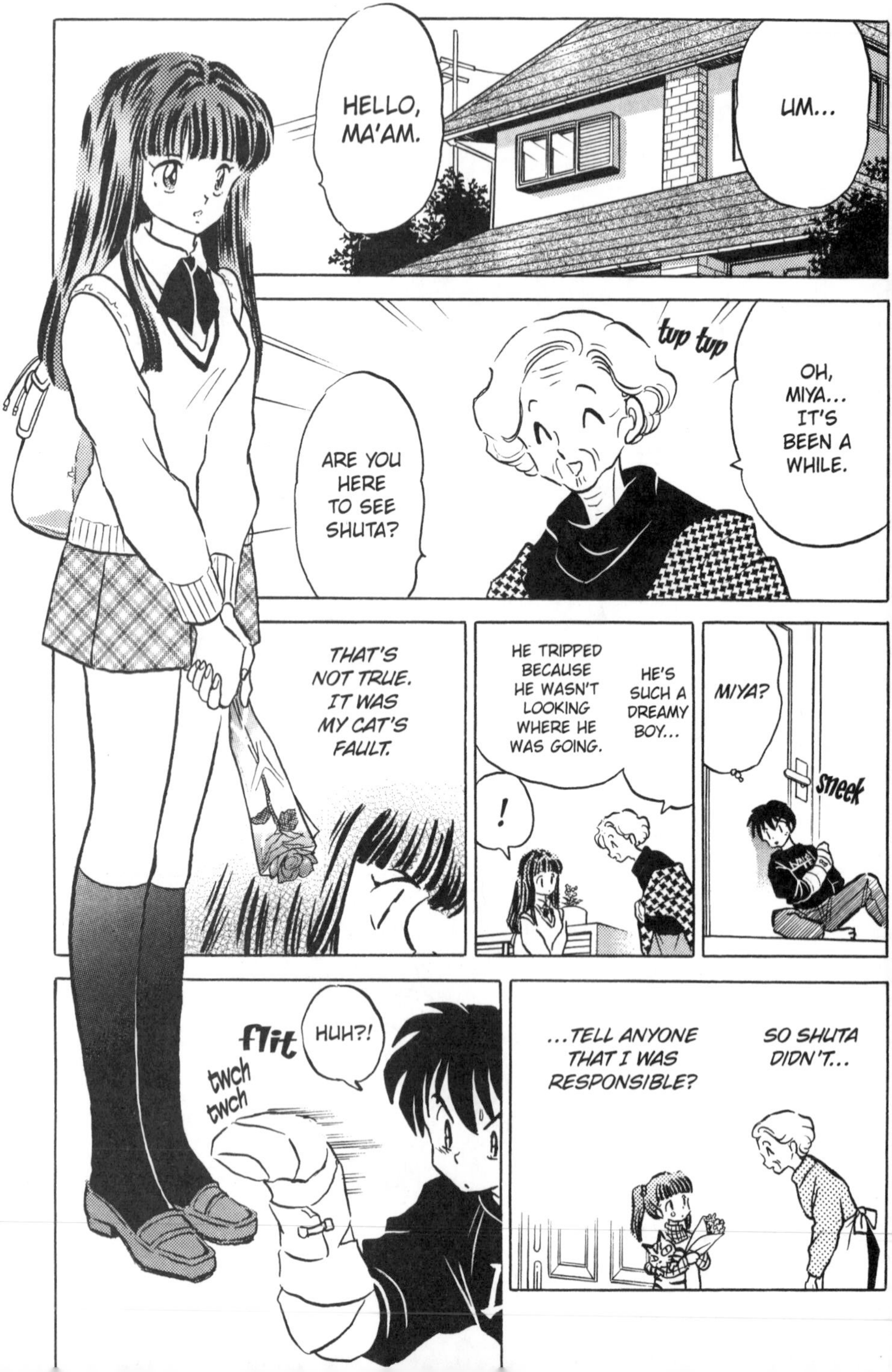
UM...
HELLO, MA'AM.
tup tup
OH, MIYA... IT'S BEEN A WHILE.
ARE YOU HERE TO SEE SHUTA?
MIYA?
sneek
HE'S SUCH A DREAMY BOY...
HE TRIPPED BECAUSE HE WASN'T LOOKING WHERE HE WAS GOING.
!
THAT'S NOT TRUE. IT WAS MY CAT'S FAULT.
SO SHUTA DIDN'T...
...TELL ANYONE THAT I WAS RESPONSIBLE?
HUH?!
flit
twch twch

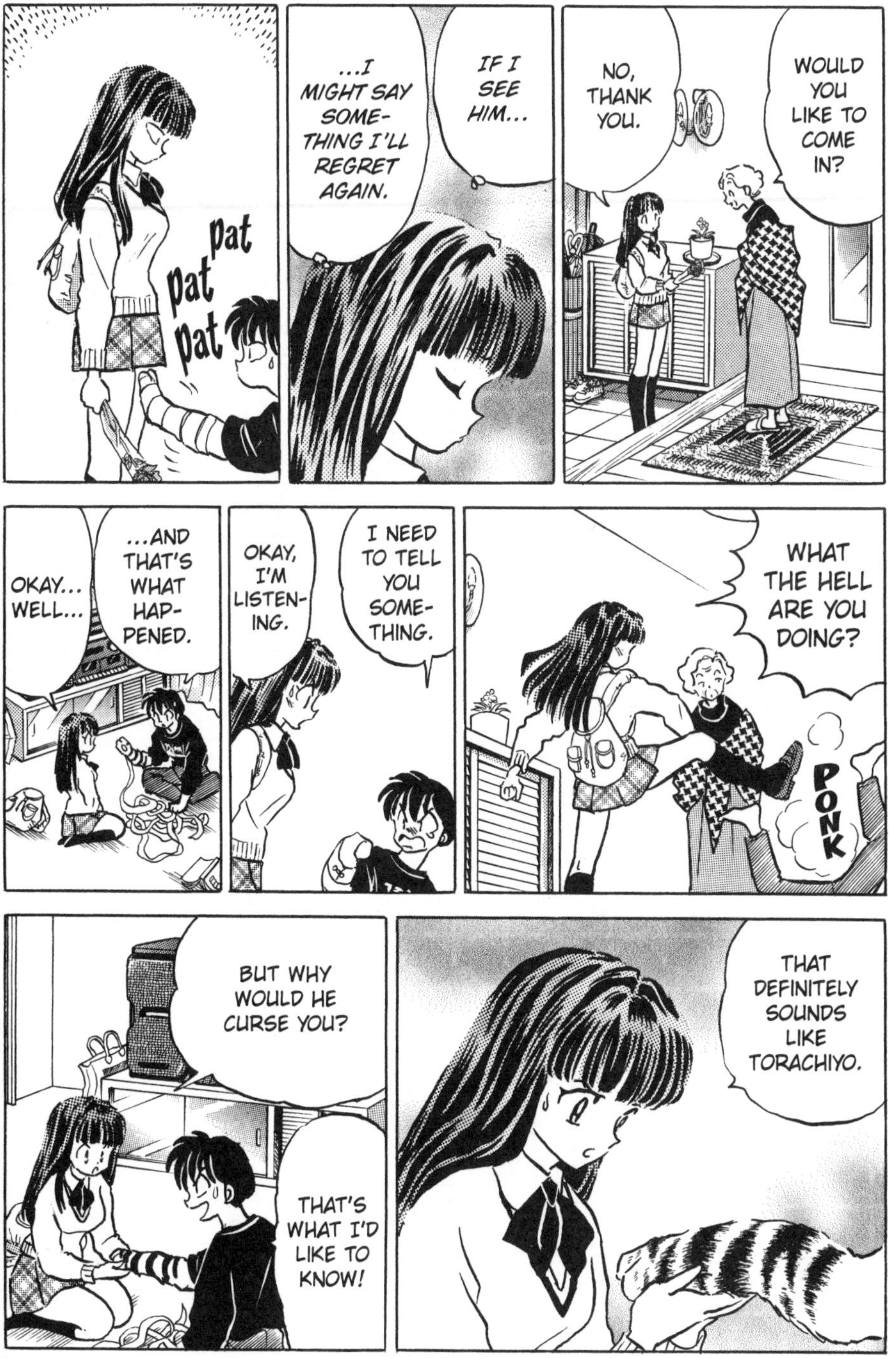
WOULD YOU LIKE TO COME IN?
NO, THANK YOU.
IF I SEE HIM...
...I MIGHT SAY SOME-THING I'LL REGRET AGAIN.
pat pat pat
WHAT THE HELL ARE YOU DOING?
PONK
I NEED TO TELL YOU SOME-THING.
OKAY, I'M LISTEN-ING.
...AND THAT'S WHAT HAP-PENED.
OKAY... WELL...
THAT DEFINITELY SOUNDS LIKE TORACHIYO.
BUT WHY WOULD HE CURSE YOU?
THAT'S WHAT I'D LIKE TO KNOW!

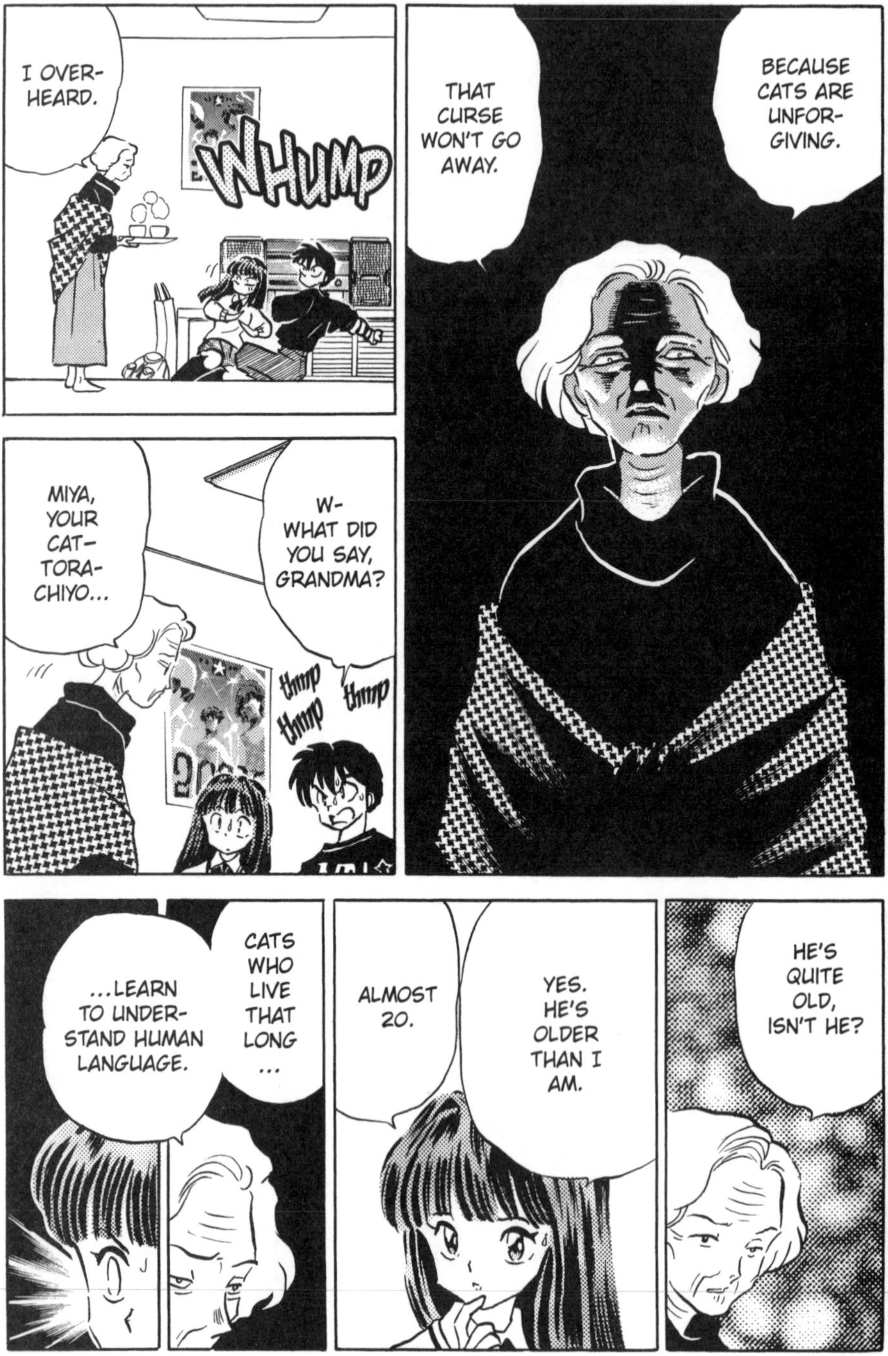
BECAUSE CATS ARE UNFOR-GIVING.
THAT CURSE WON'T GO AWAY.
I OVER-HEARD.
WHUMP
MIYA, YOUR CAT-TORA-CHIYO...
W-WHAT DID YOU SAY, GRANDMA?
thmp thmp thmp
HE'S QUITE OLD, ISN'T HE?
YES. HE'S OLDER THAN I AM.
ALMOST 20.
CATS WHO LIVE THAT LONG ...
...LEARN TO UNDER-STAND HUMAN LANGUAGE.

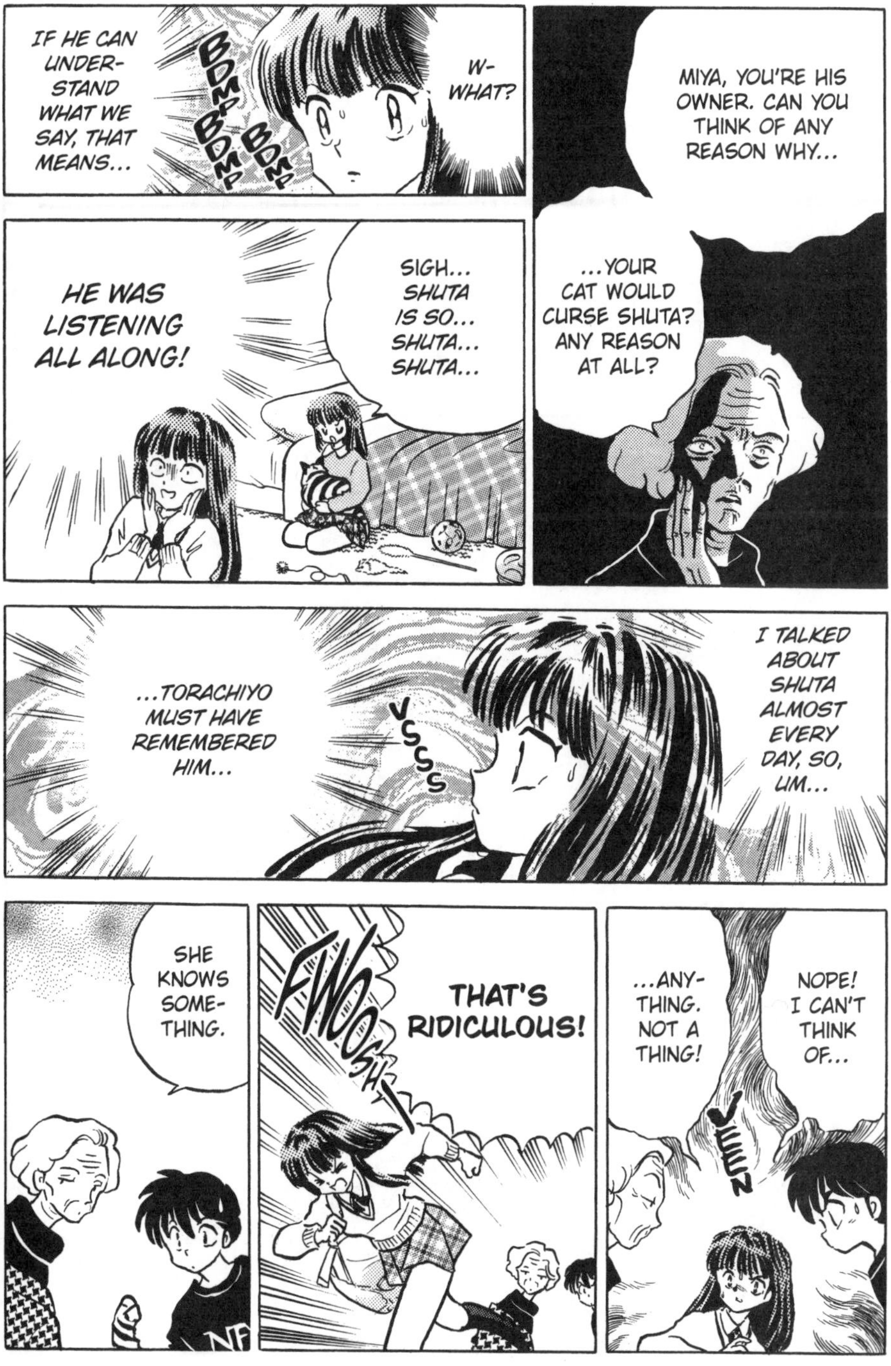
MIYA, YOU'RE HIS OWNER. CAN YOU THINK OF ANY REASON WHY...
...YOUR CAT WOULD CURSE SHUTA? ANY REASON AT ALL?
W-WHAT?
BDMP BDMP BDMP
IF HE CAN UNDER-STAND WHAT WE SAY, THAT MEANS...
SIGH... SHUTA IS SO... SHUTA... SHUTA...
HE WAS LISTENING ALL ALONG!
I TALKED ABOUT SHUTA ALMOST EVERY DAY, SO, UM...
VSSS
...TORACHIYO MUST HAVE REMEMBERED HIM...
NOPE! I CAN'T THINK OF...
...ANY-THING. NOT A THING!
JEEEN
THAT'S RIDICULOUS!
FWOOSH
SHE KNOWS SOME-THING.

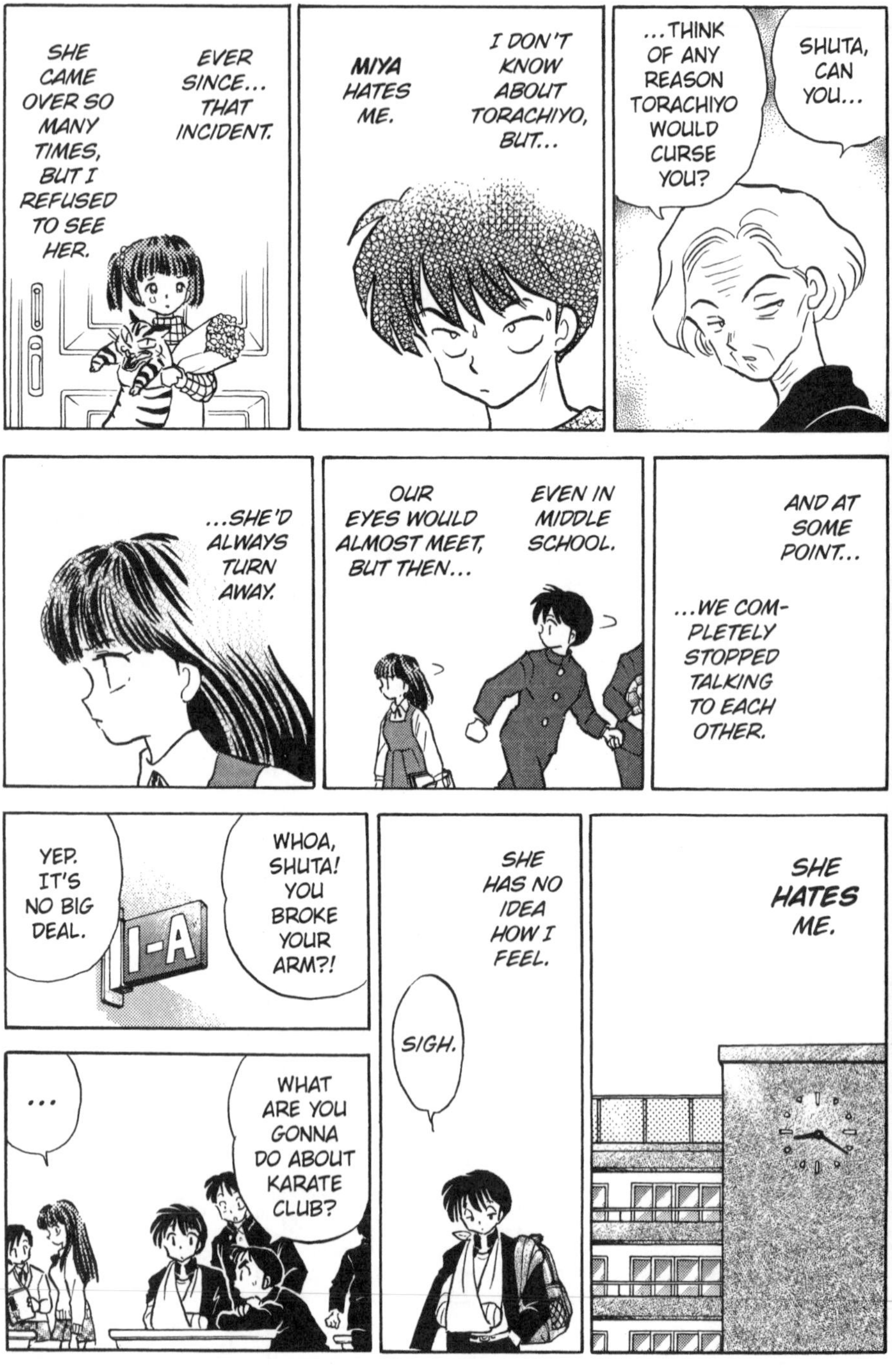
SHUTA, CAN YOU...
...THINK OF ANY REASON TORACHIYO WOULD CURSE YOU?
I DON'T KNOW ABOUT TORACHIYO, BUT...
MIYA HATES ME.
EVER SINCE... THAT INCIDENT.
SHE CAME OVER SO MANY TIMES, BUT I REFUSED TO SEE HER.
AND AT SOME POINT...
...WE COMPLETELY STOPPED TALKING TO EACH OTHER.
EVEN IN MIDDLE SCHOOL.
OUR EYES WOULD ALMOST MEET, BUT THEN...
...SHE'D ALWAYS TURN AWAY.
SHE HATES ME.
SHE HAS NO IDEA HOW I FEEL.
SIGH.
WHOA, SHUTA! YOU BROKE YOUR ARM?!
1-A
YEP. IT'S NO BIG DEAL.
WHAT ARE YOU GONNA DO ABOUT KARATE CLUB?
...

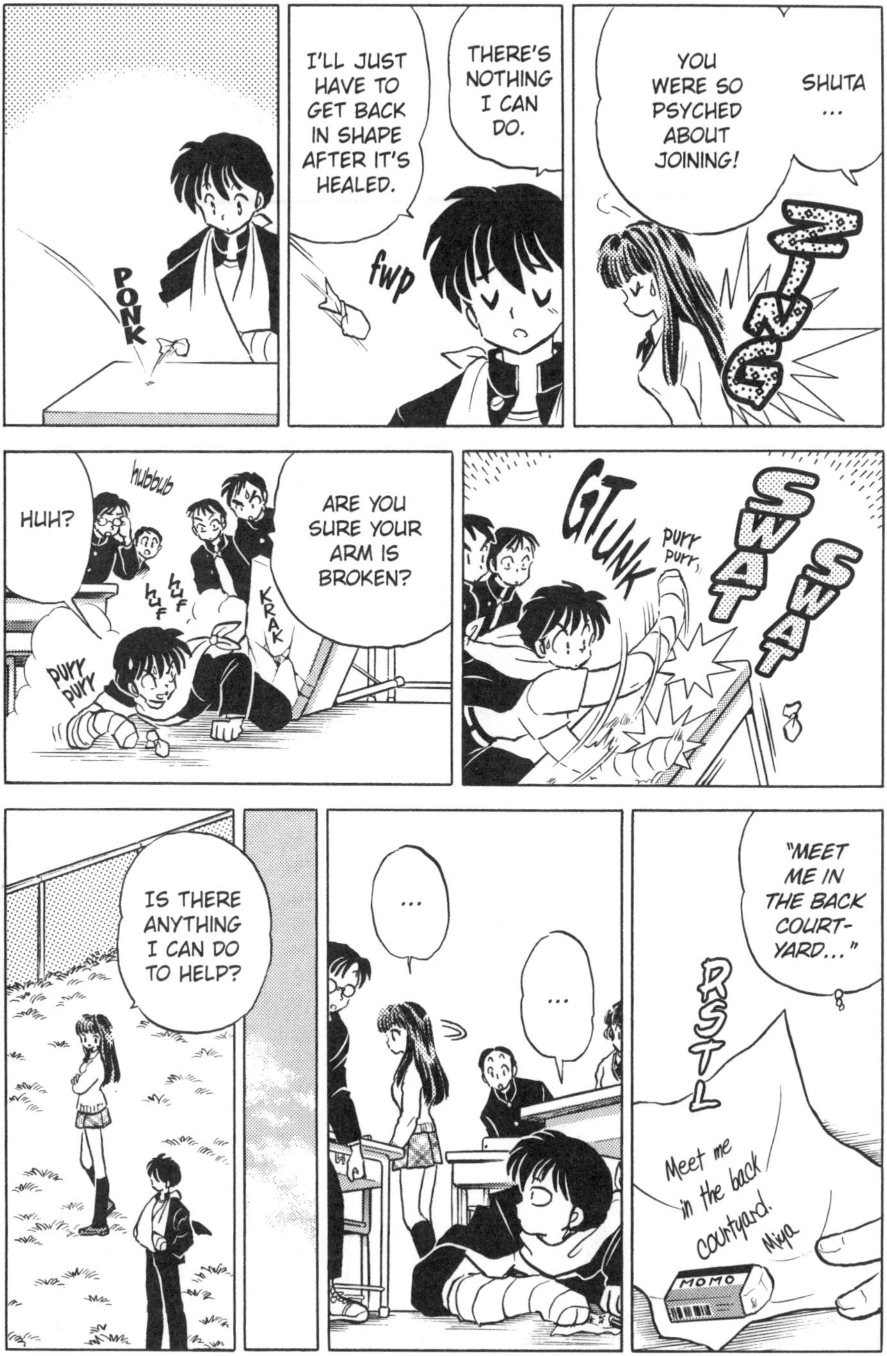
SHUTA...
YOU WERE SO PSYCHED ABOUT JOINING!
ZING
THERE'S NOTHING I CAN DO.
I'LL JUST HAVE TO GET BACK IN SHAPE AFTER IT'S HEALED.
fwp
PONK
SWAT
SWAT
GTUNK
purr purr,
ARE YOU SURE YOUR ARM IS BROKEN?
hubbub
HUH?
huff huff
KRAK
purr purr
"MEET ME IN THE BACK COURTYARD..."
RSTL
Meet me in the back courtyard. Miya
MOMO
...
...
IS THERE ANYTHING I CAN DO TO HELP?

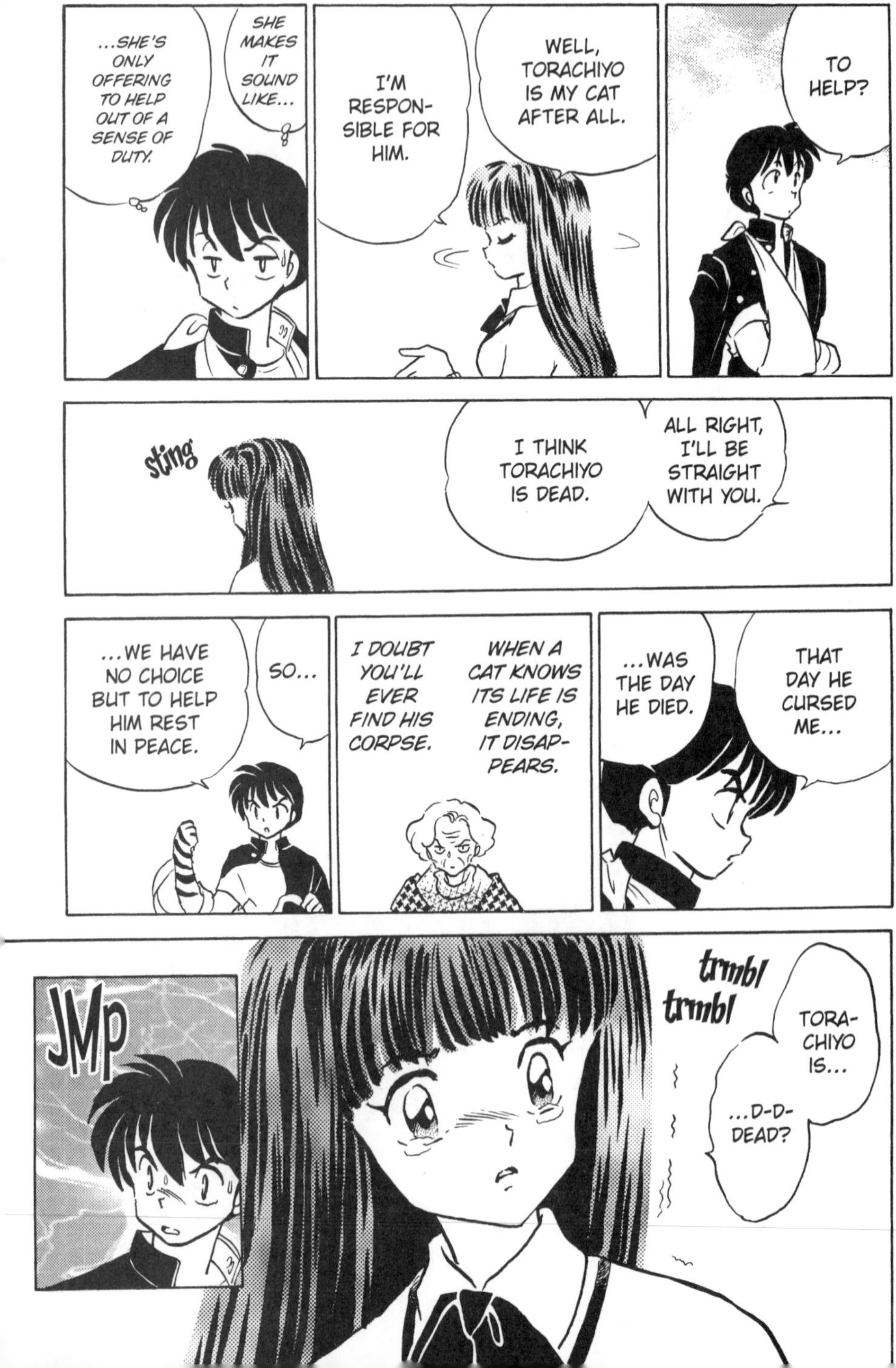
TO HELP?
WELL, TORACHIYO IS MY CAT AFTER ALL.
I'M RESPONSIBLE FOR HIM.
SHE MAKES IT SOUND LIKE...
...SHE'S ONLY OFFERING TO HELP OUT OF A SENSE OF DUTY.
ALL RIGHT, I'LL BE STRAIGHT WITH YOU.
I THINK TORACHIYO IS DEAD.
sting
THAT DAY HE CURSED ME...
...WAS THE DAY HE DIED.
WHEN A CAT KNOWS ITS LIFE IS ENDING, IT DISAPPEARS.
I DOUBT YOU'LL EVER FIND HIS CORPSE.
SO...
...WE HAVE NO CHOICE BUT TO HELP HIM REST IN PEACE.
trmbl
trmbl
TORACHIYO IS...
...D-D-DEAD?
JMP

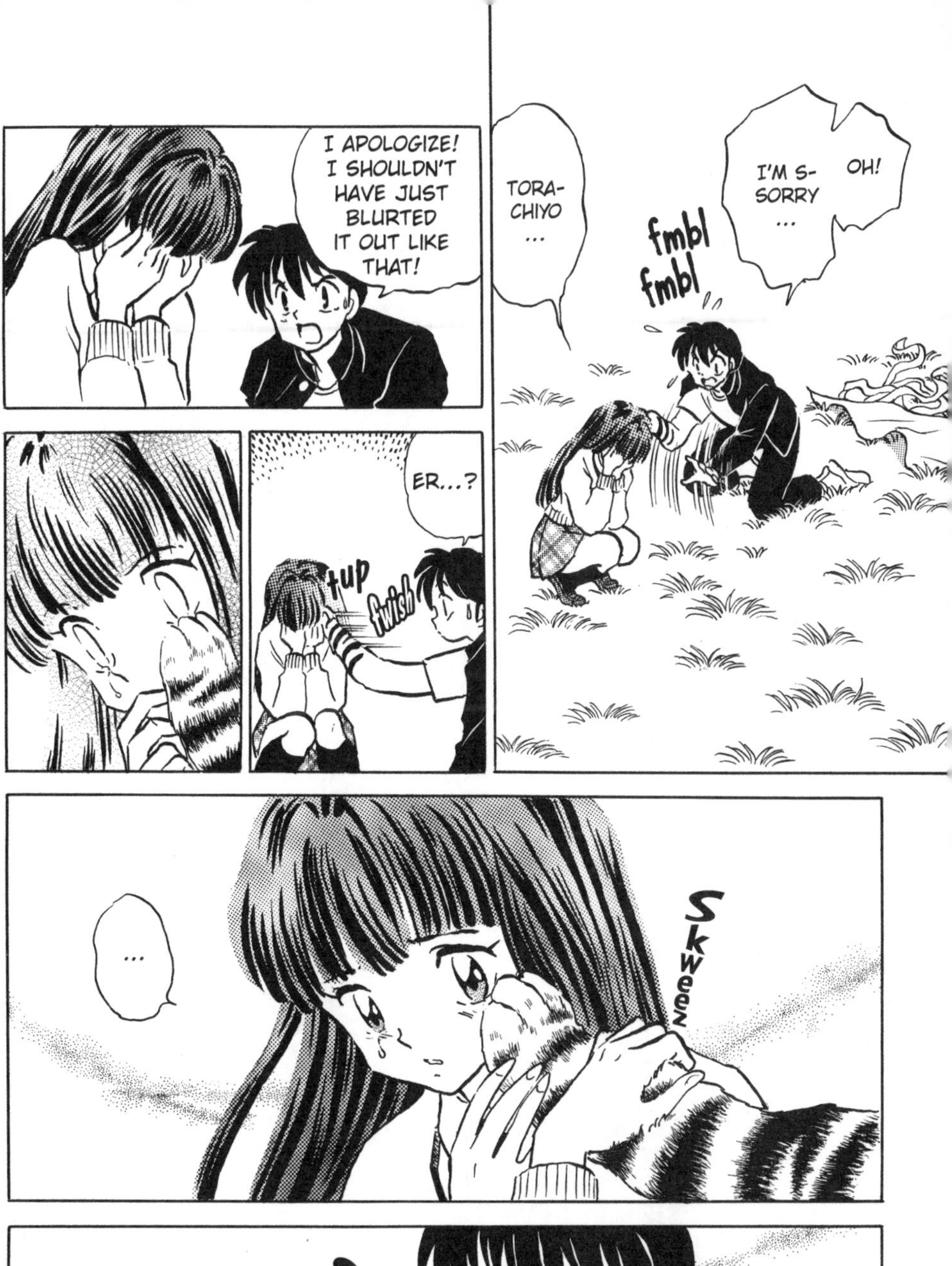

OH!
I'M S-SORRY ...
TORA-CHIYO ...
fmbl fmbl
I APOLOGIZE! I SHOULDN'T HAVE JUST BLURTED IT OUT LIKE THAT!
ER...?
tup
fwish
...
Skweez
BdMp

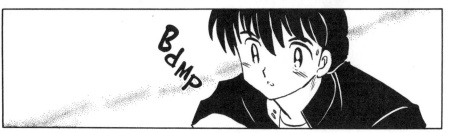

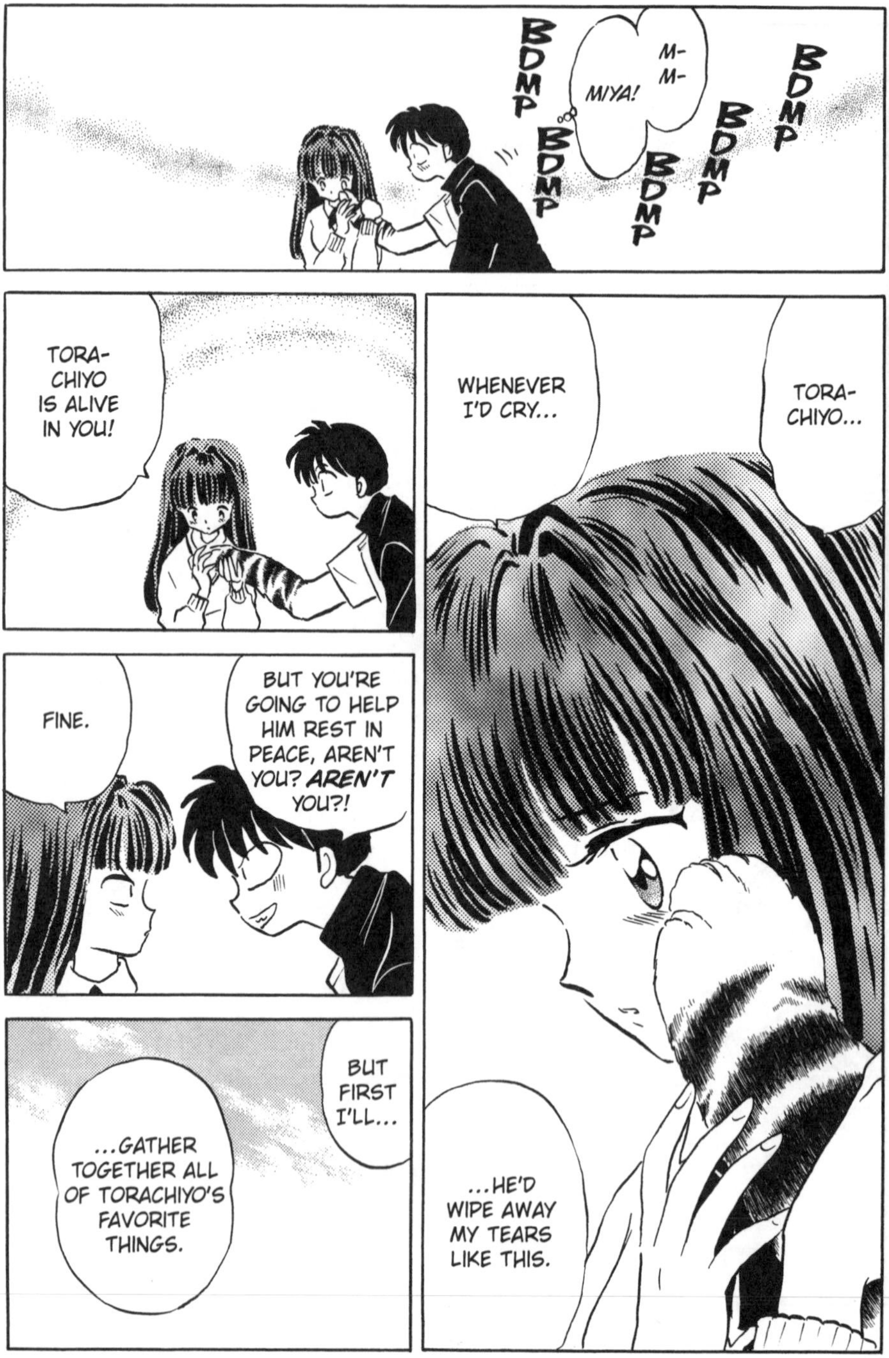
BDMP
BDMP
BDMP
M-M-
MIYA!
BDMP
BDMP
TORA-CHIYO...
WHENEVER I'D CRY...
...HE'D WIPE AWAY MY TEARS LIKE THIS.
TORA-CHIYO IS ALIVE IN YOU!
BUT YOU'RE GOING TO HELP HIM REST IN PEACE, AREN'T YOU? ***AREN'T*** YOU?!
FINE.
BUT FIRST I'LL...
...GATHER TOGETHER ALL OF TORACHIYO'S FAVORITE THINGS.

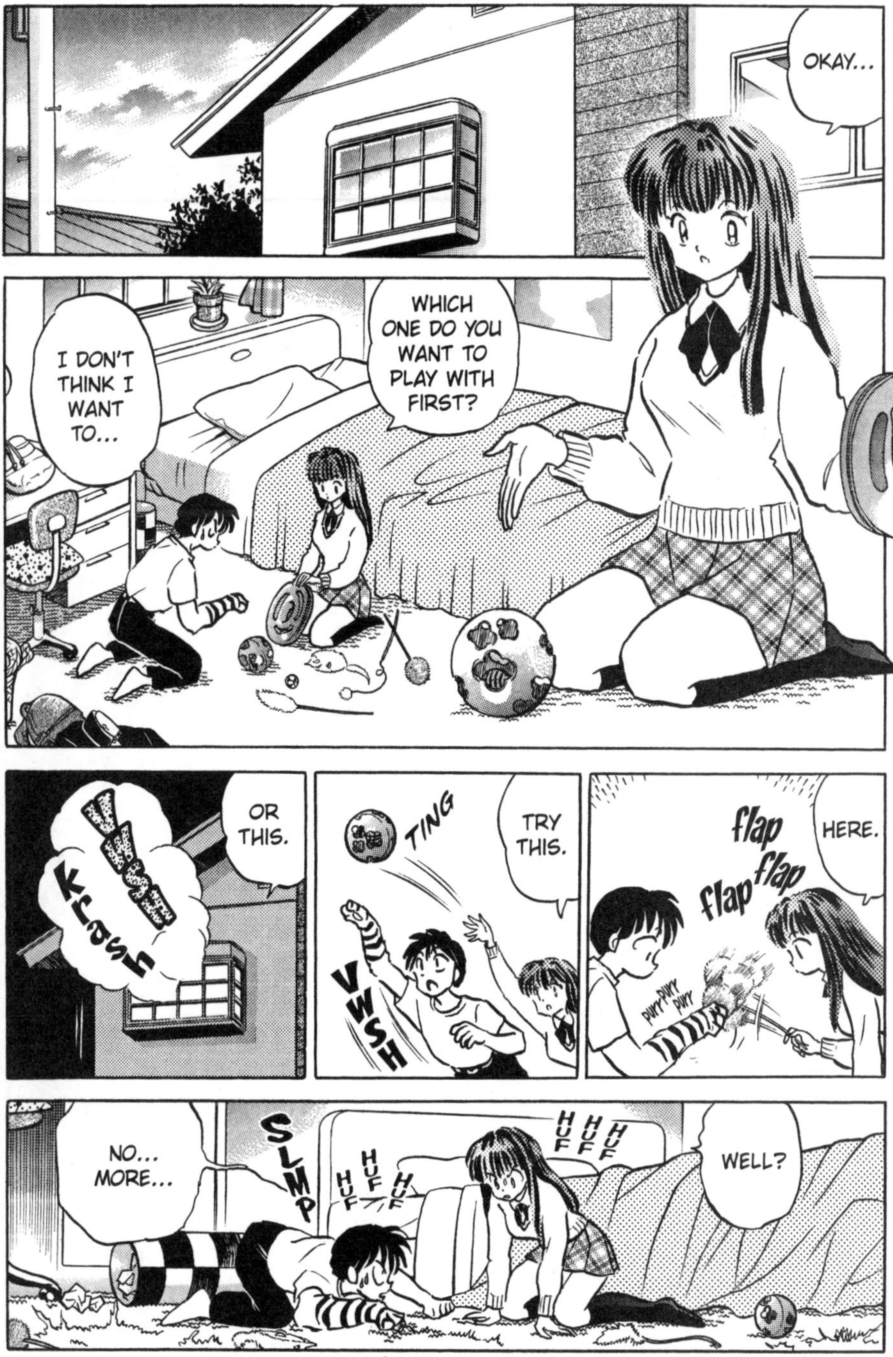
OKAY...
WHICH ONE DO YOU WANT TO PLAY WITH FIRST?
I DON'T THINK I WANT TO...
HERE.
flap flap flap
PUKY PUKY PUKY
TRY THIS.
TING
VWSH
OR THIS.
VWSH
KLASH
WELL?
HUF HUF HUF
HUF HUF HUF
SLMP
NO... MORE...

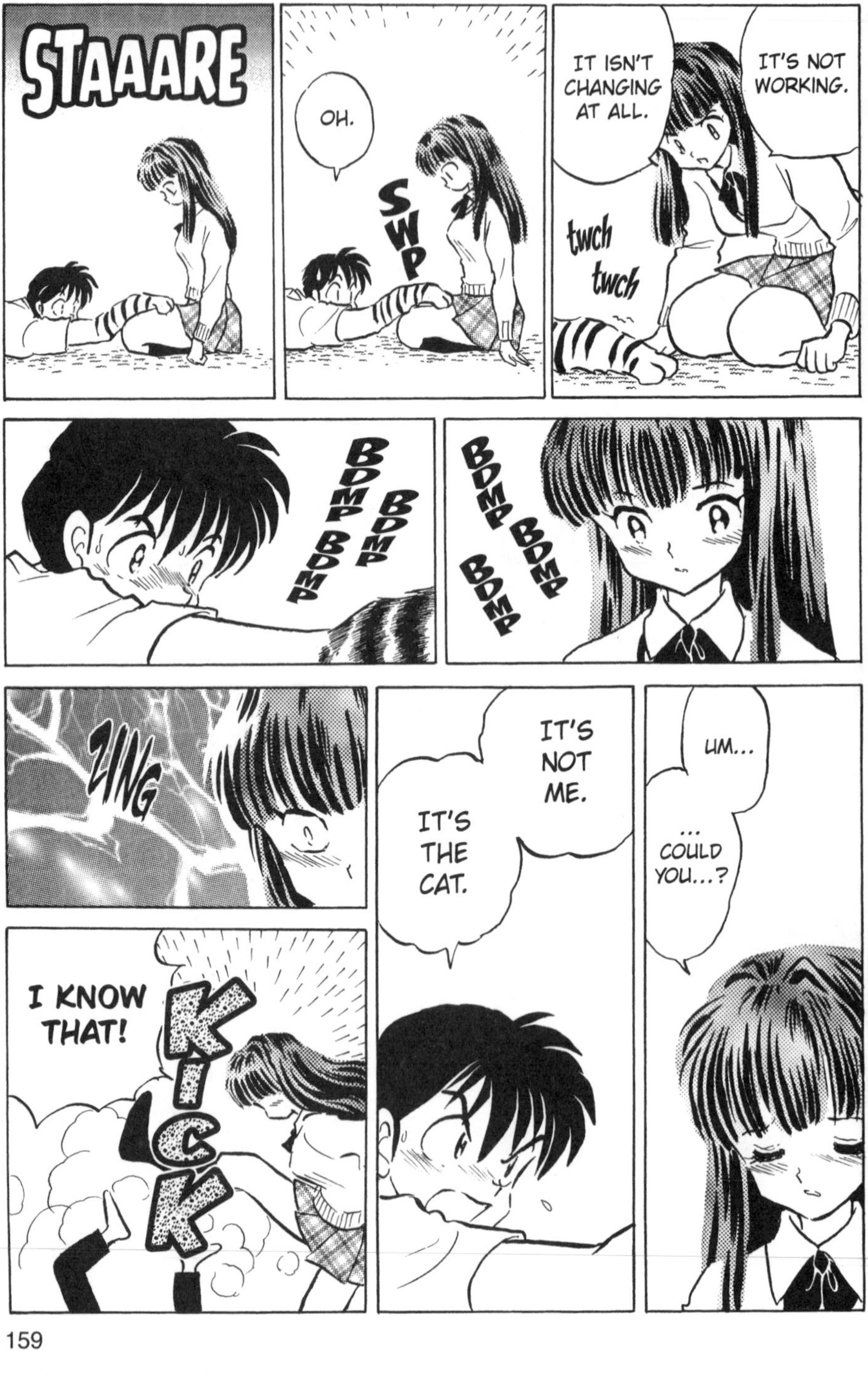
IT'S NOT WORKING.
IT ISN'T CHANGING AT ALL.
twch
twch
OH.
SWP
STAAARE
BDMP BDMP
BDMP BDMP
BDMP
BDMP
BDMP
UM...
...COULD YOU...?
IT'S NOT ME.
IT'S THE CAT.
ZING
I KNOW THAT!
KICK

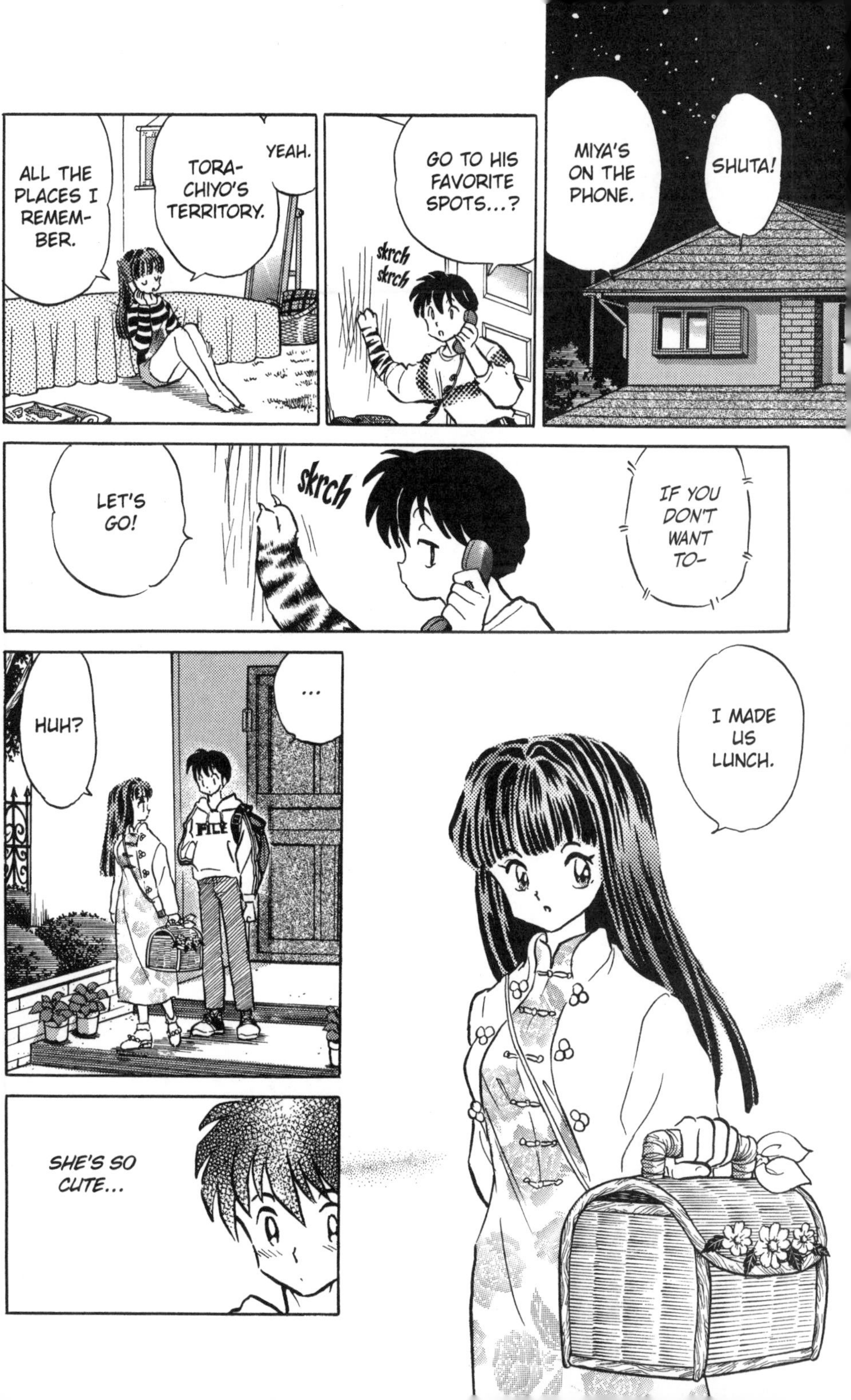
SHUTA!
MIYA'S ON THE PHONE.
GO TO HIS FAVORITE SPOTS...?
skrch skrch
YEAH.
TORA-CHIYO'S TERRITORY.
ALL THE PLACES I REMEMBER.
IF YOU DON'T WANT TO-
skrch
LET'S GO!
I MADE US LUNCH.
...
HUH?
SHE'S SO CUTE...

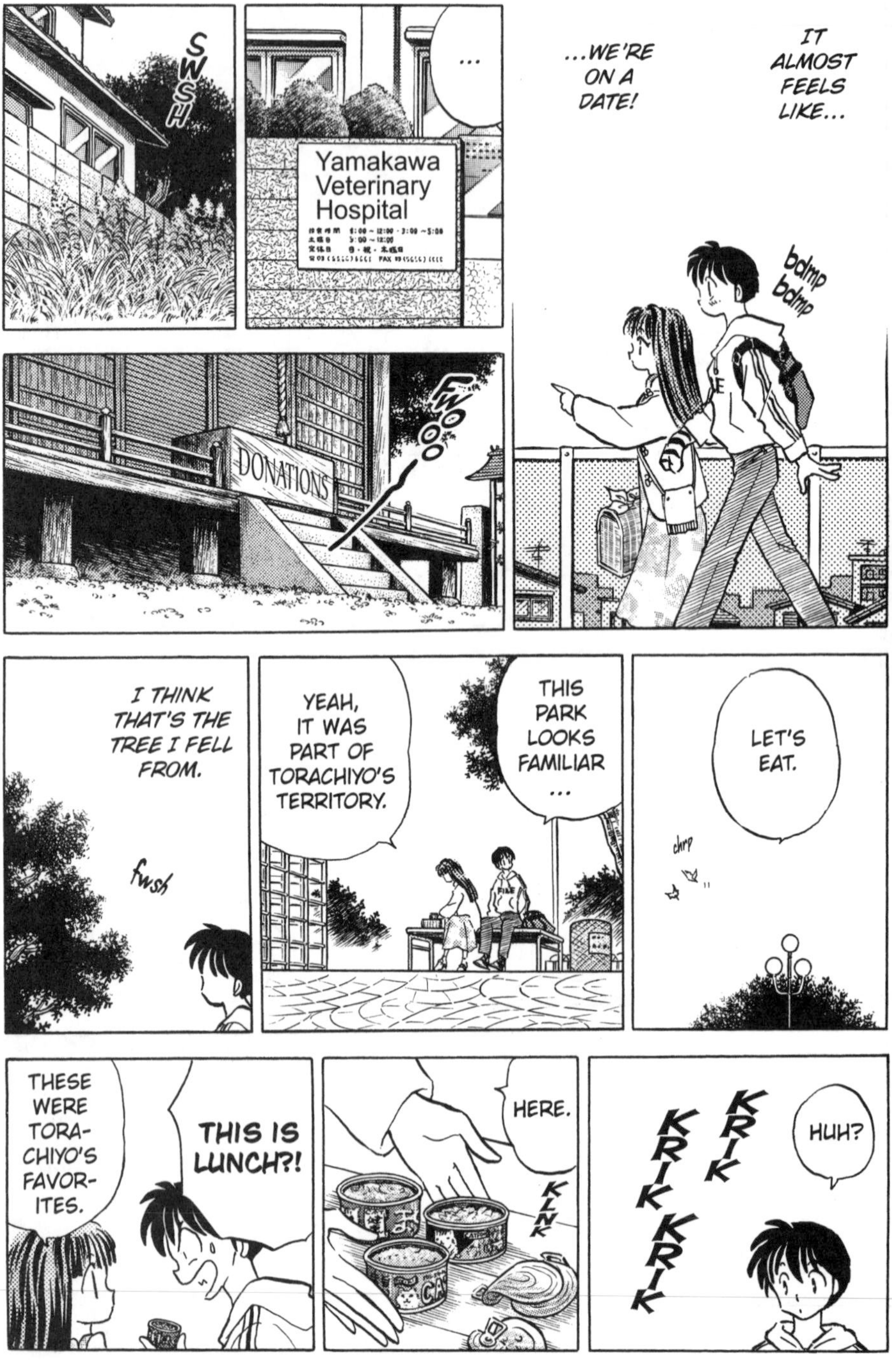
IT ALMOST FEELS LIKE...
...WE'RE ON A DATE!
bdmp bdmp
...
Yamakawa Veterinary Hospital
SWSH
FWOOO
DONATIONS
LET'S EAT.
chrp
THIS PARK LOOKS FAMILIAR...
YEAH, IT WAS PART OF TORACHIYO'S TERRITORY.
I THINK THAT'S THE TREE I FELL FROM.
fwsh
HUH?
KRIK KRIK
KRIK KRIK
HERE.
KLNK
THIS IS LUNCH?!
THESE WERE TORA-CHIYO'S FAVOR-ITES.

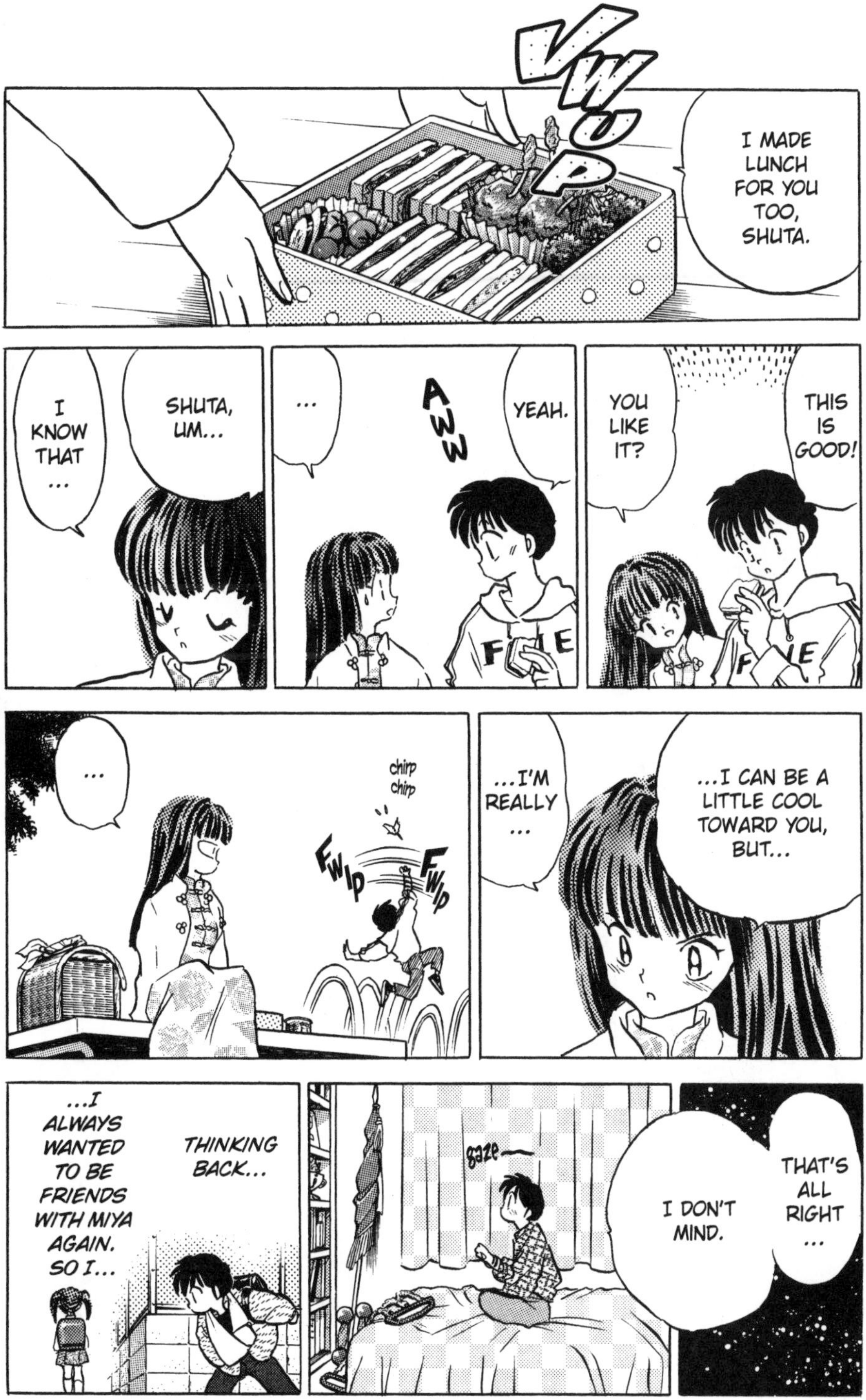
VWOP
I MADE LUNCH FOR YOU TOO, SHUTA.
THIS IS GOOD!
YOU LIKE IT?
YEAH.
AWW
...
SHUTA, UM...
I KNOW THAT ...
...I CAN BE A LITTLE COOL TOWARD YOU, BUT...
...I'M REALLY ...
chirp chirp
FWIP FWIP
...
THAT'S ALL RIGHT ...
I DON'T MIND.
gaze—
THINKING BACK...
...I ALWAYS WANTED TO BE FRIENDS WITH MIYA AGAIN. SO I...

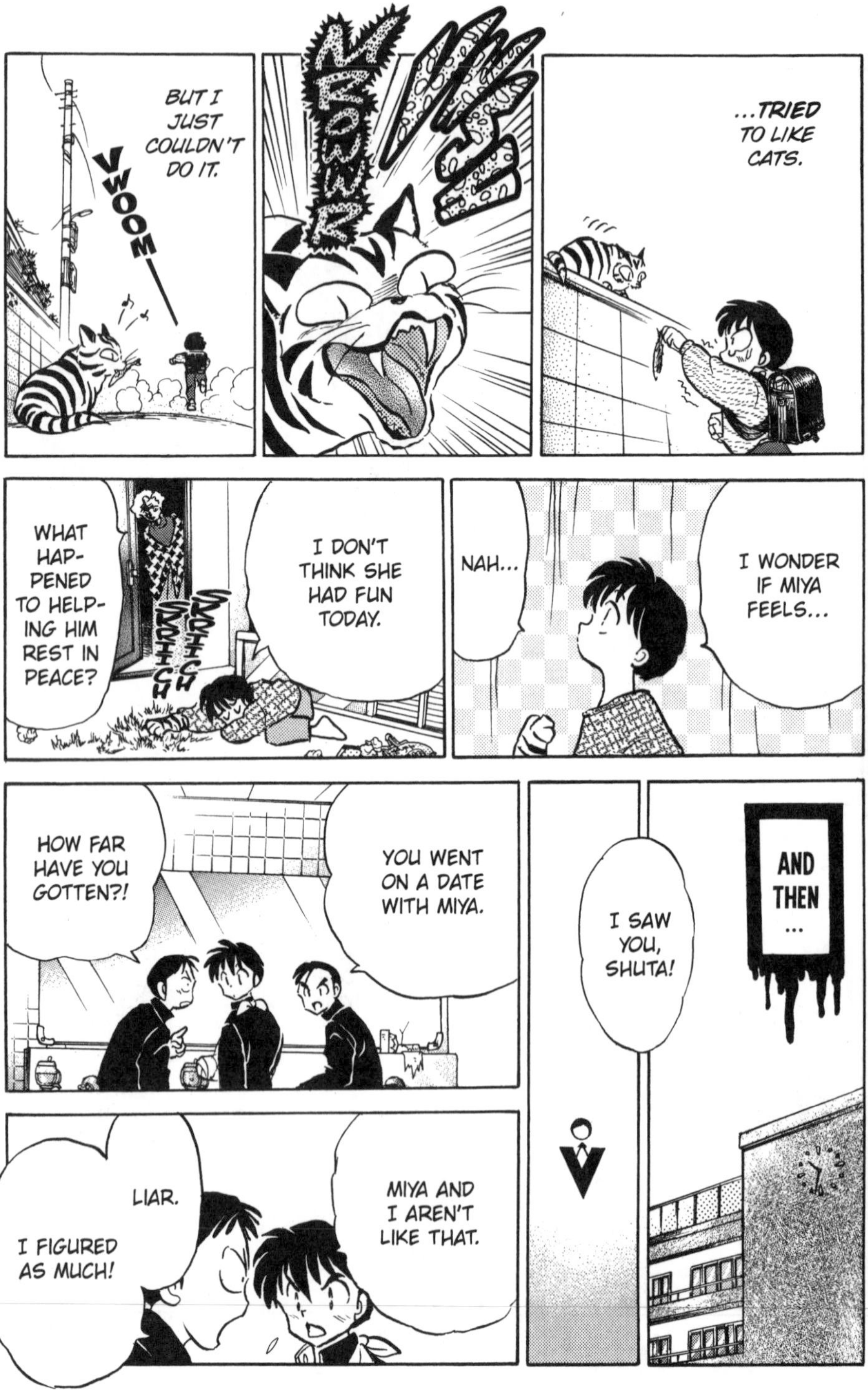
...TRIED TO LIKE CATS.
MROWR
BUT I JUST COULDN'T DO IT.
VWOOM
I WONDER IF MIYA FEELS...
NAH...
I DON'T THINK SHE HAD FUN TODAY.
SKRIICH SKRIICH
WHAT HAP-PENED TO HELP-ING HIM REST IN PEACE?
AND THEN...
I SAW YOU, SHUTA!
YOU WENT ON A DATE WITH MIYA.
HOW FAR HAVE YOU GOTTEN?!
MIYA AND I AREN'T LIKE THAT.
LIAR.
I FIGURED AS MUCH!

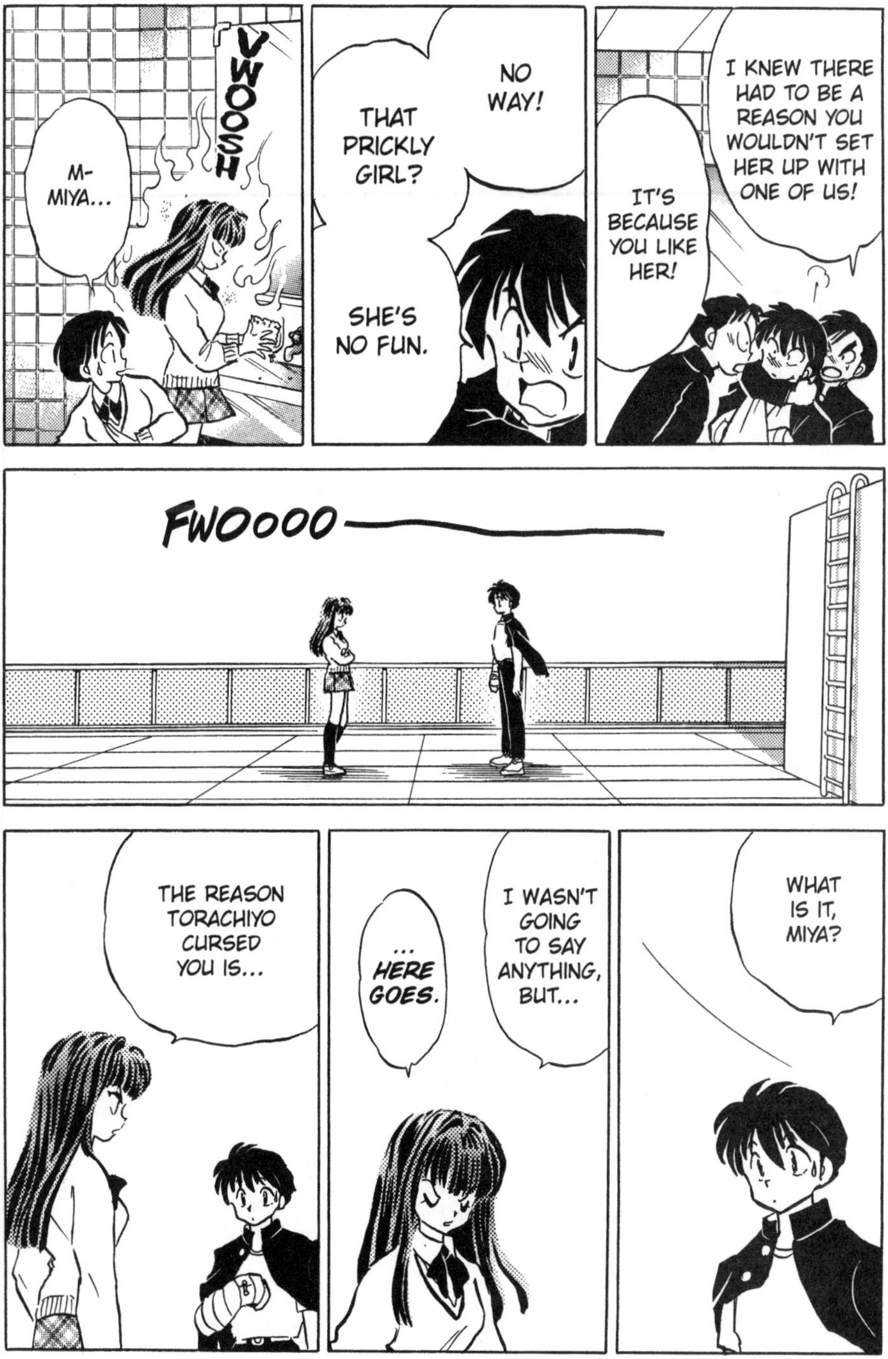
I KNEW THERE HAD TO BE A REASON YOU WOULDN'T SET HER UP WITH ONE OF US!
IT'S BECAUSE YOU LIKE HER!
NO WAY!
THAT PRICKLY GIRL?
SHE'S NO FUN.
VWOOSH
M-MIYA...
FWOOOO
WHAT IS IT, MIYA?
I WASN'T GOING TO SAY ANYTHING, BUT...
... HERE GOES.
THE REASON TORACHIYO CURSED YOU IS...

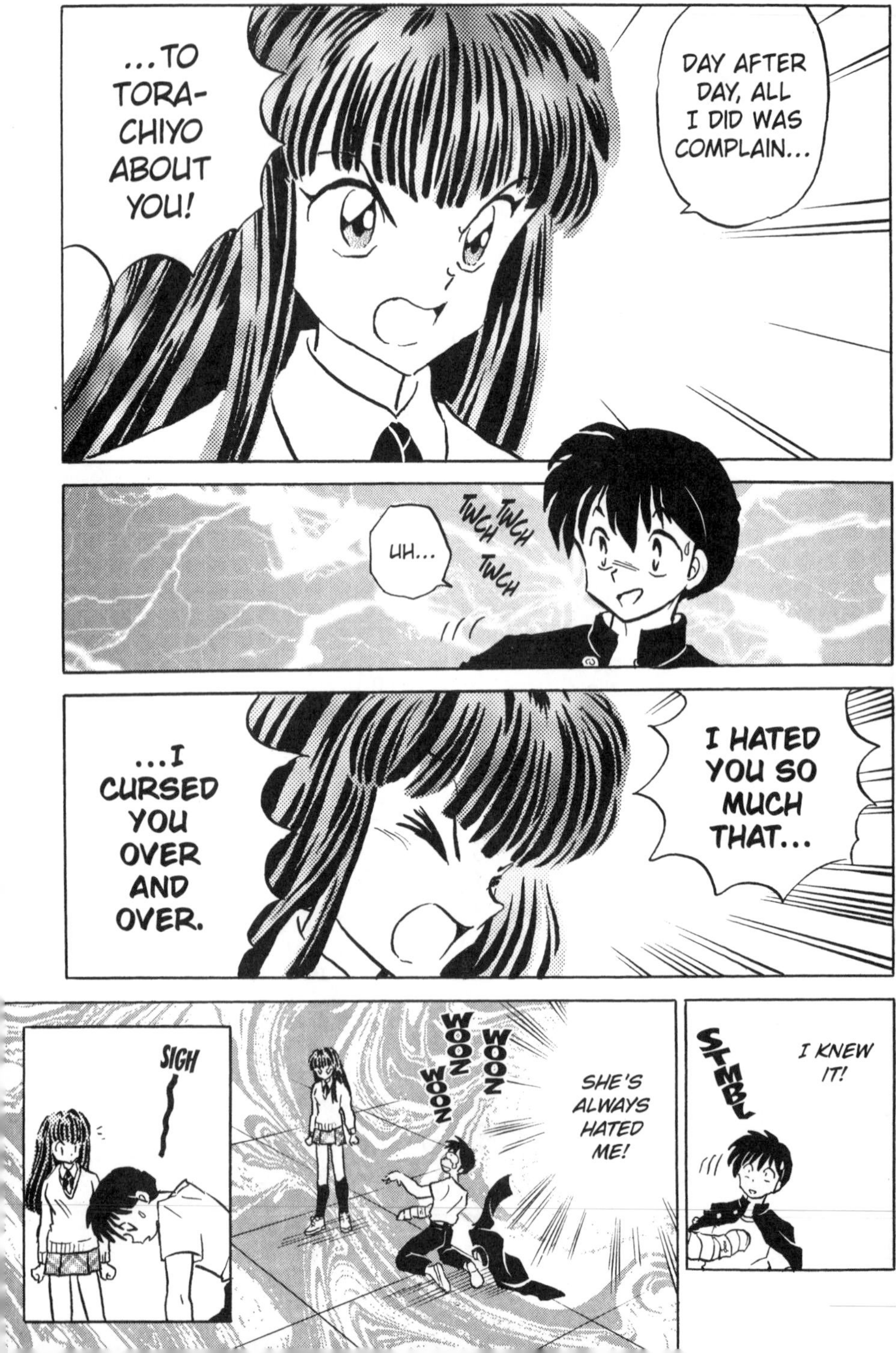
DAY AFTER DAY, ALL I DID WAS COMPLAIN...
...TO TORA-CHIYO ABOUT YOU!
TWCH TWCH
TWCH
UH...
I HATED YOU SO MUCH THAT...
...I CURSED YOU OVER AND OVER.
STMBL
I KNEW IT!
WOOZ WOOZ
WOOZ
SHE'S ALWAYS HATED ME!
SIGH

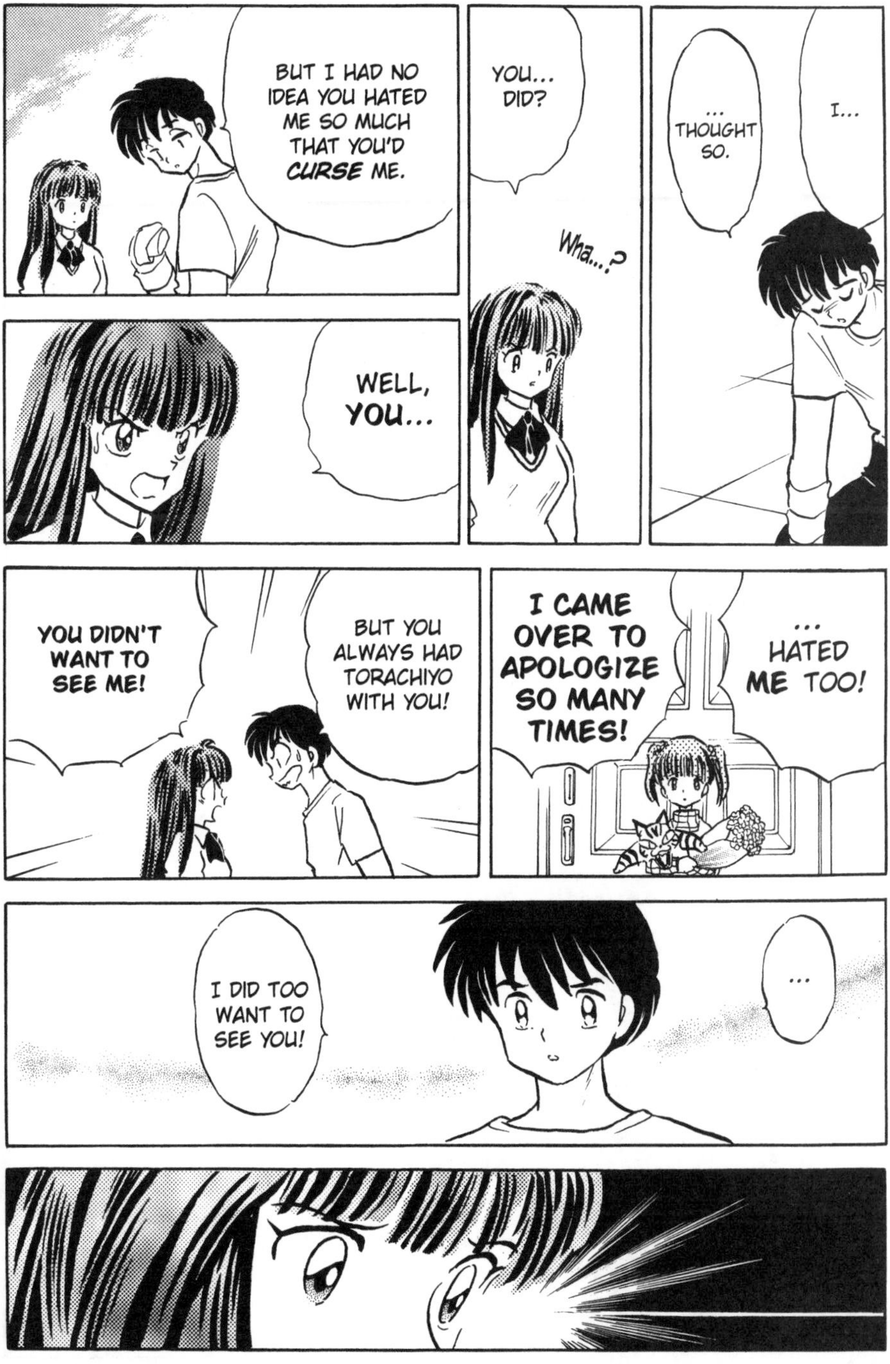
I...
...THOUGHT SO.
YOU... DID?
Wha...?
BUT I HAD NO IDEA YOU HATED ME SO MUCH THAT YOU'D CURSE ME.
WELL, YOU...
...HATED ME TOO!
I CAME OVER TO APOLOGIZE SO MANY TIMES!
BUT YOU ALWAYS HAD TORACHIYO WITH YOU!
YOU DIDN'T WANT TO SEE ME!
...
I DID TOO WANT TO SEE YOU!

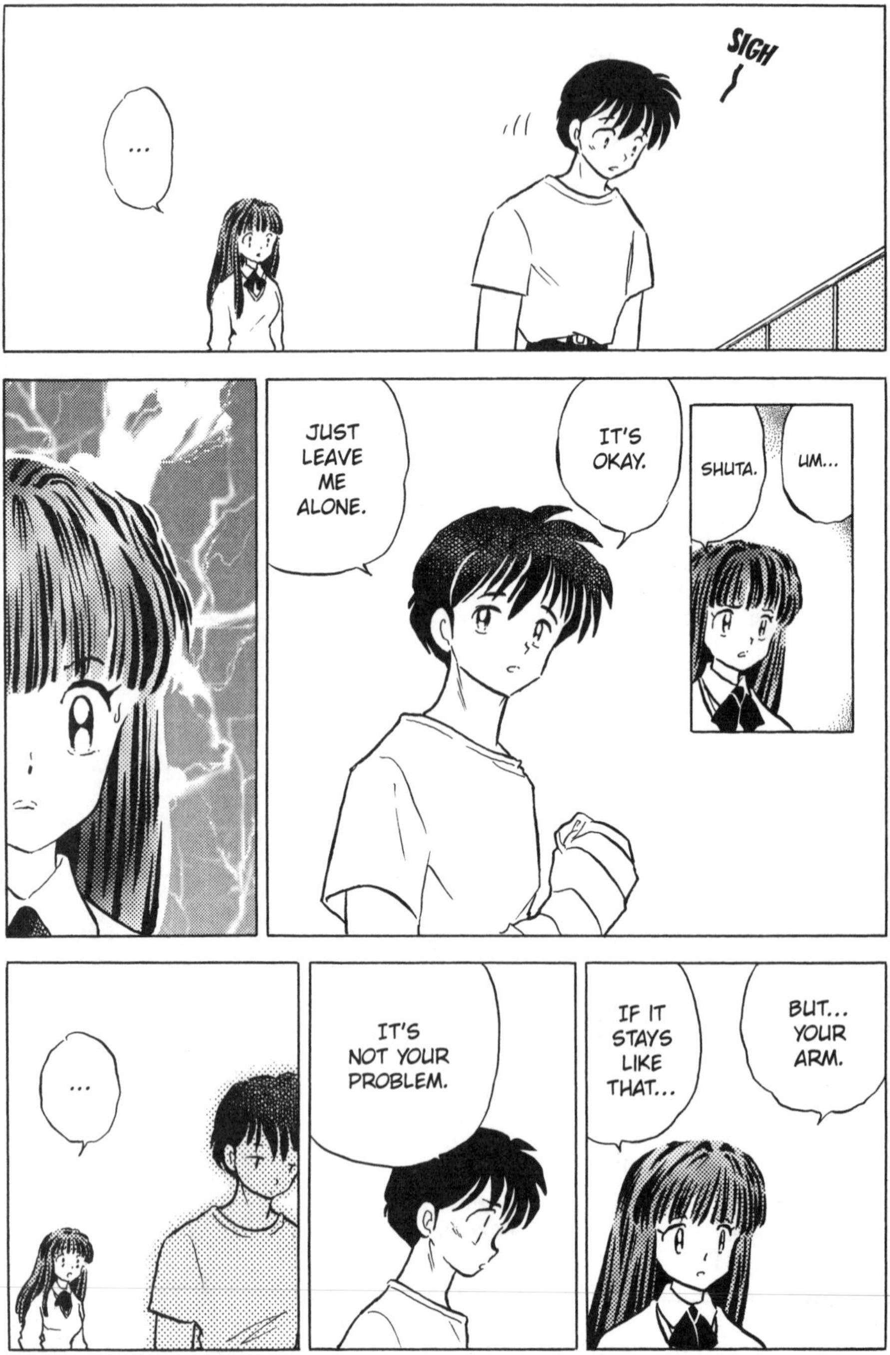
SIGH
...
UM...
SHUTA.
IT'S OKAY.
JUST LEAVE ME ALONE.
BUT... YOUR ARM.
IF IT STAYS LIKE THAT...
IT'S NOT YOUR PROBLEM.
...

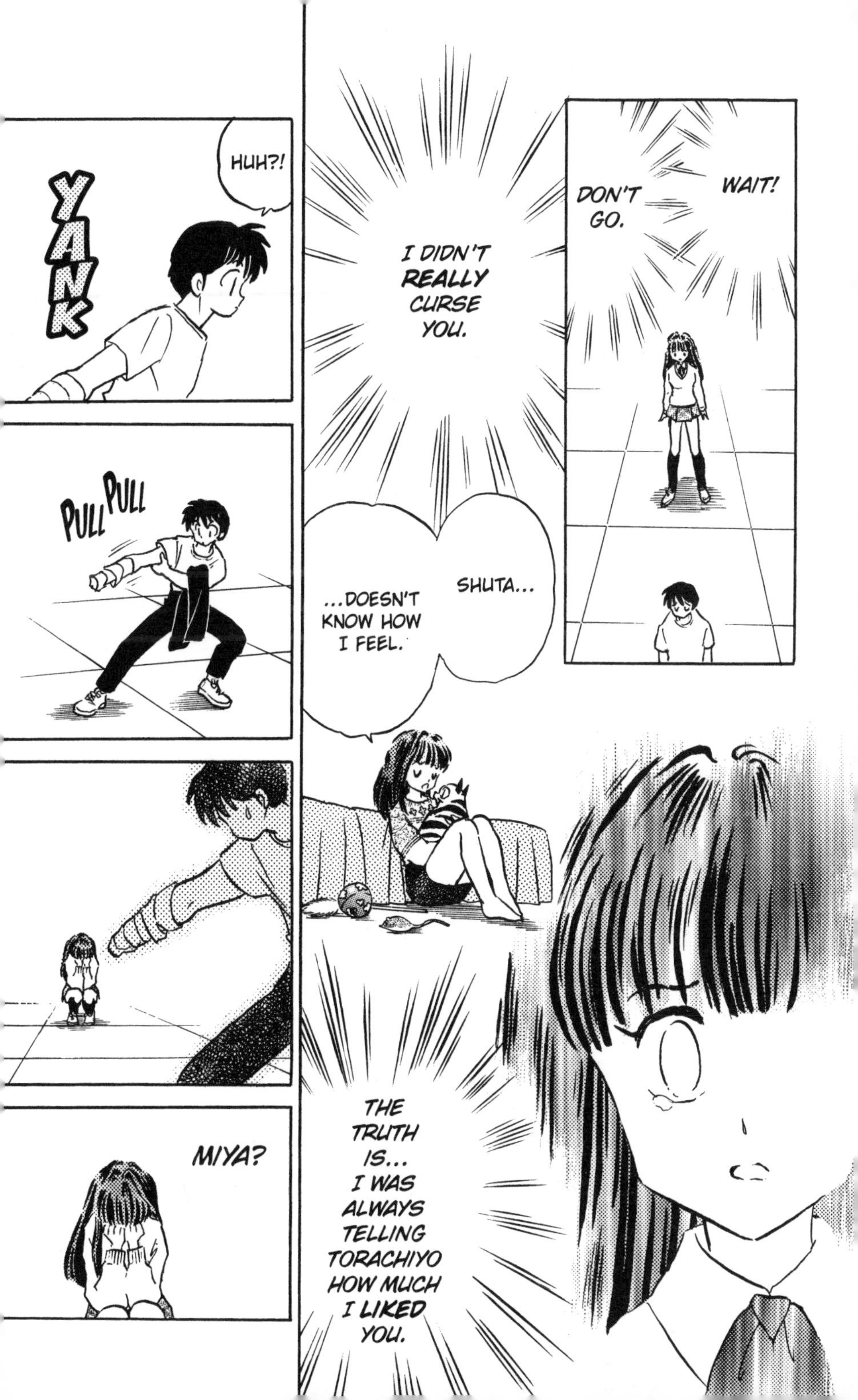
WAIT!
DON'T GO.
I DIDN'T REALLY CURSE YOU.
SHUTA...
...DOESN'T KNOW HOW I FEEL.
THE TRUTH IS... I WAS ALWAYS TELLING TORACHIYO HOW MUCH I LIKED YOU.
HUH?!
YANK
PULL PULL
MIYA?

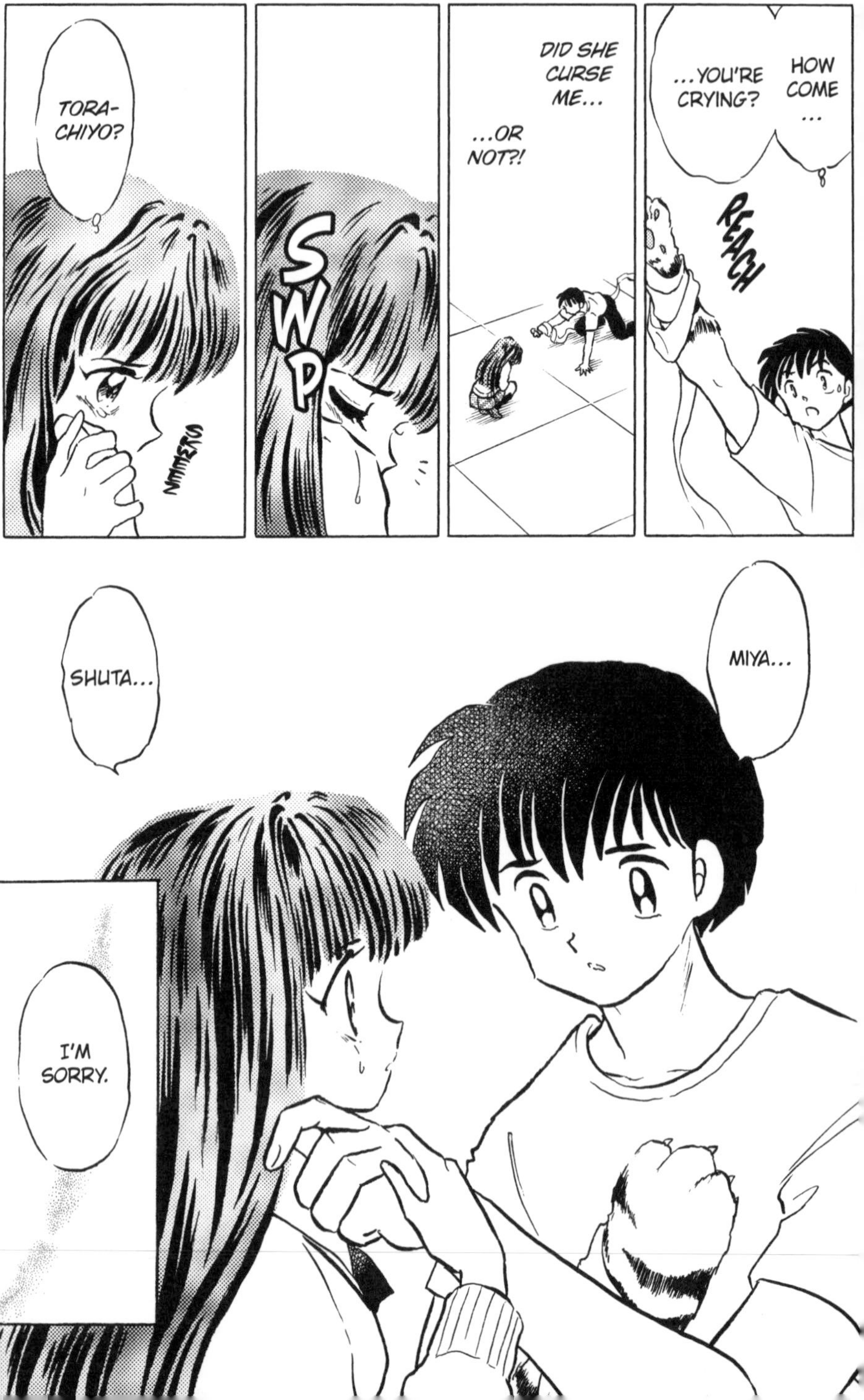
HOW COME...
...YOU'RE CRYING?
REACH
DID SHE CURSE ME...
...OR NOT?!
SWP
TORA-CHIYO?
MIYA...
SHUTA...
I'M SORRY.

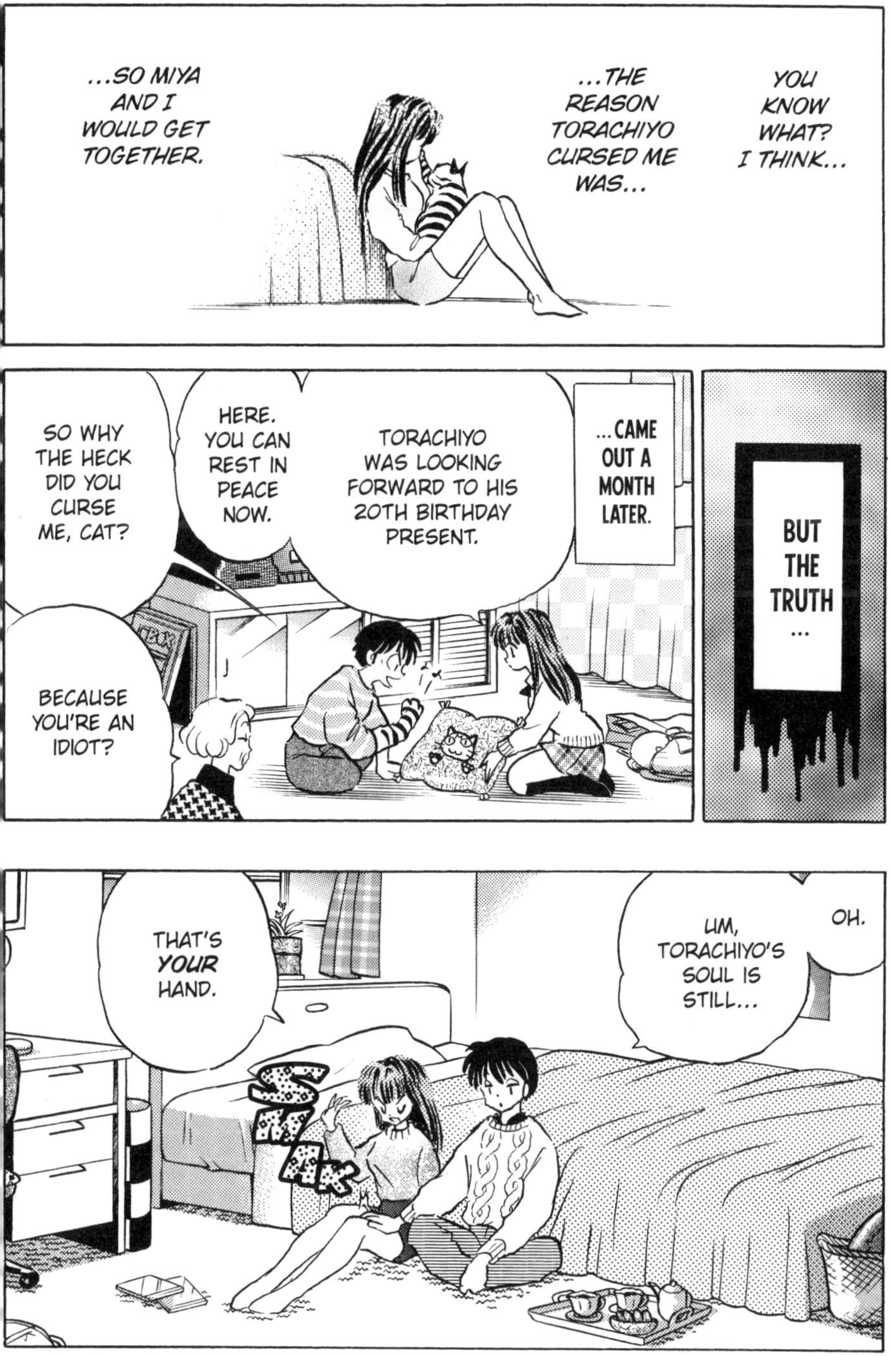
YOU KNOW WHAT? I THINK...
...THE REASON TORACHIYO CURSED ME WAS...
...SO MIYA AND I WOULD GET TOGETHER.
BUT THE TRUTH...
...CAME OUT A MONTH LATER.
TORACHIYO WAS LOOKING FORWARD TO HIS 20TH BIRTHDAY PRESENT.
HERE. YOU CAN REST IN PEACE NOW.
SO WHY THE HECK DID YOU CURSE ME, CAT?
BECAUSE YOU'RE AN IDIOT?
OH.
UM, TORACHIYO'S SOUL IS STILL...
THAT'S ***YOUR*** HAND.

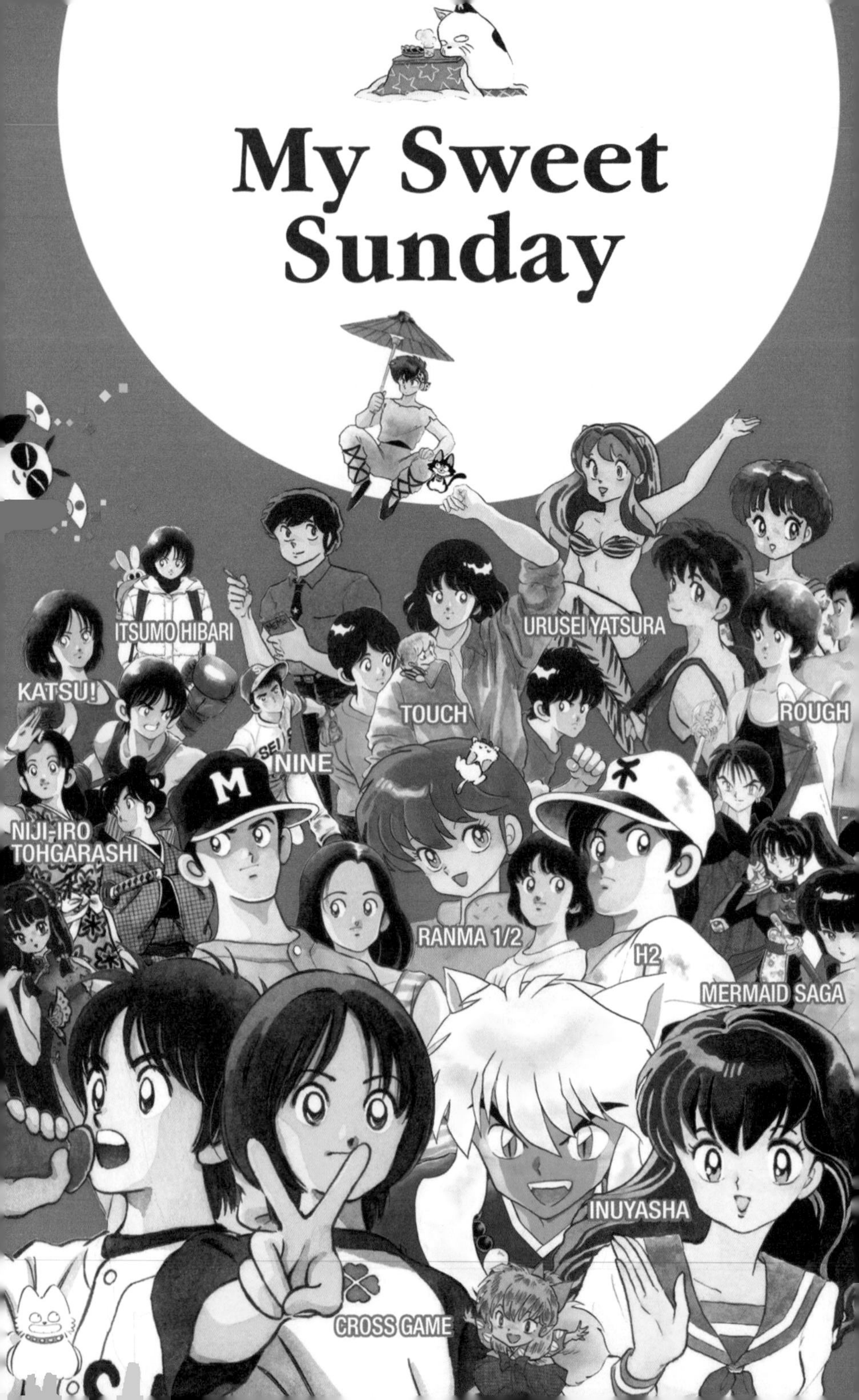
My Sweet Sunday
ITSUMO HIBARI
URUSEI YATSURA
KATSU!
TOUCH
ROUGH
NINE
NIJI-IRO TOHGARASHI
RANMA 1/2
H2
MERMAID SAGA
INUYASHA
CROSS GAME

Mitsuru Adachi

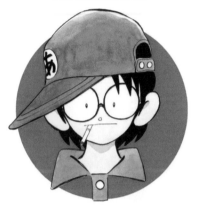

My Sweet Sunday

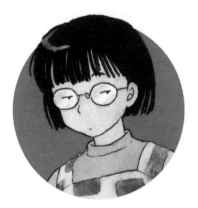

Rumiko Takahashi

Childhood

Mitsuru Adachi

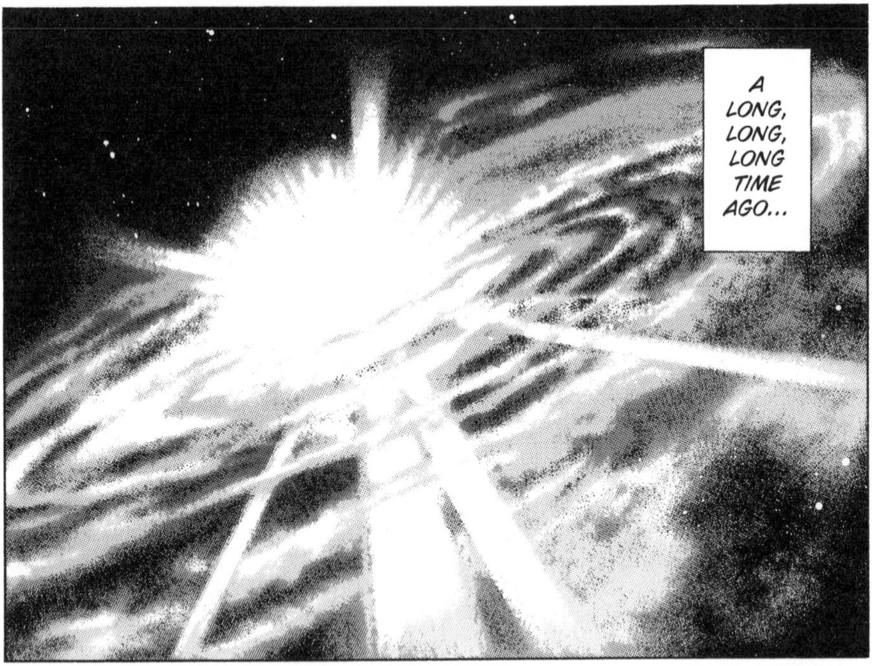
A LONG, LONG, LONG TIME AGO...

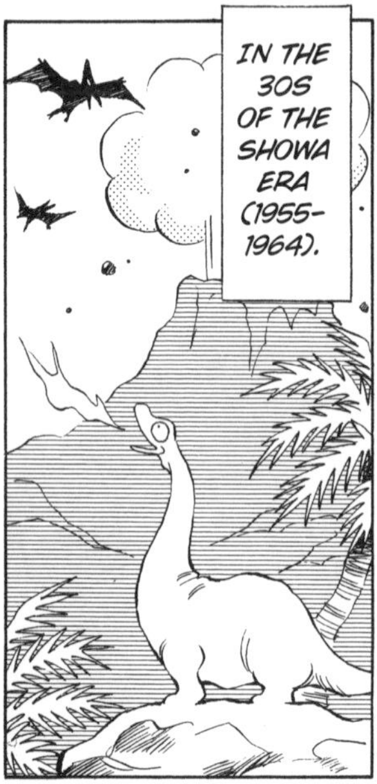
IN THE 30S OF THE SHOWA ERA (1955-1964).

Note: These drawings are full of inaccuracies and exaggerations.

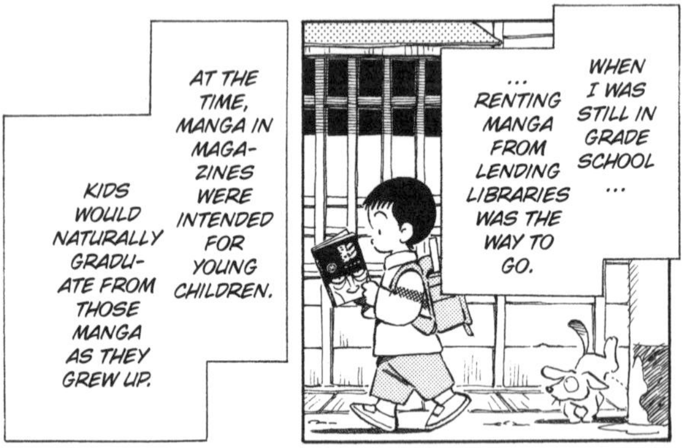
WHEN I WAS STILL IN GRADE SCHOOL ...
... RENTING MANGA FROM LENDING LIBRARIES WAS THE WAY TO GO.
AT THE TIME, MANGA IN MAGAZINES WERE INTENDED FOR YOUNG CHILDREN.
KIDS WOULD NATURALLY GRADUATE FROM THOSE MANGA AS THEY GREW UP.

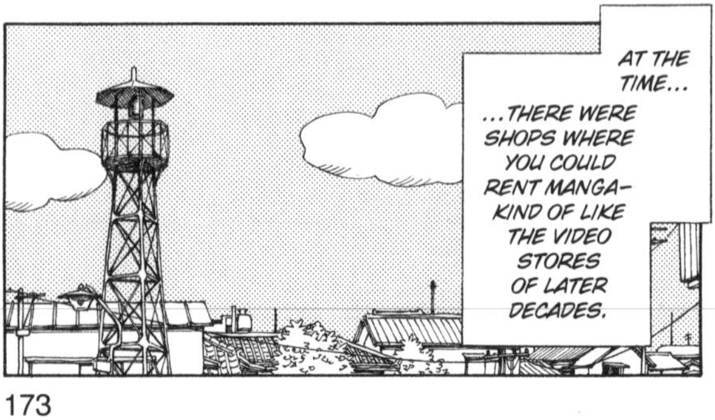
AT THE TIME...
...THERE WERE SHOPS WHERE YOU COULD RENT MANGA-KIND OF LIKE THE VIDEO STORES OF LATER DECADES.

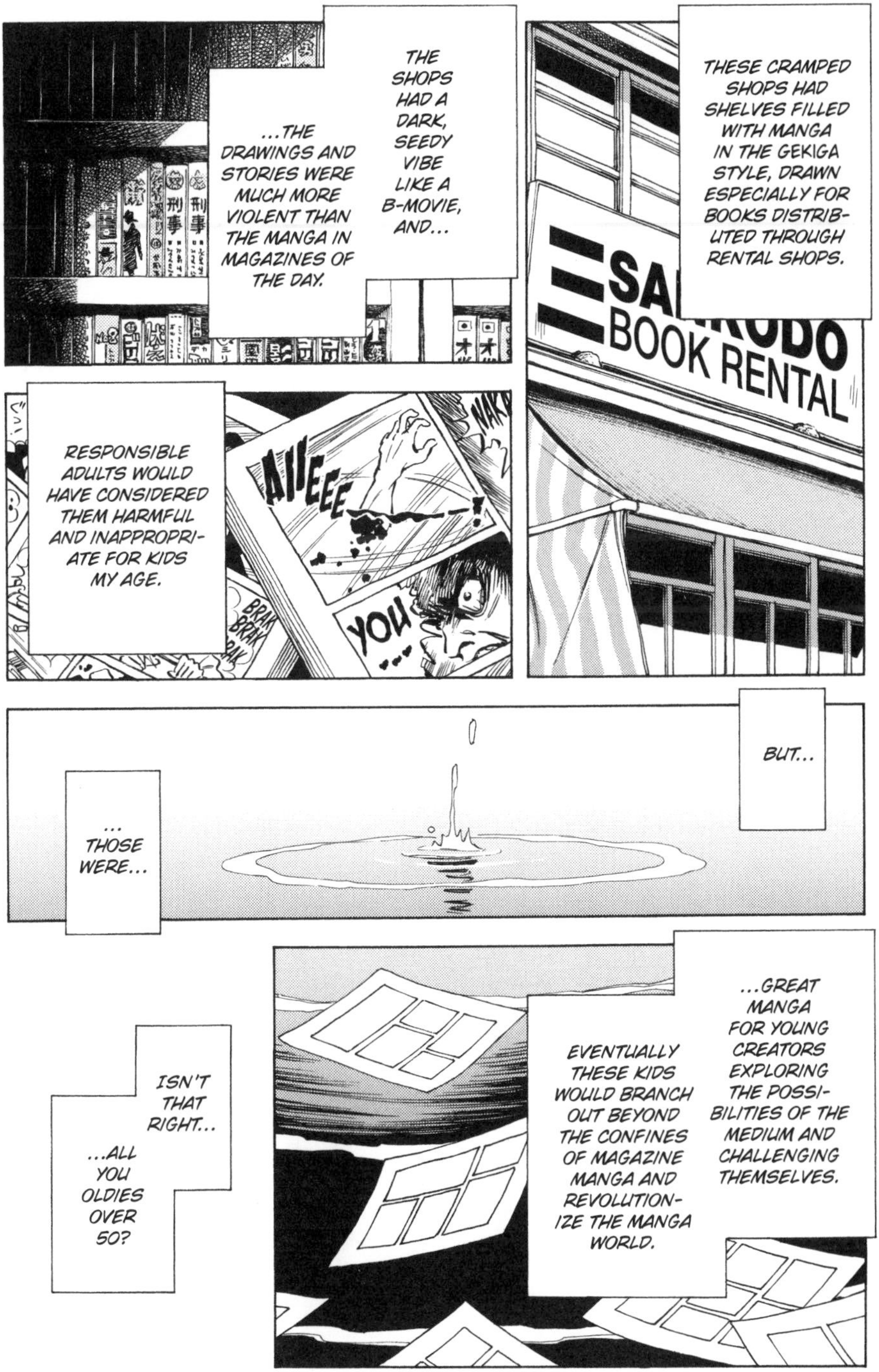

THESE CRAMPED SHOPS HAD SHELVES FILLED WITH MANGA IN THE GEKIGA STYLE, DRAWN ESPECIALLY FOR BOOKS DISTRIB-UTED THROUGH RENTAL SHOPS.
SA
KODO
BOOK RENTAL
THE SHOPS HAD A DARK, SEEDY VIBE LIKE A B-MOVIE, AND...
...THE DRAWINGS AND STORIES WERE MUCH MORE VIOLENT THAN THE MANGA IN MAGAZINES OF THE DAY.
AIIEEE—!
YOU...
BRAK BRAK
RESPONSIBLE ADULTS WOULD HAVE CONSIDERED THEM HARMFUL AND INAPPROPRI-ATE FOR KIDS MY AGE.
BUT...
...THOSE WERE...
...GREAT MANGA FOR YOUNG CREATORS EXPLORING THE POSSI-BILITIES OF THE MEDIUM AND CHALLENGING THEMSELVES.
EVENTUALLY THESE KIDS WOULD BRANCH OUT BEYOND THE CONFINES OF MAGAZINE MANGA AND REVOLUTION-IZE THE MANGA WORLD.
ISN'T THAT RIGHT...
...ALL YOU OLDIES OVER 50?

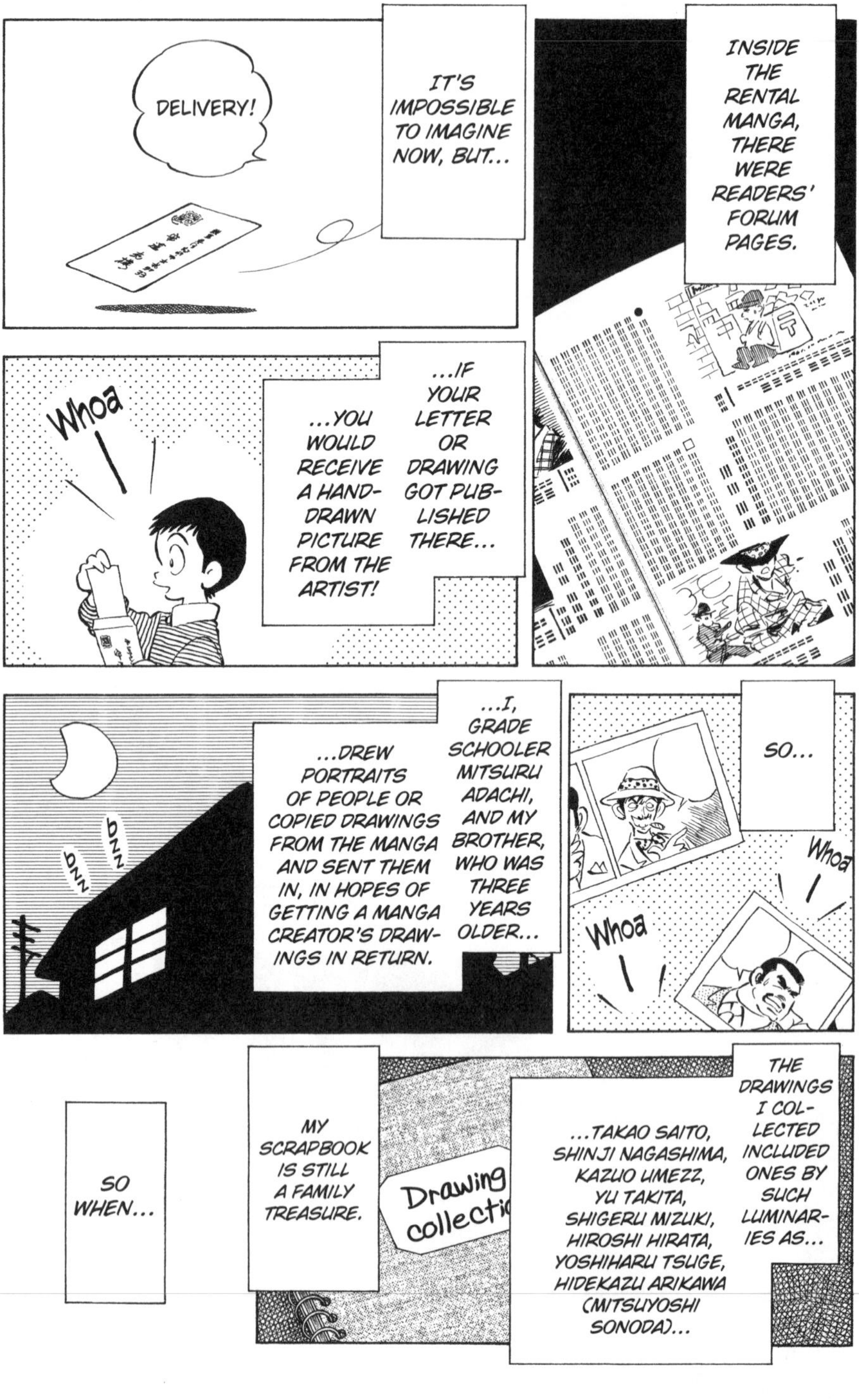
INSIDE THE RENTAL MANGA, THERE WERE READERS' FORUM PAGES.
IT'S IMPOSSIBLE TO IMAGINE NOW, BUT...
DELIVERY!
...IF YOUR LETTER OR DRAWING GOT PUBLISHED THERE...
...YOU WOULD RECEIVE A HAND-DRAWN PICTURE FROM THE ARTIST!
Whoa
SO...
Whoa
Whoa
...I, GRADE SCHOOLER MITSURU ADACHI, AND MY BROTHER, WHO WAS THREE YEARS OLDER...
...DREW PORTRAITS OF PEOPLE OR COPIED DRAWINGS FROM THE MANGA AND SENT THEM IN, IN HOPES OF GETTING A MANGA CREATOR'S DRAWINGS IN RETURN.
bzz
bzz
THE DRAWINGS I COLLECTED INCLUDED ONES BY SUCH LUMINARIES AS...
...TAKAO SAITO, SHINJI NAGASHIMA, KAZUO UMEZZ, YU TAKITA, SHIGERU MIZUKI, HIROSHI HIRATA, YOSHIHARU TSUGE, HIDEKAZU ARIKAWA (MITSUYOSHI SONODA)...
Drawing
MY SCRAPBOOK IS STILL A FAMILY TREASURE.
SO WHEN...

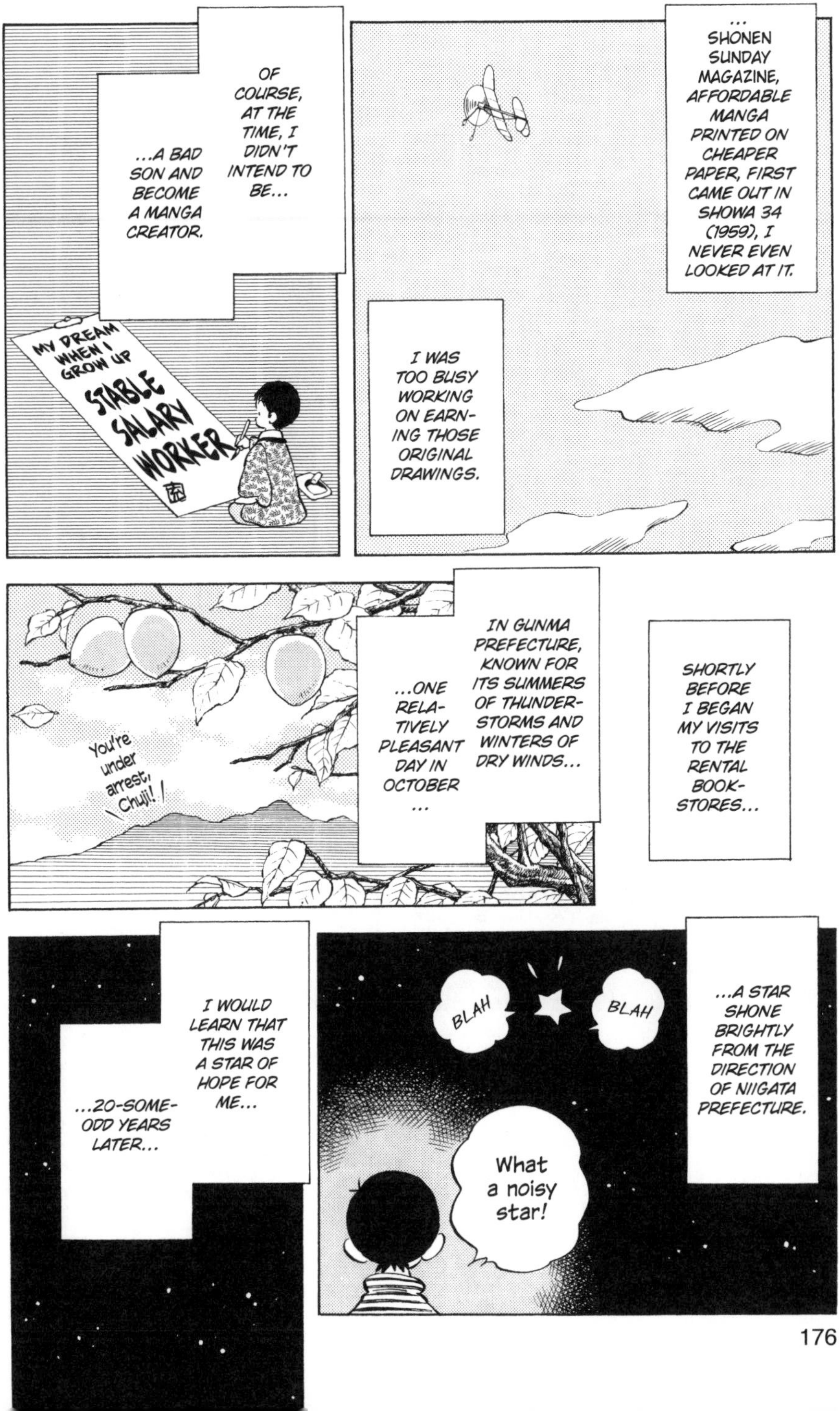
... SHONEN SUNDAY MAGAZINE, AFFORDABLE MANGA PRINTED ON CHEAPER PAPER, FIRST CAME OUT IN SHOWA 34 (1959), I NEVER EVEN LOOKED AT IT.
I WAS TOO BUSY WORKING ON EARNING THOSE ORIGINAL DRAWINGS.
OF COURSE, AT THE TIME, I DIDN'T INTEND TO BE...
...A BAD SON AND BECOME A MANGA CREATOR.
MY DREAM WHEN I GROW UP
STABLE SALARY WORKER
SHORTLY BEFORE I BEGAN MY VISITS TO THE RENTAL BOOKSTORES...
IN GUNMA PREFECTURE, KNOWN FOR ITS SUMMERS OF THUNDERSTORMS AND WINTERS OF DRY WINDS...
...ONE RELATIVELY PLEASANT DAY IN OCTOBER...
You're under arrest, Chuji!
...A STAR SHONE BRIGHTLY FROM THE DIRECTION OF NIIGATA PREFECTURE.
BLAH
BLAH
What a noisy star!
I WOULD LEARN THAT THIS WAS A STAR OF HOPE FOR ME...
...20-SOME-ODD YEARS LATER...

Early Childhood

Rumiko
Takahashi

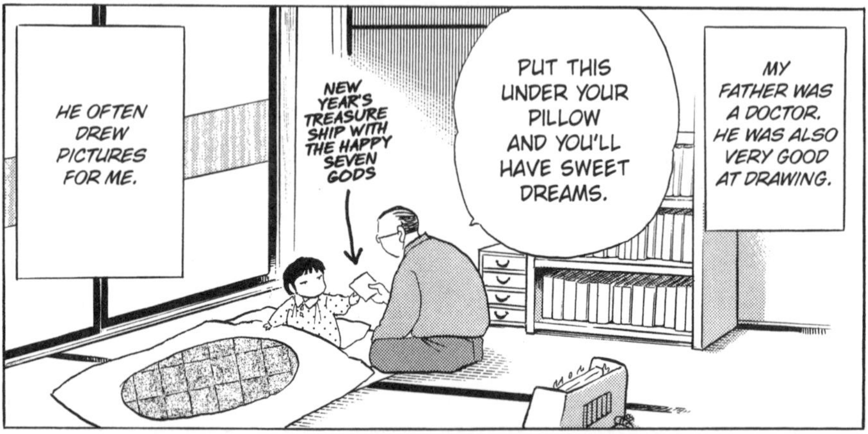
MY FATHER WAS A DOCTOR. HE WAS ALSO VERY GOOD AT DRAWING.
PUT THIS UNDER YOUR PILLOW AND YOU'LL HAVE SWEET DREAMS.
NEW YEAR'S TREASURE SHIP WITH THE HAPPY SEVEN GODS
HE OFTEN DREW PICTURES FOR ME.

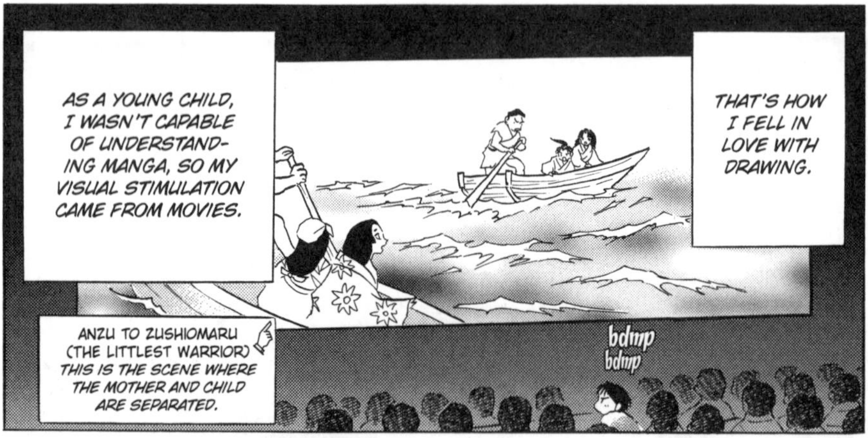
THAT'S HOW I FELL IN LOVE WITH DRAWING.
AS A YOUNG CHILD, I WASN'T CAPABLE OF UNDERSTAND-ING MANGA, SO MY VISUAL STIMULATION CAME FROM MOVIES.
bdmp bdmp
ANZU TO ZUSHIOMARU (THE LITTLEST WARRIOR) THIS IS THE SCENE WHERE THE MOTHER AND CHILD ARE SEPARATED.

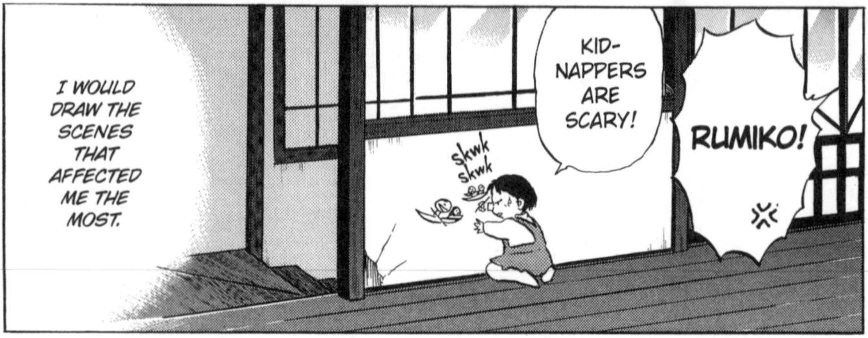
RUMIKO!
KID-NAPPERS ARE SCARY!
skwk skwk
I WOULD DRAW THE SCENES THAT AFFECTED ME THE MOST.

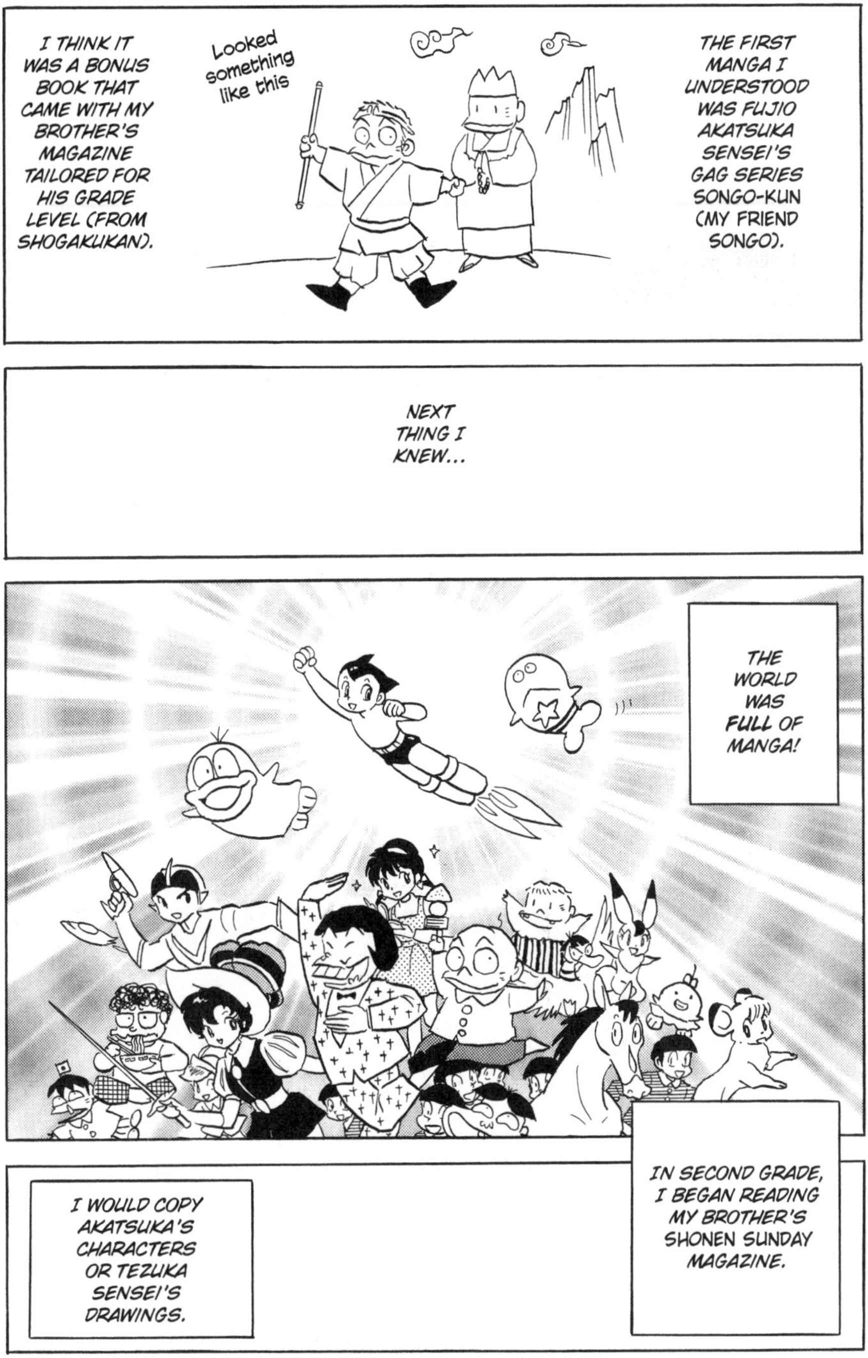
THE FIRST MANGA I UNDERSTOOD WAS FUJIO AKATSUKA SENSEI'S GAG SERIES SONGO-KUN (MY FRIEND SONGO).
Looked something like this
I THINK IT WAS A BONUS BOOK THAT CAME WITH MY BROTHER'S MAGAZINE TAILORED FOR HIS GRADE LEVEL (FROM SHOGAKUKAN).
NEXT THING I KNEW...
THE WORLD WAS **FULL** OF MANGA!
IN SECOND GRADE, I BEGAN READING MY BROTHER'S SHONEN SUNDAY MAGAZINE.
I WOULD COPY AKATSUKA'S CHARACTERS OR TEZUKA SENSEI'S DRAWINGS.

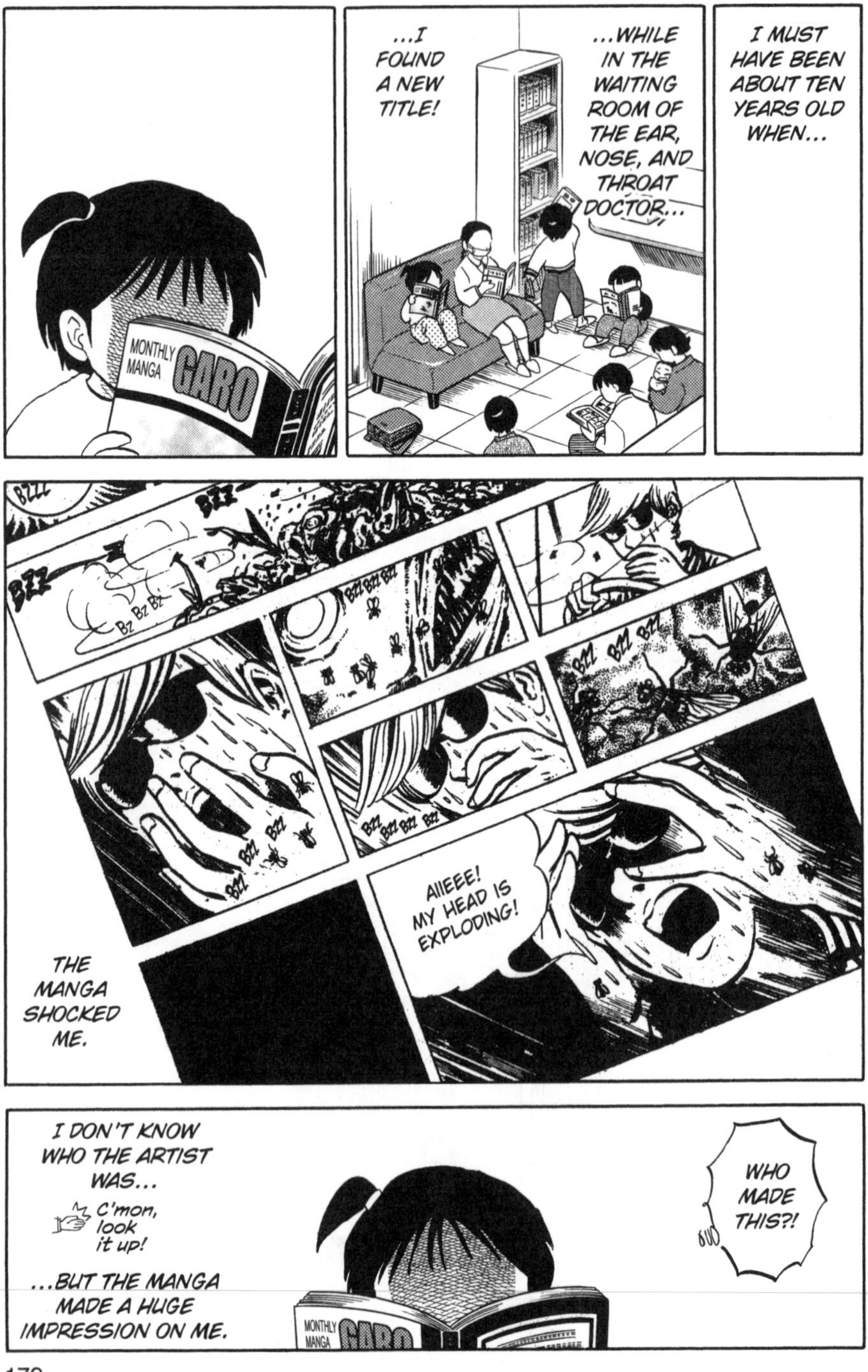
I MUST HAVE BEEN ABOUT TEN YEARS OLD WHEN...
...WHILE IN THE WAITING ROOM OF THE EAR, NOSE, AND THROAT DOCTOR...
...I FOUND A NEW TITLE!
MONTHLY MANGA GARO
AIIEEE! MY HEAD IS EXPLODING!
THE MANGA SHOCKED ME.
WHO MADE THIS?!
I DON'T KNOW WHO THE ARTIST WAS...
C'mon, look it up!
...BUT THE MANGA MADE A HUGE IMPRESSION ON ME.
MONTHLY MANGA

AROUND THE SAME TIME, MY BROTHER USED TO BUY A MANGA MAGAZINE CALLED COM. AND IN THE READER FORUM SECTION I SAW...

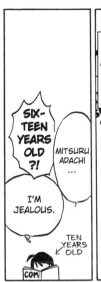

I DISCOVERED HIM!

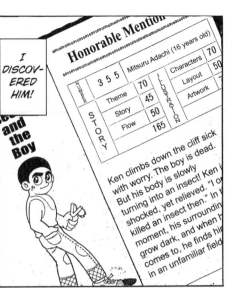

Honorable Mention

		Mitsuru Adachi (16 years old)		Characters	70
NUMBER	3 5 5		ILLUSTRATION	Layout	50
		Theme	70	Artwork	
STORY		Story	45		
		Flow	50		
			165		

Ken climbs down the cliff sick with worry. The boy is dead. But his body is slowly turning into an insect! Ken is shocked, yet relieved. "I o killed an insect then." In t moment, his surroundin grow dark, and when h comes to, he finds hi in an unfamiliar field

and the Boy

SIXTEEN YEARS OLD?!

MITSURU ADACHI...

I'M JEALOUS.

TEN YEARS OLD

COM

I SENT IN MY FIRST SUBMISSION AROUND MY FIRST YEAR OF MIDDLE SCHOOL.

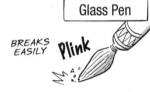

Glass Pen

BREAKS EASILY

Plink

I GRABBED A DRAWING PEN FOR THE FIRST TIME WHEN I WAS IN SIXTH GRADE.

I PASSED THE FIRST ROUND OF JUDGING.

MY NAME GOT PUBLISHED IN THE MAGAZINE!

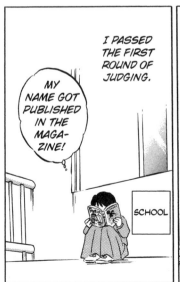

SCHOOL

I SENT OVER A DOZEN PAGES OF A FOUR-PANEL MANGA SERIES, A FAIRY-TALE STORY.

OF COURSE, I SUBMITTED TO SHONEN SUNDAY.

buzz buzz

I WANT TO GET PUBLISHED!

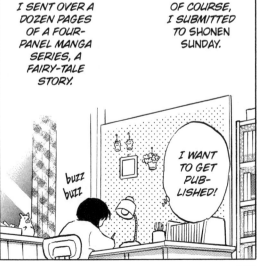

High School

Mitsuru Adachi

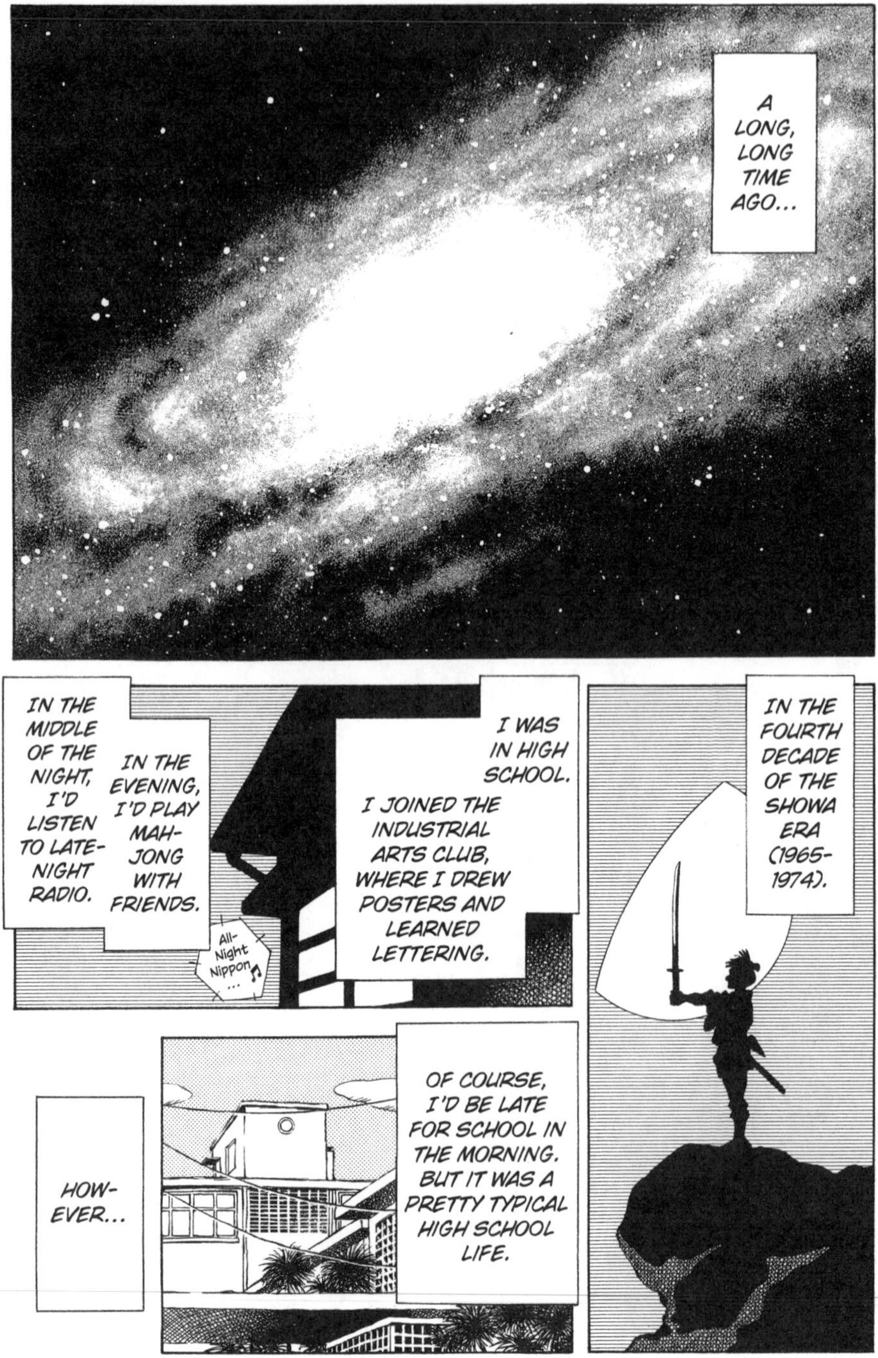
A LONG, LONG TIME AGO...
IN THE FOURTH DECADE OF THE SHOWA ERA (1965-1974).
I WAS IN HIGH SCHOOL.
I JOINED THE INDUSTRIAL ARTS CLUB, WHERE I DREW POSTERS AND LEARNED LETTERING.
IN THE EVENING, I'D PLAY MAH-JONG WITH FRIENDS.
IN THE MIDDLE OF THE NIGHT, I'D LISTEN TO LATE-NIGHT RADIO.
All-Night Nippon ♪ ...
OF COURSE, I'D BE LATE FOR SCHOOL IN THE MORNING. BUT IT WAS A PRETTY TYPICAL HIGH SCHOOL LIFE.
HOW-EVER...

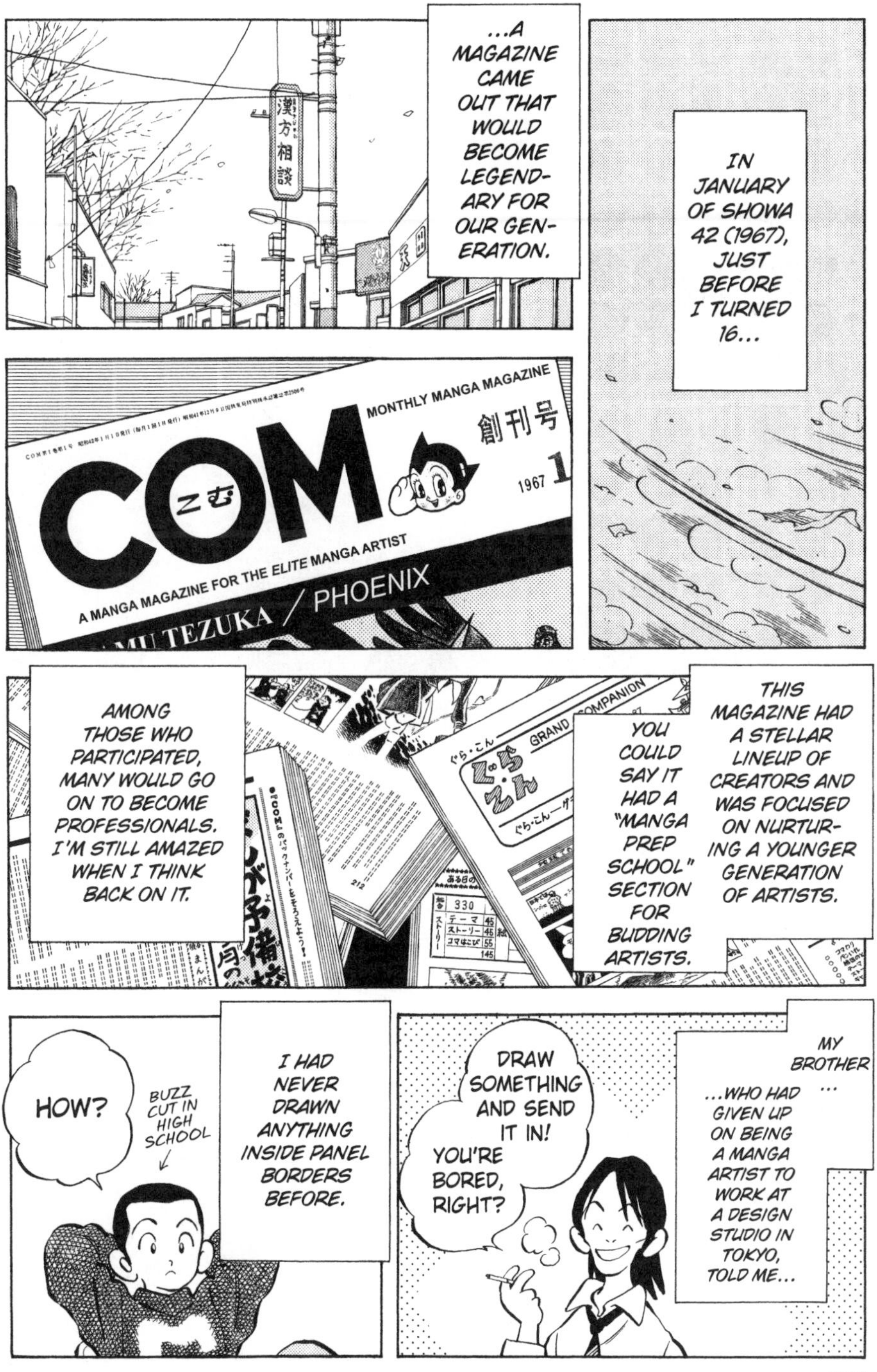
IN JANUARY OF SHOWA 42 (1967), JUST BEFORE I TURNED 16...
...A MAGAZINE CAME OUT THAT WOULD BECOME LEGENDARY FOR OUR GENERATION.
漢方相談
MONTHLY MANGA MAGAZINE
創刊号
1967 1
COM
こむ
A MANGA MAGAZINE FOR THE ELITE MANGA ARTIST
PHOENIX
THIS MAGAZINE HAD A STELLAR LINEUP OF CREATORS AND WAS FOCUSED ON NURTURING A YOUNGER GENERATION OF ARTISTS.
YOU COULD SAY IT HAD A "MANGA PREP SCHOOL" SECTION FOR BUDDING ARTISTS.
GRAND COMPANION
ぐら・こん
AMONG THOSE WHO PARTICIPATED, MANY WOULD GO ON TO BECOME PROFESSIONALS. I'M STILL AMAZED WHEN I THINK BACK ON IT.
MY BROTHER...
...WHO HAD GIVEN UP ON BEING A MANGA ARTIST TO WORK AT A DESIGN STUDIO IN TOKYO, TOLD ME...
DRAW SOMETHING AND SEND IT IN!
YOU'RE BORED, RIGHT?
I HAD NEVER DRAWN ANYTHING INSIDE PANEL BORDERS BEFORE.
HOW?
BUZZ CUT IN HIGH SCHOOL

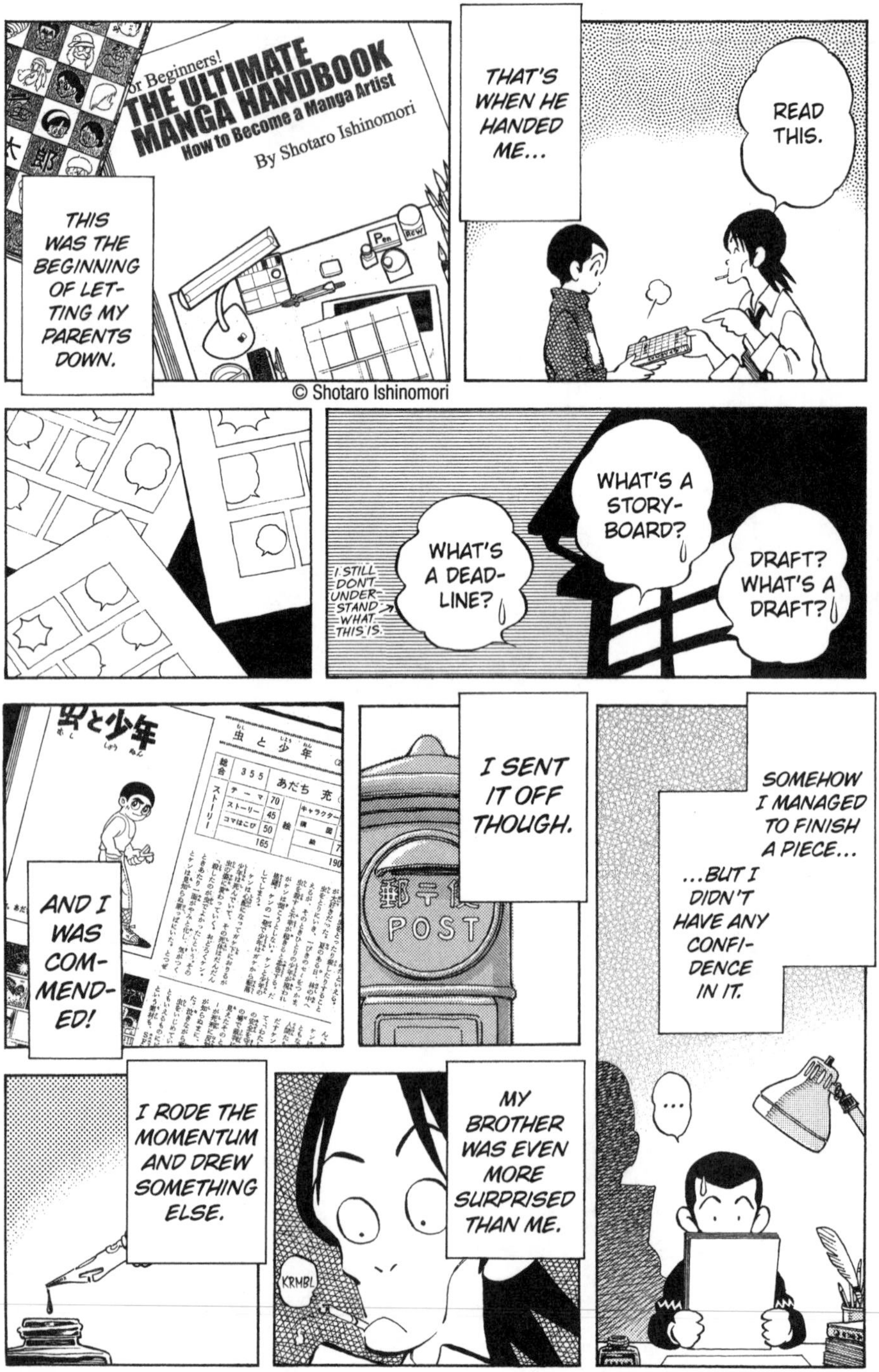
THAT'S WHEN HE HANDED ME...
READ THIS.
or Beginners!
THE ULTIMATE MANGA HANDBOOK
How to Become a Manga Artist
By Shotaro Ishinomori
THIS WAS THE BEGINNING OF LETTING MY PARENTS DOWN.
DRAFT? WHAT'S A DRAFT?
WHAT'S A STORY-BOARD?
WHAT'S A DEAD-LINE?
I STILL DONT UNDER-STAND WHAT THIS IS.
SOMEHOW I MANAGED TO FINISH A PIECE...
...BUT I DIDN'T HAVE ANY CONFI-DENCE IN IT.
...
I SENT IT OFF THOUGH.
POST
虫と少年
AND I WAS COM-MEND-ED!
MY BROTHER WAS EVEN MORE SURPRISED THAN ME.
KRMBL
I RODE THE MOMENTUM AND DREW SOMETHING ELSE.

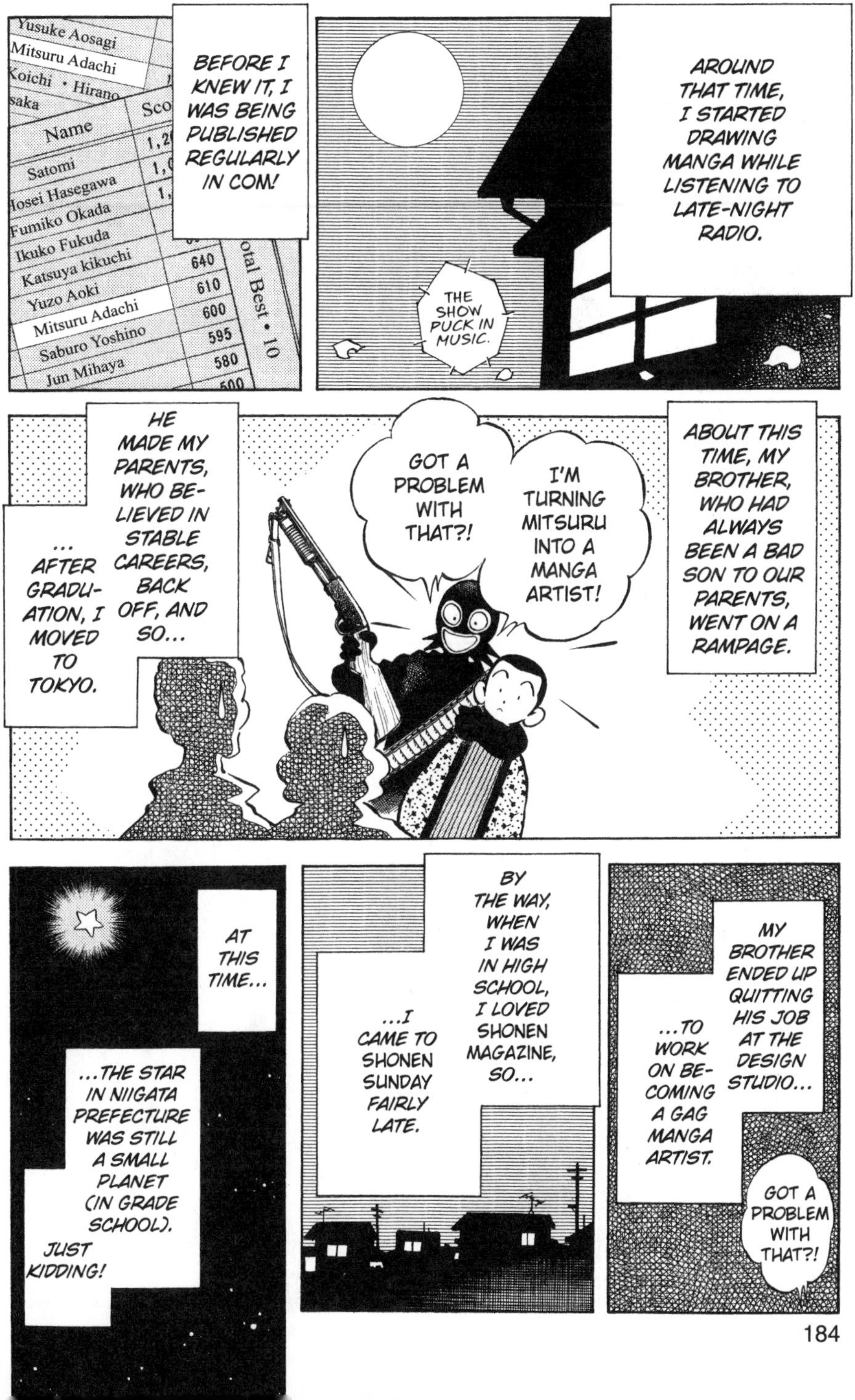

AROUND THAT TIME, I STARTED DRAWING MANGA WHILE LISTENING TO LATE-NIGHT RADIO.
THE SHOW PUCK IN MUSIC.
BEFORE I KNEW IT, I WAS BEING PUBLISHED REGULARLY IN COM!
Yusuke Aosagi
Mitsuru Adachi
Koichi · Hirano
Name
Satomi
Hosei Hasegawa
Fumiko Okada
Ikuko Fukuda
Katsuya kikuchi 640
Yuzo Aoki 610
Mitsuru Adachi 600
Saburo Yoshino 595
Jun Mihaya 580
Total Best • 10
ABOUT THIS TIME, MY BROTHER, WHO HAD ALWAYS BEEN A BAD SON TO OUR PARENTS, WENT ON A RAMPAGE.
I'M TURNING MITSURU INTO A MANGA ARTIST!
GOT A PROBLEM WITH THAT?!
HE MADE MY PARENTS, WHO BELIEVED IN STABLE CAREERS, BACK OFF, AND SO...
...AFTER GRADUATION, I MOVED TO TOKYO.
MY BROTHER ENDED UP QUITTING HIS JOB AT THE DESIGN STUDIO...
...TO WORK ON BECOMING A GAG MANGA ARTIST.
GOT A PROBLEM WITH THAT?!
BY THE WAY, WHEN I WAS IN HIGH SCHOOL, I LOVED SHONEN MAGAZINE, SO...
...I CAME TO SHONEN SUNDAY FAIRLY LATE.
AT THIS TIME...
...THE STAR IN NIIGATA PREFECTURE WAS STILL A SMALL PLANET (IN GRADE SCHOOL).
JUST KIDDING!

Middle School to High School

Rumiko Takahashi

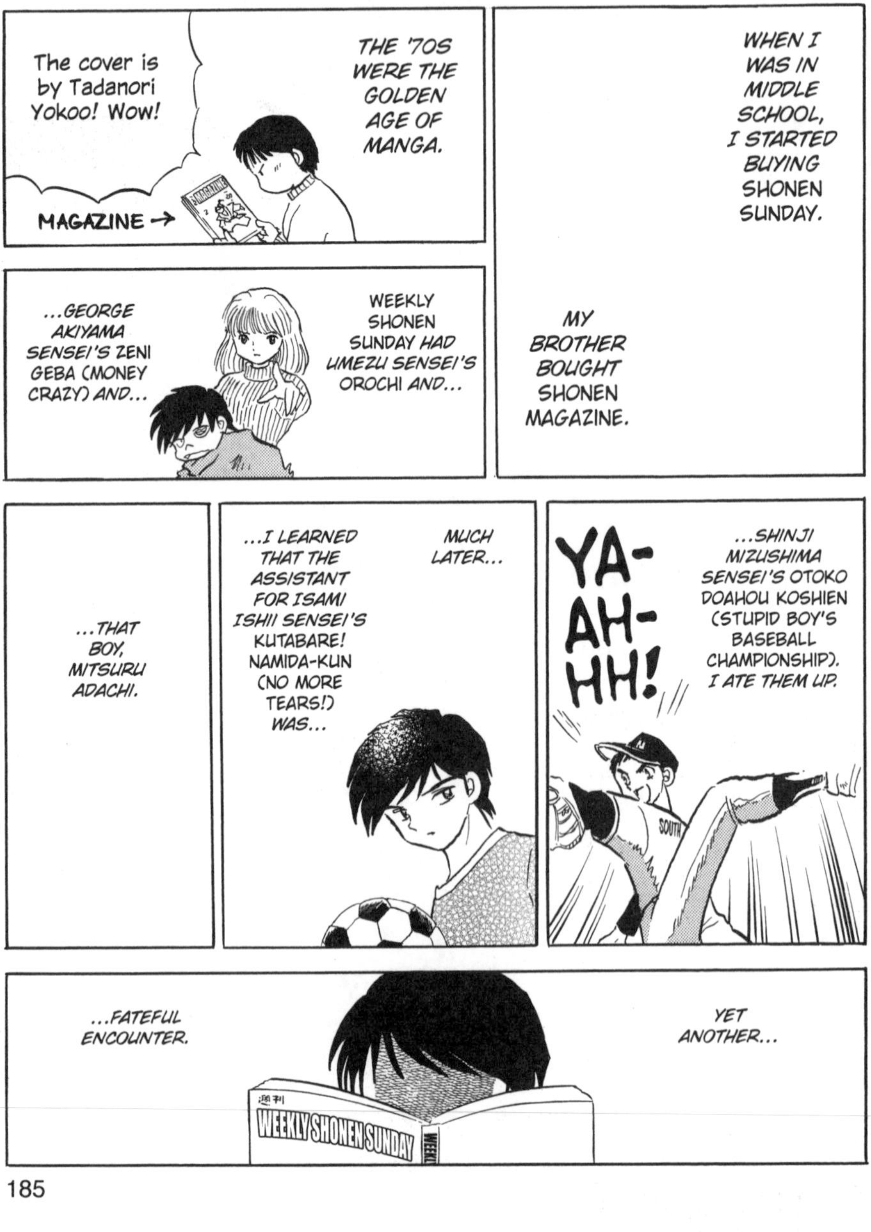
WHEN I WAS IN MIDDLE SCHOOL, I STARTED BUYING SHONEN SUNDAY.
MY BROTHER BOUGHT SHONEN MAGAZINE.
THE '70S WERE THE GOLDEN AGE OF MANGA.
The cover is by Tadanori Yokoo! Wow!
MAGAZINE →
WEEKLY SHONEN SUNDAY HAD UMEZU SENSEI'S OROCHI AND...
...GEORGE AKIYAMA SENSEI'S ZENI GEBA (MONEY CRAZY) AND...
...SHINJI MIZUSHIMA SENSEI'S OTOKO DOAHOU KOSHIEN (STUPID BOY'S BASEBALL CHAMPIONSHIP). I ATE THEM UP.
YA-AH-HH!
SOUTH
MUCH LATER...
...I LEARNED THAT THE ASSISTANT FOR ISAMI ISHII SENSEI'S KUTABARE! NAMIDA-KUN (NO MORE TEARS!) WAS...
...THAT BOY, MITSURU ADACHI.
YET ANOTHER...
...FATEFUL ENCOUNTER.
WEEKLY SHONEN SUNDAY

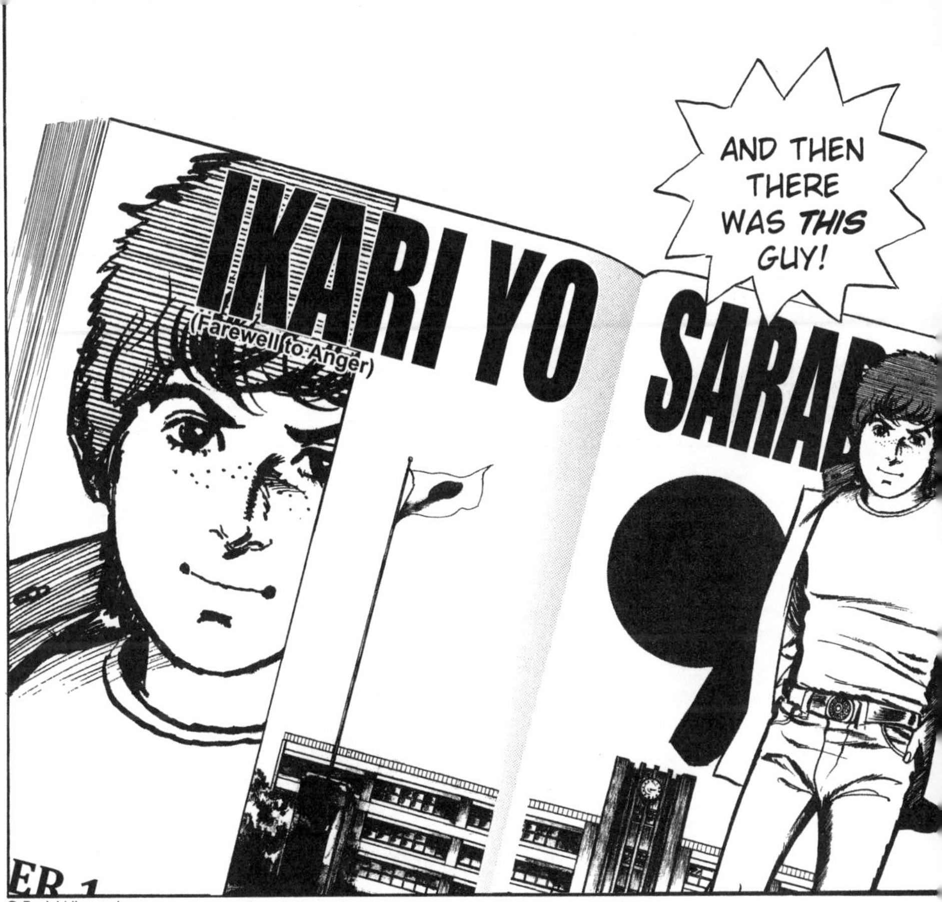
AND THEN THERE WAS THIS GUY!
IKARI YO SARAB
(Farewell to Anger)

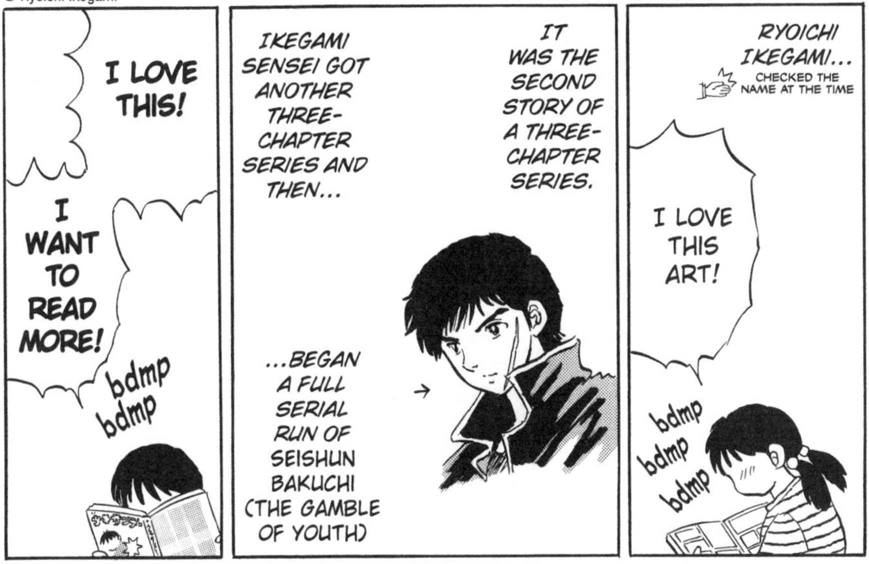
RYOICHI IKEGAMI...
CHECKED THE NAME AT THE TIME
I LOVE THIS ART!
bdmp bdmp bdmp
IT WAS THE SECOND STORY OF A THREE-CHAPTER SERIES.
IKEGAMI SENSEI GOT ANOTHER THREE-CHAPTER SERIES AND THEN...
...BEGAN A FULL SERIAL RUN OF SEISHUN BAKUCHI (THE GAMBLE OF YOUTH)
I LOVE THIS!
I WANT TO READ MORE!
bdmp bdmp

*Story by Hisao Maki Sensei

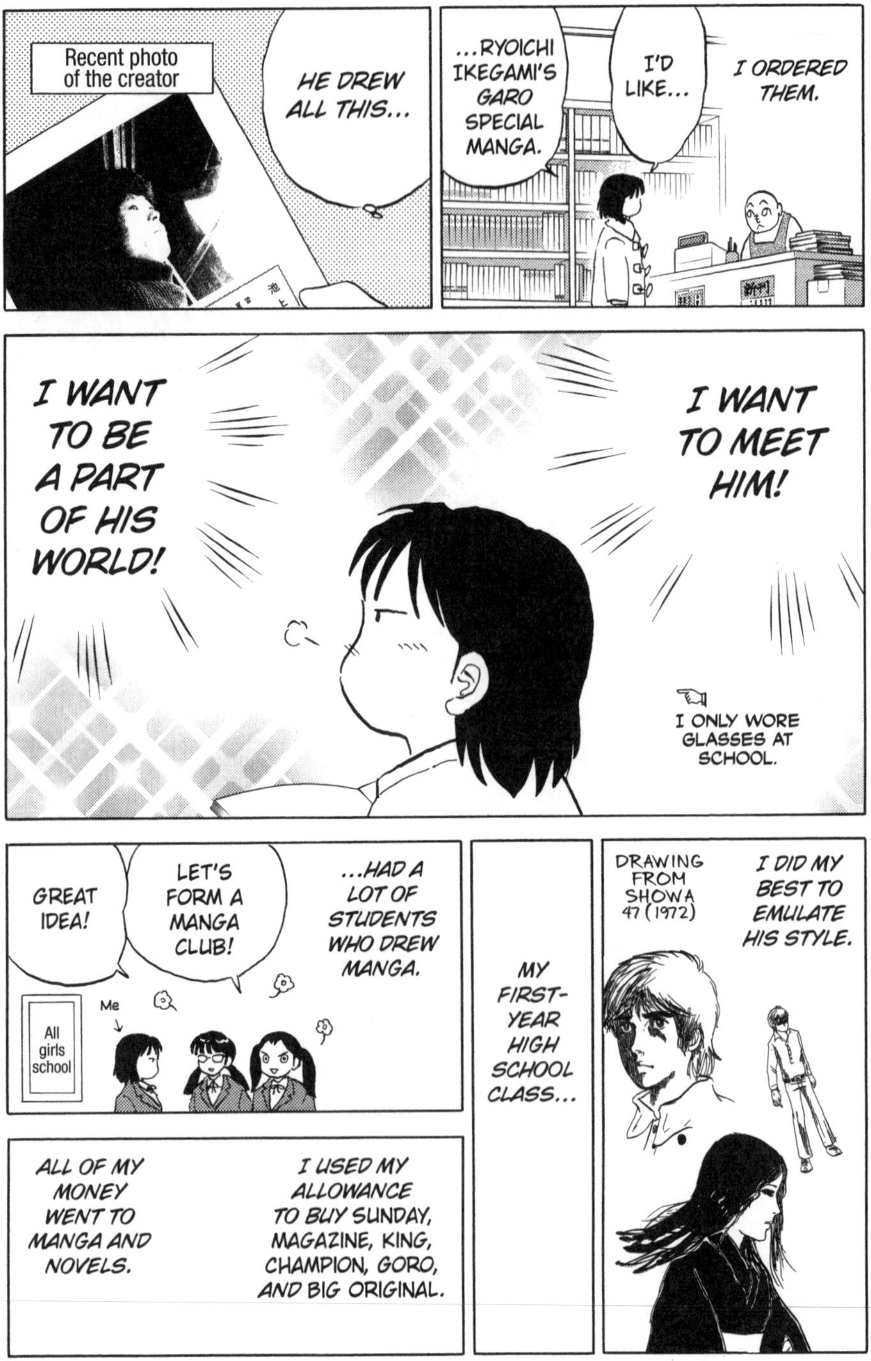
I ORDERED THEM.
I'D LIKE...
...RYOICHI IKEGAMI'S GARO SPECIAL MANGA.
HE DREW ALL THIS...
Recent photo of the creator
I WANT TO MEET HIM!
I WANT TO BE A PART OF HIS WORLD!
I ONLY WORE GLASSES AT SCHOOL.
I DID MY BEST TO EMULATE HIS STYLE.
DRAWING FROM SHOWA 47 (1972)
MY FIRST-YEAR HIGH SCHOOL CLASS...
...HAD A LOT OF STUDENTS WHO DREW MANGA.
LET'S FORM A MANGA CLUB!
GREAT IDEA!
Me
All girls school
I USED MY ALLOWANCE TO BUY SUNDAY, MAGAZINE, KING, CHAMPION, GORO, AND BIG ORIGINAL.
ALL OF MY MONEY WENT TO MANGA AND NOVELS.

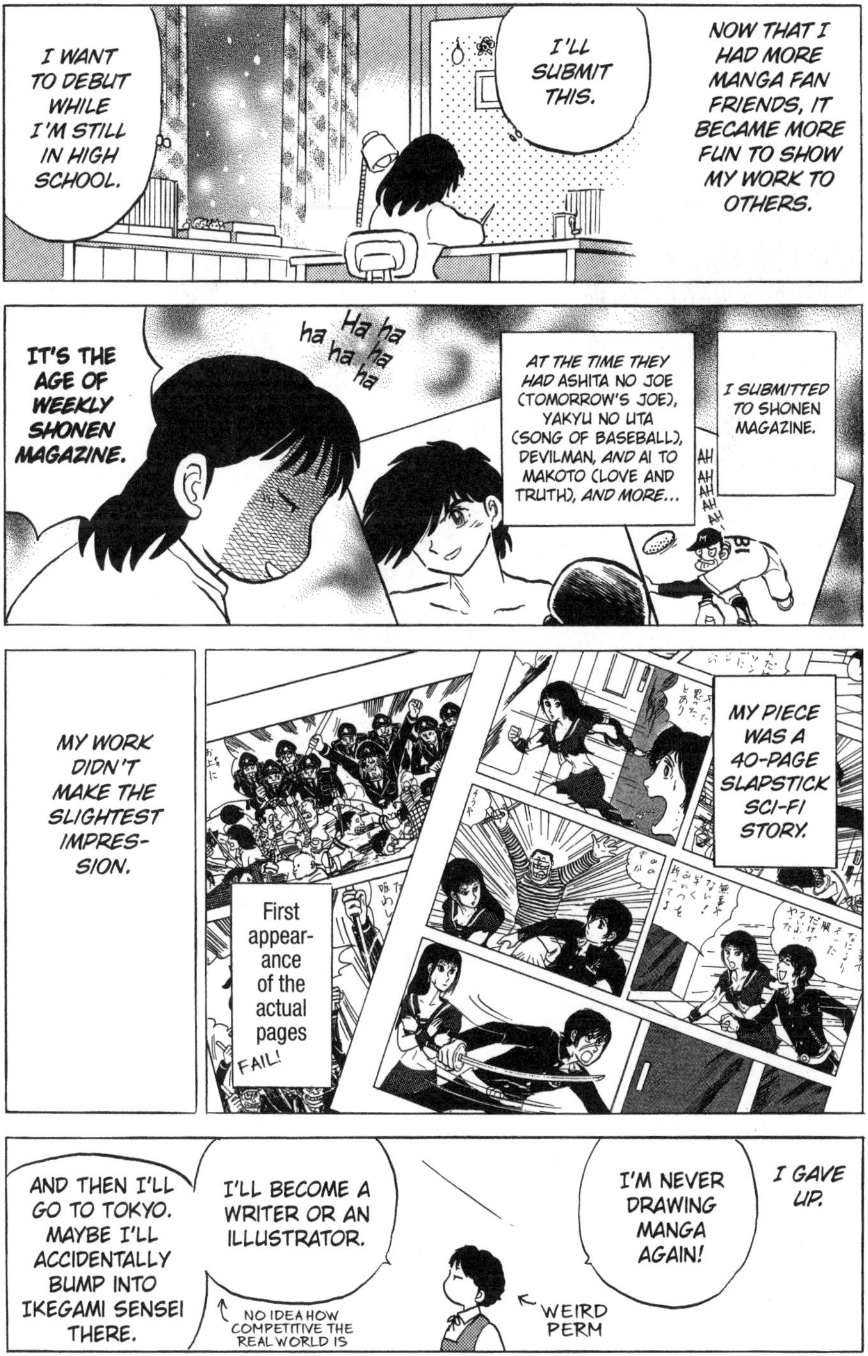
NOW THAT I HAD MORE MANGA FAN FRIENDS, IT BECAME MORE FUN TO SHOW MY WORK TO OTHERS.
I'LL SUBMIT THIS.
I WANT TO DEBUT WHILE I'M STILL IN HIGH SCHOOL.
I SUBMITTED TO SHONEN MAGAZINE.
AT THE TIME THEY HAD ASHITA NO JOE (TOMORROW'S JOE), YAKYU NO UTA (SONG OF BASEBALL), DEVILMAN, AND AI TO MAKOTO (LOVE AND TRUTH), AND MORE...
AH AH AH AH AH
Ha ha ha ha ha ha
IT'S THE AGE OF WEEKLY SHONEN MAGAZINE.
MY PIECE WAS A 40-PAGE SLAPSTICK SCI-FI STORY.
First appearance of the actual pages
FAIL!
MY WORK DIDN'T MAKE THE SLIGHTEST IMPRESSION.
I GAVE UP.
I'M NEVER DRAWING MANGA AGAIN!
WEIRD PERM
I'LL BECOME A WRITER OR AN ILLUSTRATOR.
NO IDEA HOW COMPETITIVE THE REAL WORLD IS
AND THEN I'LL GO TO TOKYO. MAYBE I'LL ACCIDENTALLY BUMP INTO IKEGAMI SENSEI THERE.

Move to Tokyo

Mitsuru Adachi

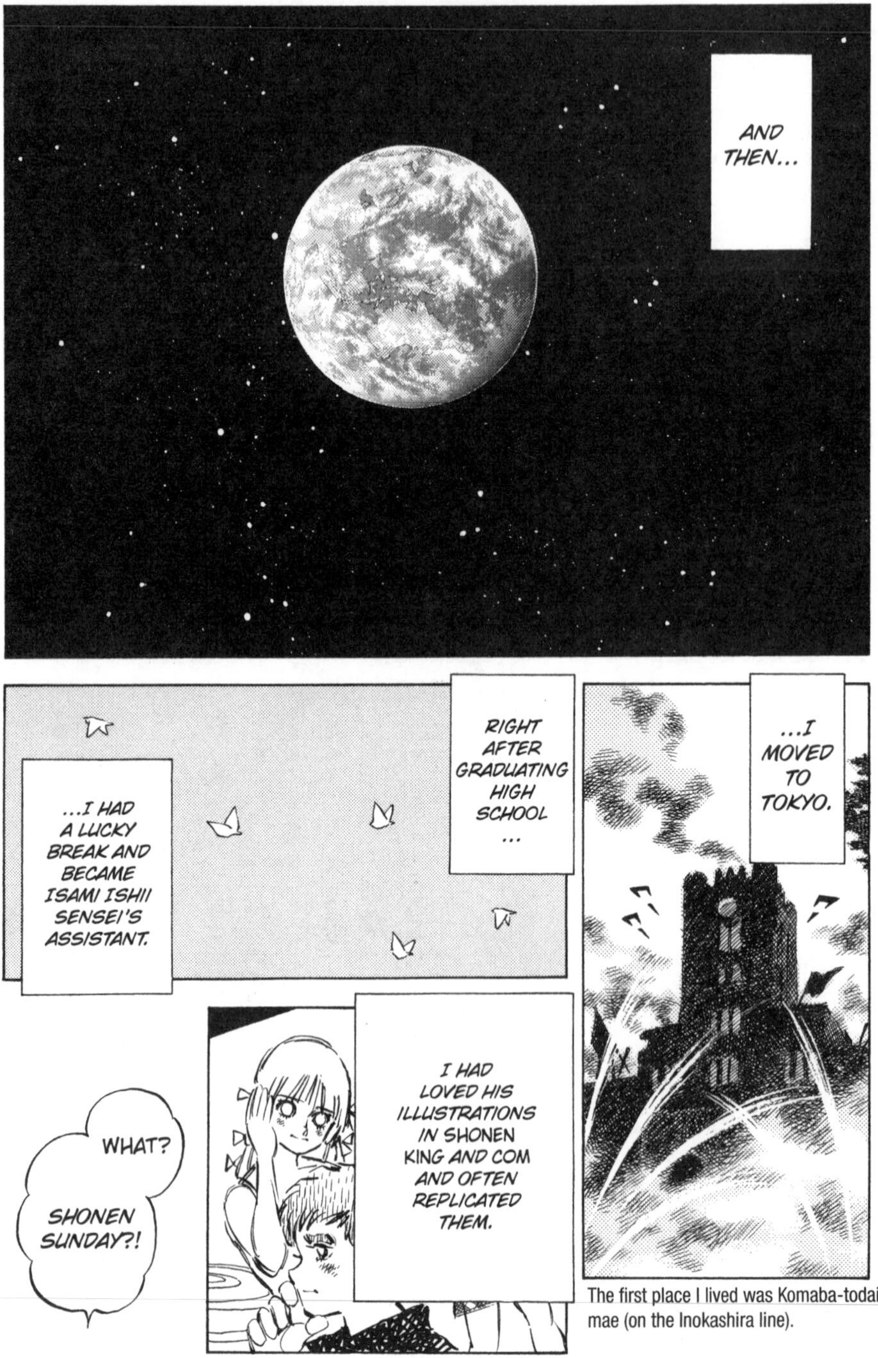
AND THEN...
RIGHT AFTER GRADUATING HIGH SCHOOL ...
...I MOVED TO TOKYO.
...I HAD A LUCKY BREAK AND BECAME ISAMI ISHII SENSEI'S ASSISTANT.
I HAD LOVED HIS ILLUSTRATIONS IN SHONEN KING AND COM AND OFTEN REPLICATED THEM.
WHAT? SHONEN SUNDAY?!

The first place I lived was Komaba-todai-mae (on the Inokashira line).

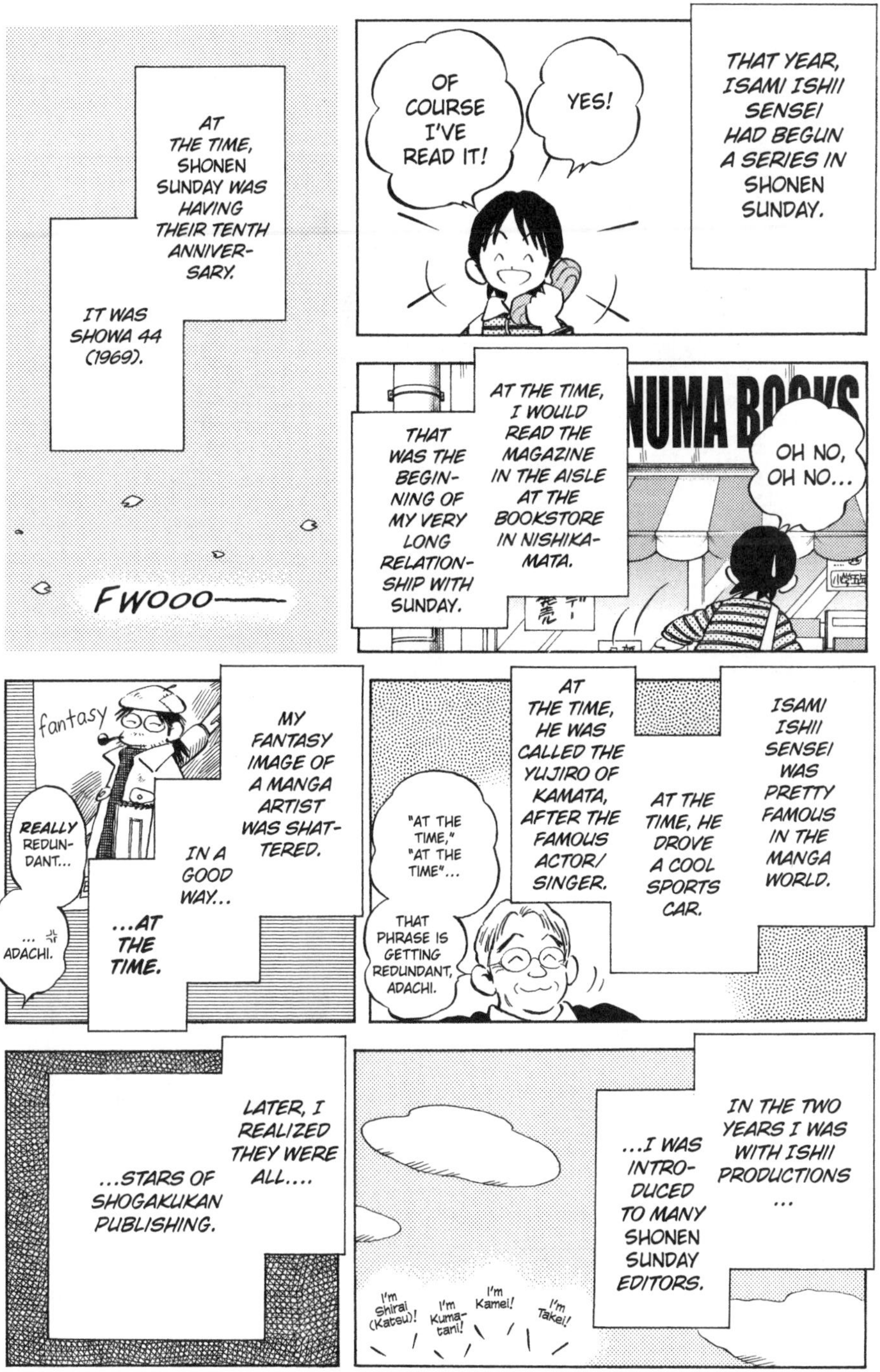

THAT YEAR, ISAMI ISHII SENSEI HAD BEGUN A SERIES IN SHONEN SUNDAY.
YES!
OF COURSE I'VE READ IT!
NUMA BOOKS
OH NO, OH NO...
AT THE TIME, I WOULD READ THE MAGAZINE IN THE AISLE AT THE BOOKSTORE IN NISHIKAMATA.
THAT WAS THE BEGINNING OF MY VERY LONG RELATIONSHIP WITH SUNDAY.
AT THE TIME, SHONEN SUNDAY WAS HAVING THEIR TENTH ANNIVERSARY.
IT WAS SHOWA 44 (1969).
FWOOO——
ISAMI ISHII SENSEI WAS PRETTY FAMOUS IN THE MANGA WORLD.
AT THE TIME, HE WAS CALLED THE YUJIRO OF KAMATA, AFTER THE FAMOUS ACTOR/SINGER.
AT THE TIME, HE DROVE A COOL SPORTS CAR.
"AT THE TIME," "AT THE TIME"...
THAT PHRASE IS GETTING REDUNDANT, ADACHI.
MY FANTASY IMAGE OF A MANGA ARTIST WAS SHATTERED.
IN A GOOD WAY...
...AT THE TIME.
fantasy
REALLY REDUNDANT...
... ADACHI.
IN THE TWO YEARS I WAS WITH ISHII PRODUCTIONS...
...I WAS INTRODUCED TO MANY SHONEN SUNDAY EDITORS.
I'm Takei!
I'm Kamei!
I'm Kumatani!
I'm Shirai (Katsu)!
LATER, I REALIZED THEY WERE ALL....
...STARS OF SHOGAKUKAN PUBLISHING.

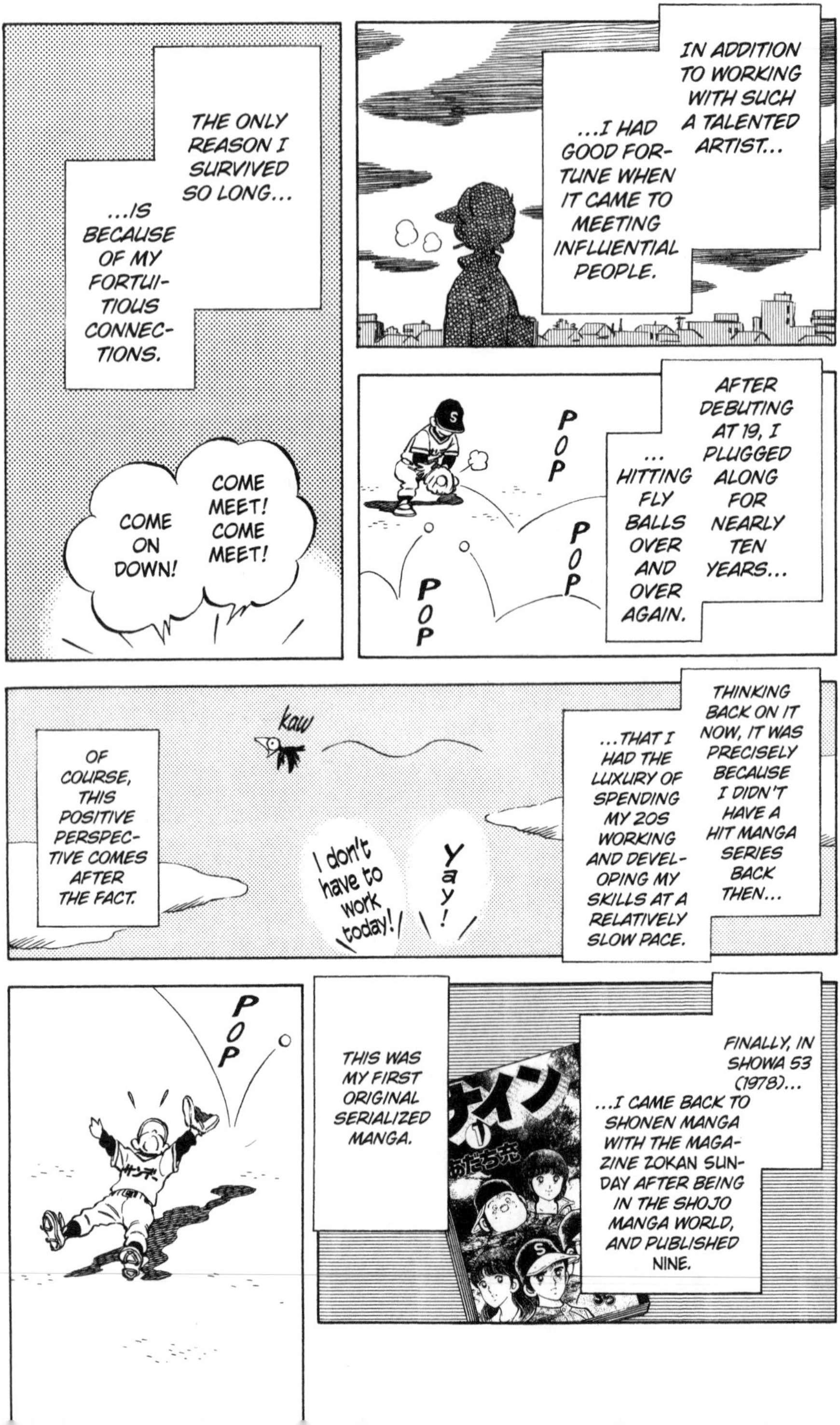
IN ADDITION TO WORKING WITH SUCH A TALENTED ARTIST...
...I HAD GOOD FORTUNE WHEN IT CAME TO MEETING INFLUENTIAL PEOPLE.
AFTER DEBUTING AT 19, I PLUGGED ALONG FOR NEARLY TEN YEARS...
...HITTING FLY BALLS OVER AND OVER AGAIN.
POP
POP
POP
THE ONLY REASON I SURVIVED SO LONG...
...IS BECAUSE OF MY FORTUITIOUS CONNECTIONS.
COME MEET! COME MEET!
COME ON DOWN!
THINKING BACK ON IT NOW, IT WAS PRECISELY BECAUSE I DIDN'T HAVE A HIT MANGA SERIES BACK THEN...
...THAT I HAD THE LUXURY OF SPENDING MY 20S WORKING AND DEVELOPING MY SKILLS AT A RELATIVELY SLOW PACE.
Yay!
I don't have to work today!
kaw
OF COURSE, THIS POSITIVE PERSPECTIVE COMES AFTER THE FACT.
FINALLY, IN SHOWA 53 (1978)...
...I CAME BACK TO SHONEN MANGA WITH THE MAGAZINE ZOKAN SUNDAY AFTER BEING IN THE SHOJO MANGA WORLD, AND PUBLISHED NINE.
THIS WAS MY FIRST ORIGINAL SERIALIZED MANGA.
POP

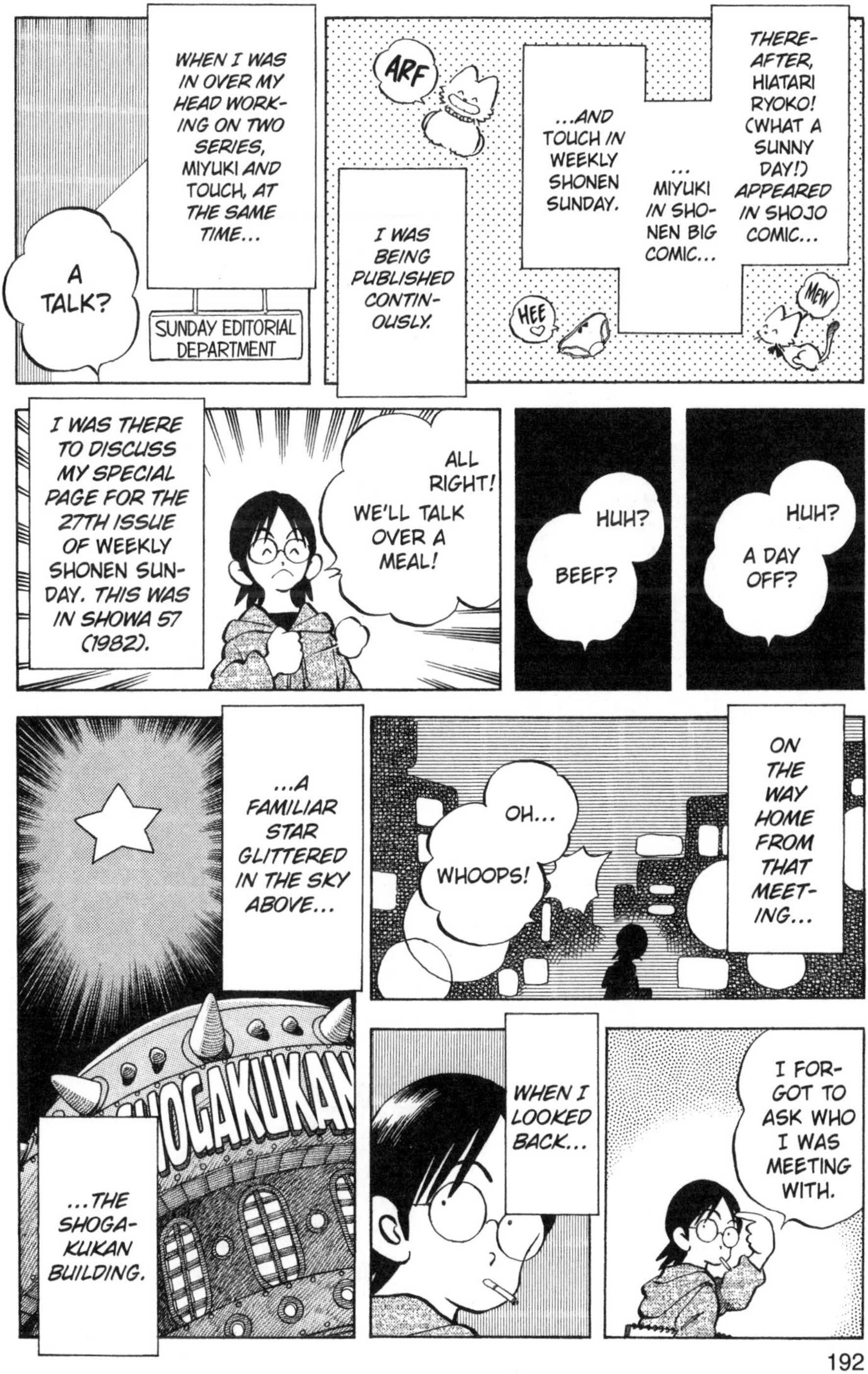
THEREAFTER, HIATARI RYOKO! (WHAT A SUNNY DAY!) APPEARED IN SHOJO COMIC...
MEW
...MIYUKI IN SHONEN BIG COMIC...
...AND TOUCH IN WEEKLY SHONEN SUNDAY.
ARF
HEE
I WAS BEING PUBLISHED CONTINOUSLY.
WHEN I WAS IN OVER MY HEAD WORKING ON TWO SERIES, MIYUKI AND TOUCH, AT THE SAME TIME...
SUNDAY EDITORIAL DEPARTMENT
A TALK?
HUH? A DAY OFF?
HUH? BEEF?
ALL RIGHT! WE'LL TALK OVER A MEAL!
I WAS THERE TO DISCUSS MY SPECIAL PAGE FOR THE 27TH ISSUE OF WEEKLY SHONEN SUNDAY. THIS WAS IN SHOWA 57 (1982).
ON THE WAY HOME FROM THAT MEETING...
OH... WHOOPS!
I FORGOT TO ASK WHO I WAS MEETING WITH.
WHEN I LOOKED BACK...
...A FAMILIAR STAR GLITTERED IN THE SKY ABOVE...
SHOGAKUKAN
...THE SHOGAKUKAN BUILDING.

Move to Tokyo

Rumiko Takahashi

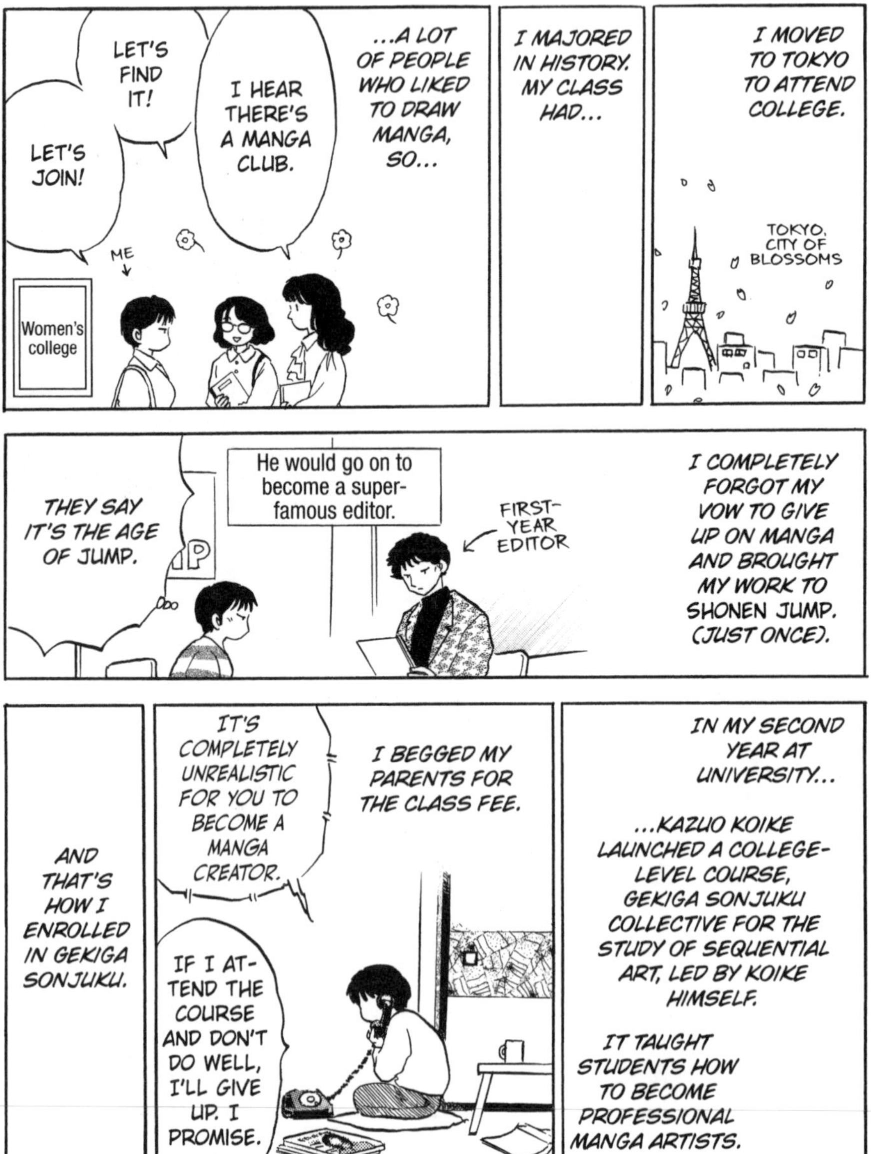
I MOVED TO TOKYO TO ATTEND COLLEGE.
TOKYO, CITY OF BLOSSOMS
I MAJORED IN HISTORY. MY CLASS HAD...
...A LOT OF PEOPLE WHO LIKED TO DRAW MANGA, SO...
I HEAR THERE'S A MANGA CLUB.
LET'S FIND IT!
LET'S JOIN!
ME
Women's college
I COMPLETELY FORGOT MY VOW TO GIVE UP ON MANGA AND BROUGHT MY WORK TO SHONEN JUMP. (JUST ONCE).
FIRST-YEAR EDITOR
He would go on to become a super-famous editor.
THEY SAY IT'S THE AGE OF JUMP.
IN MY SECOND YEAR AT UNIVERSITY...
...KAZUO KOIKE LAUNCHED A COLLEGE-LEVEL COURSE, GEKIGA SONJUKU COLLECTIVE FOR THE STUDY OF SEQUENTIAL ART, LED BY KOIKE HIMSELF.
IT TAUGHT STUDENTS HOW TO BECOME PROFESSIONAL MANGA ARTISTS.
I BEGGED MY PARENTS FOR THE CLASS FEE.
IT'S COMPLETELY UNREALISTIC FOR YOU TO BECOME A MANGA CREATOR.
IF I ATTEND THE COURSE AND DON'T DO WELL, I'LL GIVE UP. I PROMISE.
AND THAT'S HOW I ENROLLED IN GEKIGA SONJUKU.

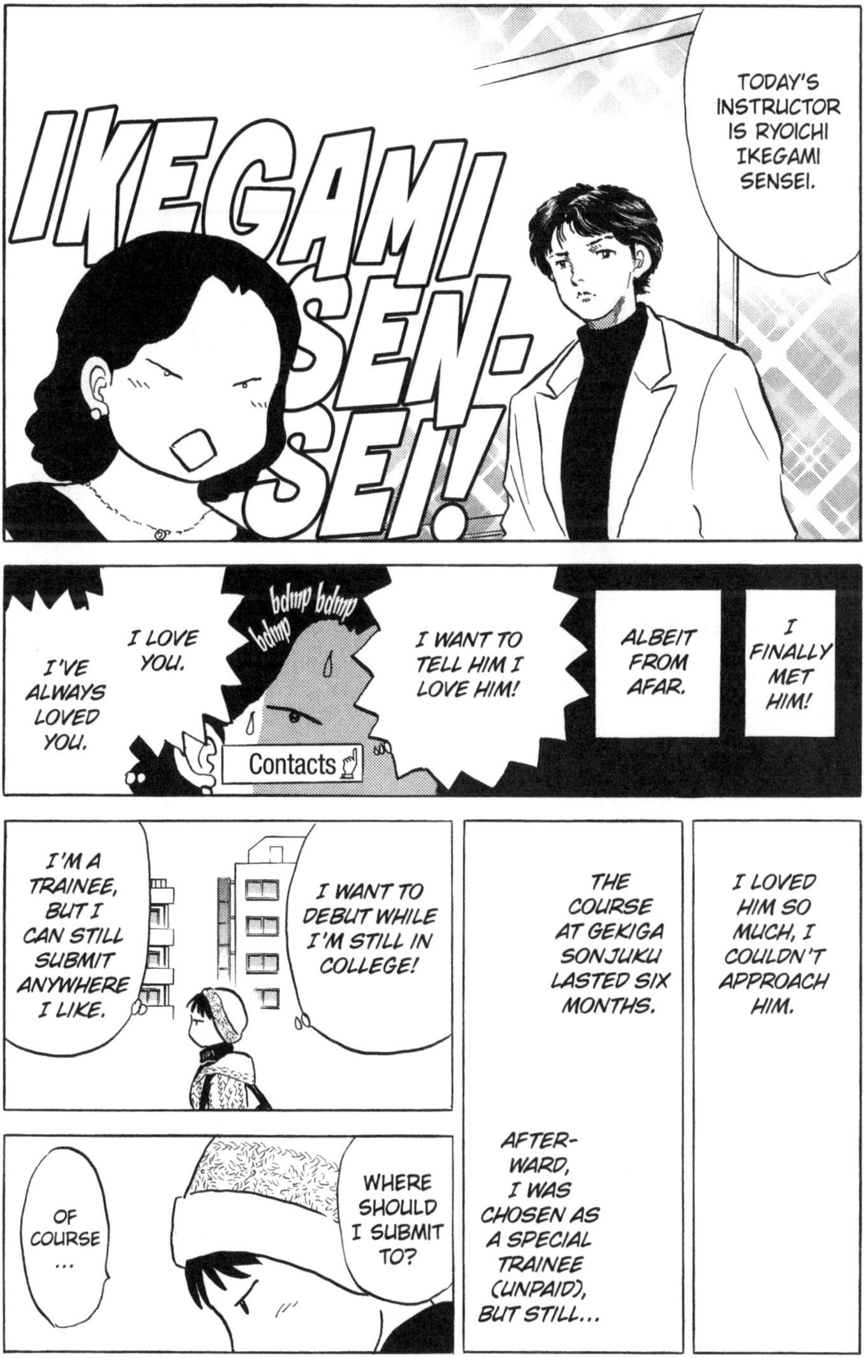
TODAY'S INSTRUCTOR IS RYOICHI IKEGAMI SENSEI.
IKEGAMI SEN-SEI!
I FINALLY MET HIM!
ALBEIT FROM AFAR.
I WANT TO TELL HIM I LOVE HIM!
bdmp bdmp bdmp
I LOVE YOU.
I'VE ALWAYS LOVED YOU.
Contacts
I LOVED HIM SO MUCH, I COULDN'T APPROACH HIM.
THE COURSE AT GEKIGA SONJUKU LASTED SIX MONTHS.
AFTER-WARD, I WAS CHOSEN AS A SPECIAL TRAINEE (UNPAID), BUT STILL...
I WANT TO DEBUT WHILE I'M STILL IN COLLEGE!
I'M A TRAINEE, BUT I CAN STILL SUBMIT ANYWHERE I LIKE.
WHERE SHOULD I SUBMIT TO?
OF COURSE...

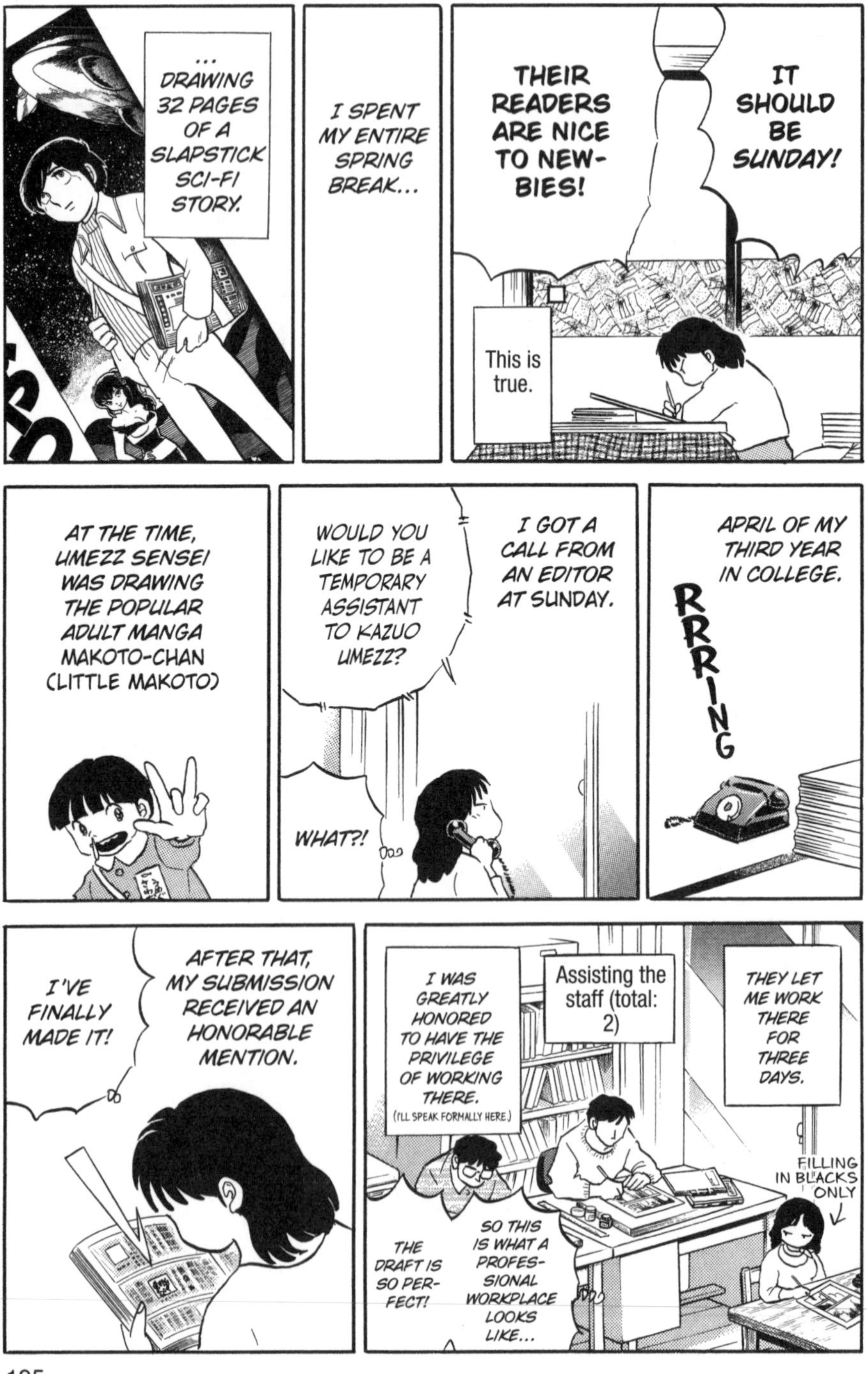
IT SHOULD BE SUNDAY!
THEIR READERS ARE NICE TO NEW-BIES!
This is true.
I SPENT MY ENTIRE SPRING BREAK...
... DRAWING 32 PAGES OF A SLAPSTICK SCI-FI STORY.
APRIL OF MY THIRD YEAR IN COLLEGE.
RRRING
I GOT A CALL FROM AN EDITOR AT SUNDAY.
WOULD YOU LIKE TO BE A TEMPORARY ASSISTANT TO KAZUO UMEZZ?
WHAT?!
AT THE TIME, UMEZZ SENSEI WAS DRAWING THE POPULAR ADULT MANGA MAKOTO-CHAN (LITTLE MAKOTO)
THEY LET ME WORK THERE FOR THREE DAYS.
Assisting the staff (total: 2)
I WAS GREATLY HONORED TO HAVE THE PRIVILEGE OF WORKING THERE.
(I'LL SPEAK FORMALLY HERE.)
FILLING IN BLACKS ONLY
SO THIS IS WHAT A PROFES-SIONAL WORKPLACE LOOKS LIKE...
THE DRAFT IS SO PER-FECT!
AFTER THAT, MY SUBMISSION RECEIVED AN HONORABLE MENTION.
I'VE FINALLY MADE IT!

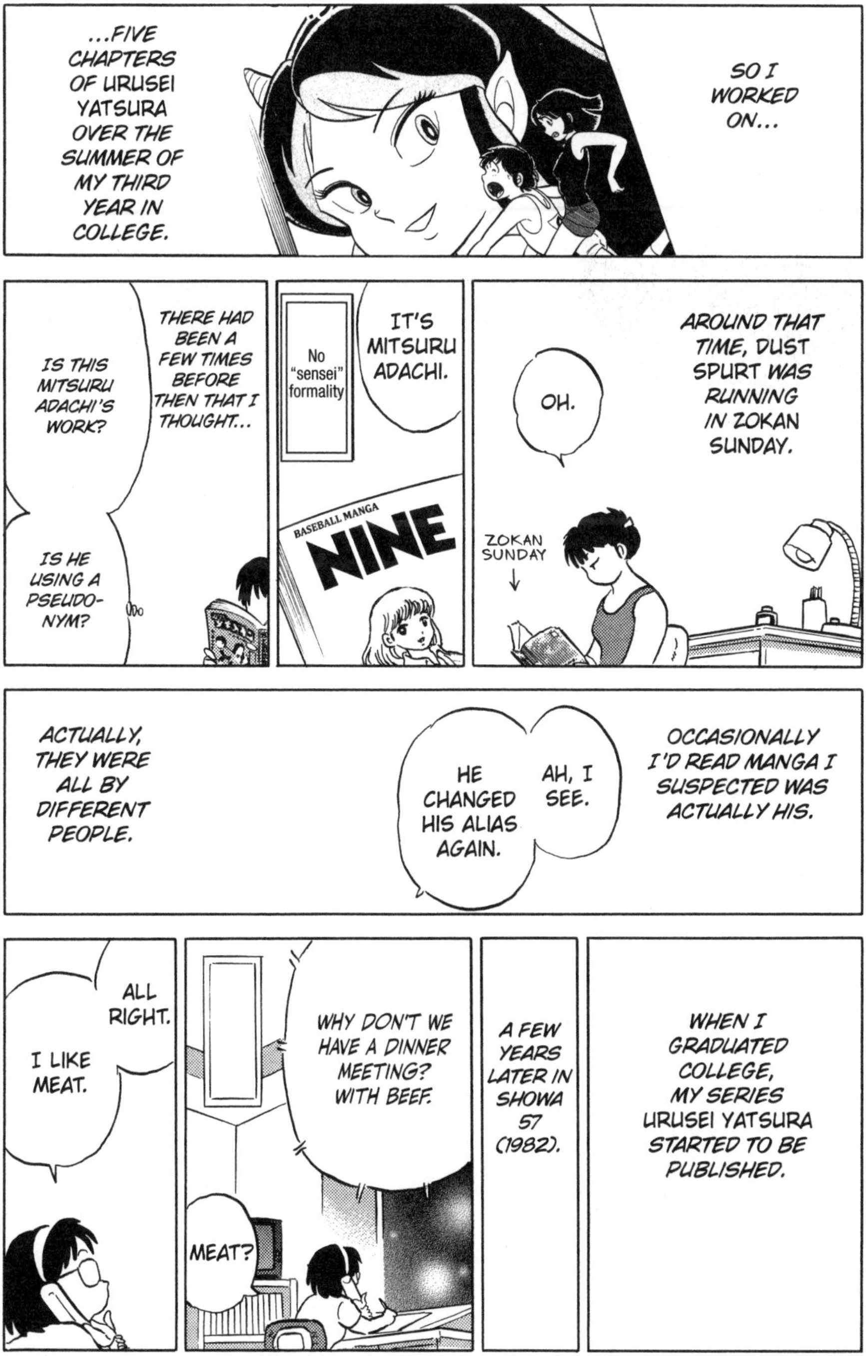
SO I WORKED ON...
...FIVE CHAPTERS OF URUSEI YATSURA OVER THE SUMMER OF MY THIRD YEAR IN COLLEGE.
AROUND THAT TIME, DUST SPURT WAS RUNNING IN ZOKAN SUNDAY.
OH.
ZOKAN SUNDAY
IT'S MITSURU ADACHI.
No "sensei" formality
BASEBALL MANGA
NINE
THERE HAD BEEN A FEW TIMES BEFORE THEN THAT I THOUGHT...
IS THIS MITSURU ADACHI'S WORK?
IS HE USING A PSEUDONYM?
OCCASIONALLY I'D READ MANGA I SUSPECTED WAS ACTUALLY HIS.
AH, I SEE.
HE CHANGED HIS ALIAS AGAIN.
ACTUALLY, THEY WERE ALL BY DIFFERENT PEOPLE.
WHEN I GRADUATED COLLEGE, MY SERIES URUSEI YATSURA STARTED TO BE PUBLISHED.
A FEW YEARS LATER IN SHOWA 57 (1982).
WHY DON'T WE HAVE A DINNER MEETING? WITH BEEF.
MEAT?
ALL RIGHT.
I LIKE MEAT.

Recently...

Mitsuru
Adachi

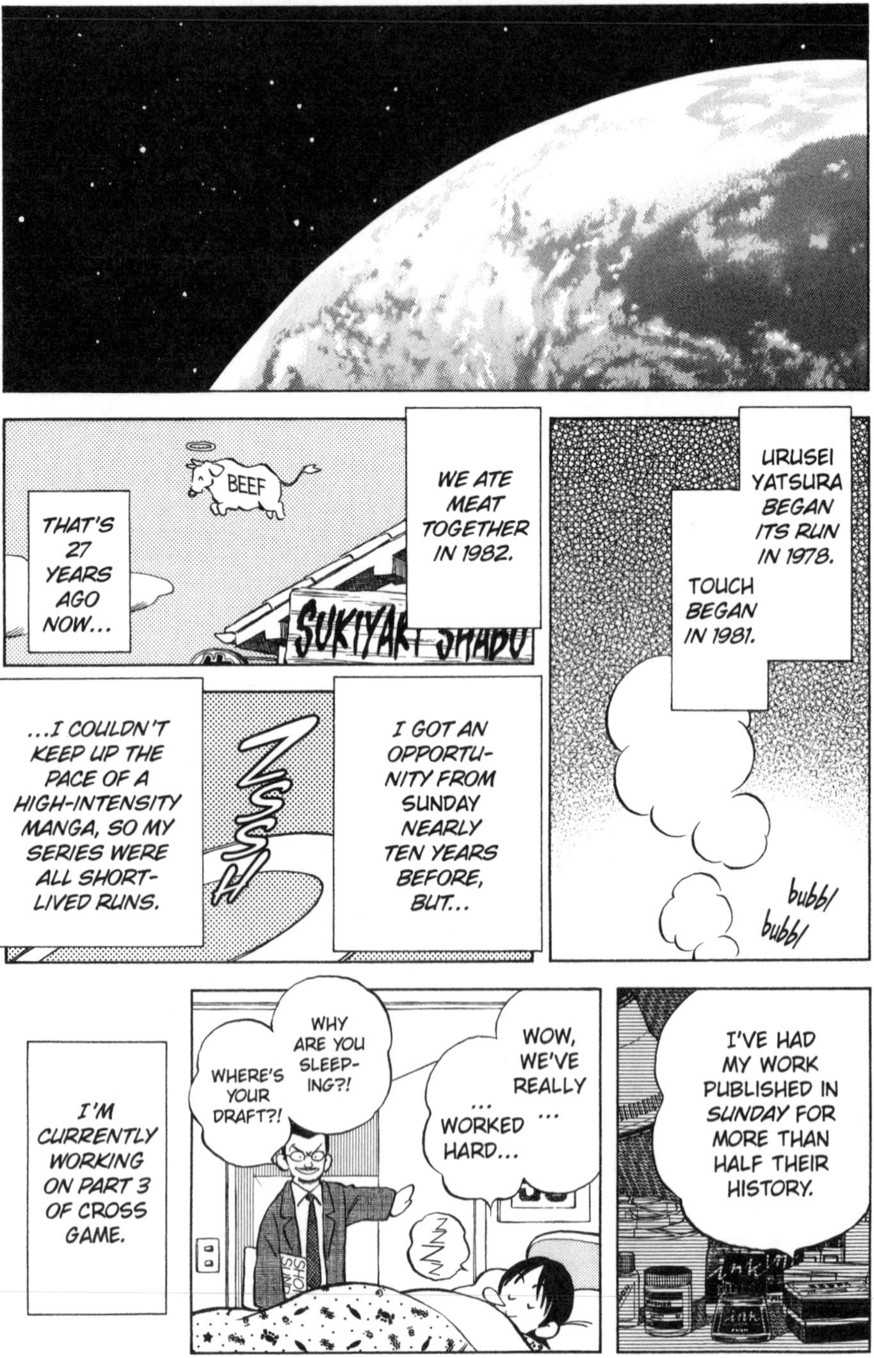
URUSEI YATSURA BEGAN ITS RUN IN 1978.
TOUCH BEGAN IN 1981.
bubbl bubbl
WE ATE MEAT TOGETHER IN 1982.
BEEF
SUKIYAKI SHABU
THAT'S 27 YEARS AGO NOW...
I GOT AN OPPORTUNITY FROM SUNDAY NEARLY TEN YEARS BEFORE, BUT...
...I COULDN'T KEEP UP THE PACE OF A HIGH-INTENSITY MANGA, SO MY SERIES WERE ALL SHORT-LIVED RUNS.
I'VE HAD MY WORK PUBLISHED IN SUNDAY FOR MORE THAN HALF THEIR HISTORY.
WOW, WE'VE REALLY ... ... WORKED HARD...
WHY ARE YOU SLEEPING?!
WHERE'S YOUR DRAFT?!
ZZZ
I'M CURRENTLY WORKING ON PART 3 OF CROSS GAME.

Recently...

Rumiko Takahashi

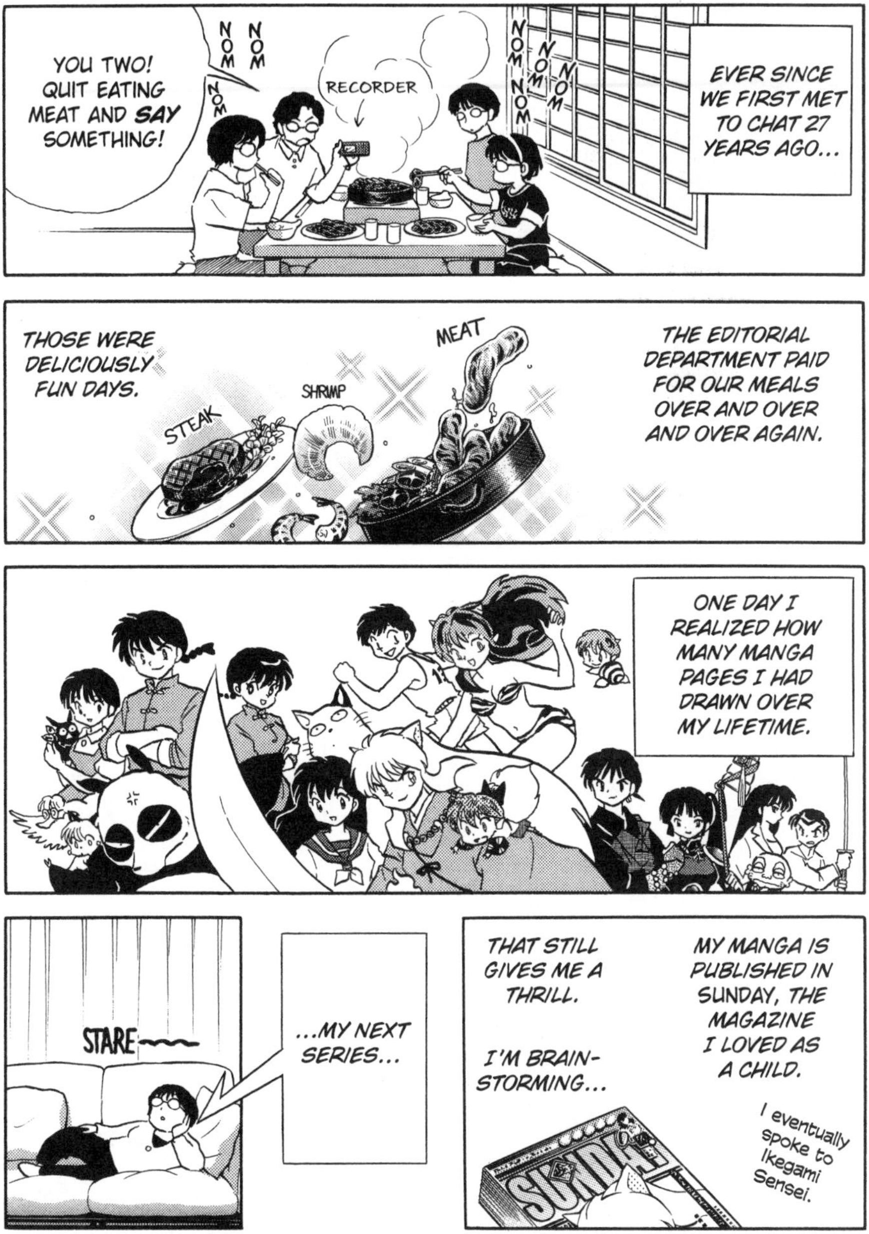
EVER SINCE WE FIRST MET TO CHAT 27 YEARS AGO...
NOM NOM NOM NOM NOM
RECORDER
NOM NOM NOM
YOU TWO! QUIT EATING MEAT AND SAY SOMETHING!
THE EDITORIAL DEPARTMENT PAID FOR OUR MEALS OVER AND OVER AND OVER AGAIN.
MEAT
SHRIMP
STEAK
THOSE WERE DELICIOUSLY FUN DAYS.
ONE DAY I REALIZED HOW MANY MANGA PAGES I HAD DRAWN OVER MY LIFETIME.
MY MANGA IS PUBLISHED IN SUNDAY, THE MAGAZINE I LOVED AS A CHILD.
THAT STILL GIVES ME A THRILL.
I eventually spoke to Ikegami Sensei.
I'M BRAIN-STORMING...
...MY NEXT SERIES...
STARE

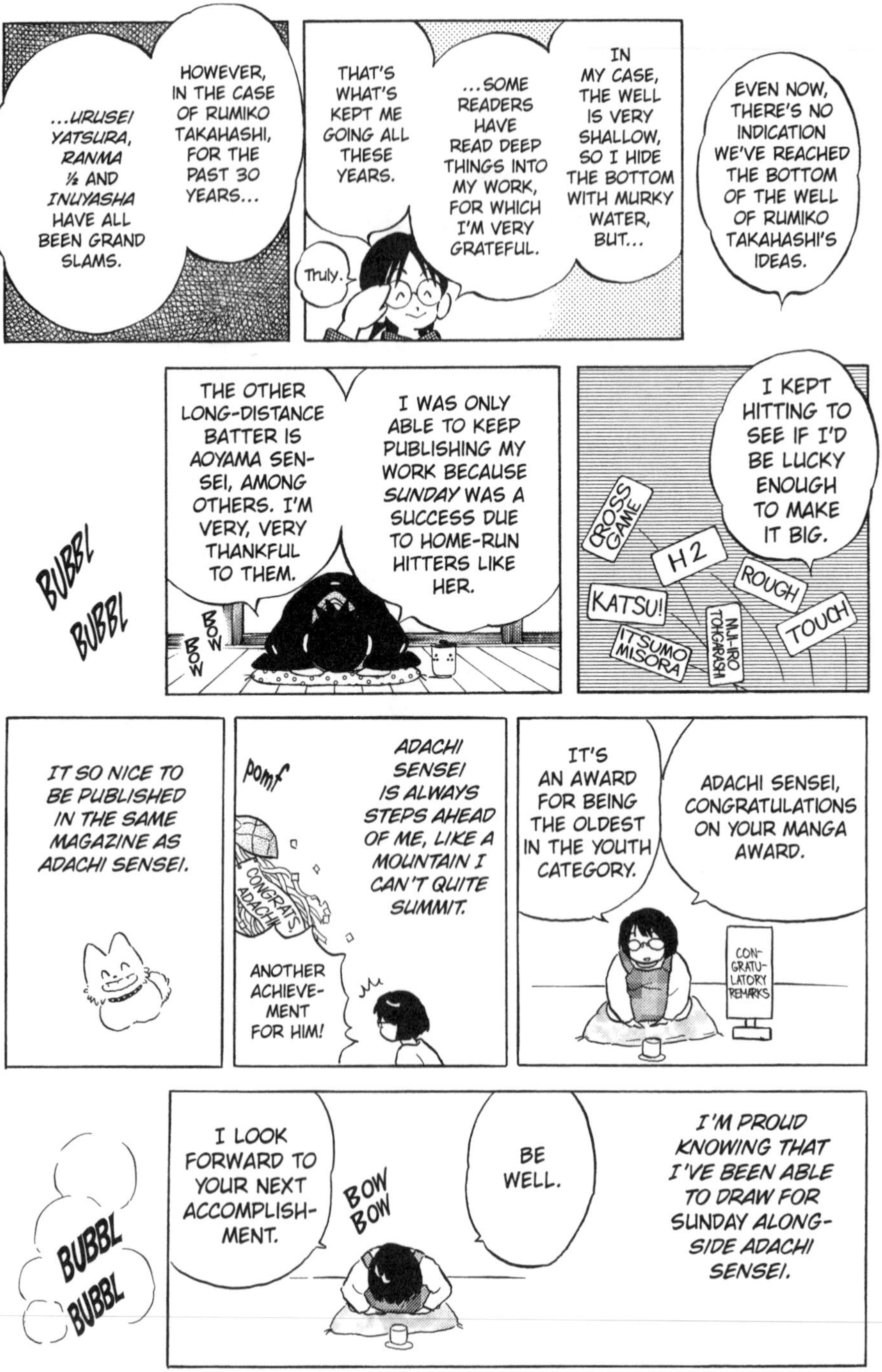
EVEN NOW, THERE'S NO INDICATION WE'VE REACHED THE BOTTOM OF THE WELL OF RUMIKO TAKAHASHI'S IDEAS.
IN MY CASE, THE WELL IS VERY SHALLOW, SO I HIDE THE BOTTOM WITH MURKY WATER, BUT...
...SOME READERS HAVE READ DEEP THINGS INTO MY WORK, FOR WHICH I'M VERY GRATEFUL.
THAT'S WHAT'S KEPT ME GOING ALL THESE YEARS.
Truly.
HOWEVER, IN THE CASE OF RUMIKO TAKAHASHI, FOR THE PAST 30 YEARS...
...URUSEI YATSURA, RANMA ½ AND INUYASHA HAVE ALL BEEN GRAND SLAMS.
I KEPT HITTING TO SEE IF I'D BE LUCKY ENOUGH TO MAKE IT BIG.
CROSS GAME
H2
ROUGH
KATSU!
NIJI-IRO TOHGARASHI
ITSUMO MISORA
TOUCH
I WAS ONLY ABLE TO KEEP PUBLISHING MY WORK BECAUSE SUNDAY WAS A SUCCESS DUE TO HOME-RUN HITTERS LIKE HER.
THE OTHER LONG-DISTANCE BATTER IS AOYAMA SENSEI, AMONG OTHERS. I'M VERY, VERY THANKFUL TO THEM.
BOW BOW
BUBBL BUBBL
ADACHI SENSEI, CONGRATULATIONS ON YOUR MANGA AWARD.
IT'S AN AWARD FOR BEING THE OLDEST IN THE YOUTH CATEGORY.
CONGRATULATORY REMARKS
ADACHI SENSEI IS ALWAYS STEPS AHEAD OF ME, LIKE A MOUNTAIN I CAN'T QUITE SUMMIT.
pomf
CONGRATS ADACHI
ANOTHER ACHIEVEMENT FOR HIM!
IT SO NICE TO BE PUBLISHED IN THE SAME MAGAZINE AS ADACHI SENSEI.
I'M PROUD KNOWING THAT I'VE BEEN ABLE TO DRAW FOR SUNDAY ALONGSIDE ADACHI SENSEI.
BE WELL.
BOW BOW
I LOOK FORWARD TO YOUR NEXT ACCOMPLISHMENT.
BUBBL BUBBL

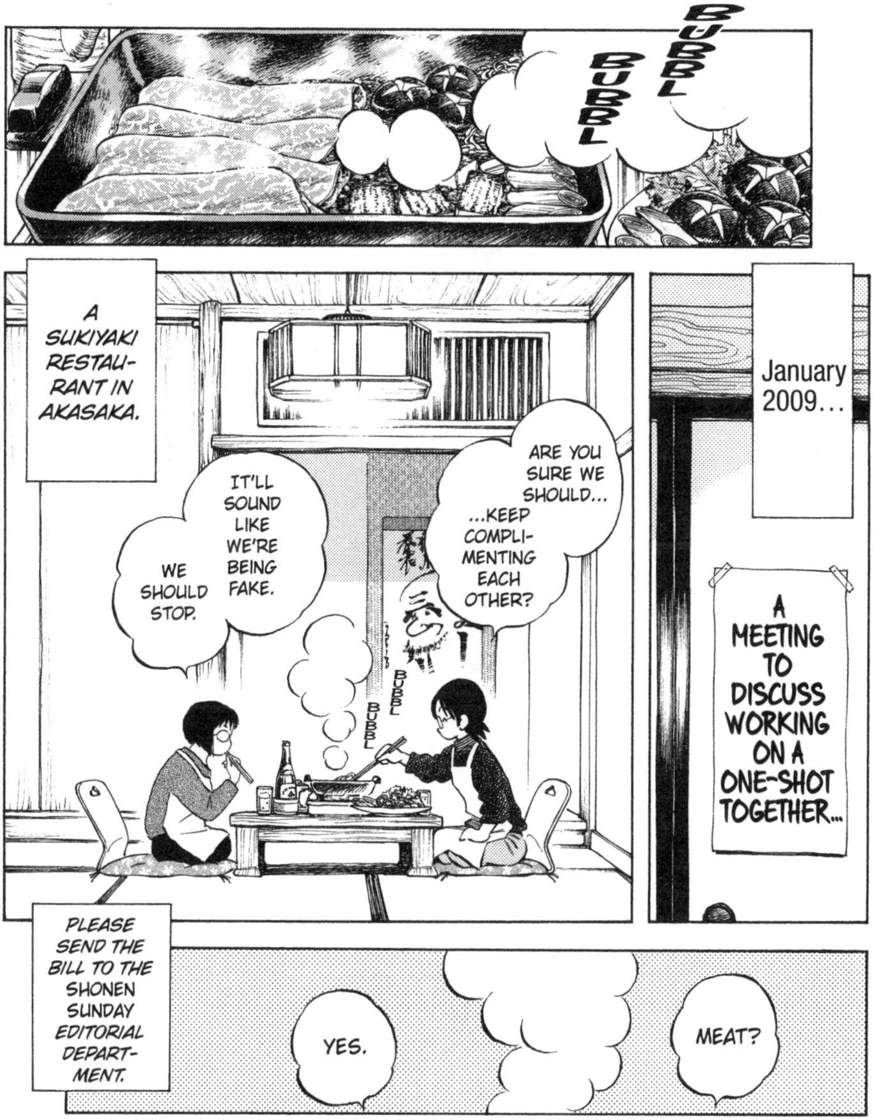
BUBBL
BUBBL
January 2009…
A MEETING TO DISCUSS WORKING ON A ONE-SHOT TOGETHER…
A SUKIYAKI RESTAURANT IN AKASAKA.
ARE YOU SURE WE SHOULD…
…KEEP COMPLIMENTING EACH OTHER?
IT'LL SOUND LIKE WE'RE BEING FAKE.
WE SHOULD STOP.
BUBBL
BUBBL
MEAT?
YES.
PLEASE SEND THE BILL TO THE SHONEN SUNDAY EDITORIAL DEPARTMENT.

Congratulations *Shonen Sunday* on your 50th anniversary

March 2009
Mitsuru Adachi
Rumiko Takahashi

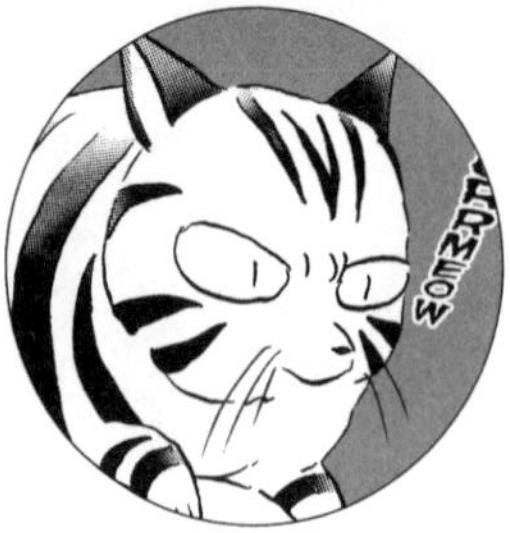
RMEOW

Rumiko Takahashi

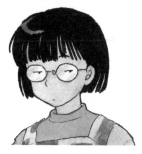

The spotlight on Rumiko Takahashi's career began in 1978 when she won an honorable mention in Shogakukan's prestigious New Comic Artist Contest for *Those Selfish Aliens*. Later that same year, her boy-meets-alien comedy series, *Urusei Yatsura*, was serialized in *Weekly Shonen Sunday*. This phenomenally successful manga series was adapted into anime format and spawned a TV series and half a dozen theatrical-release movies, all incredibly popular in their own right. Takahashi followed up the success of her debut series with one blockbuster hit after another—*Maison Ikkoku* ran from 1980 to 1987, *Ranma ½* from 1987 to 1996, and *Inuyasha* from 1996 to 2008. Other notable works include *Mermaid Saga*, *Rumic Theater*, and *One-Pound Gospel*.

Takahashi was inducted into the Will Eisner Comic Awards Hall of Fame in 2018. She won the prestigious Shogakukan Manga Award twice in her career, once for *Urusei Yatsura* in 1981 and the second time for *Inuyasha* in 2002. A majority of the Takahashi canon has been adapted into other media such as anime, live-action TV series, and film. Takahashi's manga, as well as the other formats her work has been adapted into, have continued to delight generations of fans around the world. Distinguished by her wonderfully endearing characters, Takahashi's work adeptly incorporates a wide variety of elements such as comedy, romance, fantasy, and martial arts. While her series are difficult to pin down into one simple genre, the signature style she has created has come to be known as the "Rumic World." Rumiko Takahashi is an artist who truly represents the very best from the world of manga.

Came the Mirror
& Other Tales
VIZ Signature Edition

STORY AND ART BY
RUMIKO TAKAHASHI

KAGAMI GA KITA TAKAHASHI RUMIKO TANPENSHU
by Rumiko TAKAHASHI
© 2015 Rumiko TAKAHASHI
All rights reserved.
Original Japanese edition published by SHOGAKUKAN.
English translation rights in the United States of America,
Canada, the United Kingdom, Ireland, Australia, and New Zealand
arranged with SHOGAKUKAN.

Original Cover Design: Koji INAMI + Bay Bridge Studio

Translation/Junko Goda
English Adaptation/Rebecca Packard
Touch-Up Art & Lettering/James Gaubatz
Cover & Interior Design/Yukiko Whitley
Editor/Annette Roman

Printed in Canada

Published by VIZ Media, LLC
P.O. Box 77010
San Francisco, CA 94107

10 9 8 7 6 5 4 3 2 1
First printing, February 2022

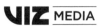

VIZ MEDIA
viz.com

VIZ SIGNATURE
vizsignature.com

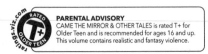

MAISON IKKOKU

STORY AND ART BY
RUMIKO TAKAHASHI

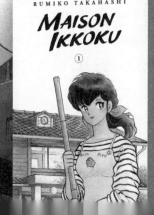

Yusaku Godai didn't get accepted into college on the first try, so he's studying to retake the entrance exams. But living in a dilapidated building full of eccentric and noisy tenants is making it hard for him to achieve his goals. Now that a beautiful woman has moved in to become the new resident manager, Godai is driven to distraction!

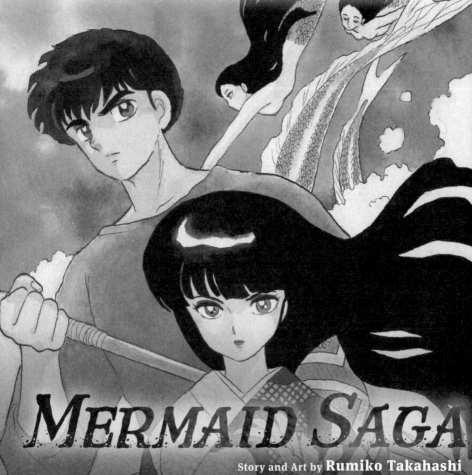
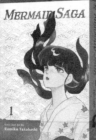
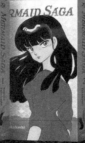

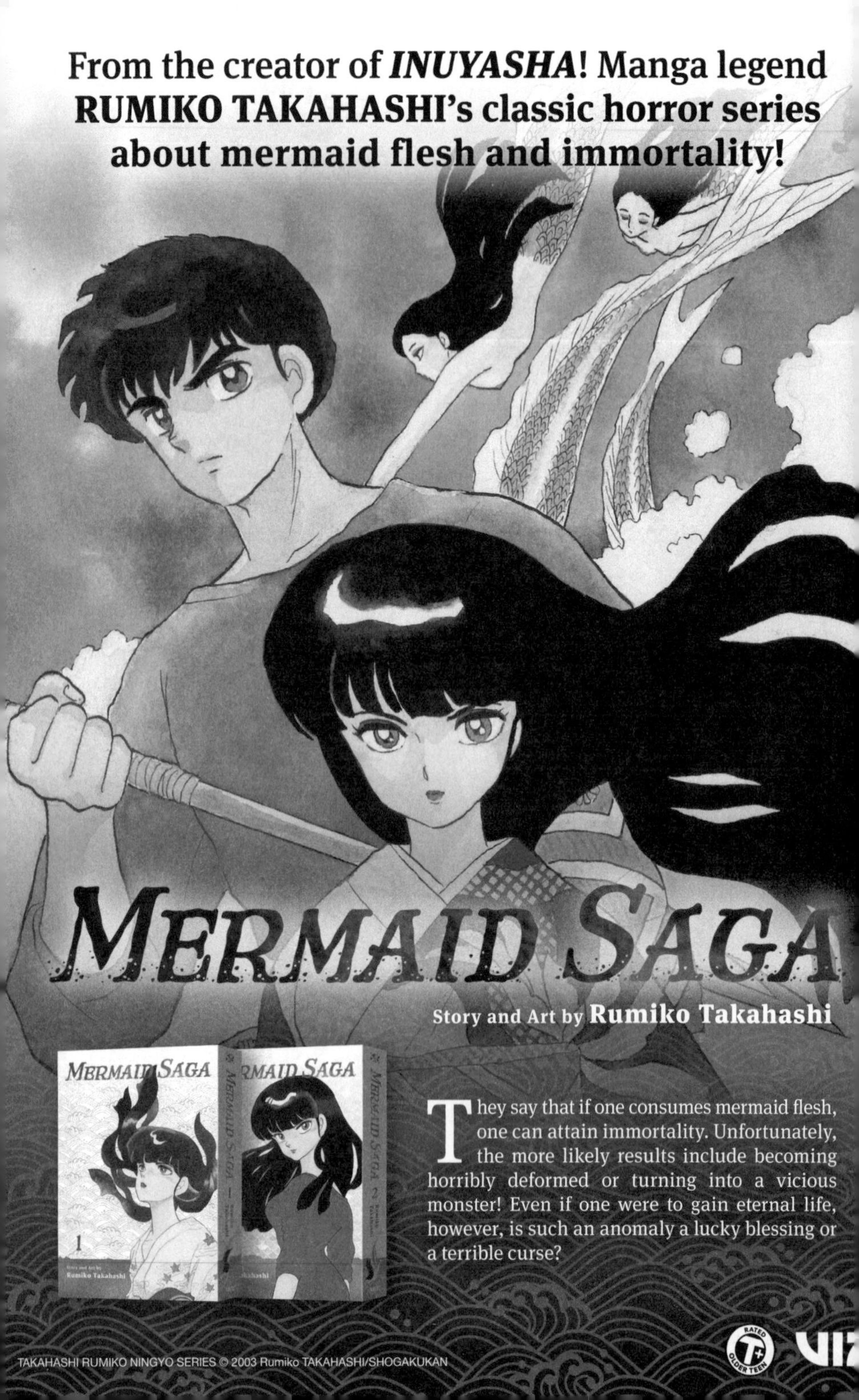

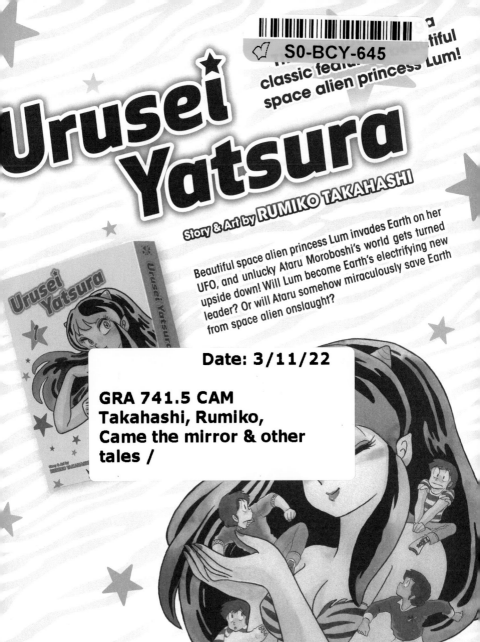

a
tiful
classic featu
space alien princess Lum!

Urusei Yatsura

Story & Art by RUMIKO TAKAHASHI

Beautiful space alien princess Lum invades Earth on her UFO, and unlucky Ataru Moroboshi's world gets turned upside down! Will Lum become Earth's electrifying new leader? Or will Ataru somehow miraculously save Earth from space alien onslaught?

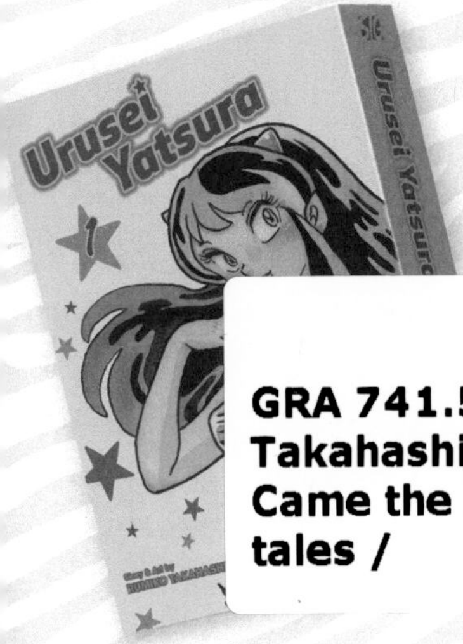
Urusei Yatsura
Urusei Yatsura
1

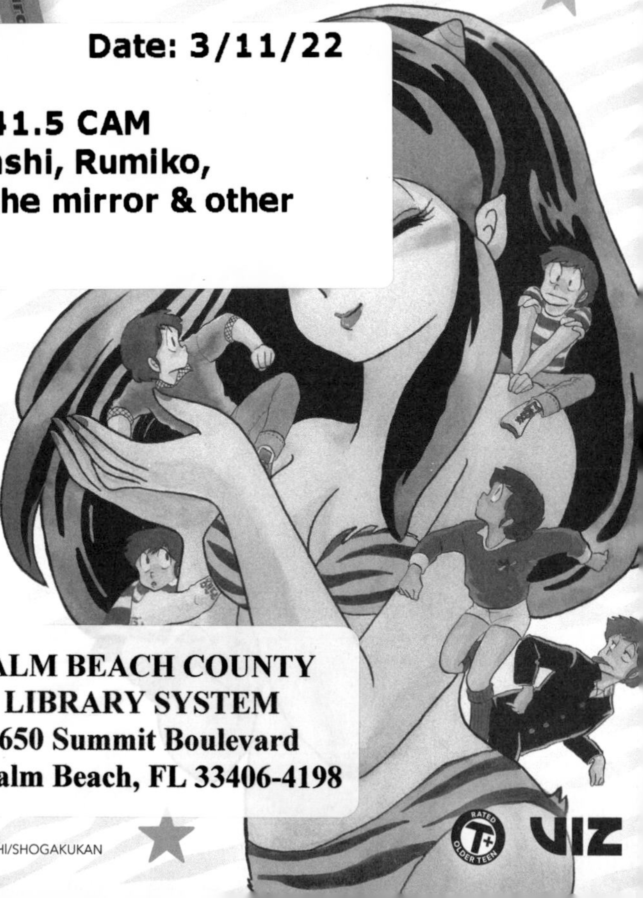

RATED T+ OLDER TEEN

VIZ